THE ONE YEAR™

Positive Mental Health

Devotional

365 Days of Going from Struggle to Strength

Drs. Les and Leslie Parrott

New York Times Bestselling Authors

TYNDALE REFRESH™

Think Well. Live Well. Be Well.

Visit Tyndale online at tyndale.com.

Visit Les and Leslie at lesandleslie.com.

The One Year Positive Mental Health Devotional: 365 Days of Going from Struggle to Strength

Cover design by Eunseo Ko

Interior design by Laura Cruise

Edited by Deb Lew

For information about special discounts for bulk purchases, please contact Tyndale House Publishers at csresponse@tyndale.com, or call 1-855-277-9400.

ISBN 979-8-4005-1951-2

Printed in the United States of America

32 31 30 29 28 27 26
7 6 5 4 3 2 1

The Lord is close to the brokenhearted;
he rescues those whose spirits are crushed.

PSALM 34:18

INTRODUCTION

Let's Be Honest

This book isn't for people with perfect peace. It's for the overthinkers, the up-all-nighters, the ones who are sometimes holding it together on the outside but unraveling somewhere deeper in.

It's also for the ones who are doing okay but craving something more grounded, more honest, more whole. People who aren't falling apart but aren't content with surface-level faith, either.

Maybe you have some quiet doubts. Maybe you've been burned by spiritual clichés. Maybe you've heard "Just pray more" or "Choose joy" and felt the sting of being misunderstood.

Maybe you've been handed toxic optimism—the kind that skips over your pain and calls it faith—instead of real hope.

Maybe you've sat in a church pew with a fake smile and a soul screaming for oxygen.

You're not alone. This devotional isn't about pretending. It's not a highlight reel or a "just trust God more" manual. It's about showing up with whatever you've got and being met with grace.

Whether you're barely holding on, quietly rebuilding, or intentionally pursuing emotional health, these pages were written for you.

Here's what you'll find each day:

- A brief Scripture quote
- A raw, reflective reading that integrates biblical truth with psychological insight
- A short anchor truth to hold on to
- A simple, heartfelt prayer
- A gentle invitation to act—a grounding practice, prompt, or next step to take

You won't find long chapters or complex theology. Not because you can't handle depth, but because sometimes your brain is fried, your spirit is flat, or your life is just a lot. These devotionals are short on purpose. They're made for real life.

The topics rotate. Half are about struggle—things like anxiety, grief, anger, trauma, self-worth. The other half are about strength—things like resilience, agency, gratitude, courage, connection. These are just a few examples. You'll see a full listing with locations in A Guide to Topics.

Over the year, you'll move through all the topics—sometimes circling back, sometimes moving forward. Because growth rarely happens in a straight line. Life doesn't come in neat emotional categories. You can be both anxious and grateful. Lonely and full of purpose. Healing and still hurting.

You don't need to be "broken enough" to read this. And you don't need to "have it all together" to benefit from it either.

What you do need—what we all need—is space to be human. And loved in the middle of it.

That's what this devotional offers. Not answers for everything. Not pressure to perform. Just presence. And a path—one small step at a time—toward deeper peace, honest faith, and lasting mental and emotional well-being.

If you sometimes feel like you're faking it, if you have days when you're white-knuckling your way through, if you've ever wondered what faith looks like when it tells the truth—you're in the right place.

Think of this journey like a branch—something small but living, a sign that even after hard seasons, growth is still happening.

Ready to begin? One day. One entry. One breath at a time.

Drs. Les and Leslie Parrott

A Guide to Topics:

STRENGTHS YOU ARE BUILDING AND STRUGGLES YOU ARE FACING

This devotional is designed to meet you in real life—not just on the calendar, but in the middle of what you're actually experiencing. Each entry is organized around a specific topic. Some reflect struggles, while others point toward strengths. You can read the devotionals day by day, or you can turn directly to the topics that speak to your current season. Each topic below includes the pages where it appears, making it easy to return to what you need most.

Return to these topics anytime,
because growth isn't linear and neither is healing.

Wired for Belonging

Then the LORD God said, "It is not good for the man to be alone."

GENESIS 2:18

You were never meant to do life alone. Not in the shallow, transactional sense of needing others to get things done—but in the deep, soul-anchoring sense of needing to be known, loved, and safe.

John Bowlby, who researched how we form relationships, made it clear: Connection isn't a luxury. It's a survival instinct.

From infancy, we're wired to reach for others. To seek proximity, safety, and comfort. That wiring doesn't disappear with age. Grown-up problems still echo childhood patterns. We reach out or shut down. We cling or retreat. And most of us are doing this dance without realizing that the choreography was learned decades ago.

But Genesis said it long before Bowlby did: "It is not good for man to be alone." This isn't just about marriage. It's about *belonging*. About how we're created for community, vulnerability, and trust.

Even God, the only self-sufficient being in existence, exists in relationship—Father, Son, and Spirit.

So if you feel that longing to be seen, to be held, to be met with presence and empathy—you're not broken. You're human.

But here's the catch: While we're wired for connection, we're also wounded by it.

Relationships are messy. Some of us learned early on that vulnerability leads to pain. So we adapted. We self-soothed. We pushed people away before they could leave. And now, decades later, the longing to connect is still there . . . but so is the fear.

That's where healing begins—not by pretending we don't need people, but by slowly, bravely opening back up to the possibility that connection can be safe. That not everyone will hurt you. That God is not distant. That healing is relational, too.

Anchor Truth

You were made for connection. You don't have to apologize for needing others.

Prayer

God, I want to belong. Heal the places in me that have stopped reaching out. Help me risk connection again—with wisdom, with courage, and with hope.

Invitation

Think about one person who helps you feel safe. Reach out to them today—just a text, a coffee, a short call. Let your need for connection lead you toward healing, not hiding.

Never Really Alone

My health may fail, and my spirit may grow weak, but God remains the strength of my heart; he is mine forever.

PSALM 73:26

Loneliness is not a glitch in the system—it's part of being human.

From the garden of Eden to the letters of Paul, Scripture doesn't shy away from it.

The words *alone*, *isolated*, and *lonely* show up repeatedly in the Bible—not just to name a problem, but to reveal a reality. Even faithful people, even heroes of our faith, wrestled with this ache.

Moses felt it on the mountain. Hagar felt it in the wilderness. Elijah, Jeremiah, David, Job—they all cried out from places of isolation, wondering where God was. And yet, again and again, God reminded them: "I am with you."

That truth didn't always change their circumstances, but it changed their experience of those events.

Clinically, we know that chronic loneliness takes a toll on our mental and physical health. But so does pretending it doesn't exist.

The healthiest path forward is neither denial nor despair; it's acknowledgment and connection. First with ourselves. Then with God. And ultimately with others.

Because even though loneliness is a universal experience, it carries a deeply personal invitation to let God meet you in the place you thought no one could.

When you stop striving to "get over it" and instead allow God to *enter it*, something shifts. That inner emptiness becomes sacred space. Not a void to fear, but a quiet room where his presence draws close.

He sees the places no one else sees. Hears the prayers you don't even speak. And sits with you when the world goes silent.

Anchor Truth

Loneliness may visit, but it does not have to define you. The one who holds the universe is holding you, even now.

Prayer

God, help me to be honest about my loneliness and to welcome you into it. Let your nearness feel more real than my isolation.

Invitation

Today, when you feel alone, pause and say aloud, "You are here with me." Let that be your refrain until the truth settles into your soul.

Ask It Again

Let us examine our ways and test them,
and let us return to the LORD.

LAMENTATIONS 3:40 (NIV)

You've asked yourself this before: *Why do I keep doing this? Why do I shut down in conflict? Why do I overcommit and then burn out? Why do I chase approval from people who rarely give it?*

You've asked. But maybe you didn't stay with the question long enough.

Real change begins when we dare to ask the same question again—and wait. Wait in the discomfort. Wait in the silence. Wait without rushing to fix.

Most people rush past this moment. We get uncomfortable, so we reach for distraction or blame. But those who grow? They lean in.

They *stay* with the question. They *stay* curious, not just about what they're doing—but why they're doing it. Curiosity makes that possible. Without it, we stay stuck on the surface, treating symptoms instead of exploring causes.

Curiosity that leads to growth is about slowing down long enough to spot a repeated behavior, track it back to its emotional source, and consider new responses.

The verse from Lamentations is a call to introspection, but also a call to hope: "Let us examine our ways and . . . return."

The goal isn't just to sit in self-critique—it's to return. To reroute. To move toward something truer, healthier, and more aligned with God's intent for our wholeness.

Jesus often responded to people by posing questions—sometimes the same one more than once. "Do you want to get well?" he asked the man by the pool.

It wasn't because Jesus didn't know the answer. It was because he wanted the man to *see himself clearly*.

Anchor Truth

Healing doesn't start with having all the answers. It starts with asking the right questions—and being willing to ask them again.

Prayer

God, give me courage to ask hard questions about myself—and grace to hear the answers without shame. Help me stay curious long enough to find what needs to change.

Invitation

Think of a behavior or emotional reaction you're tired of repeating. Ask yourself why it happens. Then ask again—and be still long enough to listen.

Sometimes It's Grief in Disguise

Even in laughter the heart may ache,
and rejoicing may end in grief.

PROVERBS 14:13 (NIV)

Jealousy doesn't always come from comparison.

Sometimes it comes from loss. You're not mad they got married. You're grieving that you haven't. You're not bitter they got the job. You're grieving the closed door you thought would open for you.

But grief wears all kinds of masks, and envy is a common one. It's easier to feel irritated at someone else's win than to feel the ache of your own deferred hope.

And if you don't recognize what's happening underneath, you'll start resenting others for having what you don't, even if they didn't take it from you.

Proverbs 14:13 says that even in laughter, the heart may ache. In other words, surface emotions don't always tell the whole story. What looks like envy might actually be unspoken sadness. And sadness that stays buried turns sour.

Self-awareness means you slow down long enough to ask, *Is this really jealousy? Or am I grieving something I haven't admitted yet?*

In therapy, this is often explored through *ambiguous grief*—the pain of what you never had, what didn't go as planned, or what's still out of reach. It's quiet. It's hard to name. But it's real. And if you're human, you have it.

Jealousy says, "They don't deserve that." Grief says, "I just wish that was part of my story too." And God says, "I see you—and I'm not rushing you past the ache."

Anchor Truth

Not all jealousy is envy. Sometimes it's unspoken grief.

Prayer

God, help me see what I'm really feeling. If jealousy is covering up sadness or disappointment, meet me in that truth. I don't want to resent others. I want to heal.

Invitation

When jealousy shows up today, ask, "Am I grieving something underneath this?" Name the loss. Let God sit with you in it. No rush. No shame.

You're Not Waiting for Permission

For God has not given us a spirit of fear and timidity, but of power, love, and self-discipline.

2 TIMOTHY 1:7

Somewhere along the line, many of us internalized the idea that we need someone to tell us it's okay to take action. To set the boundary. To say no. To make a move. To change the story. And if no one gives that green light, we stall.

But here's the truth: You don't need permission to be healthy. You don't need applause to pivot. You don't need a guarantee before you grow.

Agency means you stop waiting for someone else to bless your next step and start trusting the Spirit that's already within you.

Paul doesn't sugarcoat it: God didn't wire us for fear or shrinking back. That means chronic hesitation and self-doubt don't come from God. But power? Love? Self-discipline? Those *do*. That's what's baked into your spiritual DNA. Not recklessness, but boldness. Not self-centeredness, but Spirit-led action.

In psychology, this overlaps with what's called *self-efficacy*—your belief that you can influence outcomes. People with strong self-efficacy don't wait for someone to tell them they're ready. They act, learn, adjust, and grow. And that sense of personal agency is one of the best predictors of long-term emotional resilience.

Of course, you'll still want wisdom. You'll still need discernment. But don't confuse external permission with internal peace.

If you're walking in love, truth, and alignment with God's heart, then that next brave step might not need approval from anyone else. Just obedience.

Anchor Truth

You don't need a green light from others to grow in the direction of health.

Prayer

God, I've spent too much time waiting for permission to live with clarity and courage. Remind me today that you've already given me your Spirit. Help me move in power, love, and self-discipline—no more stalling.

Invitation

Is there something you've been waiting to do because no one "gave you permission"? Name it. Then take one small, brave step anyway. Trust the Spirit in you.

Apologizing Well

But if we confess our sins to him, he is faithful and just to forgive us our sins and to cleanse us from all wickedness.

1 JOHN 1:9

Apologizing can feel like swallowing gravel. Especially when you're not the only one at fault. Especially when you're afraid it won't be received.

But here's what most people get wrong about apologizing: They think it's about blame. Really, it's about healing.

Psychologically, a genuine apology is one of the most disarming tools for restoring connection. It signals vulnerability, empathy, and accountability—all essential ingredients for rebuilding trust.

But there's a big difference between saying "I'm sorry you feel that way" and "I'm sorry for what I did." One deflects. The other owns.

The most effective apologies follow a simple but powerful pattern:

- **Acknowledge** what you did without excuses: "I was late to dinner."
- **Name** how it impacted the other person: "You had to wait for me and may have felt like I don't respect your time."
- **Express** genuine remorse: "I'm sorry."
- **Offer** to make it right: "Next time, I'll leave earlier."

It's not about groveling. It's about taking responsibility.

And here's the clincher: Research shows that people are more likely to forgive when the apology includes *empathy*—not just admission.

James 5:16 doesn't say "explain your motives" or "justify your actions." It says *confess.*

That takes humility. It takes courage. And it leads to healing—not just for the person you hurt, but for *you.*

You're not less of a person when you apologize. You're becoming more of the person God made you to be—someone who loves well, lives honestly, and walks in grace.

Anchor Truth

A real apology doesn't shrink you. It strengthens the bridge between hearts.

Prayer

God, give me the strength to own what's mine. Help me speak with clarity, empathy, and courage. Make me someone who heals what I've broken—not with perfection, but with humility.

Invitation

Think of someone you've hurt—intentionally or not. Write out what a healthy, healing apology would sound like. Whether or not you send it today, let God use it to shape your heart.

Jesus and the Slow Burn

Jesus entered the Temple and began to drive out all the people buying and selling animals for sacrifice. He knocked over the tables of the money changers and the chairs of those selling doves.

MATTHEW 21:12

Most people think of Jesus flipping tables as a flash of holy rage, a fiery outburst of righteous indignation. But it wasn't impulsive. It wasn't reckless. It was a slow burn.

The Gospel of Mark tells us that Jesus actually went to the Temple the day before he cleansed it. He walked in, looked around, saw the injustice, and then left. He slept on it. Prayed on it. Then returned the next day, deliberate and clear.

This wasn't an emotional hijacking. It was a calibrated response. Jesus didn't react. He responded. That distinction matters.

Most of us were never taught what to do with our anger, so we default to one of two extremes: We blow up or we shut down.

But Jesus shows a third way—the way of holy restraint, intentionality, and purpose. He wasn't afraid of anger. He harnessed it.

And that's the invitation for us.

Your anger might be telling you that something needs to change. A boundary needs to be named. A lie needs to be confronted. A silence needs to be broken.

But you don't have to erupt to be effective. You don't have to react immediately to be real.

You can pause. Pray. Cool the flames. And still flip a few tables tomorrow, if love requires it.

The point isn't passivity. It's presence. Being grounded enough to let the Spirit lead your anger—not the other way around.

Anchor Truth

You can be both angry and wise. Jesus was.

Prayer

Jesus, teach me to carry anger the way you did—with clarity, courage, and compassion. Show me how to pause long enough to act with love, not just intensity.

Invitation

Think of something that angered you recently. Ask yourself what a slow, prayerful response would look like. What would it look like to flip a table—but with grace?

Doing the Right Thing Alone

But when Daniel learned that the law had been signed, he went home and knelt down as usual in his upstairs room, with its windows open toward Jerusalem. He prayed three times a day, just as he had always done, giving thanks to his God.

DANIEL 6:10

There's a specific kind of courage that doesn't get celebrated nearly enough: moral courage, the bravery it takes to do what's right when no one else is standing with you.

Ask Daniel. When he refused to compromise his values, he didn't do it for attention. He did it quietly. Without drama. Without backup.

When the decree went out that everyone could pray only to the king, Daniel didn't protest in the streets or stir up rebellion. He simply went home, opened his window, and prayed—just as he had always done. Alone. Steady. Unshaken.

That's courage.

In psychology, *moral courage* is defined as the ability to act ethically in the face of fear, shame, or risk to your reputation or relationships. It's standing up for what's right when it's unpopular or inconvenient—or when it threatens your comfort, image, or belonging.

And it's rare. Because it's hard.

Many of us were taught to keep the peace, to not rock the boat, to blend in. But peacekeeping is not the same as peacemaking.

Courage doesn't always look loud. It often looks like quiet consistency, like sticking to your convictions when no one is clapping.

And the truth is, when you act with moral clarity, you may lose something. You may feel the sting of being misunderstood or dismissed.

But you will also gain something unshakable: a stronger spine, a clearer conscience, and a life that's aligned with what matters most.

Even when you stand alone, you're not truly alone. God is near. God sees. God strengthens.

Anchor Truth

Courage doesn't always roar. Sometimes it whispers, "I will not bow to fear. Even if I'm the only one standing, I will stand with God."

Prayer

God, give me the resolve to do what's right today—even if no one notices, applauds, or agrees. Help me be faithful in private and strong in my convictions.

Invitation

Is there a situation where you've felt pressure to go along or stay silent? What would it look like to stand firm with quiet courage? Name it. Ask God for strength. And take one step toward moral courage.

What Trauma Does to You

He will not crush the weakest reed
or put out a flickering candle.
He will bring justice to all who have been wronged.

ISAIAH 42:3

You didn't ask for this. You didn't deserve it. But it happened.

And now you're left with the aftershocks—the way it shows up in your sleep, your relationships, your reactions, your body, your thoughts. Even when it feels like it's "over," it's not over inside you.

That's what trauma does. It changes you—not because you're weak, but because it rewires your nervous system. It alters your sense of safety. It teaches you to flinch, to freeze, to shut down or explode in ways you don't even recognize sometimes. It makes you feel like a stranger to yourself.

And here's what you need to know: This is not your fault. You're not broken. You're not dramatic. You're not making it up. You are someone who has *been through something*—and your pain has a reason.

The Bible doesn't gloss over trauma. It's full of people who were hurt, hunted, assaulted, betrayed, and abandoned. Job lost everything and said, "I have no peace, no quietness, no rest—only trouble comes." Elijah collapsed under the weight of fear and exhaustion, and begged God to let him die. Tamar lived in silence after being violated. Hagar ran, alone and pregnant, into the wilderness, where God found her.

Trauma has always been part of the human story. But so has the presence of a God who sees, who stays, and who never asks you to heal faster than you're able.

If no one has told you this yet: What happened to you matters. And what it did to you matters too.

You are not too fragile for God. He's not put off by your pain or rushing you to "get over it." He meets you in the rubble, and he's not going anywhere.

Anchor Truth

Trauma changes how you experience life, but it doesn't change your worth.

Prayer

God, I've been through more than I know how to say. I don't always understand why I react the way I do now. But I want to believe that you see me, that you're not ashamed of my pain, and that you won't leave me here alone.

Invitation

Give yourself permission to name something hard you've survived—even if you're still living in its shadow. Speak it aloud or write it down. God can handle your truth.

Carrying More Than You Were Meant To

Come to me, all of you who are weary and carry heavy burdens, and I will give you rest.

MATTHEW 11:28

Some burdens aren't yours to carry, but you've been lugging them anyway.

You want to be the steady one. The strong one. The dependable one who shows up when no one else does. So you say yes again. You lean in harder. You carry just a little more—because someone has to.

There's a line between love and overextension. It's often invisible until you've crossed it. It happens when you feel responsible for someone else's happiness. When you confuse your presence with their healing.

If you're suffering from carrying too much for others, it's not because you're uncaring. You're *too* caring. You've blurred the lines. You've internalized others' pain as your own.

And eventually, the soul buckles under the weight of it all.

That's why Jesus' words are so revolutionary.

He doesn't just acknowledge weariness—he *expects* it. He assumes that you're carrying more than you should be. And instead of giving you more strategies to manage the load, he offers a yoke that's lighter. One that fits you. One that honors your limits.

Even Jesus didn't try to carry everything at once. He rested when crowds were still waiting. He accepted help to carry his cross. His compassion was pure but never frantic.

So take a moment today to ask, "What burdens am I carrying that were never mine to begin with?"

Maybe it's someone else's happiness. Their sobriety. Their healing. Their approval. These aren't your burdens. They're outcomes. And they're not yours to control.

You're not the Savior. But you *know* the Savior. And he's already offering you relief.

Anchor Truth

You were never meant to carry the weight of the world. Let go of what's not yours, and rediscover the strength that comes from living within your limits.

Prayer

Jesus, I've picked up burdens that don't belong to me. Show me what I need to lay down today. Teach me the difference between helping and overreaching.

Invitation

Make two lists: burdens that are yours (responsibilities, callings, needs) and burdens that aren't yours (others' choices, outcomes, emotions). Practice releasing the second list in prayer.

Riding the Roller Coaster

[There is] a time to cry and a time to laugh.
A time to grieve and a time to dance.

ECCLESIASTES 3:4

Some people live with emotional highs and lows that feel more intense than what others experience.

The good days don't just feel good—they feel euphoric. Energizing. Limitless. You get more done in one day than most people do in a week.

But the crash comes. And when it does, it hits hard. You lose momentum. You retreat. You spiral into exhaustion, guilt, or depression. It's not laziness or drama. It's real. And confusing.

Maybe you've experienced something like this. Maybe someone you love has. Maybe you've wondered, "What's wrong with me? Why can't I stay balanced?" You're not alone.

This pattern—intense highs followed by deep lows—is often associated with *bipolar disorder*, a clinical condition that impacts millions. And while it can be profoundly disruptive, it's also very treatable. There's no shame in naming it.

The Bible doesn't label the modern diagnosis of bipolar disorder, but it does speak to the emotional range of human beings. Read David's psalms, and you'll see him move from praise to despair in a few verses. Watch Elijah, fresh off a miraculous showdown, collapse in hopelessness and beg God to take his life. These aren't weak men—they are *real* men, emotionally complex, spiritually sensitive, and deeply human.

Ecclesiastes reminds us there are times for everything—for tears *and* joy, grief *and* dancing.

Emotional fluctuations are part of life. But when they become overwhelming, relentless, or unmanageable, it's okay to seek help. That's not weakness. That's wisdom.

You are not your emotions. You are not unstable or unworthy for feeling deeply. You are not disqualified by a diagnosis. You are loved. And there is help.

Anchor Truth

Your emotional intensity doesn't scare God. He meets you in the highs and the lows—and never leaves you alone in either.

Prayer

Steady me, God. Help me feel what I need to feel—but not be ruled by it. Walk with me in the highs and hold me in the lows. Be my balance.

Invitation

If your emotional swings are more than you can manage alone, don't minimize it. Talk to someone trained to help. There is a path toward clarity—and care—and peace.

Breaking Out of Pleasantville

Therefore each of you must put off falsehood and speak truthfully to your neighbor, for we are all members of one body.

EPHESIANS 4:25 (NIV)

Some families operate like a small town with one unspoken rule: Keep it pleasant.

No raised voices. No hard questions. No mess at the dinner table—just smiles, small talk, and polite silence about the stuff that actually matters.

It's what some therapists call *emotional muting*—a system designed not around health, but around keeping the peace at all costs. Even if it means burying your grief. Ignoring the addiction. Pretending the hurtful comment didn't sting.

Growing up in "Pleasantville" might have taught you that real feelings are inconvenient. That honesty is risky. That keeping others comfortable is more important than being known.

But here's the cost: You learn to swallow your words. You become fluent in smiling while shrinking. You master the art of managing impressions and forget how to ask for what you need or reveal the real you.

But make no mistake: This kind of "niceness" isn't kindness. It's emotional suppression. And over time, it can show up as anxiety, resentment, or even depression. Because you were never meant to contort your soul to keep things smooth.

Jesus didn't avoid hard truths to keep people at ease. He spoke with grace *and* honesty. He cried. He flipped tables. He embraced emotional life in full color. And he invited others into real, raw conversations.

Authenticity means you stop stuffing your story when it's not pleasant. It means trading false peace for true connection. It means trusting that love can handle the truth, even if it's messy.

You don't have to be the keeper of calm anymore. You don't have to monitor other people's emotions. You can choose honesty over harmony. Being real over nice. Healing over image.

Anchor Truth

There's no freedom in pretending and no love without truth.

Prayer

God, help me unlearn the belief that I have to be pleasant at the expense of being real. Give me the courage to tell the truth, even when it's uncomfortable.

Invitation

If you were raised in a "keep it nice" environment, what emotion do you find hardest to express? Practice naming it today—first to yourself, then maybe to someone safe.

Gratitude for What Didn't Happen

You intended to harm me, but God intended it all for good.

GENESIS 50:20

Sometimes the deepest, most soul-shaking gratitude isn't about what went right. It's about what didn't go wrong.

You didn't end up with the person who would've wrecked your heart. You didn't get the opportunity that would've crushed your spirit. You didn't stay trapped in the version of your life you once fought to keep. You didn't see your plans come to life—and that might have saved you.

We don't often shout our thank-yous for the job we didn't get, the relationship that fell apart, or the dream that fizzled out. But buried inside those quiet noes are layers of protection, redirection, and divine mercy.

Joseph knew this kind of gratitude. He was betrayed, trafficked, falsely imprisoned, and forgotten. It was a slow-motion unraveling of everything he had once imagined for his life.

And yet, years later, he stood in a place of influence with the power to retaliate. Looking at the brothers who had betrayed him, he said, "You intended to harm me, but God intended it all for good."

That's not just forgiveness. It's clarity. It's what happens when the pain doesn't disappear, but perspective shows up. Joseph wasn't grateful for the betrayal. He was grateful for a God who met him in it—and worked through it.

Gratitude isn't just about what you can see in your hands. Sometimes it's about what God kept out of them. Trust that the hands that withheld are the same ones still holding you.

We don't need to pretend we're thankful for suffering. That's not biblical. In fact, it's just bad theology. But we *can* be thankful that even in the disappointment, God didn't waste a single moment. He was protecting, pruning, and preparing us—even when we were kicking and screaming.

Anchor Truth

You may not be able to see the full picture yet, but someday you might thank God for the thing that never happened.

Prayer

God, thank you for the times you didn't give me what I asked for. For the doors that didn't open, the relationships that didn't work out, the paths that didn't unfold. Help me trust your no as much as your yes. Even when it breaks my heart.

Invitation

Look back on a part of your story that didn't go the way you hoped. What if that detour was divine? What if that heartbreak was your rescue? Spend some time naming what didn't happen—and thank God for the mercy hidden in the mess.

Loosening the Grip of Control

Trust in the LORD with all your heart;
do not depend on your own understanding.

PROVERBS 3:5

Anxiety often disguises itself as control. You plan every detail. You rehearse conversations. You anticipate problems before they arise. And deep down, it's not because you're obsessive. It's because uncertainty makes you feel unsafe.

In psychology, this is called *safety-seeking behavior*—doing everything possible to avoid discomfort, uncertainty, or perceived danger. It's rooted in the brain's attempt to protect you, but over time, it actually reinforces fear.

Control gives the illusion of security. If you can just get it right . . . If you can just stay ahead of everything . . . If you can just hold it all together . . . Then maybe the worst won't happen.

This is a hallmark of what's known as *intolerance of uncertainty*, the struggle to function when outcomes are unpredictable. And anxiety thrives in that gap.

Control is a heavy burden. It doesn't bring peace: It steals it. It keeps your shoulders tense, your jaw clenched, your thoughts constantly scanning for threats. And worst of all, it puts you in a position you were never meant to occupy: trying to play God.

Proverbs 3:5 doesn't say to figure it all out. It says to trust.

That doesn't mean being passive. It means releasing the need to know how everything will turn out. It means loosening your grip—on outcomes, on timelines, on people—and trusting that God sees what you can't.

Loosening control isn't weakness. It's a shift from hypervigilance to surrender. It's a daily practice of saying, "I don't have to hold everything together, because God is already holding me."

Loosening control is not the same as losing it. It's surrendering to a God who never sleeps on the job. It's trusting that even when you don't understand, he does. And that's enough.

Anchor Truth

Peace doesn't come from having control. It comes from trusting the one who is in control.

Prayer

God, you know how tightly I've been holding on—how much I crave certainty, how afraid I am to let go. Help me trust you in the places I've been clenching with fear. I don't want to be in charge of everything. I want to rest in the truth that you already are. Teach me to loosen my grip on one small thing at a time.

Invitation

Make a short list of the things you are trying to control right now. Pick just one item, and ask what it would look like to release this to God, even just for today. You don't have to let go of everything at once. Start with one thing.

When Guilt Tells the Truth—and When It Lies

So now there is no condemnation for those who belong to Christ Jesus.

ROMANS 8:1

Guilt can be a teacher. Or a tyrant.

Sometimes it shows up like a warning light on the dashboard, alerting you to something that needs repair. That's healthy guilt, real guilt. It aligns with your values, helps you make amends, nudges you back on track.

But sometimes guilt lies. It clings to your shoulders even when you've done nothing wrong. It whispers that you're selfish for resting, disloyal for saying no, unworthy for falling short. That's false guilt. And it's relentless.

True guilt says, "You crossed a line that matters. Now you can take steps to make it right."

False guilt says, "You feel bad, so you must have done something wrong"—even if you didn't.

The difference? One invites growth. The other keeps you stuck.

People-pleasers often carry loads of false guilt. So do perfectionists, firstborns, and those raised in rigid religious environments.

Even your own empathy can betray you, causing you to overidentify with others' pain and take responsibility that isn't yours.

Jesus didn't die for pretend guilt. He didn't rise from the grave so you could stay buried in shame over things you didn't cause or can't control.

Healthy guilt leads to confession, repentance, and repair. False guilt leads to anxiety, self-punishment, and emotional exhaustion.

So here's your challenge: Name the guilt. Ask yourself, "Is this pointing me toward love and responsibility? Or is this just fear in disguise?"

God isn't in the business of guilt-tripping. But he is in the business of soul-restoring.

Anchor Truth

The Holy Spirit convicts with clarity and compassion. False guilt confuses and condemns. Learn to tell the difference and let go of the weight that was never yours to carry.

Prayer

God, help me discern between the guilt that heals and the guilt that harms. Quiet the lies, speak your truth, and restore my confidence in your grace.

Invitation

Pay attention to a moment today when you feel guilty. Pause. Ask, "Is this calling me to love better or just making me feel less than?" Let that clarity guide your response.

The Pressure Cooker

Fools vent their anger,
but the wise quietly hold it back.

PROVERBS 29:11

There's a reason pressure cookers come with release valves. Without them, steam builds. Heat increases. And eventually—something bursts.

That's what unprocessed anger does to the soul.

You hold it in. You tell yourself to "let it go." Smile through the tension. Numb it with productivity. Push past it with prayer and a positive attitude. But all the while, the pressure is rising. And when it hits capacity? That sharp tone. That sarcastic jab. That explosive outburst or tearful collapse—it all comes spilling out.

Unprocessed anger doesn't disappear. It goes somewhere. Often into your body, relationships, or sense of worth. You start to feel exhausted for no clear reason. You snap at small things. You struggle to concentrate. Or you withdraw—not just from others, but from yourself.

This doesn't mean you're weak or dramatic. It means you're human.

Proverbs says the wise "hold it back," not bottle it up. The Hebrew word used here implies a measured response, not suppression. Wisdom doesn't deny anger. It directs it. It recognizes what's beneath the surface and releases the steam slowly—before there's a rupture.

So what does that look like?

It looks like honest journaling instead of mental rehearsing.

It looks like giving yourself five minutes to rage-cry in the car before walking into a tough meeting.

It looks like calling a friend and saying, "I don't need solutions. I just need to vent."

It looks like speaking the truth calmly instead of stewing silently.

It looks like prayer that starts with "God, I'm mad, and I need your help."

Anger isn't the problem. Pretending you're not angry is.

Anchor Truth

Anger needs a release valve or it will find its own way out.

Prayer

God, I've held in more than I've known how to handle. Help me notice the pressure rising, and teach me how to let it out with wisdom.

Invitation

Take inventory today: Where's your anger going? Into silence? Snark? Stress? Choose one small way to release some of the pressure in a healthy direction.

The Anger Beneath the Sadness

Stop being angry! Turn from your rage!
Do not lose your temper—it only leads to harm.

PSALM 37:8

What if your sadness isn't just sadness? What if it's anger that never had a safe place to land?

Sometimes depression doesn't start with despair. It starts with fury—with things that should've been different, people who should've protected you, boundaries that were crossed or never respected in the first place.

But for some of us, anger feels unsafe. It wasn't allowed when we were growing up. It didn't feel Christian. Or it got shut down quickly. So instead of expressing it, we buried it under a smile, under shame, under the demand to be "fine." And what we bury, festers.

Anger with nowhere to go turns inward. It becomes self-blame. It calcifies into a heavy sadness that whispers, "It must be me."

Psychologists have found that unexpressed anger—especially when coupled with harsh self-judgment—is often linked to depressive symptoms. It doesn't mean you're doing something wrong. It means your pain is looking for air.

David, the psalmist, didn't bottle up his anger. He shouted it. Wrote it. Sang it. He brought the full force of his rage to God without filtering it. And somehow that expression became worship.

God can handle your fury. He's not scandalized by it. In fact, acknowledging it may be the first step toward healing.

Your sadness may be asking you to listen to your anger—not to act on it recklessly, but to name it, honor it, and stop turning it against yourself.

And remember: David didn't wait to worship until his emotions were tidy. He worshiped in the tension—grieving, raging, hoping, trusting. His psalms are proof that God meets us not after the storm, but in the middle of it. Your anger doesn't disqualify you from worship. It might just be the door into it.

Anchor Truth

Some depression is unspoken anger. Healing begins when you stop blaming yourself and start being honest about what hurt you.

Prayer

God, I'm tired of pretending. Show me if there's anger buried under this sadness. Help me bring it to you—not to destroy, but to heal.

Invitation

Think back to a situation where sadness overwhelmed you. Was there any anger under the surface? Write an uncensored prayer that gives it voice.

When You're Not Included

Turn to me and be gracious to me,
for I am lonely and afflicted.

PSALM 25:16 (NIV)

It hits differently when you weren't invited. Maybe it was a dinner with friends. A group chat you weren't added to. A celebration you only found out about after the fact, through someone else's photos or a passing comment that made your stomach sink.

The loneliness that comes from exclusion has a special kind of sting. It whispers lies: "You're forgettable." "You're not wanted." "You don't belong." And while part of you tries to brush it off—"It's no big deal"—another part aches with that quiet, familiar question, "Why not me?"

Even David, the warrior–king and "man after [God's] own heart," knew this feeling. In Psalm 25, he doesn't hide it. He names it: "I am lonely and afflicted." He doesn't minimize his ache. Instead, he brings it to God.

Loneliness from exclusion taps into our God-given need for connection. So when we're left out, it's not just disappointment—it's disorientation. It disrupts our sense of worth, even when we *know* it shouldn't.

But here's the invitation: When you're not included by others, turn toward the one who never leaves you out. Jesus knew what it felt like to be excluded, even by his closest friends. In his final hours, they fell asleep on him, denied him, abandoned him. He gets it. And yet, in that lonely place, he kept choosing love. He kept offering himself. He kept leaning into the presence of his Father. You can too.

Not being included doesn't mean you're unworthy. Sometimes it just means people are imperfect, distracted, or walking through their own stuff.

It's not always personal, but it still hurts. And God meets you in *that* place. He sees the hurt no one else does. And he whispers what your soul needs to hear: "You belong. Always."

Anchor Truth

Being left out by others doesn't mean you're left out by God. His invitation is always open, and his presence is your permanent place of belonging.

Prayer

God, you see the sting in my heart when I'm not invited, included, or remembered. Help me not to spiral into insecurity. Remind me that my worth isn't determined by who reaches out, but by the one who never lets go. Anchor me in your unshakable love, and help me become someone who includes others too.

Invitation

Was there a moment recently when you felt left out? Instead of pushing it down, bring it to God. Journal what it stirred up in you, and ask him to speak truth into those tender places. Then consider one small way you could extend belonging to someone else this week.

When the Words Just Don't Land

The instructions of the LORD are perfect, reviving the soul.

PSALM 19:7

You've heard it said your whole life: "Just read the Bible." As if it's simple. As if it's always comforting. As if opening the pages will instantly bring peace.

But what happens when it doesn't? What happens when you read it and feel nothing? Or worse—when you end up more confused than when you started? What happens when the words feel distant? Or triggering? Or tied to the very teachings you're trying to untangle?

It's sometimes referred to as *textual fatigue*—a deep mental and emotional weariness that sets in when something familiar becomes difficult to engage with, often due to unresolved tension.

Others carry something closer to spiritual *scrupulosity*—a form of anxiety and guilt where you feel immense pressure to read, understand, and apply Scripture perfectly, or you fear you're failing God.

If that's you, take a breath. You're not broken. You're not faithless. And you're definitely not alone.

Scripture is sacred, yes. But it's also ancient, complex, and sometimes confusing. And when you've been handed harmful interpretations—or even used verses as weapons against yourself—it makes sense that picking up the Bible can feel heavy.

Psalm 19 says God's Word revives the soul. But revival doesn't always happen on page one. Sometimes the soul revives slowly. Through wrestling. Through rest. Through learning to approach Scripture not as a test, but as a conversation.

God isn't waiting to scold you for struggling with his Word. He's already familiar with your questions. And he's still speaking, even when the page feels quiet.

Anchor Truth

Let God speak to you gently, and his Word will revive your soul.

Prayer

God, I want to hear from you. But sometimes your Word feels like a wall instead of a window. Help me approach it gently. Without pressure. Without fear. Just with openness. Speak to me in a way I can receive.

Invitation

What emotions come up when you try to read the Bible? Take a moment to reflect on where those feelings might be coming from.

The Masks We Wear

Fearing people is a dangerous trap,
but trusting the LORD means safety.

PROVERBS 29:25

We learn to wear emotional masks early. Maybe it was the smile you forced at the dinner table so no one would ask what was wrong. Or the version of you that performed, excelled, or kept the peace—because conflict felt unsafe or rejection stung too much.

Over time, the mask can feel like your actual face. But it's not. It's a costume stitched together by fear. Fear of disappointing. Fear of being misunderstood. Fear of being truly seen.

And Proverbs names it for what it is: a trap. A mask might shield you from the sting of rejection, but it also blocks the warmth of connection. You can't feel loved when you're not showing who you really are.

We wear masks not because we're liars, but because we're survivors. But survival is not the same as safety. The kind of safety that comes from trusting the Lord—not people's opinions, not the shifting winds of popularity, not the inner critic that says you're only as good as your performance.

Even biblical giants fell into the trap. Saul was tormented by the approval of the people. Pilate gave in to the crowd rather than doing what he knew was right.

But the opposite example is Jesus, who didn't cater to public opinion, didn't try to manage others' impressions, and never altered his truth to earn applause. He modeled congruence: His inner life matched his outer words. No mask.

Here's the thing: The people who matter most in your life—safe, mature, grounded people—don't want your mask. They want you. They want your honesty, your hesitations, even your awkward, unpolished self.

It's scary to set the mask down. But it's also the only way to be known and to rest in the safety that God offers.

Anchor Truth

You don't need a mask to be loved. God meets you in your honesty.

Prayer

God, I've spent so much energy trying to be what others expect. Help me learn the safety of your approval. Teach me to trust you more than I fear being judged.

Invitation

Take five minutes today to journal this sentence: "The mask I most often wear is . . ." Then reflect on what it costs you to keep wearing it—and what freedom might come if you took it off.

Gratitude and Humility

God opposes the proud but gives grace to the humble.

JAMES 4:6

Gratitude and humility are soul siblings. You rarely find one without the other. And when you do, something feels off.

Real gratitude doesn't swagger. It doesn't brag about being "blessed" in a way that makes others feel cursed. It doesn't look down on people who are struggling and say, "If only they had more faith." That's not gratitude. That's ego with a spiritual filter slapped on.

Humility, on the other hand, opens the door wide. It knows it didn't earn every good thing. It remembers its mess. It admits it didn't climb the ladder on grit alone. It stops pretending and starts appreciating everything.

That's why humble people are the most grateful ones in the room. They don't pretend they've got it all together. They don't owe their thankfulness to optics or obligation. They know just how fragile life can be, just how undeserved grace really is. They've lost things. They've been brought low. And still they give thanks.

Humility doesn't mean groveling. It means seeing clearly—yourself, your limits, your story. And when you see clearly, you stop needing credit for everything. You start noticing what's been gifted to you. Grace you didn't deserve. Breath you didn't ask for. People who showed up when you were falling apart.

That kind of gratitude is raw. Real. It says, "I'm not entitled to this breath, this sunrise, this second chance, this meal, this moment—but I'll receive it anyway, with open hands and an open heart."

And when you start living like that? When you walk into your life like it's all been given and none of it was owed? That's where transformation begins. That's where joy hides—in the places you stopped demanding and started delighting.

Anchor Truth

Gratitude doesn't come from having it all. It comes from knowing you don't—and still saying thank you.

Prayer

God, strip away my pride. Help me see everything good in my life as grace, not proof of my worthiness. Teach me to live low, to notice beauty, and to say thanks from a humble heart.

Invitation

Where has pride quietly taken credit for what grace provided? Where can you swap entitlement for awe? Try whispering "thank you" today for something you didn't earn.

Your Body Keeps the Score

My heart is in anguish. The terror of death overpowers me. Fear and trembling overwhelm me. I can't stop shaking.

PSALM 55:4-5

Sometimes your body knows before your brain does. Before you admit you're overwhelmed, your shoulders tense. Before you name your anxiety, your chest tightens. Before you call it grief, your energy drops and your stomach churns. That's not weakness. That's intelligence.

Your body is wired to respond to stress, fear, and emotional strain. Even when your conscious mind is pushing through, ignoring the warning signs, your nervous system is still talking. The problem is—we're often too busy, distracted, or detached to listen.

David knew something about that kind of embodied stress. In Psalm 55, he doesn't just say, "I'm upset." He describes the whole-body impact: trembling, fear, shaking. He doesn't try to hide it with poetic polish—he just tells the truth. That's self-awareness. That's holy honesty.

In trauma work and somatic therapy, this is known as *body-based awareness*. Your body often holds memories, stress, and signals your mind hasn't caught up with yet. That ache in your jaw? Could be resentment. That fatigue you can't explain? Could be suppressed grief. That urge to flee the room? Could be an old wound resurfacing.

You don't have to analyze everything you feel, but you *do* need to listen. Your body isn't trying to betray you. It's trying to bring you back to yourself.

Self-awareness grows when you learn to check in—not just with your thoughts, but with your body. It's one more way to tell the truth. And healing always starts there.

Anchor Truth

Your body often speaks what your heart hasn't said out loud.

Prayer

God, I've been living in my head. Help me listen to what my body is trying to tell me. Show me how to honor the signals—not to obsess over them, but to learn from them with grace.

Invitation

Mentally scan your body today. Where are you holding tension? Tightness? Numbness? Pause and ask, "What might this be connected to?" Don't try to fix it—just notice. That's enough for today.

When the Words Fly

The tongue is a small thing that makes grand speeches. But a tiny spark can set a great forest on fire.

JAMES 3:5

Let's talk about swearing. Not in theory, but in traffic. In arguments. In moments when your insides feel like a volcano and your mouth becomes the escape hatch. You don't plan it. It just detonates.

Some say, "It's just words." But language carries weight. It does something to us—and to the people on the receiving end. And when anger spikes, that language often comes loaded with shame, blame, or heat meant to burn.

So what's really happening?

Swearing, when fused with rage, is usually a form of *emotional discharge*. Your body is overloaded. Your nervous system is on fire. And the shortest route to relief is through the mouth. It's primal. Fast. And for a split second—satisfying.

But what happens next?

Often regret. Embarrassment. Distance. Because the words that feel like release in the moment can become wreckage in the aftermath. And if swearing becomes our default, we miss the chance to get underneath the emotion.

Swearing isn't the root problem. It's the shortcut. It's what we do instead of slowing down. Instead of saying, "That hurt." Or "I feel powerless." Or "This touched something deep in me that I haven't dealt with."

Here's the challenge: Don't just monitor your mouth, explore your mood. What are you actually feeling when you blow your top? What are you trying to say beneath the blast?

This isn't about shame. This is about power. Real power. The kind that doesn't erupt, but engages. The kind that doesn't just let words fly, but lets truth speak.

Because anyone can curse. But it takes courage to name the real wound underneath the words.

Anchor Truth

Swearing may feel powerful, but true power comes from naming what's real, not just what's loud.

Prayer

God, when I feel out of control, help me pause before I explode. Help me choose words that reflect your grace—even when I'm not feeling it yet.

Invitation

The next time you feel like cursing, ask yourself what emotion is hiding beneath the fury. What are you really trying to say? Write it down—unedited and honest.

The Martyr Complex

And what do you benefit if you gain the whole world but lose your own soul?

MARK 8:36

You sacrifice your time. You swallow your opinions. You bend over backward and call it love. But deep down, it doesn't feel like love. It feels like losing yourself—slowly, quietly, completely. That's the martyr complex. And it's a hallmark of codependency.

You wear exhaustion like a badge of honor. You're secretly proud of how little you ask for, how much you endure. You keep giving even after your soul is screaming *enough*. But what looks like selflessness is often just self-erasure. And it's not holy. It's harmful.

The martyr complex convinces you that suffering is the path to worth. That if you just hold out long enough, prove yourself sacrificial enough, one day someone will finally love you back the way you deserve. But here's the truth: God never asked you to bleed out emotionally to keep someone else comfortable.

In Scripture, we see the shadow side of this pattern in Jonah. He's not typically cast as a martyr, but when God extended compassion to Nineveh, Jonah sulked. He had sacrificed, preached, obeyed—or so he thought. But his obedience was transactional. He wanted control, not compassion. He didn't truly want to serve. He wanted to be seen as righteous, as indispensable.

The martyr complex often stems from that same root: a craving to feel needed, to gain identity through sacrifice. And when your efforts go unnoticed or unreciprocated, bitterness builds.

But you are not Jesus. You don't need to be crucified for someone else's healing. He already did that.

Anchor Truth

Sacrifice without boundaries isn't noble—it's self-abandonment. True love doesn't demand that you lose yourself to prove your worth.

Prayer

God, show me where I've confused codependency with Christlike love. Teach me to serve without surrendering my soul.

Invitation

What part of your identity has been tied to overgiving? What would it look like to set that down—not out of bitterness, but in freedom? Write it out. Name it. Then ask God to help you release it.

The Difference Between Solitude and Isolation

But Jesus often withdrew to the wilderness for prayer.

LUKE 5:16

There's a quiet kind of loneliness that heals, and a heavy kind that harms. The difference isn't in the silence—it's in the spirit behind it.

Solitude is chosen. It's a sacred pause, a place where your soul can breathe. It gives you room to hear yourself think and to hear from God.

Isolation, on the other hand, creeps in when we pull away not to rest, but to hide. It's loneliness with the door locked. It feels like safety, but it often deepens our ache and distorts our view of others—and ourselves.

Jesus modeled solitude, not isolation. He intentionally stepped away from the crowds and the chaos, not because he was burned out or bitter, but because he was deeply connected to his Father and rooted enough to know he needed that space. And when he returned, he was more grounded, more compassionate, more present.

You can step into solitude even when you feel lonely. You can turn the ache of absence into the invitation of presence—the kind that starts with God, not with people. Because healthy solitude reminds you that you are not your productivity, your popularity, or your performance.

You are a person who is deeply loved, even in the quiet. But when loneliness tempts you to shut the world out, check your motives.

Are you withdrawing to reflect and reconnect, or to nurse your wounds and reinforce the walls? One heals. The other hardens.

Anchor Truth

Solitude is space for the soul to breathe. Isolation is loneliness without light. One brings healing. The other deepens the ache.

Prayer

God, teach me to choose solitude without slipping into isolation. Let the quiet be a place where I sense your presence, not just my emptiness. Help me return from it renewed and ready to love.

Invitation

Take ten minutes today and step into solitude—not scrolling, not numbing—just sitting in silence with God. Let the quiet hold you, not haunt you.

When You're Surrounded, But Still Lonely

Why am I discouraged? Why is my heart so sad? I will put my hope in God! I will praise him again—my Savior and my God!

PSALM 42:5-6

You don't have to be alone to feel lonely. In fact, some of the loneliest moments come when you're surrounded by people—but none of them truly see you.

You smile. You show up. You keep the conversation moving. But inside? There's a quiet ache. A sense that everyone else got the memo on connection—and you're still waiting for yours.

That's the thing about loneliness: It's not about physical isolation. It's about emotional disconnection. It's the space between being *around* people and feeling ***known*** by them.

David understood this feeling. In Psalm 42, he doesn't sugarcoat his emotions. He confesses his discouragement in verse 5.

This wasn't just situational sadness—it was soul-deep solitude. But notice what he does: He names it. He turns to God. He asks for grace.

That's the first step out of the silent wilderness of loneliness. Not fixing it. Not pretending it's fine. But *naming it*—and turning toward the one who never turns away.

From a clinical lens, research shows that one of the most powerful antidotes to chronic loneliness is not *more people*, but *more authenticity*.

When you let someone—anyone—see the real you, the shame of disconnection starts to lose its grip.

So start there: Be authentic. With God. With a counselor. With a safe friend. Don't minimize your ache. And don't over-personalize it, either. Loneliness isn't proof that you're broken. It's proof that you're human.

Anchor Truth

You can feel lonely and still be deeply loved. Loneliness is a signal—not your sentence.

Prayer

God, I confess my loneliness to you. I don't want to numb it or ignore it. I want to bring it to you—the ache, the questions, the desire to be known. Thank you for seeing me even when I feel invisible. Help me move toward connection, starting with you.

Invitation

Name your loneliness today. In your journal, in your prayer, or with a trusted friend—don't let it stay buried. You're not weak for feeling this way. You're brave for telling the truth.

Curiosity Is the Gateway to Growth

Search me, O God, and know my heart;
test me and know my anxious thoughts.

PSALM 139:23

Personal growth doesn't begin with willpower. It begins with a question.

Before transformation comes exploration. You can't change what you refuse to look at, and you can't heal what you're unwilling to name. That's why curiosity is the front door to growth.

When the psalmist asks God to "search me," he's not making a poetic gesture. He's practicing spiritual curiosity—inviting insight, exposure, and revelation. This kind of self-examination isn't passive. It's brave. It says, "I want to know what's really going on inside me, even if it's messy or uncomfortable." And that's where change begins.

Social science research reveals that curiosity is known to increase cognitive flexibility, emotional intelligence, and even resilience to stress. When we remain curious, especially in the face of struggle, we're more open to possibility. More willing to reflect. Less likely to blame or shut down.

Curiosity turns "What's wrong with me?" into "What's happening in me?" It transforms "Why can't I get it together?" into "What might this pattern be trying to tell me?" It removes shame and replaces it with wonder.

And here's the kicker: When you get curious about your emotions, your habits, your relationships, your resistance—it means you're showing up. It means you're willing to learn. And that posture changes everything.

Jesus modeled this over and over. Instead of preaching at people, he asked questions. "What do you want me to do for you?" "Why are you afraid?" "Who do you say I am?"

His invitation is clear: Stay open. Keep asking. Dig deeper.

Growth isn't about having all the answers. It's about asking the right questions with a humble heart. Curiosity is how we become self-aware, emotionally agile, and spiritually mature.

Anchor Truth

The first step toward growth isn't effort—it's curiosity. God can work with an honest question more than a fake answer.

Prayer

God, give me the courage to be curious. Show me what I need to see—about myself, about others, about you. And help me resist the urge to shut down or turn away.

Invitation

Ask yourself if there's one part of your life that you've stopped being curious about. A habit? A relationship? A belief? Take five minutes today to explore it gently—with compassion, not critique.

Why Meaning Matters

You will show me the way of life,
granting me the joy of your presence
and the pleasures of living with you forever.

PSALM 16:11

If you've ever battled anxiety, you know how loud your thoughts can become. If you've felt the weight of depression, you know how quiet the world can get. If perfectionism drives you, you know how exhausting it is to never feel "enough." If insecurity shapes your choices, you know how quickly your worth feels fragile. These struggles don't all look the same, but beneath them often lies a shared ache: *What's the point of all this?*

That's why meaning matters. It's not just a philosophical concept. It's a lifeline. It's the "why" that helps us endure the "what." It's the North Star that steadies us when everything else feels unstable.

Psychiatrist Viktor Frankl, reflecting on Nietzsche's insight, often taught that people can endure almost anything if they know their "why." And that's not just theory—research backs it up. A sense of meaning has been linked to lower levels of depression, anxiety, and despair.

Meaning builds resilience. It strengthens recovery. It quiets shame. But here's the thing: The truest, deepest kind of meaning isn't something we construct on our own. It's something we receive from a God who knows us, sees us, and invites us into his story.

This is why a relationship with God matters so much in the mental health journey. He doesn't just offer coping tools. He offers identity. Purpose. Presence. A reason to keep going when nothing else makes sense.

You may still struggle. But when you know your life has meaning—not because of what you do, but because of whose you are—that truth can become a turning point.

So if you're reaching for healing, start by anchoring in meaning. Not the kind you have to hustle for, but the kind that holds you steady because it's rooted in God.

Anchor Truth

The journey to healing begins with knowing you're here for a reason, and that reason is anchored in the heart of God.

Prayer

God, I've carried confusion, fear, discouragement, and self-doubt. But in all of it, I long for a deeper purpose. Remind me that my life has meaning—not because I feel strong, but because you are with me. Help me build my healing on that foundation.

Invitation

Take one quiet moment today to ask God to show you your "why." Not your career, not your title, but your deeper purpose. Let his presence become the center of your meaning.

When Guilt Is Real

Finally, I confessed all my sins to you and stopped trying to hide my guilt. I said to myself, "I will confess my rebellion to the LORD." And you forgave me! All my guilt is gone.

PSALM 32:5

Sometimes the feeling of guilt is the soul's alarm bell ringing true. It's the soul's smoke detector blaring in the background—persistent, unsettling, and impossible to ignore. A sign that something beneath the surface is smoldering.

That was David's story. He abused his power. Violated a married woman. Tried to cover it up. Orchestrated a death. And then he went silent. And that silence nearly crushed him.

He writes in Psalm 32 that his body wasted away, that he groaned all day long. He was buried beneath the weight of real guilt. Not false guilt. But the honest-to-God awareness that he'd sinned, and it was eating him alive from the inside out.

But then he cracked open the silence: "I confessed."

That one word—*confessed*—was the beginning of his restoration. Not because confession fixed everything instantly, but because it invited God into the brokenness.

It shattered the isolation that guilt always tries to create. It put a stake in the ground that said, "I'm not going to let this fester. I'm ready to face it."

Confession isn't groveling. It's not performative penance. It's surrender. It's saying, "God, here's the mess. I own it. I'm not blaming. I'm not hiding. And I trust you with the cleanup."

David's confession didn't erase the consequences. But it did lift the guilt. It ushered in mercy. And it led to the kind of brokenness that leads to beauty. Because God doesn't despise a contrite heart. He welcomes it. Every time.

Anchor Truth

You can't outrun real guilt. But you can surrender it, and when you do, you will find mercy waiting.

Prayer

God, I don't want to hide anymore. I've carried guilt I can't fix on my own. I confess it now, fully and honestly. Not to earn your love, because I already have it. Thank you for the mercy that meets me when I stop pretending.

Invitation

If you've been avoiding confession, consider taking ten minutes in prayer today to name what's real. You don't have to fix it all. Just start with one honest sentence. Grace is already waiting.

From Perfection to Wholeness

This is what the Sovereign LORD, the Holy One of Israel, says: "Only in returning to me and resting in me will you be saved. In quietness and confidence is your strength."

ISAIAH 30:15

Striving and perfectionism promise a lot—security, approval, success, control. But what they deliver is far different—burnout, anxiety, shame, and disconnection.

You don't need a more perfect version of yourself. You need a *whole* one. Not flawless, but honest. Not polished, but present. Not admired, but deeply known and loved.

God never asked you to be perfect. In fact, Scripture reminds us that our strength is found "in returning . . . and resting . . . in quietness and confidence." This is the way forward.

Wholeness means making peace with your humanity. It's showing up with your real self, not the best version of you. It's where God meets you. Not at the finish line, but right here in the middle of your becoming.

Jesus didn't come to recruit the already-perfect. He came to restore the broken, the tired, the discouraged, the overwhelmed—the very people perfectionism wears out.

When you stop striving for perfection, you make space for joy. For peace. For grace. For God to love the real you.

You don't have to keep climbing. You can stop. Breathe. Let go. And live as someone already embraced by grace. That's where wholeness begins.

Anchor Truth

Wholeness is not the result of getting everything right. It's the result of receiving what only God can give: rest, healing, and grace.

Prayer

God, I've spent so much energy trying to be better, do more, and never mess up. But I want to rest in you. I want to live whole, not just polished. Show me what it means to trust your love right here, where I am.

Invitation

Take a breath. Then ask God, "What do you want me to carry forward? What do you want me to lay down?" Let that be your next step into wholeness.

The Illusion of Control

They promise freedom, but they themselves are slaves of sin and corruption. For you are a slave to whatever controls you.

2 PETER 2:19

It starts small. A drink to relax. A scroll to unwind. A bite to soothe. A secret to cope.

You tell yourself, *I've got this*. It's just a thing you do, nothing serious. You could stop if you wanted to. You're still in charge.

But here's the twist: Addiction rarely announces itself with sirens. It disguises itself as choice. You feel in control—until you aren't.

Psychologists often talk about the cycle of addiction. There's the *trigger*—stress, loneliness, boredom, anxiety. Then the *behavior*—the drink, the binge, the swipe, the escape. And finally, the *reward*—the fleeting sense of relief or escape. But underneath that cycle is a hidden cost: Every time you obey the urge without reflection, the illusion of control gets stronger. And the reality of bondage tightens.

This is the slow drift. You're not falling apart overnight. But you're handing over little pieces of your freedom, one compromise at a time.

Eventually, the thing you once used starts using you. You're no longer choosing—it's choosing for you.

But here's the hope: God doesn't shame you for this. He invites you to tell the truth about it. He doesn't demand perfection. He offers presence. And presence breaks the power of denial.

Healing begins not with resolve, but with honesty. Not with stronger rules, but with deeper surrender. You don't have to be "strong enough." You just have to be done pretending.

Because the moment you name what controls you is the moment you start taking it back.

Anchor Truth

Freedom begins where denial ends.

Prayer

God, I've been telling myself I'm still in control. But I now see that I've been caught. Help me walk toward freedom, one honest step at a time.

Invitation

Ask yourself, "What's something I keep saying I could quit but haven't?" Write it down. Tell one safe person. Honesty loosens the grip.

What's Underneath the Rage?

Stop being angry! Turn from your rage!
Do not lose your temper—it only leads to harm.

PSALM 37:8

Rage is a spotlight. It might not tell the whole story, but it always points to one. Beneath that outburst? A boundary crossed. Behind that clenched jaw? A wound ignored. Inside that storm? A story never validated.

Most of us weren't taught to explore our anger. We were taught to either fear it, suppress it, or let it fly—and deal with the damage later. But rage is rarely about what just happened. It's about what *keeps* happening. What keeps being buried. What still hasn't been healed.

Psychologists call anger a *secondary emotion* for a reason. Anger isn't weak. It's protective. But it often rushes in to cover up what's harder to feel—grief, shame, helplessness, fear.

And that's where compassion matters. Because unless we slow down and get curious, we'll keep reacting to the surface issue instead of tending to the source. You can spend your life managing your temper or you can start asking why it's flaring in the first place.

God doesn't ask us to pretend we're not angry. Scripture is filled with rawness and honesty. But God does ask us not to stay stuck in it. Why? Because unresolved anger hardens. It isolates. It festers. And eventually, it burns the one holding it.

So what's under your rage? What are you grieving that no one gave you space to name? What injustice have you swallowed to keep the peace? What hurt is still bleeding under the armor?

You don't have to shout it out. Just start by telling the truth—to yourself and to God. That's where healing always begins.

Anchor Truth

Rage is a signal, not a solution. Trace its source with tenderness.

Prayer

God, help me not to fear my anger but to face it honestly. Show me what's underneath the surface and lead me to healing.

Invitation

Write down a moment this week when anger surprised you. Then ask, "What was I really feeling beneath it? Grief? Shame? Powerlessness?" Start there.

The Curiosity of Nicodemus

"How are these things possible?" Nicodemus asked.

JOHN 3:9

Nicodemus had a reputation to protect. He was a respected religious leader. A man of status, intellect, and control. And yet, something about Jesus disrupted his certainty. It didn't line up with what he thought he knew. So, under cover of night, Nicodemus came with questions.

He didn't posture. He didn't argue. He didn't come to trap Jesus with theological debate like some of his peers. He simply asked, "How?" That single word is the heartbeat of curiosity.

Psychologists describe *intellectual humility* as the ability to hold our beliefs with open hands—to stay flexible, teachable, and willing to grow.

Nicodemus shows us what that looks like in real time. He models what it means to be deeply rooted in tradition, yet still open to transformation. And isn't that what spiritual maturity demands? Not blind certainty, but a readiness to learn. A willingness to be re-formed. Nicodemus asked questions not because he had weak faith, but because he longed for deeper truth. He sensed there was more to the story.

Too often we confuse faith with confidence and curiosity with doubt. But the opposite is true: Curiosity is often the evidence of a living, breathing faith—a faith that's still growing. The most dangerous posture isn't questioning. It's coasting. When you stop being curious, you start assuming. You harden. You live from a script instead of a spirit.

Nicodemus didn't get it all at once. But we later see him defending Jesus in public (John 7:50-51), and finally, showing up after the crucifixion to help bury him—no longer in the dark. His curiosity led him from cautious questions to bold allegiance.

Anchor Truth

Curiosity is not a sign of weak faith. It's often the first step toward deeper belief.

Prayer

God, give me the courage to ask questions and the humility to not need all the answers. Let my curiosity be a doorway to deeper trust.

Invitation

Is there a question you've been afraid to ask—about God, your beliefs, or yourself? Write it down. Don't try to answer it today. Just make space for it. Let it grow.

Anger with a Steering Wheel

Jesus entered the Temple and began to drive out all the people buying and selling animals for sacrifice. He knocked over the tables of the money changers.

MATTHEW 21:12

Let's be honest: Many of us don't know what to do with our anger. We either explode and regret it, or we shove it down and pretend it's not there. But Jesus? He didn't do either.

When he entered the Temple and saw how sacred space had been corrupted—had been turned into a marketplace of exploitation—he got angry. Not out-of-control, frothing-at-the-mouth angry. But intentional, righteous, fully-aligned anger. The kind that flipped tables on purpose—not because he lost his temper, but because he kept his center.

This wasn't a meltdown. It was a message. Jesus didn't react impulsively; he responded deliberately. His anger had a steering wheel, not a detonation button. That's the difference between *healthy* and *unhealthy* anger.

Unhealthy anger is reactive. It's a default setting when we feel powerless, insecure, or unheard. It often comes from a place of fear, shame, or wounded pride—and it damages trust, relationships, and our own peace.

But healthy anger? It's clear-eyed and values-driven. It rises in defense of justice, dignity, or boundaries. It tells the truth when something is out of line. And most importantly, it doesn't control you. You direct it.

Emotional regulation doesn't mean suppressing anger. It means recognizing it, owning it, and choosing how to channel it. Regulation is the spiritual and psychological work of letting anger pass *through* you without it taking *over* you.

Jesus never said, "Don't be angry." The Bible says, "In your anger do not sin." That means it's possible to be angry and holy. The key is integration. Your values stay intact. Your words are measured. Your body calms, even when your soul is stirred.

Anchor Truth

You don't have to fear your anger. When guided by truth and grounded in love, anger can become a tool for restoration rather than destruction.

Prayer

God, help me recognize when my anger is rising. Teach me to pause, to listen, and to respond, not react. Let my emotions serve your purposes, not sabotage your peace in me.

Invitation

Think of a time recently when you felt angry. Was it reactive or righteous? What values were at stake? What might it look like to use that anger to bring healing rather than harm?

God's Not Grading You

Come to me, all of you who are weary and carry heavy burdens, and I will give you rest.

MATTHEW 11:28

Somewhere along the way, you confused spiritual devotion with spiritual performance. You pray, but only in the "right" tone. You serve, but you're secretly hoping God's keeping score. You beat yourself up when you skip a quiet time. You call it discipline, but it feels a lot like pressure.

This isn't faith. It's performance anxiety dressed in a Bible verse. And here's the hard truth: Many of us aren't performing for God because he demands it. We're performing because we don't actually believe we're loved without it.

That's when we fall victim to conditional self-worth—the belief that we matter only when we achieve, produce, or meet certain standards. Spiritualize that belief, and you get a soul that's hustling for God's approval while claiming to rest in grace.

But Jesus didn't say, "Come to me with your polished résumé." He says, "Come to me, all of you who are weary." That includes the ones who overspent themselves "for the Kingdom." The ones who served while secretly hollowed out. The ones who said yes to every good thing, hoping it would silence the fear that they're not enough.

If you've been performing for God, it's time to stop. God's not watching from the bleachers with a clipboard. He's walking beside you, inviting you to trade your spiritual perfectionism for presence. Not your best version—your actual self.

This is the kind of authenticity Jesus offers. Not a project to perfect, but a person to be with. Not a grade to earn, but a grace to receive.

Anchor Truth

You don't need to impress God to be loved. He already sees, knows, and chooses you.

Prayer

God, I've spent too long trying to earn what you already gave. Help me stop performing and start trusting. Help me bring my whole, honest self to you.

Invitation

Reflect on one area where your spiritual life feels more like a performance than a relationship. What would it look like to let that guard down, even a little?

The Bedrock of Healing

He will not crush the weakest reed or
put out a flickering candle.

MATTHEW 12:20

Healing doesn't happen in harsh environments. You don't grow roots in a hurricane. You don't open up under threat. You don't become whole in the presence of shame. That's why emotional safety isn't a luxury; it's the bedrock of healing.

Safety isn't about comfort. It's about trust. It's the assurance that your heart won't be hurt. That your struggles won't be exploited. That you can show up unguarded and still be held with dignity.

When Jesus walked this earth, broken people found him safe. The bleeding woman reached out through her shame and found no condemnation. The tax collector climbed a tree and was invited to dinner. The demon-possessed man was clothed and returned to his right mind—restored, not rejected.

In his time on earth, Jesus fulfilled the prophecy that said he wouldn't crush the weakest reed or snuff out the faintest flame. That's a picture of Jesus as a safe place—tender with those who are bruised, patient with those whose spark is fading. His presence was healing because his posture was safe.

If you've struggled to heal, it may not be because you lack faith or strength. It may be because you haven't been safe. Even the strongest soul needs a refuge.

Some churches have taught people to push past their pain with more prayer and more effort, but Jesus never demanded healing on a deadline. He created space for it. And he still does.

Your healing will not take root in chaos. It will not bloom in judgment. It begins in the presence of gentleness, attunement, and grace. And Jesus offers that in full.

Anchor Truth

Healing begins in safety. Jesus offers you that space—where your wounds are seen, your story is honored, and your growth is never rushed.

Prayer

Jesus, I need you to be my safe place. I've tried to heal in hard places, and I'm weary. Help me trust your tenderness and open myself to the slow, sacred work of restoration.

Invitation

Where in your life have you been trying to heal without safety? Name it. Then invite Jesus into that space—not with performance, but with honesty.

Saying What Needs to Be Said

Let your conversation be gracious and attractive so that you will have the right response for everyone.

COLOSSIANS 4:6

It's easier to stay silent. It's easier to nod along, pretend everything's fine, and keep the peace—especially when speaking up might shake the ground beneath a relationship. But silence isn't always kind. And avoidance isn't always gentle. Sometimes the most loving thing you can do is say the thing that's uncomfortable to say.

It takes courage to speak the truth. Real courage. Especially when you're not sure how the other person will receive it. Especially when your voice shakes. Especially when your heart races and you want to backpedal. But growth—both yours and theirs—often hinges on that moment of truth-telling.

Paul urges the believers in Colossae to let their words be gracious *and* well-timed—because the right words, spoken with courage and care, can shift a conversation, a relationship, a life.

Think of Nathan confronting David after the king's moral failure. Nathan didn't come at David with rage. He came with a story, a challenge, and a truth that pierced through denial.

It was risky. But it led to repentance, healing, and redemption. Nathan's courage made space for David's transformation. The same can be true in your life.

Whether it's addressing hurt in a friendship, naming a boundary in your family, or admitting a truth you've long buried—courageous honesty, wrapped in grace, is a spiritual act.

It won't always go the way you hope. People may not respond well. But your job isn't to control the outcome. It's to be faithful in the moment.

Anchor Truth

Truth and love are not opposites; they're allies. Speaking with both is a mark of spiritual and emotional maturity.

Prayer

God, help me speak with clarity and kindness. Give me the courage to say what matters most, even when it's hard.

Invitation

What truth have you been avoiding? Is there a loving, honest conversation that's overdue? Write it out. Pray over it. Then take the step.

Finding Safe People

The heartfelt counsel of a friend is as sweet as perfume and incense.

PROVERBS 27:9

You don't need perfect people in your life. You need safe ones. People who don't flinch when you tell the truth. People who can sit in the silence with you without trying to fix it. People who don't weaponize your vulnerability later. People who can celebrate with you without competing and grieve with you without shifting the spotlight.

Safe people aren't easy to come by. If you've ever trusted someone and been met with judgment, gossip, advice-dumping, backstabbing, or awkward withdrawal, you know the cost. And if you've grown up learning to hide or perform just to keep the peace? Emotional safety can feel unfamiliar—maybe even suspicious.

But here's the truth: Emotional safety is the soil where healing grows. You were made to be known, not managed. Held, not handled.

So how do you find emotionally safe people? Start by becoming one. Practice curiosity instead of control. Respond with empathy instead of evaluation. Honor stories instead of hijacking them. The more you learn to hold space for others, the more you'll be able to recognize who can hold space for you.

Then pay attention. Do they listen well? Do they respect boundaries? Do they apologize when they blow it? Do they stay steady when you're messy? Safe people won't be perfect, but they'll be humble and willing to grow. That's what makes them safe.

Even Jesus had circles. He didn't bare his soul to the crowds. He took Peter, James, and John with him into Gethsemane. He let them see him sweat blood, break down, and beg God for another way. Even the Son of God needed people nearby in his hour of anguish. And you do too.

But don't let past hurt convince you that safe people don't exist. They do. And you are worthy of finding them. You are not too needy. You are human—with human needs wired by a relational God. You were created for connection, and the road to healing doesn't begin with self-sufficiency. It begins with the courage to seek out people who can sit with the unedited you and stay.

Anchor Truth

Emotionally safe relationships are sacred ground. You deserve to be known by people who don't make you pay for it.

Prayer

God, give me the courage to seek out safe people and the wisdom to recognize them. Help me be the kind of friend who holds space for others without judgment, and help me find those who can do the same for me.

Invitation

Who in your life feels safe? What makes them that way? If no one comes to mind, ask God for the discernment and boldness to begin looking again. Healing often begins in the presence of someone who simply stays.

What Humility Really Is (and Isn't)

Don't be selfish; don't try to impress others. Be humble, thinking of others as better than yourselves.

PHILIPPIANS 2:3

We tend to think of humility as a soft-spoken shrug that says, "Oh, I'm nothing." But true humility isn't self-deprecation. It's not self-hatred. And it's definitely not thinking you have nothing to offer. That's just insecurity wearing a modest disguise.

Healthy humility isn't about putting yourself down. It's about *right-sizing* yourself in the world. It's about recognizing your value without making everything about you. It's strength under control. Awareness without arrogance.

In clinical terms, humility is correlated with greater psychological flexibility, higher self-awareness, and lower levels of defensiveness. It's being secure enough in your identity to admit faults, apologize well, defer when needed, and celebrate others freely. Humility does not mean being a doormat. It's having a grounded enough sense of self that you don't need to dominate the room to know your worth.

Jesus embodied this perfectly. He had nothing to prove, yet he knelt and washed feet. He had all authority, yet he used it to serve. His humility didn't diminish his power; it *defined* it.

We often confuse humility with humiliation. But they're not the same. Humiliation is what happens when dignity is taken from you. Humility is what happens when you freely lay it down—not because you're less valuable, but because love leads the way.

Humility isn't a posture of weakness. It's a position of quiet strength. It frees you from the exhausting need to impress, defend, or dominate. When you live humbly, you stop playing the comparison game. You show up fully, love freely, and live rooted in something deeper than applause.

It's a paradox. When you stop striving to prove your worth, you begin to embody it. And in a world obsessed with spotlight and status, true humility shines brighter than pride ever could.

Anchor Truth

Humility isn't thinking less of yourself. It's thinking of yourself less and others more.

Prayer

God, help me stop confusing humility with weakness. Show me how to be grounded in your truth—not puffed up with pride and not deflated with insecurity. Teach me to live with quiet strength, open hands, and a heart that listens first.

Invitation

Where have you mistaken humility for self-shrinkage? Today, practice humble strength: speak the truth with kindness, admit something small you got wrong, or celebrate someone else without comparing.

When You're Tired of Being Overlooked

The last will be first, and the first will be last.

MATTHEW 20:16 (NIV)

Jealousy and resentment don't always start loud. Sometimes they build slowly, in the background, like pressure rising in a sealed jar.

You work hard. You show up. You stay faithful. But someone else gets the spotlight. Someone else gets the promotion. The recognition. The moment. And even if you smile on the outside, inside something twists. You're left wondering, *What about me? Don't I matter too?*

This isn't just about envy. It's about feeling *invisible*. It's the ache of being overlooked when you've done everything right. The weariness of watching someone else get what you've been praying for.

And if you're not careful, that ache can calcify into resentment. Not just toward others—but toward God. You start thinking, *If goodness really gets rewarded, where's mine?*

Jesus told a story in Matthew 20 about workers in a vineyard. Some were hired early. Some were hired late. But at the end of the day, they all received the same wage. And the ones who worked longer? They grumbled. They felt cheated. But the landowner reminded them, "I'm not being unfair—I'm being generous."

That's what grace does. It's not fair. And if you're addicted to fairness, grace will offend you.

But here's the truth: You haven't been forgotten. God's economy runs on timing, not timelines. And your unseen faithfulness is not wasted—not by the one who sees in secret.

Anchor Truth

Feeling overlooked isn't proof you've been forgotten.

Prayer

God, when I feel invisible, remind me that you see it all. Help me resist the pull of resentment when others are recognized. Teach me to trust your timing.

Invitation

If jealousy today feels like Why them?, *gently ask yourself what you are feeling—unseen, unrewarded, or unheard? Name it. Then invite God to meet you in that exact place.*

The Fear Behind the Fence

Such love has no fear, because perfect love expels all fear.

1 JOHN 4:18

You've built fences. We all have. Invisible boundaries that keep people just far enough away to avoid rejection, judgment, disappointment.

You smile, you make small talk, maybe even share bits of your story. But the parts that hurt? The parts that feel tender or unlovable? You keep those tucked out of reach. Why? Because vulnerability is terrifying. What if they don't understand? What if they think less of you?

But here's the truth: The fences you've built for protection can easily become your prison, walling you off from healthy relationships. Real connection can't happen without risk. And growth—true, transformative growth—requires exposure.

You can't heal what you pretend doesn't hurt. You can't deepen relationships if you never let anyone past your surface.

That's where courage steps in. Courage is what lets you open the gate a little wider. It's what helps you say, "Here's the real me—mess and all." And when you do, you might discover something surprising: The people who matter don't pull away. They draw near.

First John reminds us that love and fear don't share space. When you let yourself be truly seen and truly loved, fear starts to loosen its grip. You begin to realize you're not as alone—or as unworthy—as shame once told you.

Jesus modeled this kind of vulnerable courage. In Gethsemane, we see him in anguish, sweat like blood, asking for another way. He didn't pose. He didn't pretend.

He brought his rawest self to the Father and invited his closest friends to witness it. That's not weakness. That's strength.

Anchor Truth

You can't grow if you're always hiding. Courage invites you to let the right people in and let love drive out fear.

Prayer

God, I'm tired of holding back. Give me the courage to open up—to risk vulnerability so I can experience deeper connection and healing.

Invitation

What fence have you built to protect yourself? What's one way you can open the gate, just a bit, this week?

The Problem with Christian Clichés

When they saw Job from a distance, they scarcely recognized him. Wailing loudly, they tore their robes and threw dust into the air. . . . Then they sat on the ground with him. . . . No one said a word.

JOB 2:12-13

You've probably heard these statements before: "Everything happens for a reason." "God won't give you more than you can handle." "It's all in God's timing." "Too blessed to be stressed." "Let go and let God."

They're meant to help. To comfort. To wrap your pain in something tidy. But instead, they land like vinegar on an open wound. Because life is not always tidy. And real faith doesn't always rhyme.

It's known as *emotional invalidation* when someone, even with good intentions, responds to your pain in a way that dismisses or minimizes it. And in Christian culture, this often comes in the form of polished phrases that bypass the depth of what someone is actually carrying.

Job's friends started out well. When they saw him broken and grieving, they didn't throw theology at him. They didn't offer social media–ready advice or postable truth bombs. They sat in silence for seven days.

Sometimes the holiest thing we can do for someone in pain is nothing at all. No explanations. No sermons. Just presence.

If you've been on the receiving end of clichés—if people quoted verses when you needed validation or gave you formulas when you needed friendship—it's okay to feel angry. Or sad. Or unseen. And if you've handed out clichés yourself, there's grace for that too.

God is not a sound bite. And his comfort doesn't come in prepackaged lines. It comes in presence. Stillness. Truth told gently.

So let's be done with pretending that easy answers can heal deep pain. Let's sit in the silence. And trust that God is already there.

Anchor Truth

Pain can only be healed through presence—not clichés.

Prayer

God, I've been on both sides of this. I've said things that ended up hurting others and I've heard things that made me feel small. Help me speak less and listen more. Help me remember that presence is more powerful than platitudes.

Invitation

What phrase have you heard when you were hurting that felt more dismissive than helpful? If someone in your life is hurting, resist the urge to fix it. If you're the one hurting, try saying this: "I don't need advice right now. I just need someone to be with me."

Receiving Help with Grace

Pride leads to disgrace,
but with humility comes wisdom.

PROVERBS 11:2

Some people would rather limp alone than lean on someone else. They say things like "I've got it" or "I don't want to be a burden" or "I'll figure it out." But behind that self-reliance is often something more tender: Fear of being seen as weak. Or worse—needy.

But here's the truth: Healing almost always happens in community. You cannot become whole while pretending you already are.

One of the strongest predictors of mental health improvement is a person's *openness to help*. Whether it's support from a friend, guidance from a counselor, or simply allowing someone to sit with you in your pain—healing depends on connection. And connection requires humility.

Humility says, "I need." Pride says, "I'll manage." And guess which one God blesses?

Scripture consistently links humility with wisdom, grace, and growth. The proud resist help because they're convinced they shouldn't need it. But the humble? They become wiser, stronger, freer—because they allow themselves to be human. Dependent. Receptive.

Even Jesus, when carrying the cross, accepted help from Simon of Cyrene. He didn't turn it into a solo act. And if the Son of God could receive help without shame, so can you.

Anchor Truth

You don't get stronger by pretending you're not struggling. You grow by reaching out, letting in, and receiving what grace wants to give you.

Prayer

God, help me receive what I need with open hands and a humble heart. Quiet the voice that says I have to prove myself. Teach me to accept love, support, and guidance as gifts from you.

Invitation

Where are you trying to go it alone? Invite someone into that space today—whether it's a friend, mentor, or counselor. Practice saying "I need help" and let it be holy, not humiliating.

Don't Believe Everything You Think

Fix your thoughts on what is true, and honorable, and right, and pure, and lovely, and admirable.

PHILIPPIANS 4:8

Your mind is a narrator. Every day it spins stories about your worth, your future, and what kind of day it's going to be.

But here's the kicker: Not everything it says is true. That voice in your head that says, "This will never get better," "Everyone's farther along than you," "Why even try?" That's not discernment. That's distortion.

It's called *cognitive bias*—the brain's tendency to fixate on what's wrong, dangerous, or disappointing. It's a survival instinct. But if left unchecked, it becomes a worldview. Optimism, then, isn't about silencing your thoughts. It's about challenging the ones that don't serve you. Or the ones that won't shut up.

Paul wasn't suggesting some sanitized version of thought control when he wrote Philippians 4:8. He was offering a filter. A test. A way to separate truth from the tangle. Is this thought true? Is it hopeful? Is it rooted in God's grace—or my fear?

You don't have to entertain every thought that walks through the door. You can say, "Thanks for stopping by," and show it out. "Be on your way now." And the more you practice this—the more you call out distorted thinking and replace it with something grounded—the more your optimism becomes resilient.

You don't have to become a sunshine-and-rainbows person. But you *can* become someone who holds space for the good. Someone who doesn't believe every anxious prediction. Someone who replaces internal criticism with curiosity.

That's what optimism does: It breaks the echo chamber of fear and creates room for something truer, lighter, and more aligned with the Spirit of God.

Anchor Truth

Not every thought deserves your agreement.

Prayer

God, help me pay attention to my inner dialogue. Interrupt the loops that wear me down—and plant new ones that lift me up.

Invitation

Write down one negative thought that's been circling your mind lately. Now ask, "Is this true?" Replace it with one statement that reflects grace, not fear.

The Courage to Heal

Do you want to get well?

JOHN 5:6 (NIV)

Some of the boldest steps you'll ever take won't be public or dramatic. They'll be internal. Invisible. Unapplauded. But life-altering.

It takes courage to admit you're not okay. It takes courage to go to therapy. To tell the truth about your past. To stop numbing the pain and finally feel it. To face the pattern you keep repeating. To forgive someone who will never apologize. To forgive yourself.

Jesus asked a bedridden man lying beside a healing pool, "Do you want to get well?" It sounds like an odd question. Of course he wanted to get well, right?

But healing comes at a cost. It requires letting go of what's familiar, even if it's broken. It means stepping out of resignation and into responsibility. And that takes guts.

In psychology, it's called *approach-oriented coping*—when you move *toward* what's painful in order to resolve it, rather than avoiding or denying it.

People who face their emotional wounds head-on, rather than burying or bypassing them, tend to report better long-term well-being and resilience.

But it's not easy. It takes intention. It takes support. It takes a holy kind of bravery.

Courage isn't just found on battlefields or big stages. It's found in the small, quiet "yes" to healing. It's the resolve to become whole, even when staying fractured feels safer. It's refusing to let your pain become your identity.

Jesus didn't shame the man for being stuck. But he didn't let him stay there either. Healing wasn't forced. It was *invited.* And that same invitation is extended to you.

Anchor Truth

Courage is choosing to move toward healing, even when it's painful, slow, or uncertain. The first step may not feel heroic, but it's holy.

Prayer

God, give me the courage to face what I've avoided. Heal what's broken in me. Help me step toward wholeness—even when it's scary.

Invitation

What part of your life needs healing? Don't try to fix everything at once. Just take the next courageous step—make the call, name the wound, ask for help. Healing begins with that.

When Caring Becomes Crushing

Give all your worries and cares to God, for he cares about you.

1 PETER 5:7

You don't have to be a nurse or counselor to experience compassion fatigue. If you've ever shown up for someone while silently running on fumes, you already know what it feels like.

It's the ache beneath the smile. The numbness behind the "I'm fine." The resentment that sneaks in when giving stops feeling like love and starts feeling like obligation.

Compassion fatigue—often described as *the cost of caring*—sits at the intersection of burnout and emotional depletion. It's what happens when you carry the emotional weight of others without tending to your own.

And you don't have to be in a formal helping profession to feel it. Parents. Pastors. Friends. Spouses. Adult children of aging parents. Leaders. Listeners. Fixers. Even those who simply carry the emotional weight of too much news, too much need, too much noise.

It can feel noble at first—you're the one people count on. But over time, something shifts. You start waking up tired. You feel irritated more often. You lose empathy. You check out emotionally or withdraw altogether. You wonder, "What's wrong with me?" when the better question is, "What have I been carrying for too long without relief?"

Even Jesus—the very image of divine compassion—stepped away from the crowds. He sought quiet. He withdrew to be alone. He said no. If he modeled limits, why do we pretend we're limitless?

The first step out of compassion fatigue is naming it. You're not weak. You're not failing. You're human. And you need rhythms of rest, replenishment, and honesty about what you can (and can't) carry. You were never meant to carry every burden alone. Not even the burdens of those you love most.

Anchor Truth

Caring deeply doesn't mean carrying endlessly. True compassion includes compassion for yourself.

Prayer

Jesus, I'm tired in places no one can see. I've stretched too far, carried too much, and tried too hard for too long. Help me rest in your presence—not just physically, but emotionally and spiritually. Teach me how to let go.

Invitation

Ask yourself honestly, "What am I carrying that's not mine to hold?" Write down one step you can take to lighten that load this week—whether it's rest, boundaries, asking for help, or simply saying no.

Naming What's Yours

Pay careful attention to your own work, for then you will get the satisfaction of a job well done, and you won't need to compare yourself to anyone else.

GALATIANS 6:4

You can't own what you won't name. And one of the first steps to reclaiming your agency is getting clear on what's *actually yours*. Your time. Your energy. Your attitude. Your effort. Your boundaries. Your voice.

We lose track of that list quickly, especially when we're trying to keep everyone else happy. Before we know it, we're carrying emotions that aren't ours, trying to control outcomes that don't belong to us, or shrinking to make others comfortable. That's not agency. That's emotional outsourcing. And it's exhausting.

Paul's words in Galatians aren't about self-absorption. They're about self-responsibility. "Pay careful attention to your own work," he says. Not your friend's. Not your boss's. Not your spouse's. Yours.

Why? Because that's where the satisfaction lives—not in comparison, not in control, but in showing up fully to the work God has given you.

In therapy, this is called *locus of control*—the belief about what's within your influence. A healthy internal locus means you understand what's yours to change. People with a strong sense of agency don't try to control everything, but they do take ownership of their choices. They stop waiting for someone to rescue them, and they start participating in their own healing.

That's not selfish. That's spiritual maturity.

So today, do a mental audit. What are you carrying that was never yours? What are you avoiding that *is*? The path to peace isn't paved by people-pleasing or avoidance. It's built one brave, honest choice at a time.

Anchor Truth

Agency begins when you take responsibility for what's yours and release what isn't.

Prayer

God, show me where I've taken on too much and where I've let go of what matters. Give me the wisdom to know the difference and the courage to take back what's mine to carry. Not out of pride, but out of trust.

Invitation

Take sixty seconds today and list what is yours to steward.

The Freedom of Not Having to Win

Don't be selfish; don't try to impress others. Be humble, thinking of others as better than yourselves.

PHILIPPIANS 2:3

There's something exhausting about always needing to be right. The mental gymnastics. The spiraling thoughts. The subtle—or not-so-subtle—dig to prove your point. It's not just relational friction, it's emotional erosion.

But what if peace matters more than proving yourself? This quiet gift of humility frees you from the compulsion to win. You stop seeing every disagreement as a battlefield and start seeing it as an opportunity to understand. You stop defending your ego and start defending the relationship.

Look at Abigail in 1 Samuel 25. Her husband, Nabal, insulted David—who was furious and ready for bloodshed. Abigail stepped in, not to defend Nabal's behavior, but to keep the peace. She humbled herself, defused the tension with wisdom and grace, and prevented disaster. That's power without pride. That's strength dressed in humility.

Or consider Paul and Barnabas, who parted ways over a sharp disagreement about John Mark. Rather than battling for dominance, they both continued in ministry separately and fruitfully. They didn't need to "win" the argument to keep living out their calling.

Humility says, "I don't need to have the last word." It shifts the goal from being right to being wise. From conquering to connecting.

Clinically, this kind of mindset reduces anxiety, fosters deeper empathy, and improves communication outcomes. It also protects your energy because you don't have to spin every disagreement into a debate. You can simply say, "I see your side. Let me think about that."

Philippians 2:3 flips the script of pride, inviting you to take the posture of humility. Not to diminish yourself, but to elevate connection. When you're not trying to impress or overpower, you're finally free to love well.

Letting go of the need to win isn't weakness. It's wisdom. And it just might save your sanity, your relationships, and your soul.

Anchor Truth

Humility isn't about shrinking. It's about choosing what matters—peace, grace, and people—over being right.

Prayer

God, help me quiet the part of me that needs to prove something. Grow in me the strength to stay humble when I feel defensive. Teach me to value people over pride and peace over winning.

Invitation

In your next disagreement, pause before speaking. Ask yourself, "What would humility sound like here?" Then choose the words that build a bridge, not a wall.

Panic Isn't the Whole Story

He led me to a place of safety;
he rescued me because he delights in me.

PSALM 18:19

Panic is a hijacker. It grabs you without warning. Your heart races. Your thoughts blur. Your body sends every signal that you're in danger—even when there's no visible threat.

It's terrifying, disorienting, and isolating. And afterward, you're often left with shame. Embarrassment. Exhaustion. Maybe even self-disgust.

Clinicians call this *post-episode shame*—a secondary wave of distress that often follows the panic itself. Many people feel like they've failed somehow, even though they haven't.

So hear this clearly: Panic is not your fault. And it's not your identity. It's a physiological storm, not a moral failure. It's a moment, not the measure of your faith.

This distinction is crucial. Learn to detach your identity from the episode. You are not your panic. You are someone experiencing a moment of *dysregulation*—an inability to manage or control emotional or physiological responses. And it will pass.

You can experience panic and still be deeply loved by God. You can sit on the bathroom floor gasping for air and still be worthy of kindness, dignity, and care.

The psalmist says God led him to a place of safety—not because he had it all together, but because God delighted in him. That's your story too. Your panic may be loud, but it's not the final word. It's not the sum total of who you are.

Panic disorder may explain part of your experience, but it doesn't define your identity. Your value is never up for debate. There is more to you than your moments of feeling overwhelmed. You are more than your lowest hour.

Panic may visit, but it doesn't get to define you. God's rescue, his presence, his delight in you—those are what matter.

Anchor Truth

Panic may feel like the whole story, but God knows the pages you haven't lived yet—and he's not finished.

Prayer

God, when panic takes over, I feel weak, ashamed, and out of control. Help me remember that even when I can't hold it together, you're still holding me. Remind me that I'm more than this moment. Let your love speak louder than my fear

Invitation

Think of one word or phrase that reflects who you are beyond anxiety. (Examples: "Beloved." "Resilient." "Still standing." "Held.") Write it somewhere you'll see it. Speak it over yourself when panic tries to take center stage.

When Helping Isn't Helping

Put me on trial, LORD, and cross-examine me.
Test my motives and my heart.

PSALM 26:2

You call it compassion. You say you're just being supportive. But deep down, you know: This isn't healthy. You're not just helping anymore—you're rescuing. Managing. Covering.

You're absorbing consequences so someone else doesn't have to face them. And it's not love that's driving you. It's fear. Fear that they'll fall apart. Fear that they'll leave. Fear that if you stop holding everything together, it will all come undone, including you.

This is what codependency often looks like: a hidden deal we make in relationships. *I'll be what you need so you'll never leave me.* Or *I'll fix your chaos so I don't have to face mine.* But rescuing isn't the same as loving. One enables dysfunction. The other empowers growth.

When Paul wrote in Galatians 6 that "each one should carry their own load," he wasn't suggesting we stop caring for one another. He was inviting us to own what's ours and let others own what's theirs. That includes emotions, decisions, and consequences.

Some of us were raised in homes where care meant control. Where love meant appeasement. We learned to scan the emotional weather in every room and adjust ourselves accordingly. That's not connection. That's emotional survival.

Real love doesn't require you to vanish. It doesn't demand that you betray yourself to stay in good standing. And it certainly doesn't thrive when one person plays savior while losing their own soul.

If you're stuck in a cycle of rescuing, ask yourself, "What am I afraid will happen if I stop?" Let that answer surface. Name it. Then bring it to God. Sometimes the bravest thing you can do in love is step back—not to punish, but to let another person grow.

Anchor Truth

Love empowers responsibility but doesn't erase it. When you carry someone else's load out of fear or guilt, you rob them of growth—and yourself of peace.

Prayer

God, show me where I've confused rescuing with loving. Help me release what's not mine to carry and trust you to be the Savior I keep trying to be.

Invitation

Ask yourself today, "Where am I rescuing instead of relating?" Write it down. Then take one small step back, just enough to breathe again.

When They Won't See It

Have I now become your enemy because
I am telling you the truth?

GALATIANS 4:16

Few things are as gut-wrenching as watching someone you love spiral—and refuse to see it. You try to help. You offer facts, empathy, gentle warnings, even a tearful plea. But they brush it off. Get defensive. Call you critical. Or go silent.

Denial isn't just frustrating. It's devastating. Because it's not just that they're rejecting truth. It feels like they're rejecting *you.*

But here's the hard truth: You can't make someone see what they're not willing to face. No amount of convincing, confronting, or crying will force insight into a heart that's not ready.

Even Jesus couldn't force change. He looked over Jerusalem and wept—not because he didn't speak truth, but because they wouldn't listen. He knew the heartbreak of watching people choose blindness over healing. And he still loved them.

So what can you do? Let go of control, but not of compassion. Stay honest without becoming hostile. Pray like it matters, because it does. And stop letting their refusal to face truth define your own peace.

Sometimes love means stepping back instead of charging in. Sometimes it's silence, not speeches. A boundary, not a breakdown.

Sometimes the most faithful thing you can do is *not* rescue them. Because facing truth is an inside job. And the Spirit is better at it than you'll ever be.

Anchor Truth

You're not called to be someone's savior, only their witness. Stay faithful. Stay grounded. Stay free.

Prayer

God, it hurts to watch someone I love avoid the truth. Help me release the need to fix them. Give me grace to love without losing myself, and the courage to let your Spirit do what only you can.

Invitation

If you're carrying the burden of someone else's denial, take a moment to name it. Then release it—literally write it down and hand it to God. Trust that you can be faithful without being responsible for their awakening.

You Can Start Over Mid-Sentence

The faithful love of the LORD never ends! His mercies never cease. Great is his faithfulness; his mercies begin afresh each morning.

LAMENTATIONS 3:22-23

There's a myth that starting over has to be dramatic. Quit the job. End the relationship. Move across the country. Change your life in one big, sweeping gesture.

But most of the time? Starting over looks way smaller. It's pausing mid-spiral and taking one deep breath. It's stopping yourself in the middle of a harsh sentence and saying, "Let me try that again." It's noticing you're slipping into a familiar pattern and choosing a new response before the whole day derails.

That's not weakness. That's agency. In fact, this kind of micro-reset is one of the most powerful moves you can make. Because it means you're not letting a bad moment define a whole day. You're not letting shame steer the car. You're recognizing that you still get to pivot.

Lamentations 3 reminds us that God's mercies are new every morning. But here's the thing: You don't have to wait until morning. The clock doesn't have to hit midnight for grace to reset. You can start over mid-conversation, midafternoon, or mid-sentence. That's the beauty of being human and being loved. Change is always on the table.

Therapists sometimes call this *pattern interruption*—when a person actively disrupts a destructive or automatic behavior and swaps in a healthier response. It's a small move, but over time it rewires the brain. And the more you do it, the more you remember: *I'm not stuck. I have a say.*

So when today goes sideways—and let's be honest, it might—don't wait for perfect conditions to change course. Agency doesn't need an invitation. It just needs a willingness to try again.

Anchor Truth

You don't need a new day to make a new choice.

Prayer

God, thank you for mercies that don't run out. When I mess up, spiral, or react in old ways, remind me that I can start again—right in the middle of the mess. Help me reset without shame.

Invitation

Catch yourself mid-pattern today. Instead of spiraling, pause. Take one deep breath and say, "I get to start over." Then do just that.

Say It Anyway

Instead, we will speak the truth in love, growing in every way more and more like Christ.

EPHESIANS 4:15

Some truths come easy. But others? They shake things up. You know the ones: The words that might disappoint. The confession that could change the dynamic. The honest boundary that risks being misunderstood. The question that challenges the groupthink.

So we hesitate. We water it down. We change the subject. We smile instead of speaking. We tell ourselves it's more loving to keep the peace.

But peacekeeping isn't the same as peacemaking. And silence, though polite, can be its own kind of dishonesty.

Authenticity doesn't mean saying everything you think, whenever you think it. But it *does* mean being faithful to the truth, especially when that truth costs you comfort. It's not just what you say: It's what it costs you not to say it.

Chronic inauthenticity comes at a price: anxiety, resentment, even disconnection from your own core self. When you bury your truth long enough, you bury your sense of self with it. What begins as people-pleasing often ends as soul-fading.

The truth doesn't always keep the room calm, but it does keep your heart aligned. And alignment—congruence between your values, voice, and actions—is a hallmark of psychological health.

Jesus never used truth as a weapon. But he never used silence as a shield, either. He disrupted expectations. He upset power structures. He spoke plainly. And he loved people too much to leave them unchallenged.

You're not here to be liked. You're here to be real. And sometimes the most loving thing you can do is tell the truth kindly—even if it shakes the room.

Anchor Truth

Authenticity means loving enough to be honest, even when it's hard.

Prayer

God, give me wisdom to know when to speak and courage to say what's true with love and grace. Help me choose integrity over approval.

Invitation

Is there a conversation you've been avoiding? A truth you've been holding back? Write it out first. Practice it with God. Then, when the time is right, say it with humility and strength.

Forging When You Can't Forget

[Love] keeps no record of being wronged.

1 CORINTHIANS 13:5

You've said the words, maybe more than once: "I forgive them." But the memory still stings. It pops up uninvited—at stoplights, in conversations, when you're trying to fall asleep. And you wonder, *Did I really forgive them if I can't forget?*

That question has haunted a lot of good-hearted people trying to live like Jesus. But here's the truth: Forgiveness is a decision. Forgetting is not. Your brain holds on to painful moments to protect you. Not being able to forget doesn't mean your forgiveness didn't count. In fact, forgiving when you can't forget may be the most Christlike thing you do.

Forgiveness isn't pretending something didn't hurt. It's choosing not to get even. It's releasing your right to replay the offense and building your boundary with wisdom instead of revenge. (Boundaries are especially important when the hurt runs deep.)

You can forgive someone and still say, "I can't be in close relationship with you right now." That's not holding a grudge. That's holding on to your mental health. And for those who've hurt you but continue to minimize, gaslight, or deny? Forgiveness doesn't require their permission. It's between you and God. It's your soul choosing freedom over festering pain.

First Corinthians 13 says that love doesn't keep score, but it doesn't say love erases memory. God is not asking you to forget. He's inviting you to live free, even with a scar. In fact, remembering can become part of the healing. When you remember and still choose grace, when you recall the pain but no longer carry its weight—that's redemptive. That's holy.

Forgiveness isn't proven by forgetting, it's proven by how you live *after* the wound. And with God, even what you remember can be reshaped into strength.

Anchor Truth

Forgiveness is a choice to release, not erase. You can forgive fully even when the memory still lingers.

Prayer

God, help me forgive what I can't forget. Let your grace fill the gaps between what I've released and what I still remember. Give me the courage to set boundaries that protect my heart, and the mercy to keep choosing freedom.

Invitation

Is there someone you've forgiven, but the memory still burns? Bring it to God. Speak the release again—not because you're weak, but because you're strong enough to stop carrying what's not yours to hold.

Picture the Good—and What Might Get in the Way

Faith shows the reality of what we hope for; it is the evidence of things we cannot see.

HEBREWS 11:1

You've probably been told to "just think positive." But that advice is about as helpful as telling someone to "just relax" in the middle of a panic attack. It's not that you don't want to be hopeful. It's just hard to get there when reality keeps punching holes in your confidence.

But optimism—the real kind—isn't naive. It's not about pretending life is smooth sailing. It's about deciding to face the waves with your eyes open and your faith intact.

Psychologist Gabriele Oettingen calls this *mental contrasting*—a practice that builds grit and grounded hope by pairing your dreams with real obstacles.

Here's how it works:

Name what you hope for. Get specific. Don't water it down. What's the outcome you actually want? "I want to exercise every morning before work."

Name what's likely to get in the way. Is it fear? Fatigue? Old patterns that keep pulling you off track? "I have a hard time focusing, and I'm afraid I'll be hungry all morning if I start the day with a workout."

Then, build a plan. If this obstacle happens, here's how you'll respond. "I'll listen to my favorite podcast while exercising and have a healthy snack afterward. If I feel like quitting, then I'll remind myself why I started."

This process rewires your brain, increasing follow-through, motivation, and emotional resilience. Now your hope isn't floating in fantasy. It's anchored in strategy.

Faith works the same way. Hebrews 11:1 doesn't define faith as blind optimism. It's trust in something *unseen*—not something *imaginary*. So let's stop settling for shallow mantras and start building your faith muscle.

Hope doesn't mean you don't anticipate resistance. It means you don't let resistance win.

Picture what healing might look like. What restoration, joy, or peace might feel like. Then name the junk that could block the path—and meet it with grace and grit.

Anchor Truth

Strong hope stares down obstacles. And still believes.

Prayer

God, I won't fake positivity. But with open eyes and a willing heart, I will choose hope. Help me walk toward the life I long for with trust and truth.

Invitation

Name a desire that feels just out of reach. Now name what's most likely to get in the way. Create one "if-then" plan and give your hope a spine.

The Fear of Letting People Down

Obviously, I'm not trying to win the approval of people, but of God. If pleasing people were my goal, I would not be Christ's servant.

GALATIANS 1:10

It starts young—the desire to be liked, to be accepted, to make people proud. But for many, that desire quietly evolves into something heavier: the fear of disappointing others. You become the one who always shows up, always follows through, always says yes—even when it costs you. You overextend, overcommit, overperform. Not out of joy, but out of fear. Because what if they're disappointed? What if they think less of you?

This fear doesn't just shape your schedule. It shapes your identity. You start believing your worth depends on being perceived as dependable, competent, or admirable. But beneath the surface lies anxiety. Resentment. Disconnection.

Paul understood the pull of people-pleasing and perfectionistic tendencies. But he named it clearly: "If pleasing people were my goal, I wouldn't be following Christ." That's not a license to be careless. It's a call to be free. Free from the trap of living for everyone else's expectations.

Even Jesus disappointed people. The religious leaders. The crowds. Even his own disciples didn't always understand him. But he didn't compromise his mission to keep them happy. He stayed aligned with his Father.

The truth is that disappointing someone doesn't mean you're doing something wrong. It might mean you're finally doing something *true.*

Your job is not to meet every expectation. It's to live with integrity and love—guided by God's voice, not by fear. If your goal is to never let anyone down, you'll end up letting yourself go.

Choose truth over approval. That's where peace begins.

Anchor Truth

You weren't created to meet everyone's expectations—only to walk faithfully with the one who knows you best.

Prayer

God, I want to love others well, but sometimes I confuse love with approval. Free me from the fear of disappointing people. Help me care deeply without carrying what isn't mine. Let me live from your truth, not their opinions.

Invitation

Pay attention today when you say yes. Is it out of love or out of fear? Practice saying a kind but honest no if needed. Disappointment may happen, but so can freedom.

Is Faith Supposed to Be This Fragile?

God might kill me, but I have no other hope.
I am going to argue my case with him.

JOB 13:15

Faith is supposed to be unshakable. That's what they say, right? But no one mentioned how much it can tremble.

All it takes is one unanswered prayer, one spiritual disappointment, one deep disillusionment—and suddenly faith feels paper-thin. Brittle. Breakable. You worry that if you tug on one loose thread, the whole thing might unravel.

But faith isn't porcelain. It's not meant to be kept in a glass case. It's meant to be lived with. Handled. Wrestled with. Even doubted.

In psychology, there's a term called *distress tolerance*—the ability to remain present in discomfort without rushing to escape or shut it down. That's what real faith often looks like. Not the absence of fear or uncertainty, but the willingness to remain in relationship with God even when the ground feels unsteady.

That's what Job modeled. After unimaginable loss, he didn't walk away from God. He *argued* with him. "God might kill me," he says, "but I have no other hope." That's not sanitized spirituality. That's a gritty, relational kind of faith—one that dares to speak honestly and still stay near.

You don't need to fake faith. You don't need to tie up your questions with a bow. You just need to stay in the conversation. Fighting for your faith doesn't mean it's failing. It might mean it's maturing. It's not about having the answers. It's about staying open.

Faith doesn't mean suppressing doubts or sanitizing your struggle. Faith can stretch. It can wrestle. It can even rage—and still survive. In fact, it often grows stronger when it's allowed to bend.

So if you're arguing your case with God right now, that's okay. It's not a sign of failure. It's a sign that you're taking your faith seriously. You're asking it to hold real weight. And that takes courage.

Anchor Truth

Faith might feel fragile, but it can survive being stretched. It's okay to argue your case with God.

Prayer

God, I don't even know if you're hearing me, but I need more confidence in my faith. I don't want to have to argue with you. I need to see that faith doesn't have to mean certainty. Thank you for holding on to me when I don't know how to hold on to you.

Invitation

Today, notice where your faith feels stretched. Don't rush to patch it. Just sit with it. Breathe. Say, "God can handle questions—even this one."

The Myth of "I Had No Choice"

Don't copy the behavior and customs of this world, but let God transform you into a new person by changing the way you think.

ROMANS 12:2

We say it all the time: "I didn't have a choice." But more often than not, what we really mean is, "I didn't like the choices I had." Or "I wasn't aware I had any."

When you're feeling overwhelmed or afraid, your brain's decision-making systems can go offline. It's a phenomenon called *cognitive narrowing*. Your mind zooms in on the threat and blocks out creative alternatives. That's useful when you're facing an actual emergency. But in daily life, it can make you feel trapped in false binaries: fight or freeze, quit or explode, push through or shut down.

That's where agency begins—not in having perfect options, but in learning to pause and say, "Wait. Is this really the only way?"

Romans 12:2 tells us not to conform to the patterns of the world, but to let God transform us by renewing our minds. Transformation doesn't just happen in the soul—it happens in the synapses. *Neuroplasticity* is the brain's capacity to rewire itself over time, especially as we start to think differently. Which means new choices *can* emerge, even if they're small at first.

So when you catch yourself saying, "I didn't have a choice," try slowing down. You may not like the cost of the better choice. You may not feel strong enough to act on it yet. But that doesn't mean it isn't there.

Agency doesn't mean having a hundred options. It means finding one that aligns with your values and taking it.

Anchor Truth

You always have a choice. It just may not be easy, obvious, or comfortable.

Prayer

God, sometimes I feel stuck, cornered, or out of options. Remind me that I don't have to live on autopilot. Change the way I think. Help me notice the small but meaningful choices I do have—and give me the courage to act on them.

Invitation

Today, when you feel stuck, ask, "Is there a third option I haven't seen yet?" Even a tiny shift counts. Write it down and take the first step.

Borrowed Belief

Encourage those who are timid. Take tender care of those who are weak. Be patient with everyone.

1 THESSALONIANS 5:14

Some days hope is easy. Other days it feels like lifting a thousand pounds.

When optimism runs dry, it's not a personal failure. It's part of being human. That's why God gave us each other.

There will be days when someone else has to believe for you. When a friend's prayer carries more faith than your own. When a line of Scripture feels too distant—but someone else is close enough to whisper it over you. This is the power of *borrowed belief.*

Psychologists refer to something similar as *vicarious hope*—the idea that seeing someone else hold hope, heal, or rise again can spark the same possibility inside you. Even if just for a moment.

The early church knew this well. Paul's letters are full of commands to "encourage," "lift up," "carry one another." Not because people were weak, but because this life is *hard.* And nobody's optimism survives in a vacuum.

So if today feels heavy, let someone else's light leak into your darkness. Read the psalm you're not sure you believe. Let a worship lyric sink in, even if your heart's not there yet. Call the friend whose faith hasn't wavered this week and let them speak hope over you.

And if you *are* the one feeling strong right now, don't waste that gift. Pour some of it into someone else. Write the note. Say the prayer. Lend the hope. We take turns believing. And that's how we make it through.

Anchor Truth

When your hope runs low, someone else can hold it for you.

Prayer

God, thank you that I don't have to muster hope alone. Surround me with people who speak life, and help me do the same for them.

Invitation

Think of one person who has helped carry you through a hard time. Text or call them to say thanks, or pay it forward to someone who needs the lift today.

Shame and Self-Blame After Trauma

Those who look to him for help will be radiant with joy;
no shadow of shame will darken their faces.

PSALM 34:5

After trauma, it's common to turn the pain inward. You replay the moment. You question your choices. You wonder what you could have done differently. And even when logic says, "This wasn't your fault," your heart still whispers, "But maybe it was."

This is the cruel trick of trauma. It doesn't just wound you, it also makes you feel like you're the reason you're wounded.

You might blame yourself for not seeing it coming. For not speaking up. For freezing instead of fighting. For being too trusting. Or too vulnerable. Or too much. Or not enough.

But here's the truth: You did not deserve what happened.

And your reaction was not a failure: It was survival. Your body, your brain, your heart—they did what they had to do to protect you. And you are still here. That is not weakness. That is resilience.

Shame says, "It was because of me." Grace says, "It was never yours to carry."

Psalm 34 says that those who look to God will be radiant, with no shadow of shame darkening their faces. That's not just poetry—it's a promise.

God doesn't look at you with blame. He looks at you with compassion. And he longs to lift the weight of shame that trauma unfairly placed on you.

Jesus carried more than your sin on the cross. He carried your shame. He saw it. Named it. And said, "That's not who you are anymore." You don't have to carry shame for what you lived through. What happened was not your choice, but healing still can be.

Anchor Truth

Shame is a liar. God is not ashamed of your story.

Prayer

God, I've carried shame that doesn't belong to me. I've blamed myself for what I didn't choose. Help me release that weight. Speak truth where lies have lived for too long. Let your love rewrite how I see myself.

Invitation

Today, write down one thing you've blamed yourself for. Speak this over it: "That wasn't my fault. God sees the whole story, and he does not shame me."

The Loneliness of a Shifting Belief

Do not turn your back on me. Do not reject your servant in anger. You have always been my helper. Don't leave me now; don't abandon me, O God of my salvation!

PSALM 27:9

Doubt, even if it's sporadic, can feel like exile.

It's not just the inner wrestling—it's the fear of saying it out loud. You start to realize that voicing your questions might mean disappointing the people who once celebrated your faith. Or being quietly pushed to the margins. Or just . . . misunderstood.

So you keep it quiet. You nod. You smile. And you feel a little more invisible every time.

This is the emotional weight of *disenfranchised grief*—a form of loss that isn't openly acknowledged or supported by your community. When your beliefs shift, you may grieve the version of faith you once held, but no one brings a casserole for this kind of mourning.

You may also experience what psychologists call *social disconnection*—not just being alone, but feeling relationally unsafe in your questions. When spiritual doubt is seen as betrayal, it becomes isolating, even when you're around people.

David felt that too. "Don't leave me now; don't abandon me," he wrote. He wasn't doubting God's existence—he was doubting God's nearness. And that's what so many of us feel when faith starts to change: not just uncertainty, but *abandonment*. From God. From others. Sometimes both.

But your questions don't make you unlovable. They don't make you unsafe. They make you real. And being authentic has never been a deal-breaker for God.

If you feel alone in this, please hear this clearly: You're not the only one. And you're not too much.

This path may be quieter than the one you used to walk, but it is not empty. Even in the silence, you are still seen. Still held. Still loved.

Anchor Truth

Doubt tells us we are alone. God says he is still with us.

Prayer

God, I feel isolated in my questioning. I miss the comfort of certainty. Help me believe that you are still with me, even in the quiet. Bring someone into my life who can sit with me in this—not to fix it, but to be present.

Invitation

Think of one person who might be safe enough to hear your questions. Not to debate, just to listen. Reach out with a simple message: "Hey, can I share something I've been wrestling with?"

Recovery Is Reconnection—with Yourself

Love your neighbor as yourself.

MARK 12:31

Codependency fractures your relationship with yourself. You become so tuned in to everyone else's moods, needs, and reactions that your own thoughts and emotions get drowned out. You might stop asking, "What do I need? What do I want? What do I think?" Because somewhere along the way, you believed that being a "good" person meant disappearing.

But healing from codependency isn't about becoming colder or more distant. It's about becoming whole. It's about recovering your voice. Your preferences. Your agency. And most importantly, your self-worth.

Jesus' words are often quoted: "Love your neighbor as yourself." But many of us skip over the second half. You *can't* love others well if you're not connected to yourself. You'll either disappear in the name of peace or manipulate in the name of love.

Recovery begins when you turn toward yourself—not in narcissism, but in compassion. When you start honoring your limits instead of overriding them. When you stop apologizing for having needs. When you make decisions from inner clarity instead of outer pressure.

This isn't selfish. It's spiritual. It's a return to how God designed you: with boundaries, with a soul, with worth apart from anyone else's opinion.

Think about the woman who had experienced constant bleeding (Mark 5:25-34). She spent years being overlooked, dismissed, and drained. But healing came when she reached out—boldly, vulnerably—for what *she* needed. And Jesus didn't scold her. He honored her. Called her "daughter." Affirmed her faith. That's the tone of divine healing. Not shame. Not duty. Not martyrdom. But dignity.

Recovery from codependency is not about getting someone else to change. It's about changing your own patterns. Relearning how to trust yourself. Reclaiming the space you were always meant to take up.

Anchor Truth

Healing from codependency isn't about turning away from others. It's about finally turning toward yourself with truth, compassion, and courage.

Prayer

God, help me return to myself. Heal the parts of me that believed I wasn't worthy of care, and teach me to love myself the way you already do.

Invitation

What's one small way you can reconnect with yourself today? A quiet moment? A journal entry? A "no" that honors your energy? Take the step. Healing begins there.

Making Less of Yourself on Purpose

He must become greater and greater,
and I must become less and less.

JOHN 3:30

John the Baptist didn't have a self-promotion strategy. No polished social presence. No curated highlight reel. Just camel hair, locusts, and a message people couldn't ignore.

He had followers—lots of them. A crowd, a reputation, influence. And then Jesus showed up.

John's response? Not defensiveness. Not jealousy. Not "Hey, I was here first." It was surrender: "He must increase; I must decrease." That may sound noble and poetic, but it's deeply disruptive.

Imagine willingly stepping aside while your influence fades. Imagine celebrating someone else's rise, especially when your platform begins to shrink. That's not passive resignation. That's active humility.

John knew who he was—and who he wasn't. He said plainly, "I am not the Messiah." He understood his role: to prepare the way, not to stay center stage.

And that's one of the purest forms of humility: knowing your purpose, playing your part, and letting go of the spotlight when it's time.

John the Baptist teaches us that humility isn't thinking you have nothing to offer. It's offering what you have, and then gladly handing the mic to someone else.

In a world obsessed with recognition, humility doesn't compete. It clears the way.

Anchor Truth

Humility is knowing who you are—and who you're not.

Prayer

Jesus, help me loosen my grip on being seen. Let my life point to you, not to me. Teach me to celebrate others, even when it costs me attention. Make me small in all the right ways.

Invitation

Is there someone you've struggled to celebrate because their success feels like your loss? Pray for them today. Then find a way to honor or encourage them without needing anything in return.

Your Reaction Has a Backstory

People may be pure in their own eyes,
but the LORD examines their motives.

PROVERBS 16:2

You lose it over something small—a comment, a delay, a look. And afterward you think, *Where did that come from?*

Here's a clue: It probably didn't start there. Most reactions aren't just about the moment in front of you.

They're about something underneath—something older, deeper, more vulnerable. You snapped at your partner, but the real issue was feeling unheard . . . again. You over-apologized in the meeting, but it was really about that voice in your head saying, "Don't mess this up." You felt jealous when your friend shared good news, but under that was a fear that you're falling behind.

Self-awareness doesn't shame the reaction. It traces it. It slows you down just long enough to ask, "What's this really about?"

Proverbs 16:2 reminds us that while we often justify our behavior, God sees the motives underneath. Not to condemn us, but to call us into honesty. Because without that honesty, you're stuck managing symptoms instead of healing the source.

In therapy, this process is tied to *emotional triggers*—intense reactions that come from unprocessed pain or unmet needs. Triggers aren't proof you're broken. They're proof something inside you is still asking to be seen, heard, and healed.

God isn't intimidated by your strong reactions. But he is inviting you to get curious about them. Because the more honestly you explore your backstory, the more compassion and clarity you'll bring to your present.

Anchor Truth

A strong reaction is often a signal, not a flaw.

Prayer

God, when I react strongly, help me pause instead of spiral. Help me ask better questions—not to justify my behavior, but to understand it. Lead me into truth that sets me free.

Invitation

Today, when you feel a strong emotional spike—anger, shame, fear—pause.

The Happiness Pie

Yet true godliness with contentment is itself great wealth.

1 TIMOTHY 6:6

Want to know what makes you happy?

Research reveals that about 50 percent of your happiness is wired into your DNA. It's your "set point," how naturally upbeat (or not) you tend to be. You didn't choose it. And you don't control it.

Another 10 percent comes from your circumstances. Things like income, relationship status, job situation, even where you live. Which means the stuff we obsess over changing only accounts for a tiny sliver of our well-being.

That leaves 40 percent, the chunk you actually have influence over. Your daily choices. Your habits. Your responses. What you focus on, dwell on, and make room for.

This is called the *happiness pie*, and it's good news. Because it means you don't have to wait for life to get easier, your job to get better, or your personality to shift. You can start cultivating joy right now—right where you are. And Paul knew this long before psychologists put it in a chart.

Sitting in a prison cell, writing to his young protégé Timothy, he penned this truth: Godliness with contentment is great wealth. In other words, a life shaped by spiritual integrity and grounded in quiet satisfaction? That's gold.

You can't control your DNA. You can't always change your situation. But you can choose to show up to your life with humility, gratitude, and grace. And when you do? You start to rewrite the narrative of your own well-being—one decision, one moment at a time.

Anchor Truth

Happiness isn't about what happens to you. It's about what you cultivate in you.

Prayer

God, I can't control everything. But I want to steward what I can. Teach me to make space for joy, even when it's hard. Show me how to live with contentment, not comparison.

Invitation

Today, ask yourself, "What's one small habit or shift I can make in my 40 percent?" Maybe it's stepping outside. Sending a kind message. Starting a gratitude list. You don't have to overhaul your life to shape your happiness. Just start somewhere.

When Peace Feels Out of Reach

I am leaving you with a gift—peace of mind and heart. And the peace I give is a gift the world cannot give. So don't be troubled or afraid.

JOHN 14:27

Anxiety is not just a feeling. It's a full-body experience. Your thoughts race. Your chest tightens. Your stomach knots. You replay past conversations and fear future ones. You may feel like you're always bracing for something, even if you can't name what.

That's your nervous system trying to protect you, sounding an alarm that never quite turns off.

In clinical terms, anxiety is a *stress response*—your brain's way of protecting you from a threat. When your mind perceives danger—real or imagined—it sends signals through your body to prepare for fight, flight, or freeze. That's biology, not brokenness. But in a world of constant demands, our systems can stay stuck in chronic activation—always scanning, always tensing.

That's why Jesus' words in John 14:27 matter so much. He isn't offering a surface-level platitude. He's giving a gift no therapist, self-help book, or achievement can provide.

"Peace of mind and heart," he says. Not just the absence of fear, but the presence of something deeper: the internal safety of being held.

This peace is different from the world's version. It doesn't depend on your to-do list being cleared or your feelings behaving. It's not always immediate. And it may not silence your symptoms. But it does promise this: You are not alone, and you are not expected to be untroubled before you are embraced.

If you've been made to feel like your anxiety disqualifies you from spiritual maturity, please know this: Jesus gave this promise before the cross, before the resurrection, and knowing full well that his disciples would still be afraid. He gave it because he knew we'd need it.

That's nervous system regulation at its deepest level—not just a change in your biology, but a reminder that you are safe, loved, and never abandoned.

You may not feel peaceful today. But that doesn't mean the gift has been revoked. Even if peace feels out of reach, it's already been given.

Anchor Truth

Peace isn't the absence of anxiety. It's the presence of Jesus in it.

Prayer

Jesus, I want your peace, but sometimes it feels just out of reach. Teach me to stop striving for calm and instead rest in you. Help me understand my anxiety without shame. Thank you for staying close, even when I feel far from okay.

Invitation

If your body feels tense, pause. Place one hand over your heart. Breathe in slowly and say, "God is here." Breathe out slowly and say, "I am safe."

Let Them

We are not trying to please people but God, who tests our hearts.

1 THESSALONIANS 2:4 (NIV)

You saw the invite go to everyone but you. You noticed they stopped reaching out. You heard how they spoke about you—dismissive, inaccurate, maybe even cold. And the temptation is strong: Prove your worth. Defend your place. Fix the narrative. Pull them back in.

But what if the holiest thing you could do is *let them*? Let them misunderstand you. Let them move on. Let them choose something or someone else. Not because you don't care, but because you're done begging to be seen.

That's the spiritual practice of release. It's not passive-aggressive. It's not bitter. It's just honest. You stop grasping. You unclench. You say, "I won't build my identity around people who are determined not to see me clearly." That's hard. Especially when jealousy and resentment creep in. Especially when the rejection feels personal, because sometimes it is.

But Paul reminds us that we're not living to earn approval from people. God knows the heart. He sees beyond the optics. And he's not running your story through someone else's filter.

It's called *boundary work*—letting go of what you can't control (other people's behavior) and taking full ownership of what you can (your response, your peace, your path forward).

So the next time you feel the itch to defend, prove, or chase—pause. Notice the heat rising in your chest. The urge to send the text. The spiral of overthinking. Then take a breath. And whisper—not in anger, not in bitterness—"Let them."

Let them think what they want. Let them choose what they choose. Let them walk away if they're going to. Not because you don't care. But because you care enough about your soul not to tie it to people who won't hold it with care.

This is not about giving up. It's about giving yourself back to peace.

Anchor Truth

You don't have to fight to stay where you're not being valued.

Prayer

God, I confess I want to be included, understood, defended. But I don't want to lose myself trying to hold what's not mine. Help me release what I can't control—and trust you with what's next.

Invitation

If jealousy or resentment shows up today in response to someone's behavior, ask, "What am I clinging to that I might need to release?" Say these words: "Let them." And see what loosens inside you.

When You're Called Insecure—But You're Not

People may be pure in their own eyes,
but the LORD examines their motives.

PROVERBS 16:2

Ever had someone throw the word *insecure* at you like an accusation? Maybe you drew a boundary. Maybe you spoke up for yourself. Maybe you weren't trying to win—just trying to be wise. But then came the label, "You're just insecure." It can feel like a gut punch, especially when it's not true.

Here's the thing: Standing in your God-given worth can make some people uncomfortable, especially those who've benefited from you staying small. What they call insecurity might actually be growth. What they call low self-esteem might be a strong sense of identity they just don't recognize or like.

Yes, there are times when you act from insecurity. We all do. But just because someone accuses you of being insecure doesn't mean you actually are. And it certainly doesn't mean you have to internalize it.

God examines your heart, not just your behavior. He knows whether you're acting out of fear or out of faith. He sees when you're trying to honor him by standing firm in truth, even when others don't get it.

When someone mislabels you, pause. Ask God, "Is there something in me that needs refining—or is this about them?" That kind of spiritual self-check keeps you grounded in humility without giving away your identity.

You don't owe anyone the version of you that keeps them comfortable. You're not here to be palatable—you're here to be whole. Let them call you what they want. Let God call you by name. You are his. You are growing. And you are not insecure just because someone couldn't handle your strength.

Keep showing up with courage. Keep listening to his voice over theirs. And walk like someone who's already accepted, even when you're misunderstood. Because you are.

Anchor Truth

You don't have to prove your worth to people who misunderstand you. You only need to stay rooted in the one who sees you clearly.

Prayer

God, help me stay secure in you when others question or mislabel me. Search my heart. Strengthen my spirit. And remind me that I don't need to shrink to stay in someone's favor. I just need to stand in your truth.

Invitation

If you've been called "insecure" by someone who didn't understand your boundaries or voice, let that label fall off today. Ask God to affirm what's true, and walk in that truth with quiet confidence.

When Resentment Starts Running the Show

Get rid of all bitterness, rage, anger, harsh words, and slander, as well as all types of evil behavior. Instead, be kind to each other, tenderhearted, forgiving one another, just as God through Christ has forgiven you.

EPHESIANS 4:31-32

Resentment is the slow burn you tell yourself isn't that big of a deal. It's quieter than rage, sneakier than jealousy, and sometimes even dressed in righteousness. But it sticks to your soul like a film you can't scrub off.

You replay the offense. You rehearse what you wish you'd said. You stew. And every time you think you're over it, it bubbles back up.

Resentment doesn't just poison your peace. It rewrites your story—making you the victim, always owed, never free. It builds invisible walls in your relationships, narrows your vision, and keeps you tangled in the very thing you say you want to release. It tells you that holding on gives you control. But that's a lie. You're not holding it, it's holding you.

Here's the hard truth: Resentment feels justified when the wound is real. And maybe it is. Maybe they *did* betray you. Ignore you. Belittle you. And it cost you. But forgiveness doesn't mean pretending it didn't hurt. It means refusing to let that hurt write the next chapter.

Paul's words to the Ephesians are both a challenge and a lifeline. "Get rid of it," he says. Not because you're weak, but because bitterness is weakening. It's corrosive. It steals energy that could be spent healing. And the only way to stop resentment from running your inner world is to name it, grieve what was lost, and choose to release it—even when you have to do it again tomorrow.

Forgiveness isn't soft. It's spiritual strength. It doesn't erase justice. It makes room for it—on God's terms, not yours.

Anchor Truth

Resentment doesn't protect you. It traps you. Letting go may not change the past, but it can change what's still possible.

Prayer

God, I don't want to keep replaying what hurt me. Teach me how to release the grip resentment has on my heart. Even if it takes time, even if I have to do it in layers, help me to forgive. Not just for them, but so I can be free.

Invitation

Is there someone or something that keeps reactivating your anger? Write it down. Talk to God honestly about it. And ask, "What would it look like to begin letting this go?"

Desire Isn't the Problem

Take delight in the LORD,
and he will give you your heart's desires.

PSALM 37:4

Desire gets a bad rap. Especially when you're battling an addiction or a compulsion, it can feel like your longings are the enemy. Wanting becomes dangerous. Feeling becomes suspect. Craving gets confused with failure. So we try to shut it all down. We numb. We avoid. We say, "If I could just stop wanting, I'd be free."

But here's the thing: *Desire isn't the problem.* Desire is holy. It's a sign you're alive. That you're made for more.

The problem is when your desire gets misdirected—when it's twisted by pain, masked by shame, or buried beneath years of disappointment. That drink? That scroll? That one-night escape? Those are just stand-ins.

They're counterfeit versions of something truer, deeper: Comfort. Connection. Control. Relief. Desires for something real—but reached for in the wrong way. You don't need to kill your longing. You need to listen to it.

Ask, "What is this craving trying to say?" "What hurt is it trying to soothe?" "What ache is it trying to numb?" Because every addiction is a signal. Every craving points to something underneath.

God doesn't ask you to erase your desire. He wants to *redeem* it. To reshape it. To lead it back to its truest source.

The gospel isn't about eradicating desire—it's about satisfying it with living water. You were made to want. But you weren't made to settle.

Anchor Truth

Your craving isn't a curse. It's a compass, if you let it lead you to the truth.

Prayer

God, I'm tired of being afraid of my desires. Show me what they're pointing to. Teach me to bring them to you instead of chasing shadows.

Invitation

Think of a recent craving. What deeper longing might it have been masking? Instead of judging it, explore it with honesty and compassion.

What If They're Right?

To learn, you must love discipline;
it is stupid to hate correction.

PROVERBS 12:1

You know the feeling. Someone offers you feedback—maybe even gently—and your body tightens. Your heart races. Your defenses kick in before your brain has time to process. You get sarcastic. You shut down. You fight back.

Defensiveness is a reflex. Curiosity is a choice. It takes real courage to pause that internal alarm and ask, "What if they're right?" Or at least, "What truth might be hiding in what they're saying?"

Most of us don't like being wrong. And we especially don't like being told we're wrong. But curiosity can turn those moments of tension into moments of growth.

People with a "growth mindset" tend to lean into constructive feedback. They ask questions. They explore patterns. They want to understand—not just be understood. Why? Because they believe they can change. They know that God isn't finished with them yet.

Curiosity in the face of criticism isn't passive. It's not just nodding while seething inside. It's an active effort to sift the helpful from the harmful. To resist the urge to protect your ego and instead prioritize your growth.

The writer of Proverbs doesn't pull punches: Hating correction is stupid. Harsh, but true. Wisdom requires discipline. Growth requires feedback. And curiosity is what opens the door to both.

Jesus himself wasn't above receiving questions or challenges. He engaged. He listened. He asked questions right back. Jesus never operated from a place of fragile ego, but from grounded identity. And that's what allowed him to stay curious even with those who misunderstood or opposed him.

The next time you feel defensive, don't shame yourself. Get curious. Why did that comment land so hard? Is there something unresolved that it's bumping into? Is this an opportunity to learn something about myself?

You don't have to agree with every critique. But you'll never grow from the ones you refuse to examine.

Anchor Truth

Feedback doesn't have to threaten your identity. With curiosity, even hard truths can lead to growth.

Prayer

God, help me stay open when it's easier to shut down. Teach me to listen, reflect, and grow, even when it stings.

Invitation

Think of a recent moment when you got defensive. Replay it with curiosity and ask, "What was said? What did I feel? Why did I react that way?" Invite God to show you what's beneath the surface.

Gratitude and Relational Health

Always be humble and gentle. Be patient with each other, making allowance for each other's faults because of your love.

EPHESIANS 4:2

Gratitude is the glue that holds relationships together. It softens sharp edges. It turns irritation into appreciation. It shifts the spotlight from what's lacking to what's already good.

When gratitude is absent, relationships feel entitled, brittle, and transactional. But when it's present, even imperfect relationships feel rich with grace.

Instead of nitpicking what someone forgot, you notice what they offered. Instead of replaying the last offense, you remember the last kindness. Gratitude reorients your heart toward the bigger picture—and the best parts of the people in front of you.

Research confirms it: People who regularly express appreciation toward their partner, friends, and coworkers report higher satisfaction, stronger connection, and even fewer conflicts. Why? Because gratitude creates emotional safety. It invites vulnerability. It quiets defensiveness. It makes you want to give more—not out of guilt, but joy.

And this goes for your relationship with God, too. Gratitude reminds you that you're not merely tolerated by him—you're treasured. That his mercies didn't run dry yesterday and won't run dry tomorrow. That every breath, every sunrise, every undeserved do-over is grace stacked on grace. And when you thank him—not just for the big, miraculous moments, but for the simple daily mercies—you're training your soul to stay close, not wander.

Gratitude is how we love better. It's how we stay tender. It's how we honor the image of God in others—and recognize it in ourselves.

Gratitude isn't just a nice gesture—it's relational oxygen. Without it, love gasps. But with it, even weary relationships can catch their breath again.

So don't hold it in. Say the thank-you. Write the note. Whisper the prayer. Let your gratitude be the lifeline that keeps connection alive.

Anchor Truth

Gratitude deepens connection. With people. With God. With your own soul. It builds bridges where resentment would burn them.

Prayer

God, help me to see the good in the people around me, even when it's hard. Give me the grace to speak thanks more often than complaints. And help me draw near to you with a grateful heart that stays open.

Invitation

Who in your life could use a dose of appreciation today? A partner, friend, parent, or child? Tell them—specifically—why you're grateful. Watch what it does to your connection.

When You Don't Feel Like Enough

I praise you because I am fearfully and wonderfully made; your works are wonderful, I know that full well.

PSALM 139:14 (NIV)

Low self-worth doesn't always show its face, but it shapes everything. It might wear the face of *low self-esteem*—a constant sense that you're less than others. Sometimes it takes the form of *insecurity*—a hyperawareness of how you're perceived. Or maybe it shows up as a nagging sense of *inadequacy*—a deep-down belief that something is fundamentally wrong with you.

Whatever you call it, it's the inner whisper that says you're not enough. Not smart enough. Not attractive enough. Not spiritual enough. It's the ache of feeling unseen in a crowd, the shame that shadows your every accomplishment, the fear of being found out as a fraud.

Sometimes it wears the mask of overachievement—trying to earn love or approval. Other times it masquerades as withdrawal—fear to take up space or speak too loudly. Either way, it's exhausting. And it's deeply personal.

Low self-esteem is formed through early wounds, constant comparison, or trying to live up to impossible ideals. Over time, we internalize the lie that something is wrong with us. God never intended for us to live under that weight.

In fact, Scripture doesn't avoid insecurity; it names it. Moses felt inadequate. Gideon said he was the least in his tribe. Leah just wanted to be loved. And still, God didn't sideline them. He saw them. Chose them. Used them.

God doesn't love you *because* you're worthy. He makes you worthy because he loves you. This isn't about self-inflation or pretending you're perfect. It's about letting your value be rooted in something unshakable—your identity as God's beloved. Your worth isn't earned. It's bestowed.

So if you've been living under the burden of not-enoughness, it's time to step out. To stop agreeing with shame. And to start living as someone who is deeply seen, deeply loved, and deeply valuable—because your Maker said so.

Anchor Truth

You are not what others say about you or even what you say about yourself. You are who God says you are: wonderfully made, fully known, and unconditionally loved.

Prayer

God, you know every corner of my heart, even the ones where insecurity hides. Teach me to see myself through your eyes. Help me to rest in the love you've already given me.

Invitation

Where does your inner critic show up most? Name one lie you've believed about your worth and counter it today with truth from God's Word. Write it down. Speak it aloud.

What Didn't Happen

Even if my father and mother abandon me,
the LORD will hold me close.

PSALM 27:10

Sometimes addiction isn't about what happened—but about what didn't happen. The hug you never got. The safe place that didn't exist. The parent who wasn't able to see you, soothe you, or stay.

These are called *attachment wounds*—early relational injuries that shape how we give and receive love. And often, how we cope with pain. If your core need for connection went unmet, your nervous system learned to self-soothe however it could. Maybe through food. Or fantasy. Or substances. Or overfunctioning. Not because you were weak, but because your wiring was trying to protect you.

Addiction often traces back to unmet needs for safety, comfort, nurture, or being known. When that foundational trust was fractured early, it doesn't just disappear with time. It resurfaces—in our patterns, our triggers, our relationships. That's not your fault, and it doesn't make you broken.

But healing means naming it. It means recognizing that the thing you reach for in your lowest moments might not be just a habit. It might be a *substitute for attachment.* A placeholder for the comfort that never came. But the gospel speaks directly into this space: "The LORD will hold me close."

God does not recoil from your wounds. He draws near. He becomes the parent who never left. The embrace that never flinched. The one who stays.

You can begin to unlearn patterns of self-protection. You can learn to feel safe in love again—real love, not the numbing kind. But first, be gentle with yourself. That addiction you're trying to quit may have been a survival strategy long before it became a problem.

Anchor Truth

Addiction often grows where attachment was missing. But healing begins in safe connection.

Prayer

God, I've learned to go it alone. To self-soothe, to self-manage. Help me learn trust again in safe relationships. And meet me in the places I still feel unheld.

Invitation

Notice when your craving flares. What emotional need might be underneath? Instead of fixing it, just name it. Then ask, "What would comfort look like in a safe relationship?"

Take a Good, Honest Look

Pay careful attention to your own work, for then you will get the satisfaction of a job well done, and you won't need to compare yourself to anyone else.

GALATIANS 6:4

Sometimes the bravest thing you can do is tell yourself the raw, unfiltered state of your soul. Are you weary? Are you angry more than you want to admit? Have you been showing up for others while quietly falling apart?

Compassion fatigue rarely announces itself with sirens. It creeps in subtly—through irritability, disengagement, cynicism, or feeling numb. It's when you show up physically but check out emotionally. It's when your ability to care starts to feel like a burden instead of a gift.

The first step out of this spiral is simple but not easy: honest self-assessment. It's the discipline of sitting down with yourself and asking hard questions: What's my energy level really like? Have I lost joy in things that used to fill me? When's the last time I felt deeply connected to God—or anyone? Am I meeting needs out of love or out of guilt?

Science backs this up. Self-awareness is the foundation of emotional intelligence. When you know what you're feeling—and why—you're better equipped to set boundaries, seek support, and stop the slow bleed of emotional depletion.

Biblically, we see David model this kind of introspection in Psalm 139:23-24. That prayer wasn't about shame. It was about alignment. About returning to a place of clarity and wholeness.

Galatians 6:4 reminds us to examine our own work, not in comparison to others, but as a reflection of our inner life. This kind of introspection takes courage.

It means telling the truth about what's unsustainable, what's not working, what needs to change. It means naming the ways you're spiritually dry, emotionally tapped out, or physically worn thin—and doing so without shame.

Self-assessment isn't selfish. It's stewardship. Tuning in to your own well-being is the only way to offer something real to others. You don't need to fix everything today. But you do need to stop pretending you're fine if you're not.

Anchor Truth

You can't heal what you won't name. Telling yourself the truth is the first act of grace.

Prayer

God, give me the courage to be honest with myself. Reveal what I've been avoiding. Show me where I'm empty, where I'm hurting, and where I need your help. I don't want to live numb—I want to live whole.

Invitation

Take five minutes alone. Journal your honest answers to this question: What am I really feeling lately? *No filters. No edits. Just truth. Let that be your starting point.*

Holy vs. Harmful Anger

Jesus made a whip from some ropes and chased them all out of the Temple. . . . Then his disciples remembered this prophecy from the Scriptures: "Passion for God's house will consume me."

JOHN 2:15, 17

Not all anger is created equal. Some anger is holy. Fierce, but not reckless. Rooted in justice. Anchored in love. That's the kind of anger Jesus displayed when he overturned tables in the Temple. His passion wasn't about pride, but about people being exploited and God's house being dishonored.

Then there's another kind of anger—the harmful kind. The kind that demands control, attacks, escalates. The kind that's less about love and more about ego. That kind damages relationships and distorts truth, even when it feels justified.

But here's the hard part: Holy anger and harmful anger can feel the same in your body. The difference isn't in the adrenaline. It's in the intention. One kind fights *for*. The other fights *at*. Harmful anger says, "You crossed me. You'll pay." Holy anger says, "This matters too much to let slide." And yet it's easy to confuse them—especially when we feel personally attacked, overwhelmed, or burned out.

We call it "righteous indignation," but really it's reactivity. We might lash out in the name of honesty, but it's venting, not truth-telling. We might say we're defending what's right, but we're defending our pride.

Holy anger doesn't hide or explode: It constructs. It takes a stand without dehumanizing. It speaks without shaming. It refuses to stay silent in the face of injustice, but it does so with self-control, humility, and intention.

You're allowed to be angry. But ask, Is this anger rooted in love? In truth? In something bigger than yourself? Because holy anger doesn't leave destruction in its wake—it leaves clarity, accountability, and sometimes even healing.

Anchor Truth

Holy anger protects. Harmful anger punishes.

Prayer

God, when I feel anger rise, help me pause and examine it. Shape my response so it reflects your love and your wisdom.

Invitation

Think of a time when your anger led to harm and a time when it led to healing. What was the difference? What might holy anger look like in your life today?

Triggers Aren't Excuses

Don't sin by letting anger control you.
Think about it overnight and remain silent.

PSALM 4:4

We all have triggers. They're real. They're any external stimulus—a word, tone, look, memory, situation, or even silence—that evokes a strong emotional reaction. They're tied to your past, your wiring, your wounds.

And when they get poked, your amygdala, your brain's alarm system, goes off fast. It floods your body with adrenaline, and before you know it, you're saying or doing something you'll wish you hadn't. That's not because you're a bad person. It's because you're human.

But here's the deal: Although triggers explain your reaction, they don't excuse your behavior. Emotional regulation is what allows you to feel the fire without letting it burn someone else. It's the second thought. The grown-up decision to own your choices instead of blaming your buttons.

It takes work. Neuroscience shows that while your brain is designed to react quickly in moments of perceived threat, it's also capable of rewiring. That's called *neuroplasticity*—and it means you can train yourself to slow down, reflect, and respond more wisely over time. Not overnight, but over time.

David, in Psalm 4, gets this. He's angry, but he doesn't let his anger rule him. He doesn't lash out. He steps back. Reflects. Sleeps on it. He models what many of us need to practice: noticing the emotion but not being ruled by it.

This doesn't mean you ignore your triggers. It means you *tend to them*. Get curious about where they come from. Talk to a counselor. Journal about them. Bring them to God in prayer.

Your triggers are trying to tell you where healing is still needed. Your triggers are not an excuse; they're an invitation. To pause. To examine. To grow.

Anchor Truth

Your past may shape your triggers, but your present choices shape your growth. You're responsible for what you do with what stirs you.

Prayer

God, help me recognize my triggers without using them as weapons or excuses. Teach me to pause, to breathe, and to respond with wisdom instead of reflex.

Invitation

What situation or person tends to trigger you the most? Today, name the trigger. Then take one small step toward responding with intentionality rather than instinct.

Boundaries and Forgiveness

Forgiving one another . . . just as God through Christ has forgiven you.

EPHESIANS 4:32

Forgiveness and boundaries are often mistaken for opposites, like you can't hold both at once. But that's a myth.

Forgiveness doesn't mean open-door policies. It doesn't mean pretending the hurt didn't happen or exposing yourself to more of the same. In fact, real forgiveness sometimes *requires* boundaries.

Forgiveness is about releasing resentment. Boundaries are about protecting what's still tender. You can forgive someone and still say, "I can't keep having that same conversation." You can forgive someone and still say, "I'm not coming to the family gathering this time." You can forgive someone and still say, "This relationship needs to change if it's going to continue."

Forgiveness isn't about erasing consequences. It's about refusing to be poisoned by bitterness. And boundaries are what keep you from returning to the scene of the wound just because you think grace demands it.

God's forgiveness is full and free. But it also calls us into wisdom. The prodigal son was welcomed home with open arms, but he didn't get a credit card and the keys to the estate the next day. Grace and trust aren't the same thing. So don't confuse forgiveness with access.

You're not being hard-hearted to draw a boundary. You're being honest about what's healthy—and what's not. Setting a boundary isn't a sign that you haven't forgiven. It's a sign that you're healing. And healing well means loving others *and* yourself enough to honor what's true, safe, and right.

Grace can coexist with limits. In fact, sometimes that's where grace shines brightest.

Anchor Truth

Forgiveness is an act of grace. Boundaries are an act of stewardship. Both are holy.

Prayer

God, thank you for forgiving me fully, even when I didn't deserve it. Help me extend that same grace to others—without compromising the wisdom and peace you've given me. Give me courage to set boundaries where needed and compassion to keep my heart soft.

Invitation

Is there someone you've forgiven but still feel unsure around? That tension might be your soul asking for a boundary. Ask God for clarity and the strength to honor it.

Borrowed Meaning

Two people are better off than one, for they can help each other succeed. If one person falls, the other can reach out and help. But someone who falls alone is in real trouble.

ECCLESIASTES 4:9-10

Maybe you're in a place where meaning feels out of reach. You're not inspired. You're not energized. You're just . . . existing. And the more people talk about purpose and passion, the more disconnected you feel from it all. When that happens, it's tempting to think something is wrong with you. But here's the truth: None of us are meant to manufacture meaning on our own.

We're wired for connection. And sometimes, when your own sense of purpose goes dim, you're allowed to borrow someone else's light. Borrow it from a friend who still believes in you. From a mentor who helps you see the bigger picture. From a parent, a counselor, a pastor, or a prayer. From Scripture, where stories of perseverance remind you that your chapter isn't finished.

This isn't weakness. This is spiritual interdependence. It's Ecclesiastes 4:9-10 in real time—people in community reaching out and helping each other, including when the struggle of meaning feels too heavy to wrestle with alone. Jesus modeled this when he leaned on his inner circle in Gethsemane, asking them to stay awake and pray. He knew the value of not facing the darkness alone.

Psychologists call this a *scaffold of meaning*—a temporary support structure until you're strong enough to stand again. And it works.

In recovery from depression or trauma, healing often begins with connection, not clarity. You don't have to feel purposeful to be living with purpose. Sometimes just staying tethered to someone who sees hope is itself an act of resilience.

Anchor Truth

You don't have to carry meaning alone. When you can't find your own, you can borrow someone else's faith in you until your own voice returns.

Prayer

God, I feel unmotivated and unsure of what my purpose is right now. Thank you for the people who hold space for me and believe in me when I don't. Help me receive their support as a gift. And remind me that I don't have to figure it all out today.

Invitation

Reach out to someone whose steadiness can help anchor you. You don't have to show up with a plan, just a willingness to stay connected. Let their encouragement be the thread that keeps you moving forward.

Shame Behind the Mask

But while he was still a long way off, his father saw him and was filled with compassion for him; he ran to his son, threw his arms around him and kissed him.

LUKE 15:20 (NIV)

Perfectionism doesn't just push you to perform; it also trains you to hide. To wear the smile. Maintain the image. Say "I'm fine" when your soul is fraying at the edges. Because underneath all the striving is often something far more tender: shame. The quiet belief that if people *really* knew you—your doubts, your weaknesses, your messy emotions—they'd turn away.

So you hide. You manage appearances. You try harder, do more, stay polished. This is the mask of perfectionism—not just to impress, but to protect.

But here's the tragedy: When you live behind a mask, you may be admired, but you won't feel loved. Because only what is seen can be truly known. And only what is known can be truly loved.

Even in Scripture we see this pattern. Adam and Eve, after the fall, covered themselves and hid. Not just physically, but emotionally. Shame was the instinct. But God came looking. Not with condemnation, but with a question: "Where are you?" (Genesis 3:9). That's what he still asks us. We don't need to keep pretending.

God's love doesn't depend on your flawless presentation. He sees the you behind the mask and he comes running to you, ready to wrap you in his arms.

Shame tells you to hide. Grace tells you to come out. Because God doesn't love the version of you that you've perfected. He loves *you*. You're not too messy to be loved. You're just too loved to keep hiding.

Anchor Truth

God's love reaches the parts of you that perfectionism tells you to cover.

Prayer

God, I've worn a mask for too long, afraid of what others might see. Help me step into the light of your love. Remind me that I don't have to be flawless to be fully known and fully accepted.

Invitation

Today, take a small step out of hiding. Share something honest with someone safe. Or be honest with God. Let grace meet the real you.

What If It Works Out?

I am confident I will see the LORD's goodness while I am here in the land of the living.

PSALM 27:13

Sometimes pessimism feels like protection. If you assume things will go wrong, maybe the disappointment won't sting as much when they do. If you expect the worst, maybe you'll be ready for it. But the shield of pessimism is heavy, and it rarely works the way we hope. It doesn't prevent pain. It just drains our joy in advance.

Optimism isn't denial. It's not plastering on a smile or pretending everything is fine. It's choosing to believe that something good is possible, even when you're not sure how or when it will come.

In psychology, this mindset is part of what's called your *explanatory style*—the internal script that explains why things happen.

People with a more optimistic explanatory style tend to interpret setbacks as *temporary* ("This is hard, but it won't last forever"), *specific* ("This one area is tough, not my whole life"), and *external* ("This happened to me—it doesn't define me").

That style doesn't just boost mood. It fuels perseverance. Optimism often leads to action. And action opens the door for change.

Biblically, optimism is anchored not in yourself, but in the goodness of God. In Psalm 27, David didn't say, "I sure hope things will turn around eventually." He said, "I am confident I will see the LORD's goodness"— not "in heaven someday"—but "while I am here in the land of the living." That's not naive. That's faith at work.

So today, what if you asked a different question? Not "What if it all falls apart?" but "What if it works out?" And then, "What if I live like it might?"

Anchor Truth

Optimism isn't pretending. It's trusting that goodness is still on the table.

Prayer

God, help me lift my eyes again. Not in denial, but in trust. Give me the courage to expect goodness even when I don't see it yet.

Invitation

Where are you bracing for disappointment? What would shift if you approached it with sacred optimism instead? Name one action you'd take if you believed something beautiful could still happen.

God and the Silence After Trauma

Behold, I go forward, but he is not there, and backward, but I do not perceive him; . . . But he knows the way that I take; when he has tried me, I shall come out as gold.

JOB 23:8, 10 (ESV)

After trauma, silence can feel unbearable. Not just from people, but also from God. You pray, and nothing stirs. You open your Bible, and the words fall flat. You go through the motions of faith, but your heart feels numb or hollow.

And in that stillness, the questions creep in: *Where were you, God? Why didn't you stop it? Why do you feel so far now—when I need you most?*

This is a sacred ache, one that Job knew well. In Job 23, he describes looking for God in every direction and finding nothing—just absence. Silence. And yet, even there, he says, "He knows the way that I take." Even when Job couldn't feel God, he dared to believe God still saw him. Still held him. Still had not walked away.

The silence after trauma can feel like divine abandonment. But silence is not the same as absence. Sometimes God is near in ways we don't yet feel.

Sometimes healing begins with the honesty of sitting in the silence and not faking your way out of it. Even Jesus cried out from the cross, "My God, my God, why have you forsaken me?" That wasn't a lack of faith. It was the deepest kind of trust—to bring the silence to God.

When God is quiet, he is not gone. When he feels distant, he still draws near. Even in the silence, he is holding your story. Even in the silence, healing is happening in ways you can't yet see.

Your cries are not lost in the dark. God hears them all, and he holds every tear like a treasure.

Anchor Truth

God's silence is never the end of the story.

Prayer

God, I don't know where you are in this pain. I don't know why you feel so far. But I'm still reaching. Still hoping. Still whispering your name. If you're near, help me feel it. And if I can't feel it, help me trust it anyway.

Invitation

If God feels silent, don't run from the quiet. Sit with him there. Light a candle. Breathe. Say just one word if that's all you can manage. He is listening, even in the stillness.

Ask Before You Assume

Fools think their own way is right,
but the wise listen to others.

PROVERBS 12:15

Assumptions are easy. Curiosity is work. It's easier to assume your spouse is being selfish, your coworker is out to get you, or your friend is ignoring you on purpose than it is to pause and ask what else might be going on.

Assumptions shut down connection, but curiosity opens it up.

In relationships, curiosity is like a pressure release valve. It de-escalates tension and defuses defensiveness. It allows us to approach others not with accusations, but with openness.

Psychologist Marshall Rosenberg emphasized the power of observations without evaluations. Instead of leaping to judgment, lead with curiosity. Ask things like "Help me understand what happened." "I noticed this—am I missing something?" "Can you walk me through how you were feeling?"

These questions take courage. But they also create space for empathy.

This principle plays out all over Scripture. Jesus, again and again, asked questions—not because he didn't know the answers, but because he knew people needed to be seen, heard, and drawn out. "What do you want me to do for you?" "Why are you afraid?" "Do you want to get well?"

These questions weren't rhetorical. They were relational. They broke down barriers and built bridges.

Try this in your own relationships. The next time you feel hurt, irritated, or misunderstood, resist the urge to leap to a conclusion. Ask a question instead. Get curious about their motives, their emotions, or their perspective.

It's not always easy. But it's a powerful step toward connection.

Anchor Truth

Assumptions create distance. Curiosity builds bridges. Ask questions before writing stories in your head.

Prayer

God, help me resist the lure of assumption and choose the humble path of curiosity. Teach me to see others with fresh eyes and to listen with love.

Invitation

Think of someone you've felt misunderstood by recently. What is a curious question you could ask to draw them closer, not push them away? Write it down, and when you're ready, ask.

The Body Remembers

My health may fail, and my spirit may grow weak, but God remains the strength of my heart; he is mine forever.

PSALM 73:26

Sometimes anxiety shows up in your body before your mind can name it. Your shoulders tighten. Your stomach knots. Your chest gets heavy. You can't concentrate, can't sit still, can't breathe deeply.

You might feel silly or confused, like your body is reacting to something that isn't happening. But here's what many people don't realize: Your body stores what your mind tries to forget.

This is called *somatic memory*—the body's way of holding on to past pain, even when the mind has tried to move on. It's why symptoms show up long after the stressful moment is over.

Even if you've moved on from a stressful season or survived a difficult relationship, your nervous system may still be in protection mode. That's not weakness. That's wiring.

When the body has lived in a state of hypervigilance—constantly scanning for danger—it doesn't always know how to come down, even when the threat is gone. It takes time to relearn safety.

When you've experienced ongoing stress or trauma, your brain adapts to stay alert. And long after the danger is gone, your body may keep bracing—tightening, clenching, overreacting to ordinary moments like they're threats. It's frustrating. But it's not failure. It's your body asking for care. And compassion—not criticism—is what helps it heal.

In trauma recovery work, we say "the body keeps the score"—but with the right care, it can also learn a new rhythm of rest. And faith can be part of that restoration. God knows your frame. He formed every cell, every nerve, every muscle. He doesn't shame your physical response. He meets you in it. When your strength fails—emotionally, spiritually, physically—he does not.

So if you can't explain the heaviness, if you're tired of feeling tense without reason, take heart. You're not losing it. You're remembering something your body hasn't yet released. And God is still your refuge, even there.

Anchor Truth

Your body isn't betraying you. It's trying to protect you. And God is patient in the healing process.

Prayer

God, I don't always understand what's happening inside me. My body reacts before my mind can catch up. Help me meet myself with compassion, not shame. Thank you for being gentle with my limits. Teach me to listen to what my body is trying to say and to trust that you are with me in every part of it.

Invitation

Take a few minutes today to check in with your body. Where are you carrying tension? Where are you holding your breath? Stretch, walk, or place a hand gently over your heart. Say, "You're safe now." Let your body hear what your mind already knows: God is near.

What's Draining You, Really?

Come to me, all of you who are weary and carry heavy burdens, and I will give you rest.

MATTHEW 11:28

You know the feeling—you're worn out, short-fused, running on fumes. You call it burnout, but can't quite name what caused it. The meetings? The inbox? The video calls? The group chat? Maybe. But maybe that's just the surface.

Because sometimes what drains you isn't what's *on* your calendar. It's what's *underneath* it. The pressure to be impressive. The weight of unspoken expectations. The emotional labor of managing other people's moods. The constant inner commentary telling you that you're not doing enough. The silence between you and someone you used to be close to.

Self-awareness means slowing down long enough to ask, "What's really depleting me right now?" Not just what's happening, but what's happening *in* me as it happens?

Jesus says, "Come to me, all of you who are weary and carry heavy burdens, and I will give you rest." But rest isn't just sleep or vacation. Sometimes rest starts with self-honesty. You can't release a burden you haven't recognized. You can't ask for relief from something you haven't admitted is heavy.

Notice, for example, where emotional stress is showing up in your body. That tight chest, that clenched jaw, that back spasm, that exhaustion that doesn't go away with sleep? That's data. It's your body trying to tell you the truth that your mind is pushing past.

You are allowed to stop. You are allowed to name what's too much. You are allowed to be tired—for real reasons. Not to wallow in it, but to find the path out. And that starts with naming what's really draining you.

It might not be the crowded schedule. It might be the pressure to prove your worth. The way you say yes when you mean no. The fear that rest makes you look lazy. The quiet grief you haven't made time to feel. Or the constant scanning of the room, trying to keep everyone else okay while you disappear in the process.

It's no wonder Jesus doesn't just offer us advice—he offers us rest. And rest starts with truth. And truth starts with paying attention.

Anchor Truth

You can't find rest if you won't name what's wearing you out.

Prayer

God, I'm tired in ways I don't fully understand. Help me trace the source—not to complain, but to come clean. I want to lay it down, not just carry it better.

Invitation

Take five minutes today and ask, "What's costing me energy right now—emotionally, mentally, spiritually?" Write it down. Even just naming it is a form of rest.

When Medication Helps the Healing

Whatever is good and perfect is a gift coming down to us from God our Father.

JAMES 1:17

For many people walking through trauma, the decision to take medication is layered with fear, shame, or even spiritual doubt. You might think, *Shouldn't I be able to pray my way through this?* Or, *If I trust God, shouldn't that be enough?* Or maybe someone told you that needing medication is a sign of weakness, lack of faith, or failure. It's not.

Let's be clear: Taking medication for your mental health is not a failure. It's not a sin. It's not a shortcut. It's care. And sometimes it's lifesaving.

Medication doesn't erase your pain or bypass the hard work of healing, but it can steady the ground beneath your feet long enough for you to breathe, think clearly, and begin to heal.

Medication can quiet the constant noise of panic or soften the sharp edges of depression. It can bring your nervous system out of fight-or-flight and into rest-and-repair. And all of that makes space—for counseling, for prayer, for community, for clarity, for grace.

James 1:17 says that whatever is good and perfect is a gift from God. That includes medicine. Doctors. Therapists. Neuroscience. God can work through all of it.

He doesn't need you to suffer more to prove your faith. He wants you well. Jesus didn't shame people who were sick for using physical remedies. He healed with mud and spit and touch and time. He met people where they were—and that includes you.

Taking medication doesn't make you weak. It means you're tending to your wounds with wisdom, and God can meet you right there.

Anchor Truth

Medication isn't a lack of faith. It can be a vessel of God's mercy.

Prayer

God, you know how hard it is for me to admit I need help. Thank you for the tools you've made available. If medication is part of my healing, help me receive it with courage and peace. Let it make space for your presence to move in deeper ways.

Invitation

If you're taking medication, pause to give thanks for it today. If you're considering it, bring your fears honestly to God. Let him be part of that decision—and trust he can use any tool for your good.

When Words Are Weapons

Don't repay evil for evil. Don't retaliate with insults when people insult you. Instead, pay them back with a blessing. That is what God has called you to do, and he will grant you his blessing.

1 PETER 3:9

They don't want a conversation. They want a reaction. That's the twisted game of the troll—someone who deliberately posts inflammatory, offensive, or disruptive content online to provoke others, stir up conflict, or get attention.

Whether in your inbox, your comment section, or a public post—trolls don't show up to connect. They show up to control. They're motivated by a need to dominate by provoking emotion. It's not about logic. It's not even about you. It's about their need to feel powerful, even if that power is wielded through cruelty.

Trolling thrives in anonymity but lands in your real-life nervous system. You feel it as adrenaline. Tight muscles. An internal churn that begs you to fire back. But here's the thing: You don't have to engage to prove your strength.

Jesus was trolled. Not online, of course, but to his face—mocked, baited, twisted, and misrepresented. Yet he responded not with retaliation, but with restraint. Not because he was weak, but because he was anchored. You can be too.

You don't need to clap back to protect your worth. You don't need to win the thread to defend your character.

The moment you recognize the troll for what they are—a trap dressed in commentary—you reclaim your peace. Not everything deserves your reply. Especially not someone who's looking for a fight, not a conversation.

Anchor Truth

You don't fight trolls with fire. You fight them with groundedness. God calls you to respond not with venom, but with clarity, peace, and sometimes silence.

Prayer

God, help me resist the urge to defend myself where no defense will satisfy. Guard my heart from the poison of other people's projection. Teach me to recognize what is not mine to carry and give me the strength to let it go.

Invitation

Next time someone tries to provoke you, pause. Ask yourself, "What do I gain by replying?" If the answer is nothing meaningful, step back. Your peace is worth more than their bait.

Self-Compassion Is Not Self-Indulgence

Then he lay down and slept under the broom tree. But as he was sleeping, an angel touched him and told him, "Get up and eat!"

1 KINGS 19:5

Resilience is not just about pushing through. Sometimes it's about pausing with kindness. We live in a world that confuses self-compassion with weakness—or worse, self-pity. But research tells a different story.

Self-compassion—the ability to respond to your pain with gentleness instead of judgment—is one of the strongest predictors of long-term emotional health. It lowers anxiety, softens shame, and boosts resilience more than self-esteem alone.

In Scripture, Elijah gives us a picture of what burnout and breakdown can look like, even for people of deep faith. After a spiritual high on Mount Carmel, he crashes into despair. He runs. He hides. He prays to die. And what does God do? He doesn't lecture Elijah or call him dramatic. He doesn't say, "You just need to believe more." Instead, God sends an angel with a meal, saying, "Get up and eat." Then Elijah sleeps again. And the angel returns a second time, still gently saying, "The journey is too much for you." That's compassion. That's how God treats the exhausted.

Or think of Hannah, whose pain spilled out in the form of silent sobs and trembling prayers (1 Samuel 1:9-18). Eli, the priest, misjudged her. But God didn't. God met her in the anguish and honored her honest, tear-soaked request.

Self-compassion doesn't mean you stop growing. It means you stop growing through self-hate. It means you let yourself rest, grieve, and be human, because that's what builds the strength to rise again.

Beating yourself up doesn't make you stronger. Being gentle with yourself does. That's not indulgence. That's wisdom.

Anchor Truth

Self-compassion is how you tend to the parts of you that are still healing.

Prayer

God, I've been hard on myself. I've called it discipline, but deep down, it's shame. Teach me how to treat myself the way you do—with truth, yes, but also tenderness. Help me build strength from grace, not guilt.

Invitation

Notice your inner voice today. Is it harsh? Demanding? Critical? Gently interrupt it. Say to yourself what God might say: "You're tired. You're doing your best. I'm with you." Then take one compassionate action, just for you.

The Power of the Follow-Up

You must show sincere love to each other as brothers and sisters. Love each other deeply with all your heart.

1 PETER 1:22

Most conversations skim the surface: "How are you?" "Busy." "Same."

We nod, move on, and call it connection. But the truth is, most people are starving to be known. And one of the simplest, most overlooked ways to help someone feel seen is the follow-up question. Not the first question. That one's easy.

The follow-up is what signals presence. Curiosity. Honor. It says, "I heard you, and I want to understand more." That second question is often where the real conversation begins.

Research backs this up. In a study published in the *Journal of Personality and Social Psychology*, people who asked more follow-up questions—especially "how" and "why" questions—were rated as more likable and engaging conversationalists.

Why? Because follow-ups communicate interest. They invite depth. They say, "I'm not here to impress you. I'm here to know you."

Jesus modeled this masterfully. In John 4, his conversation with the woman at the well doesn't just stop at "Give me a drink." He engages. He asks. He listens. And then he asks again. His questions draw her out of shame and into dignity. And when she runs back to her village, she says, "Come and see a man who told me everything I ever did!" (John 4:29). What she remembers isn't just his answers. It's his attention.

In a world where most people are simply waiting for their turn to speak, a well-placed follow-up can feel like love in action. It shows that you're not just playing the part of a friend—you're actually showing up with curiosity and care.

Follow-up questions can be simple: "What was that like for you?" "How did that make you feel?" "What happened next?" And the greatest of all: "Tell me more."

It's not about prying. It's about presence.

Anchor Truth

Real connection lives in the second question.

Prayer

God, help me slow down enough to really hear people. Give me ears to listen, a heart that cares, and the courage to follow curiosity into deeper connection.

Invitation

In your next conversation, ask one thoughtful follow-up question. See what unfolds. Let your curiosity be a gift.

Taking Your Last Guilt Trip

He has removed our sins as far from us
as the east is from the west.

PSALM 103:12

You've packed the bags. Boarded the train. Punched the ticket. And off you go—on another guilt trip. The destination? Self-condemnation. The return time? Indefinite.

It's amazing how many of us take this journey without even realizing it.

We replay the same scenes in our mind. We rehearse the words we wish we hadn't said. We imagine what we should have done differently. And we call it humility. But it's not.

Living in perpetual guilt isn't a sign of spiritual maturity. It's a sign you haven't let grace sink all the way in.

Psalm 103:12 says God has *removed* your sin. Not just forgiven—*removed.*

He didn't file it away for later review. He didn't mark it "pending." He didn't keep it on your permanent record to remind you of who you used to be.

He cast it so far away that you couldn't find it again if you tried. And yet, how many of us keep returning to it? As if penance will earn back what grace already gave. The cross was never about making you feel worse. It was about setting you free.

Jesus didn't endure the weight of sin so you could carry a piece of it around in your back pocket. He carried it *all.*

So maybe today is the day you cancel the trip. Unpack the bags. Step off the train. Make God's grace your final stop. There's nothing more to prove.

Anchor Truth

Grace means never having to earn your way back. Jesus already made the way. You don't have to keep punishing yourself for what he already paid for.

Prayer

God, help me stop reliving what you've already released. Teach me to trust in your grace more than my guilt. I want to live free—starting now.

Invitation

Is there a mistake you keep replaying in your mind? Write it down, and then tear it up. Let that physical act remind you of what's spiritually true: In Christ, it's gone for good.

This Doesn't Have to Be the End of the Story

He will yet fill your mouth with laughter
and your lips with shouts of joy.

JOB 8:21 (NIV)

You've been through a lot. Maybe more than anyone knows. The unraveling. The grief. The silence. The ache of not knowing where you stand. The version of faith you once held has changed or maybe even disappeared altogether. And some days, you wonder if you've come to the end of your spiritual story.

But what if you haven't? What if this isn't the end, but the middle? The messy, unformed, still-being-written part?

Psychologists talk about something called *post-traumatic growth*—the idea that people who go through deep struggle don't just bounce back, they can grow forward. Not despite the pain, but through it.

They develop deeper empathy. A clearer sense of purpose. A more grounded identity.

That doesn't mean the struggle disappears. It means something new is being formed—slowly, invisibly, in the dark.

The Bible is full of people who thought their story was over. Sarah. Job. Elijah. Peter. Thomas. But God met them right in their disillusionment. Not with platitudes, but with presence.

Job, who sat in ashes and wished he'd never been born, was eventually told, "He will yet fill your mouth with laughter."

Yet. That word matters. You don't have to rush into a new chapter. You don't need to pretend everything is resolved. But you *can* hold space for the possibility that this isn't how it ends.

Maybe faith is returning in quieter ways. Maybe healing is happening even when you can't feel it. Maybe you're not going back to what was; you're becoming something new.

This doesn't have to be the end of the story. Not with God. Not ever.

Anchor Truth

Your struggles are part of your journey, not the end of it. Your story with God is still unfolding.

Prayer

God, I've come so far, but I'm still unsure of so much. I don't want to close the book if you're still writing. Help me stay open to what comes next.

Invitation

Take a walk. Listen to music. Light a candle. Do one small thing that reminds you, "I'm still here. I'm still becoming. This story isn't over."

The Amygdala Hijack

Understand this, my dear brothers and sisters: You must all be quick to listen, slow to speak, and slow to get angry.

JAMES 1:19

You didn't mean to blow up. You didn't want to say that. But in the moment, something took over and logic left the room. That "something" has a name: the amygdala.

It's a tiny, almond-shaped part of your brain that acts like a fire alarm. The moment it senses a threat—emotional or physical—it triggers your fight, flight, or freeze response. Heart rate spikes. Muscles tense. Blood rushes. And higher reasoning goes offline. Fast.

This is what psychologists call an *amygdala hijack*—when your brain is flooded with reactive emotion before your prefrontal cortex (the rational part) can weigh in. It's why you say things you regret. Why you slam the door. Why the email you shouldn't send feels so necessary in the moment.

But the Bible says be slow to get angry. And that kind of slowness doesn't come naturally when your brain thinks you're under attack. It has to be trained.

Self-regulation starts with awareness. Noticing your body. Your breath. The early signs of escalation. And then choosing—however awkwardly—not to react immediately.

That might mean walking away to breathe. Waiting ten minutes before replying. Splashing cold water on your face. Or even praying aloud, "God, help me respond with wisdom, not just instinct."

You're not weak for feeling hijacked. You're wired that way. But you're also not powerless.

The more you practice pausing, the more space you create between your trigger and your response—and that's where transformation happens. Not in pretending you're calm, but in slowing the surge long enough for grace to rise.

Anchor Truth

Anger floods fast. Wisdom flows slow.

Prayer

God, you designed my brain, and you know how quickly I can be swept up in emotion. Help me pause. Help me breathe. Help me choose response over reaction.

Invitation

Today, when you feel yourself reacting quickly, take a breath—literally. One deep breath activates your nervous system's calming mechanism and gives your brain time to reengage.

Everyday Acts of Bravery

Whoever can be trusted with very little can also be trusted with much.

LUKE 16:10 (NIV)

The bravest moments in your life may never go viral. They're the private, personal acts of courage that often get overlooked. Saying "I was wrong." Walking into a room where you feel invisible. Setting a boundary with someone you love. Leaving a toxic job without a new one lined up. Admitting to your child that you lost your temper.

These aren't small things. They're seismic. And they're the kind of bravery that builds character over time.

Jesus didn't just demonstrate courage by facing the cross: He showed it in small daily ways. By touching the untouchable, by calling out injustice at his own risk, by speaking plainly when others wanted him to flatter or soften the truth. He lived a life of steady, principled courage.

That's the kind of courage Luke 16:10 points us toward. It's easy to imagine that God is looking for big, impressive acts. But over and over again, Scripture reminds us that God watches how we show up in the little things. The hidden things. The moments no one applauds.

The test of courage isn't only in the battle. It's in the quiet, internal choices we make every single day. And when we choose integrity over image, honesty over comfort, and faithfulness over convenience, we prove trustworthy—not only to others but to ourselves.

Every small, brave decision shapes who we're becoming. And God takes notice.

You don't need a stadium of onlookers to be brave today. You need one moment of resolve. Just enough light to take the next step.

Anchor Truth

You don't have to do something dramatic to be brave. Every time you act in alignment with your values, especially when it costs you, you're practicing real courage—and growing into someone God can trust with more.

Prayer

God, give me the strength to do the right thing today—even when no one's watching, even when it's hard, even when I'm afraid. Help me choose truth over comfort, and help me be faithful in the little things.

Invitation

What's one small act of bravery you can take today? A hard conversation? A confession? A step toward healing? Write it down. Then take it.

Don't Believe Everything You Feel

The human heart is the most deceitful of all things, and desperately wicked. Who really knows how bad it is?

JEREMIAH 17:9

Anxiety has a way of making everything feel urgent. Final. Unfixable. It doesn't just whisper lies; it makes them feel true. You feel like you've messed everything up. You feel like everyone is judging you. You feel like it will always be this way.

This is known as *emotional reasoning*—when the intensity of your feelings convinces you something must be true, even when there's no evidence to support it.

But feelings aren't facts. They're real. They're powerful. But they're not always accurate. Your emotional response can be based on your history, trauma, exhaustion, or plain old stress.

Anxiety often twists thinking through patterns called *cognitive distortions*—like *catastrophizing* ("My headache must mean something's wrong with my brain and I'm going to die"), *personalization* ("My coworker was short with me, so she must be upset with me"), or *black-and-white thinking* ("If this presentation doesn't go perfectly, I'll be a total failure").

Sometimes anxiety takes an ordinary moment and wraps it in fear, shame, or panic. That doesn't mean your faith is failing: It means your system is sounding an alarm.

God doesn't ask you to ignore your feelings. He invites you to test them. To slow down and ask, "Is this true? Is this from God? Does this align with grace?"

This is a core practice in both faith and therapy called *compassionate self-inquiry*. It helps you create space between what you feel and what is true.

Even David, in the Psalms, regularly questioned his own despair: "Why am I discouraged? Why is my heart so sad?" (Psalm 42:5). That question wasn't weakness. It was wisdom.

So yes, listen to your emotions. But don't hand them the keys. You are not at the mercy of your feelings. You can honor them without obeying them. You are allowed to feel deeply without letting every feeling steer your day.

Anchor Truth

Your feelings are valid, but they are not the voice of God. Truth is steadier than emotion.

Prayer

God, I confess that sometimes my feelings take over. They feel louder than truth. More convincing than hope. But I don't want to live at the mercy of every emotion. Help me pause and remember that you are the same, even when I am not. Speak truth into the places where fear has taken root.

Invitation

When a strong feeling hits, pause and ask yourself three questions: "What am I feeling?" "What do I know to be true?" "What would I say to a friend feeling this way?" Your anxiety might shout, but truth speaks quietly and kindly.

People Can't Read Your Mind

Even fools are thought wise when they keep silent;
with their mouths shut, they seem intelligent.

PROVERBS 17:28

Some people don't talk about what they need because they've been taught that needing anything is a sign of weakness. Others keep their feelings quiet because they've been burned before—dismissed, ignored, or misunderstood. And still others hope that someone, somewhere, will simply know what they're going through and respond without them having to explain.

But know this: People can't read your mind. Not your friend. Not your spouse. Not your pastor. Not even your therapist. And certainly not your barista.

Connection depends on communication. And communication requires vulnerability. When we hope others will just "get it" without us saying a word, we set ourselves up for disappointment, resentment, or disconnection. Not because others failed us, but because we never gave them the chance to show up.

We, too, often assume others see the world as we do, feel what we feel, or somehow intuit what we're hoping they'll offer. But people aren't mind readers. Most are trying to navigate their own emotional chaos and may not even notice what you're hiding behind that well-crafted smile. Even in close relationships, assumptions erode intimacy.

That's why clarity is a kindness—both to yourself and to others. If you need something—support, space, affirmation, truth-telling, companionship—say it. Let people rise to meet you instead of silently scripting your disappointment.

Scripture calls us to live in the light, to speak the truth in love, and to bear one another's burdens. That can't happen in secrecy.

Start small if you need to: "I could use a friend today." "That comment hurt." "I'm not okay, but I don't need a solution, just someone to sit with me." It may feel awkward. But over time, it builds the kind of honest connection your soul is wired for.

Anchor Truth

Unspoken needs are rarely met.

Prayer

God, give me the courage to speak up—not for attention, but for truth. Help me stop expecting people to guess what's going on inside me. Teach me to name what I need, and help me trust you to meet me through others.

Invitation

This week, express one need out loud to someone safe. It could be practical or emotional. Resist the urge to downplay it. Practice honesty, and notice how it deepens connection.

When You Find Your Why

I cry out to God Most High,
to God who will fulfill his purpose for me.

PSALM 57:2

Sometimes the ache of insecurity isn't really about how we see ourselves. It's about not knowing why we're here. When you wake up without purpose, your sense of worth can begin to drift. You second-guess your choices, compare your path to everyone else's, and wonder if you're falling behind—or worse, if you don't even matter.

But purpose grounds you. When you catch even a glimpse of the "why" behind your life, it reshapes your "who." Not in a self-glorifying way, but in a quietly confident way. Because now you know: You're part of something bigger. You're not random. You're not an accident. You're here on purpose *for* a purpose.

Take Esther. She didn't set out to be a queen who would save her people. She was young, orphaned, and likely unsure of herself.

But when the opportunity came, her cousin Mordecai reminded her of something bigger: "Perhaps you were made queen for just such a time as this" (Esther 4:14). That truth shifted her focus from fear to purpose—and purpose gave her courage.

In psychological terms, purpose is one of the most powerful antidotes to low self-worth. Researchers have consistently found that people with a clear sense of purpose experience better mental health, greater resilience, and even longer life spans.

Purpose doesn't have to be flashy. It just has to be *real.*

So how can you find yours? Start with what breaks your heart. What stirs your compassion or frustration in a way that makes you want to do something about it? Consider your gifts—what comes naturally to you that lifts others? And don't discount your story. Often our greatest wounds become the very places we're called to bring healing.

Your purpose doesn't need a spotlight. It needs your surrender. Let God shape your "why" and watch your self-worth grow from the inside out.

Anchor Truth

You are not here by accident. God is writing a bigger story, and you have a part to play.

Prayer

God, I want to live with purpose. Show me the work you've prepared for me, and help me walk in it with confidence, not fear.

Invitation

Write down one thing that matters deeply to you—something that energizes or burdens your heart. Ask God to show you how it connects to your unique purpose.

When the Truth Gets Twisted

The LORD detests lying lips,
but he delights in those who tell the truth.

PROVERBS 12:22

Gaslighting isn't just a buzzword. It's emotional manipulation in its most insidious form. It happens when someone tries to distort your perception of reality—downplaying your emotions, rewriting history, or twisting facts—until you're no longer sure what's true.

It starts subtly: "That never happened." "You're too sensitive." "You're overreacting." Over time, you begin to question your memory. Your instincts. Your sense of self.

That's what makes gaslighting so damaging: It attacks your confidence at the root. It's not just about being lied to. It's about being made to feel foolish for even believing you knew the truth in the first place.

Clinically, gaslighting is a hallmark of emotional abuse. Spiritually, it's the very opposite of what God invites us into. The God of Scripture is a God of truth, not confusion. Of clarity, not distortion. Jesus didn't tell people they were imagining their pain. He validated it, met them in it, and called things what they were.

So if you're in a relationship where gaslighting has taken root, hear this clearly: Your confusion isn't weakness. It's a signal that something isn't right.

You don't need to explain your pain perfectly in order for it to matter. And you don't have to stay tangled in someone else's distortion to prove you're loyal, loving, or forgiving.

The truth will always lead you toward freedom, even if it's uncomfortable. And God delights in that kind of truth. Not just doctrinal truth, but emotional, relational, grounded-in-reality truth. Because truth is where healing begins.

Anchor Truth

Gaslighting dims your sense of reality, but God is never the author of confusion. His voice steadies your mind, anchors your heart, and reaffirms what's true.

Prayer

God, help me recognize the voices that twist the truth—both around me and within me. Give me the courage to name what's real and the wisdom to seek help where needed. Help me walk in your truth, no matter who tries to rewrite the story.

Invitation

If you've experienced gaslighting, don't walk it alone. Talk to a counselor, pastor, or trauma-informed mentor. Begin journaling the facts of your experiences. It's a powerful step in regaining clarity and reclaiming your story.

Start by Getting Curious About You

Search me, O God, and know my heart;
test me and know my anxious thoughts.

PSALM 139:23

Most of us aren't as self-aware as we think. We get stuck in patterns—snapping at people, procrastinating, numbing out—without ever stopping to ask why. We assume our reactions are just "who we are," when in fact they're usually telling us something.

Curiosity is the antidote to self-judgment and self-avoidance. Curiosity invites you to notice your patterns with compassion, not condemnation. When you get curious about your internal world, you can begin to connect the dots between your emotions, behaviors, and deeper needs.

Instead of berating yourself for being reactive, curiosity asks, "What just got triggered?" Instead of spiraling into shame, curiosity wonders, "What need was I trying to meet?" Instead of suppressing your sadness, curiosity gently asks, "What's the deeper grief underneath this?"

This is how real transformation begins. Psychologists call this *metacognition*—the ability to think about your thinking. It's a foundational skill for emotional regulation and healthy relationships. The more curious you are about yourself, the more aware you become of what drives you—and the more intentional you can be in your actions and responses.

David's prayer in Psalm 139 models this kind of God-honoring self-curiosity. He doesn't hide. He invites God into his inner world: *Search me. Know me. Test me.* That's not a prayer of fear. It's a prayer of trust. A prayer of someone who believes that being fully known is the first step toward being truly transformed.

It's easy to stay on autopilot. But the life you want doesn't grow there. It grows in the honest, messy, curious work of self-awareness.

Anchor Truth

Growth starts with self-awareness. Curiosity about your inner world leads to healing, clarity, and deeper connection with God and others.

Prayer

God, help me slow down and get honest with myself. Show me what's beneath my reactions. Search my heart and help me see what you see.

Invitation

Pay attention today to a moment you felt reactive, overwhelmed, or shut down. Pause and ask yourself, "What was really going on beneath the surface?" Let that moment be a doorway to greater understanding.

Shoulder to Shoulder

Then they sat on the ground with him for seven days and nights. No one said a word to Job, for they saw that his suffering was too great for words.

JOB 2:13

Grief isn't always obvious. It doesn't always look like what you would imagine—especially in others. Sometimes it looks like your friend zoning out mid-conversation. Or showing up but saying almost nothing. Or canceling plans. Again.

And when you care, you feel it too. Their ache presses into your chest like it's yours. You want to fix it, to say something profound. But grief doesn't need fixing. It needs presence.

Sometimes love looks like sitting beside someone in their unspoken sadness. No pep, no platitudes. Just warmth. A hand on their back. A silent nod that says, "You're not alone."

When your friend loses a parent or a marriage or a job they wrapped their identity around, it doesn't matter if the words get clumsy. What matters is that you showed up. That you stayed.

Scripture doesn't tell us to offer perfect comfort. Galatians 6:2 tells us to "share each other's burdens." That means sitting on the floor when they can't get off it. Bringing dinner when they haven't cooked in days. Remembering the date they dread. Asking how they're really doing, even when they say, "I'm fine."

Look at Job. His friends got it terribly wrong when they started talking. But when they first showed up and just sat with him in silence for seven days, they got it right.

When you walk with someone through grief, you mirror the heart of God. Psalm 34:18 says he is "close to the brokenhearted." Not hurrying them. Not lecturing them. Close.

Why does this matter? Because grief isolates. And your presence bridges the gap.

You may not have the perfect words, but you don't need them. Because when you walk with someone in their sorrow—unhurried and unafraid—you become living proof that God hasn't left them. And that kind of love doesn't just comfort the grieving. It changes their world.

Anchor Truth

God's presence is the model for how we grieve with others—close, compassionate, and patient.

Prayer

God, help me resist the urge to fix what can't be fixed. Teach me to offer my presence without pressure, my empathy without explanation, and my heart without hesitation. Show me how to love like you do—shoulder to shoulder.

Invitation

Think of someone in your life who is grieving—big or small. Reach out today. Not with solutions, but with presence. A text. A memory. An offer to sit in silence. Be the safe place where they don't have to hold it all together.

Worship as the Ultimate Expression of Gratitude

Let all that I am praise the LORD;
with my whole heart, I will praise his holy name. . . .
He fills my life with good things.

PSALM 103:1, 5

Gratitude isn't just saying "thank you" with our lips. It's offering our whole selves in response to what God has done. That's what worship is.

Worship is where gratitude gets legs and lungs. It moves from a mental note—*I should be grateful*—to a bodily expression through raised hands, bent knees, whispered prayers, full-on tears. It's how we give God what no one else can: our delight in him.

Psalm 103 doesn't just remind us to be thankful. It is David preaching to himself, "Let all that I am praise the LORD."

He's not half-hearted about it. Gratitude, for him, is a full-body, full-soul experience.

This kind of worship doesn't require a band or a stage. Sometimes it happens at the kitchen sink or in the car or the hospital room. It can be quiet or loud. It can be weeping or dancing.

But underneath it all is a grateful heart that recognizes: *I didn't earn this breath. I didn't orchestrate this grace. I didn't carry myself here. God did.*

Worship transforms gratitude from a feeling into a force. It shapes your posture toward life, bending your focus away from scarcity and toward abundance—not in what you have, but in who God is.

Gratitude may start as a whispered prayer. But it ends in worship.

Anchor Truth

Worship is what gratitude looks like when it reaches full expression—body, heart, and soul responding to the goodness of God.

Prayer

God, you are worthy of more than a passing thank-you. Stir my heart toward worship, not just when things are good, but because you are good—always.

Invitation

Today, let your gratitude become embodied. Turn on worship music. Go for a walk and thank God aloud. Write a psalm of your own. Let all that you are praise the Lord.

When Hypocrisy Breaks Your Trust

What sorrow awaits you teachers of religious law and you Pharisees. Hypocrites! For you are like whitewashed tombs—beautiful on the outside but filled on the inside with dead people's bones and all sorts of impurity.

MATTHEW 23:27

You were taught to trust people who called themselves Christians. To believe that what they said matched how they lived. To assume that love, honesty, and humility came with the label. But somewhere along the way, the mask slipped—and you saw too much.

Maybe it was a family member who preached grace but never gave it. A friend who quoted verses on forgiveness but kept score like a pro. A community that talked about love—until you needed it. Or a roommate who name-dropped Jesus but lived like none of it applied to them.

You saw the double standards. The judgment. The passive aggression baptized in Scripture verses. The kindness that had conditions. And suddenly faith didn't just feel confusing—it felt *contaminated.* Because how do you trust the message when the messengers are faking it?

Jesus had strong words for this kind of spiritual performance. He didn't shame people for struggling. Instead, he called out the ones who pretended not to—those who wore faith like a costume to cover control, pride, or fear.

Psychologists call this *cognitive betrayal*—that deep rupture that happens when someone who should have been safe, wasn't. And when that betrayal happens in God's name, it cuts even deeper.

If you've been let down by people who claimed to follow Jesus but acted nothing like him, you're not bitter. You're not broken. You're awake. And Jesus was too.

He flipped tables in the Temple—not because he hated faith, but because he hated fraud. He wanted real connection, not performance. Real hearts, not hollow routines.

So don't let the hypocrisy of others push you away from the Jesus they misrepresented. There is still a kind of faith that rings true. There are still people trying, failing, and being honest about both. And Jesus is still worth following, even when others aren't.

Anchor Truth

Hypocrisy is fraud. True faith is honest and humble.

Prayer

God, I've seen people use your name for power. I've felt betrayed by those I trusted. Help me separate what's true from what's toxic, and give me courage to follow you, not just those who claim to.

Invitation

How has the hypocrisy of others shaped your faith? Write down what parts of it still feel worth reclaiming.

You Don't Have to Be Special to Live a Meaningful Life

Make it your goal to live a quiet life, minding your own business and working with your hands, just as we instructed you before.

1 THESSALONIANS 4:11

You were likely told at some point, "You're special." And it's true. You are fearfully and wonderfully made.

But somewhere along the way, "special" got twisted. It became code for "extraordinary." Unforgettable. Impressive. The pressure to live a big, visible life is everywhere. Be unique, be exceptional, leave a mark.

Here's the thing: Chasing specialness can actually suffocate meaning. It turns life into a performance. It tricks you into thinking that quiet faithfulness doesn't count. That ordinary love isn't enough. That unless you're seen, you're failing.

Scripture offers a different vision: "Make it your goal to live a quiet life," Paul writes. Not a flashy one. "Work with your hands." Not for applause, but for the joy of contribution. Not for fame, but for faithfulness.

Think of Andrew the disciple. He's not the one who walked on water or preached to the multitudes. But he brought Peter to Jesus. That one act changed everything. And yet, Andrew mostly stayed in the background. Faithful. Steady. Meaningful.

Psychologists call this *intrinsic value orientation*—living from inner conviction rather than outer validation. It's tied to stronger well-being, less anxiety, and deeper joy. Meaning doesn't require standing out. It requires showing up.

Your worth isn't in being spectacular. It's in being sincere. And some of the most meaningful lives are the ones no one notices, except the people they loved well.

So drop the pressure to impress. Meaning isn't earned through impact. It's revealed through intention.

Anchor Truth

A meaningful life isn't about being special. It's about being present, faithful, and real.

Prayer

God, free me from the pressure to prove myself. Quiet the voice that says I have to be impressive to matter. Help me love well in the life I already have. Let faithfulness be enough for me.

Invitation

Do something today that no one may see, but do it with love. Let go of applause. Practice presence. Live like meaning is already in the moment, not waiting for a spotlight.

The Search for Happiness

Blessed are all who hear the word of God and put it into practice.

LUKE 11:28

Everyone wants to be happy. But let's be honest: Most of us are terrible at figuring out how. We chase it through achievement, accumulation, distraction, and even perfection. We think if we fix ourselves, our families, or our finances, we'll finally get there.

But happiness slips through our fingers when it becomes a performance. And for some, even the word itself feels like a setup—a standard we're supposed to meet, but can't seem to sustain. That's because happiness isn't something we achieve. It's something we align with.

Psychologists define happiness as a combination of life satisfaction and emotional well-being. But in Scripture, the word often translated as "blessed" (Greek: *makarios*) carries the meaning of deep, soul-level flourishing. It's not just about a fleeting good mood. It's about wholeness. Integrity. Living in sync with what's good, true, and life giving.

That's why Jesus flips the script. He says happiness doesn't come from getting your way. It comes from getting in step with God's way.

Even neuroscience backs this up. Research shows that happiness isn't about constant pleasure. It's about purpose. Meaning. Connection.

And people who live by their values—who practice gratitude, compassion, faith, and service—report more lasting happiness than those who pursue only momentary highs. Which means your happiness isn't on layaway. It's not waiting until life's perfect. It begins where you are, when you say yes to what matters most.

Anchor Truth

Happiness isn't the absence of pain. It's the presence of purpose. And it grows when you live in step with the truth.

Prayer

God, I'm tired of chasing happiness in all the wrong places. Teach me what it means to truly flourish—to follow your way, to ground myself in what matters, and to find joy, even here.

Invitation

Today, notice where your pursuit of happiness has led to striving instead of peace. What if happiness is closer than you thought—waiting in obedience, gratitude, or stillness? You don't have to earn it. Just begin again.

This Might Sting a Little

You desire honesty from the womb,
teaching me wisdom even there.

PSALM 51:6

There's a version of you that's easy to live with. The version that's composed, generous, self-controlled. The version you show to others—and sometimes even to yourself.

But real growth doesn't come from polishing the image. It comes from facing the stuff you'd rather avoid. Self-deception isn't always loud. Sometimes it whispers, "I'm fine." "This isn't a big deal." "That's just how I am." "If I ignore it long enough, it'll go away."

But here's the truth: You can't grow around the truth. You can only grow *through* it.

David knew this. After hiding, deflecting, and spinning his story, he finally came clean in Psalm 51. And what does he say? "You desire honesty in the womb, teaching me wisdom even there." Even in the womb. Even in the beginning. Even in the broken places.

God doesn't demand perfection. He asks for truth. Because truth is the soil where wisdom grows.

This kind of truth brings about the kind of transformation that doesn't just modify behavior but addresses core beliefs. And insight starts with honesty. Not public confession. Not performance. Just quiet, courageous truth-telling inside your own soul.

You don't need to fear the truth. God already sees it. He's not disappointed that you're human. He's just inviting you to stop pretending.

Sure, the truth might sting a little—not because it's cruel, but because truth tends to press on the places we've tried to protect.

But when you finally stop managing your image and start listening to your soul, something shifts. Not into shame, but into freedom.

Anchor Truth

Honesty with yourself is the first act of spiritual courage.

Prayer

God, I don't want to live in denial, not even the subtle kind. Help me see myself clearly. Not to tear myself down, but to let your truth set me free.

Invitation

What's one uncomfortable truth you've been avoiding? Name it privately. You don't have to solve it today—just stop pretending it's not there.

When Guilt Becomes a Weapon

Do not judge others, and you will not be judged. Do not condemn others, or it will all come back against you. Forgive others, and you will be forgiven.

LUKE 6:37

Some people don't ask for what they need. They hint. They sulk. They guilt. And when guilt is your go-to strategy for getting others to comply, connect, or come through—that's not love. It's control dressed up as concern.

If you've been on the receiving end of this, you know the feeling: The heavy sense that no matter what you do, it will never be quite enough. The lingering suspicion that you're responsible for someone else's mood, peace, or pain. The obligation to respond—not out of care, but out of dread. This is guilt gone rogue.

It's not uncommon. Guilt is easy to weaponize. It doesn't scream—it sighs. It doesn't demand—it insinuates. "I guess I'll just do it myself" or "I wouldn't have expected you to understand." These subtle arrows don't leave bruises, but they leave you bleeding internally.

And if you grew up in an environment where this was normal, it can be hard to recognize. You might even think you owe guilt a response. That it's godly to feel bad. But guilt isn't always holy—and it's definitely not harmless.

God doesn't guilt you into change. He *calls* you. He invites you. And his conviction never leads to anxiety, just restoration.

So if someone in your life is constantly triggering false guilt, it's okay to step back. To clarify. To ask yourself, "Is this mine to carry?" And to let their disappointment be theirs, not yours.

If you're the one using guilt—pause. What do you really need? How could you express it with courage instead of manipulation?

Because real love doesn't require guilt to grow. It flourishes in freedom.

Anchor Truth

Guilt doesn't get to be in charge. Where there is no condemnation, there is no obligation to shrink, to prove, or to perform.

Prayer

God, help me see guilt for what it is, whether I'm drowning in it or dishing it out. Replace shame with clarity. Replace manipulation with love. Show me how to live and relate from a place of freedom.

Invitation

If guilt has become the background noise in one of your relationships, notice it. Name it. And if needed, disrupt it—with honesty, boundaries, and grace.

When Pleasing Becomes Losing

If you try to hang on to your life, you will lose it. But if you give up your life for my sake, you will save it.

MATTHEW 16:25

People-pleasing feels like self-sacrifice. You say yes, you avoid conflict, you put others first. On the surface, it looks like servanthood. Noble. Kind. Christlike, even. But sometimes it's not.

Sometimes it's fear in disguise. Fear of disapproval. Fear of disappointing someone. Fear of what might happen if you set a boundary, say what you really think, or simply stay silent instead of scrambling to fill the silence with something agreeable.

Over time, this fear wears you down—not just emotionally, but existentially. You lose your edges. You forget what you want, what you value, what you even like. You're still showing up, but it's not really *you* anymore. And the scariest part? You've said yes to so many things for so long that your true self—the self that Christ called you to become—has been buried under a pile of expectations and obligations.

Jesus calls us to lose our lives for his sake. But people-pleasing is a counterfeit version of that call. It asks you to lose yourself for *their* sake—for the comfort and preferences of others, not for the sake of truth, love, or calling.

There's a difference between self-denial and self-erasure.

Jesus never invited you to become a hollow version of yourself. He invited you to become your truest self by laying down your ego, not your identity. Following him doesn't mean dissolving into what everyone else wants. It means becoming grounded enough in who you are in him that you can love freely, without the need to be liked in return.

Anchor Truth

Jesus doesn't ask you to disappear. He invites you to become who you truly are.

Prayer

Jesus, I want to follow you—not fear, not approval, not obligation. Help me reclaim the self you've shaped in me, and teach me how to serve without losing my soul.

Invitation

Reflect on a recent time you said yes when you wanted to say no. What motivated that decision? What might a Christ-centered response have looked like instead?

Staying Curious When You Want to Shut Down

Listen to advice and accept discipline,
and at the end you will be counted among the wise.

PROVERBS 19:20 (NIV)

Curiosity sounds lovely—until it doesn't. Until someone pushes back. Until your ego gets bruised. Until the mirror shows you something you didn't want to see. That's when curiosity gets real.

It's easy to be curious when the answers are flattering. But what about when curiosity means facing a blind spot? Or asking someone how they experience you—without interrupting to defend yourself? Or examining a habit that once soothed you but now stunts your growth?

That kind of curiosity is not soft. It's steel. It's called *non-defensive curiosity*—the ability to stay open and ask questions even when your emotional armor wants to clamp down. It's what emotionally healthy people do. They pause, they wonder, they notice. And they resist the urge to flee, fix, or fight.

In Scripture, we see examples of people who shut curiosity down, like Pharaoh hardening his heart. But we also see those who stay open. Think of Nathan confronting David. Nathan didn't accuse him; he told a story. And David, to his credit, stayed curious long enough to say, "I have sinned against the Lord." That moment of curiosity changed the trajectory of his life.

Here's the truth: Shutting down is easy. Curiosity is costly. It requires humility, emotional regulation, and a deep belief that growth is worth the discomfort. But it's also a pathway to wisdom, connection, and healing.

Every time you ask, "What's really going on here?" instead of reacting, you take a step toward wholeness. Every time you say, "Tell me more," instead of shutting someone down, you make space for grace.

Anchor Truth

Curiosity isn't weak. It's resilient. Staying open—especially when it's hard—is one of the most courageous choices you can make.

Prayer

God, help me resist the urge to defend or deflect. Keep my heart soft. Help me listen, ask, reflect, and grow.

Invitation

When was the last time you felt yourself get defensive? Revisit that moment. What question could you have asked instead of reacting? Write it down and consider trying it the next time.

When Perfectionism Wears a Halo

The old way ends in death; in the new way, the Holy Spirit gives life.

2 CORINTHIANS 3:6

Spiritual perfectionism is sneaky. It doesn't just demand excellence, it demands righteousness, flawlessly executed. It says, "Be more disciplined. Be more faithful. Be more holy. And if you fail, don't let anyone know."

It sounds like spiritual maturity, but it's actually spiritual pressure. And it often leads to hidden shame, burnout, and a distorted view of God.

Perfectionism, in this form, convinces you that God is mostly disappointed with you. That if you pray more, read more, try harder—then maybe you'll be good enough to be loved.

But Scripture tells a different story: The Spirit gives life; the law brings condemnation. God is not interested in your performance. He's after your heart. Jesus confronted spiritual perfectionism head-on. He saw it in the religious leaders, who were outwardly polished but inwardly hollow. They followed every rule but missed the deeper point—mercy, love, humility, grace. He didn't condemn their discipline. He condemned their pride. Their pressure. Their pretense.

And maybe, if you're honest, you've felt that pressure too. To be the "strong Christian." To always have the right answer. To appear spiritually "together," even when you're crumbling inside.

But Jesus says, "Come to me, all you who are weary . . . and I will give you rest." That includes people weary from trying to be spiritually perfect. You don't have to earn your way to grace. You already have it.

Holiness isn't flawlessness. It's closeness. And that means you can stop performing and start receiving.

You were never meant to be a flawless example. You were meant to be a loved child. So take a deep breath, drop the act, and rest in this truth: Grace meets you where striving ends.

Anchor Truth

Grace, not performance, is the path to transformation.

Prayer

God, help me see the difference between loving you and trying to impress you. Set me free from the burden of spiritual performance. Teach me to walk with you in truth, not pretense.

Invitation

Let go of one spiritual "should" today—the thing you do out of pressure, not joy. Replace it with a quiet moment of honesty with God. That's where real connection begins.

Held by a Steady God

He will not let you stumble;
the one who watches over you will not slumber.

PSALM 121:3

Anxiety makes you feel like everything depends on you. Hold it together. Keep it all afloat. Don't let anyone down.

But when the pressure builds and your grip weakens, fear creeps in: "What happens if I drop the ball? If I break down? If I can't hold it all up anymore?"

This is often rooted in what's called *hyper-responsibility*—a pattern where you feel personally accountable for outcomes beyond your control. It's common among those with anxiety and can be driven by a deep fear of failure or disappointing others.

That fear runs deep because we've been taught to stay strong, stay composed, stay in control. But Scripture paints a different picture. It doesn't tell us to hold it all together. It tells us we're already being held.

Psalm 121 says God never slumbers. He doesn't blink. He doesn't miss the moments when you feel like you're slipping. He doesn't get distracted or tired of your needs. While you're overwhelmed, he's attentive. While your strength wavers, his stays firm.

This kind of safety is what psychologists call *secure attachment*—knowing that someone steady is always there, no matter how chaotic life feels. And in faith, that someone is God.

You may feel like you're walking on the edge, but you're not alone on that ledge. There's a hand beneath you, steady and sure.

God doesn't just lift you when you fall. He keeps you. He carries you. He holds you. So take a deep breath.

Let your nervous system exhale the pressure of being the one who holds it all. You are not the one holding the world together. You are being held by the one who already does.

Anchor Truth

God's steadiness is not dependent on yours. When your grip loosens, his never does.

Prayer

God, I'm tired of trying to hold everything up. My strength feels small, and I'm afraid of what will happen if I let go. Remind me that you are not asking me to carry more than I can bear. You are already holding me. Teach me to rest in your steadiness, even when mine runs out.

Invitation

Find something small to hold in your hand today—a stone, a coin, a smooth piece of wood. Let it remind you that you are also being held. Not by your own effort, but by grace that never slips.

The Risk of Being Real

Confess your sins to each other and pray for each other so that you may be healed.

JAMES 5:16

Vulnerability sounds like soft stuff: Tears. Talk. Touchy-feely confessions.

But in reality? Vulnerability is courage in its rawest form. It's choosing to let someone see your fear. Your failure. Your longing. It's risking rejection to make room for real connection. And for many of us, that risk feels impossible.

Because somewhere along the line, we learned that being seen might lead to being shamed. So we built walls. We got good at keeping it surface-level. We laughed off the hard stuff. We became masters of disguise.

But Scripture doesn't let us stay hidden. James writes that confession—honest, unpolished, mutual confession—is what *heals* us. Not just spiritually, but emotionally. Because what we hide festers.

What we reveal has a chance to be met with love—and, slowly, healed. It's called *attachment repair* when someone meets your vulnerability with empathy instead of judgment.

It rewires something deep inside you. It teaches your nervous system that you're not alone. That you can be seen and still safe. That you don't have to perform to be loved.

It doesn't always go perfectly. Sometimes people won't know how to hold your truth. Sometimes it will sting. But without vulnerability, there's no bridge. No intimacy. No healing. No real love.

The cross itself is the ultimate act of vulnerability—Jesus exposed, emptied, misunderstood, and yet still choosing love. When you show up with your real story, your real struggle, your real need—you echo that courage. And you invite others to do the same.

Anchor Truth

Healing begins at the place where honesty meets grace.

Prayer

God, I want to be brave enough to live unhidden. Give me wisdom to know when to open up and the courage to risk being fully seen.

Invitation

Share one honest thing today with someone you trust. Just one. Start small. But start. Vulnerability is a muscle, and every use makes it stronger.

Not Today, Shame

So now there is no condemnation for those who belong to Christ Jesus.

ROMANS 8:1

Shame will shut you down faster than fear. Fear says, "This might not work." Shame says, "You don't work."

And when shame wins, agency goes out the window. You stop showing up. You shrink. You stall. You tell yourself things like, "I should've figured this out by now." "Other people don't struggle with this." "If I mess this up again, what's the point of trying?" Sound familiar?

This is what shame does. It convinces you that you don't have a right to move forward until you're "better." It's not just an emotion, it's a barrier. One that blocks growth, healing, and spiritual momentum—not because God has turned away from you, but because shame has you turning away from yourself.

Romans 8:1 is a mic-drop verse. It cuts through shame's noise with a clear and final word: *No condemnation.* Not less. Not a little. *None.*

If you belong to Christ, shame doesn't get the last say. Full stop.

From a clinical standpoint, researchers have shown that shame thrives in secrecy and silence. But it loses power when it's met with empathy and truth. That's where agency comes back online—not through perfection, but through *permission.* Permission to be in process. Permission to try again. Permission to act without apologizing for existing.

So today, when shame starts whispering old scripts in your ear—"You're too much" or "You're not enough" or "You'll never get it right"—pause and push back. Not with ego, but with truth.

"Not today, shame. I still get to choose."

Anchor Truth

Shame is loud, but it doesn't get to drive. Grace does.

Prayer

God, I don't want shame calling the shots in my life anymore. When I freeze or spiral, remind me that I'm not condemned. Give me the courage to act—not because I'm perfect, but because I'm yours.

Invitation

Write down one choice shame has been talking you out of. Then take a small step in that direction. Let grace walk with you, not guilt.

The Freedom of Being Unliked

If the world hates you, remember that it hated me first.

JOHN 15:18

Let's get brutally honest: Part of you wants to be liked by everyone, even people you don't particularly like. You want them to think well of you. Approve. Admire. Maybe even envy. And when they don't? It stings.

But here's a hard truth: Living for approval is a life sentence. No matter how carefully you curate your words, your tone, your image—someone will still misunderstand. Misjudge. Dislike. Disagree. What then?

Jesus didn't chase universal approval. In fact, the closer he walked in obedience to God's mission, the more controversial he became. Some adored him. Others plotted his death.

He loved them all, but he wasn't controlled by their opinions. This is where freedom lives.

Psychologists call this *differentiation*—the ability to stay grounded in your values and identity even when others disapprove. It's a key marker of emotional maturity. Low differentiation means you crumble under criticism or contort yourself for affirmation. High differentiation means you can love people without letting their approval define you.

Not everyone will like you. Even if you're kind. Even if you're generous. Even if you do everything "right."

People bring their own baggage into the way they see you—and sometimes their disapproval has nothing to do with you at all.

So what if you stopped living on the tightrope of public opinion? What if you stopped twisting yourself into something palatable and just told the truth? What if you trusted that the people who really matter—the ones who love you in truth—can only find you when you stop pretending?

There's peace in knowing that being unliked isn't fatal. Sometimes it's even holy.

Anchor Truth

You don't need to be liked by everyone to be deeply loved by the one who matters most.

Prayer

God, I confess I've made approval an idol. I've traded authenticity for applause. Teach me to walk in your love even when others reject me. Let my worth be rooted in your truth.

Invitation

The next time you feel disliked, don't panic or placate. Just notice. Then remind yourself, "I wasn't made to be everyone's favorite. I was made to be free."

Known and Still Loved

O LORD, you have examined my heart
and know everything about me.

PSALM 139:1

One of the deepest longings of the human soul is to be fully known and still loved. Not tolerated. Not pitied. Not accepted under certain conditions. But truly seen and embraced without needing to curate, filter, or perform.

That kind of connection is rare. Many of us have learned to present only the parts of ourselves that feel safe to show. We hide the rest—fears, flaws, compulsions, regrets—believing they disqualify us from belonging.

But the irony is that the very thing we think will bring us connection—performing or pretending—is the thing that keeps us lonely. As Brené Brown puts it, "Authenticity is the daily practice of letting go of who we think we're supposed to be and embracing who we are." Vulnerability—not perfection—is the gateway to true connection.

Psychologists have long observed that meaningful connection requires both *exposure* and *acceptance*. Attachment research shows that our emotional well-being is directly tied to how safe we feel in being ourselves with others. When someone sees the mess and stays—that's where healing happens. That's where shame loses its grip.

David's prayer in Psalm 139 reminds us that God knows *everything* about us—every secret, fear, and failure—and still chooses to stay. Not reluctantly. Not out of duty. But with love. If that's true, you don't have to hide anymore.

Still, it's terrifying to let others in. It takes discernment, courage, and time.

But when you dare to be seen, you create space for intimacy—the real kind, not the social media version. And every time you experience that safe, honest connection with another person, you taste something holy.

Anchor Truth

You don't have to hide to be loved. Real connection begins with honesty.

Prayer

God, it's scary to be seen. Help me trust that I am safe in your love, and give me courage to let others see the real me too.

Invitation

Ask yourself, "What part of me have I been hiding to keep people close? What would it look like to let someone safe see more of the real me today?"

The Sacred Pause Before a Meal

Then Jesus took the loaves, gave thanks to God, and distributed them to the people.

JOHN 6:11

It's easy to blow past it. The food is hot. The conversation is flowing. The day has been long. But there's something sacred about that moment when you stop, bow your head, and whisper thanks.

Jesus did it. Before multiplying bread and fish for thousands. Before breaking bread in the upper room. Even walking toward the cross, he took the cup, gave thanks, and passed it.

Gratitude was his rhythm. His reflex. Not just a ritual—but a declaration. *This life is a gift. This food is a provision. This moment is holy.* And for us, it's a reset. A sacred pause. A way to push back against hurry and entitlement, and to ground ourselves—again and again—in the truth that we're being cared for, moment by moment.

Sure, it can become mechanical. Just words. Habit. But isn't that kind of the point?

When life spins fast and hard, we need rituals that remind us of what's true. We need anchors. We need built-in breathers—like giving thanks before a meal—to reframe what we're experiencing. To whisper to ourselves and to God, "I didn't earn this. I didn't make this grow. I'm not the source. But I'm grateful."

Even the smallest meal becomes a practice in presence. A reminder that God provides in all kinds of ways—not just what's on the plate, but who's at the table and how far we've come.

Every mealtime prayer is a chance to push back against forgetfulness. A built-in rhythm that says, "God, I see your hand—even here."

Anchor Truth

Gratitude before a meal isn't just about the food. It's about cultivating a posture of humility and awareness, one bite at a time.

Prayer

Jesus, thank you for showing me how to live with a grateful heart, even in the ordinary. Help me not to rush past these moments. Teach me to pause and remember that every good thing—big or small—has your fingerprints on it.

Invitation

Slow down before your next meal. Put your fork down. Take a breath. Offer real thanks—not just for the food, but for the unseen ways God is sustaining you right now.

When Loneliness Becomes a Lie

Elijah replied, "I have zealously served the LORD God Almighty. But the people of Israel have broken their covenant with you, torn down your altars, and killed every one of your prophets. I am the only one left, and now they are trying to kill me, too."

1 KINGS 19:10

Loneliness isn't always honest. It might show up as that hollow ache in your chest, or the quiet that feels louder than any noise.

And sometimes loneliness lies. It tells you that no one sees you. That you don't matter. That your absence wouldn't affect a single soul. And the longer you sit with that lie, the more convincing it starts to sound.

But listen: Loneliness can't be trusted to tell you the truth about your worth. This is where the mental health side of things gets real. Psychologists call it *cognitive distortion*—when your brain takes a difficult emotion and spins a story around it that isn't accurate. The emotion is valid. The story is not.

Scripture is full of people who wrestled with that exact dynamic. Take Elijah. After a stunning spiritual victory on Mount Carmel, he flees into the wilderness and says, "I am the only one left." But he wasn't. He just felt like it.

God didn't scold him. God met him with food, rest, and truth. He corrected Elijah gently—not just spiritually, but emotionally and physically. That's what real love does.

Your loneliness may be real, but the conclusion it draws is not. You are not forgotten. Not invisible. Not alone.

You are loved by a God who sees what others overlook—and who refuses to let the voice of loneliness have the final word.

Anchor Truth

Loneliness is a feeling, not a fact. God sees you, knows you, and walks with you—even when no one else seems to.

Prayer

God, when loneliness tries to tell me who I am, remind me of who you are. Help me quiet the lies and hear your truth. Thank you for never leaving, even when I feel alone.

Invitation

Pay attention to the story your loneliness is telling you today. Challenge it. Then reach out—to a friend, to a support group, to God in prayer. You don't have to sit in the silence alone.

The Quiet Saboteur

A peaceful heart leads to a healthy body;
jealousy is like cancer in the bones.

PROVERBS 14:30

Jealousy rarely shows up waving red flags. It whispers. It hides. It pretends to be ambition or discernment or concern. But underneath it all, it's just pain masked as comparison.

You see someone else's win and feel your own worth shrink a little. Their vacation, their relationship, their recognition, their "effortless" joy—it all stings just enough to make you feel behind or less than. And before you know it, your happiness is bleeding out slowly through the wound of comparison.

Psychologists have found that nothing corrodes well-being quite like jealousy. It rewires your focus from gratitude to scarcity. It tells you there's not enough to go around. It distorts someone else's gain as your personal loss.

But Scripture cuts through the noise: "Jealousy is like cancer in the bones." It eats away quietly. Relentlessly. Even the happiest moments get tainted when jealousy is at the wheel. The smile feels forced. The celebration feels fake. The soul feels restless.

So what's the antidote? It's not denial. It's not shame. It's honesty. Name what you're feeling. Tell God the truth.

Then choose celebration on purpose, especially when it's hard. Gratitude and rejoicing aren't just spiritual practices, they're emotional reprogramming. They break the jealous cycle and open your heart to joy again. Because someone else's joy doesn't steal yours. And their success doesn't mean your story is stuck.

God's goodness isn't pie. You're not getting a smaller slice because someone else already got theirs. Let that settle in. You're not in a competition for joy. You're not behind. You're not forgotten.

God's goodness isn't scarce. There is still a beautiful, unfolding story for you.

Anchor Truth

Jealousy quietly drains happiness, but gratitude restores it. You can rejoice with others without losing anything yourself.

Prayer

God, I confess that I sometimes compare and come up short. Help me to be honest about the jealousy that sneaks in. Rewire my heart toward celebration. Fill me with peace as I trust that your goodness has room for me, too.

Invitation

When jealousy hits, flip the script. Say something kind about the person you're tempted to compare yourself to. It's not fake. It's freeing.

Why Do They Get to Be So Free?

For the Lord is the Spirit, and wherever the Spirit of the Lord is, there is freedom.

2 CORINTHIANS 3:17

Some jealousy doesn't come from what people have. It comes from how light they seem. They laugh easily. They dance at weddings. They don't overthink every text or rehearse every conversation in their head before hitting send. And something in you tightens.

Not because you don't want them to be happy—but because it doesn't seem fair.

You're working hard to hold it all together, managing old wounds, childhood trauma, maybe a diagnosis or a divorce. You're exhausted from the emotional labor of just being okay. And those other people? They float.

This is the kind of jealousy we don't talk about much. It's not envy of success, but envy of freedom. You're not bitter. You're tired. And their joy feels like a mirror, showing you what you wish you could feel without effort.

Sometimes the ache behind jealousy is a question: *Why does it seem so easy for them to live the life I'm still trying to recover from?* But 2 Corinthians 3:17 doesn't say freedom comes from ease. It comes from presence.

Where the Spirit of the Lord is, there is freedom. And that means freedom isn't just for the emotionally unscarred. It's not reserved for the lucky or the unburdened.

Freedom is for you. Right here. In the mess, the overthinking, the overfunctioning. In therapy, this realization is often the turning point—when we stop resenting ease in others and start reclaiming emotional liberation for ourselves.

The question isn't, *Why do they get to feel that way?* The better question is, *How might I move toward a little more freedom of my own?* Even if it's one breath at a time.

Anchor Truth

Freedom isn't for the flawless. It's for the willing.

Prayer

God, when I feel jealous of someone's ease, meet me there. Remind me that freedom isn't about circumstances. It's about you, present with me, even here.

Invitation

Notice someone today who seems emotionally free. Instead of comparison, let it stir curiosity. Ask, "Where might I need more lightness in my life? And what's one small way I can invite it in?"

Signs Your Boundaries Might Be Too Loose (or Too Rigid)

Let your "Yes" be "Yes," and your "No," "No."

MATTHEW 5:37 (NKJV)

You say yes to things you dread. You stay quiet when you should speak up. You give more than you have—and feel resentful afterward. Or maybe you never let anyone in. You say no before they even ask. You keep your guard up and your heart sealed.

When it comes to boundaries, both ends of the spectrum—too loose or too rigid—can sabotage your well-being and relationships.

Loose boundaries look like

- Saying yes out of guilt or fear
- Feeling responsible for others' emotions
- Having trouble identifying your own needs
- Letting others override your limits without consequence

Rigid boundaries look like

- Keeping people at arm's length
- Assuming you can't count on others
- Refusing help or vulnerability
- Cutting people off at the first sign of discomfort

In both cases, it's about protection. But one is self-sacrificing, the other self-isolating. Healthy boundaries aren't about control; they're about clarity. And they always require courage. Especially if you've been conditioned to avoid conflict or carry the weight of someone else's expectations.

Jesus didn't live with loose or rigid boundaries. He was openhearted but not open-doored to everything and everyone. He showed up with empathy and truth. He wasn't reactive—he was rooted.

Clinical wisdom confirms that healthy boundaries improve self-esteem, reduce stress, and foster healthier relationships. But they take practice. At first, saying no can feel unnatural. Voicing your needs might feel awkward. But discomfort isn't the enemy—*disconnection is.*

Anchor Truth

When your boundaries are rooted in love and clarity, they don't push people away. They show them where you stand so connection can grow.

Prayer

God, help me see where my boundaries are off-kilter—too soft in some places, too hard in others. Give me wisdom to adjust them with grace and courage to follow through. Teach me to live with truth and love.

Invitation

Reflect on one relationship in your life that feels draining or distant. What boundary might be too loose or too rigid? Take one small step toward adjusting it this week.

What's Really Going On Here?

Examine yourselves to see if your faith is genuine. Test yourselves.

2 CORINTHIANS 13:5

You snap at your partner. You withdraw from your friends. You overreact to something small. And later, when the dust settles, you wonder, "What was that really about?"

Most of us don't pause long enough to ask that question. We just move on. But emotional autopilot is a dangerous place to live. It keeps us reactive, not reflective. Defensive, not discerning.

Curiosity slows you down. It invites you to look under the hood of your emotions, to ask what's really going on. What fear, story, or wound is shaping this moment? The key is simple: Naming what you feel and why.

Research shows that just identifying your emotions reduces their intensity. The amygdala—the brain's fear center—calms down. The prefrontal cortex—the rational part of your brain—comes back online. It's not magic. It's self-awareness. And it starts with curiosity.

Instead of beating yourself up for the outburst, try a different script: "Why did that bother me so much?" "What did that interaction remind me of?" "Is there something I'm avoiding or afraid to feel?"

Even Jesus asked questions to reveal deeper truth: "Why are you so afraid?" "What do you want me to do for you?" "Do you want to get well?" He didn't rush to fix; he paused to explore.

And Paul's words to the Corinthian church echo that same rhythm: *Examine yourself. Test your faith.* He knew that spiritual growth is stunted when we never stop to ask hard questions.

So don't just push past your emotions. Get curious about them. Let your reactions be road signs that point to something deeper. The more honest you are with yourself, the more room you give the Spirit to move.

Anchor Truth

When you get curious instead of reactive, your emotions become signals, not enemies.

Prayer

God, help me pause when I'm triggered. Give me the courage to ask hard questions and the grace to hear the answers.

Invitation

Today, when you feel yourself overreacting—or shutting down—stop and ask, "What's this really about?" Don't rush past it. Let curiosity lead you into greater clarity and peace.

Counting Your Blessings

Let all that I am praise the LORD;
may I never forget the good things he does for me.

PSALM 103:2

We've heard the phrase so often it feels like a cliché: Count your blessings. But what if that worn-out phrase is one of the most scientifically and spiritually sound habits we could ever adopt?

Research has consistently shown that *gratitude journaling*—deliberately counting blessings and naming what you're grateful for—can rewire your brain for happiness. It's not just fluff. Studies show it boosts mood, reduces depression, and increases resilience.

It's been proven: People who write down what they were thankful for each week feel more optimistic and better about their lives overall. The psalmist beat these social scientists to it by a few thousand years: "May I never forget the good things he does for me."

That's what counting blessings really is. Remembering. Rehearsing. Choosing to see what's easy to overlook when you're busy or beaten down. Because when life is hard, we forget. We zero in on the problem and filter everything else through it. But blessing-counting flips the lens. It says, "Yes, this hurts. Yes, I'm tired. But also—God has been good to me."

David, who wrote this psalm, knew pain. Betrayal, loss, regret—you name it, he experienced it. But he trained his soul to *bless the Lord* and remember. That's spiritual resilience.

Try it: Right now, count three things that are true today. Name them out loud. Write them down. They might be obvious. Or subtle. Or deeply personal. But they're there. And when you name them, your spirit starts to shift.

Anchor Truth

Counting your blessings isn't denial. It's defiance. It says, "I see the hard, but I won't be blinded by it."

Prayer

God, help me remember the good when life feels heavy. Open my eyes to the quiet graces tucked into ordinary days. Teach my heart to rehearse your faithfulness even when my circumstances feel like anything but.

Invitation

Don't wait until life feels easy to start counting blessings. Start today. Write down three. Speak them out loud. Let gratitude slowly bend your heart back toward joy.

I'm Not a Perfectionist . . . Am I?

People judge by outward appearance,
but the LORD looks at the heart.

1 SAMUEL 16:7

You may not color-code your closet or alphabetize your spice rack. You might even laugh off mistakes, miss deadlines, or leave dishes in the sink—and for that reason, you've probably thought, *I'm not a perfectionist.*

But perfectionism isn't just about performance. It's about pressure. And it shows up in your inner dialogue. In the way you second-guess what you said. In the way you delay starting something important because you're scared it won't be "right." In how hard it is to rest without guilt. In the silent, sinking feeling that you're not enough. That's perfectionism too—just without the glossy exterior.

Sometimes it's loud and obvious. Other times it's subtle. Quiet. Internalized. But either way, perfectionism keeps you stuck and steals your peace.

Scripture reminds us that people look at appearances, but God looks deeper—at the heart. He sees not just what you do, but why you do it.

God sees the pressure you carry, even if no one else does. And he doesn't meet that pressure with more demands. He meets it with grace.

You don't have to call yourself a perfectionist to start healing from it. You just have to notice where fear is driving your choices and invite God into those places. You may not be striving for perfect results, but are you still chasing a perfect version of yourself?

You don't need that "perfect" person. You need Jesus. You don't have to prove anything to belong.

Let grace meet you in the real, messy middle and remind you: You're already enough.

Anchor Truth

Perfectionism doesn't always look like perfection. But it always feels like pressure, and God invites you to lay it down.

Prayer

God, I didn't think I struggled with perfectionism, but now I see the pressure I've been living under. Help me recognize the quiet ways I've been trying to prove myself. Teach me to live from your grace, not my standards.

Invitation

Pay attention today to the quiet pressure beneath your decisions. When you notice it, pause and ask, "Why am I doing this—out of love or out of fear?" Let grace reshape your "why."

Sorrow Upon Sorrow

But God had mercy on him, and not on him only but also on me, to spare me sorrow upon sorrow.

PHILIPPIANS 2:27 (NIV)

Paul was a spiritual giant, yes. But he was also deeply human. In Philippians 2, he's writing about Epaphroditus, a friend and fellow worker who nearly died.

Paul doesn't sugarcoat the situation. He doesn't dismiss it with a platitude or theological spin. He says that if Epaphroditus had died, it would have meant "sorrow upon sorrow." That phrase—that gut-deep honesty—matters.

Because many of us were taught, whether directly or indirectly, that real faith means pushing past sorrow, not admitting it. But Paul—who wrote much of the New Testament, who endured persecution, imprisonment, beatings, and betrayal—names his pain. And he doesn't flinch.

Grief doesn't disqualify your faith. It reveals your capacity to love deeply. And layered sorrow doesn't mean you're failing. It means you're human, just like Paul.

We live in a world where losses pile up. Some sharp and sudden, others slow and chronic. And some days, it really is sorrow upon sorrow. Paul gets that. And more importantly, God gets that.

What's striking is that Paul didn't spiritualize the moment. He didn't say, "It's fine, God is in control," and leave it at that.

He acknowledged that mercy sometimes looks like relief from one more heartbreak.

Sometimes the most spiritual thing you can do is admit you're barely holding it together—and trust that even then, God is holding you.

Anchor Truth

Grief doesn't mean you've lost your faith. It's often where faith goes to grow.

Prayer

God, I admit it—some days I feel like I'm drowning in layer after layer of sorrow. Help me not to hide it, not to fake a smile, but to bring my honest grief to you. Meet me there with mercy like you did for Paul.

Invitation

What would it look like to name your layered sorrow today instead of minimizing it? Try journaling it or simply whispering it to God. You don't have to hold it all alone.

The Problem You Can't See

Who can discern their own errors?
Forgive my hidden faults.

PSALM 19:12 (NIV)

Have you ever been driving with the sun in your eyes and almost missed a car in the next lane? That's the thing about blind spots. They're not about stupidity. They're about your line of sight. Perspectives.

What you can't see can still hurt you—or someone else. And it's not just a driving problem; it's a human problem.

We all carry behaviors, assumptions, or emotional habits we've learned to live with so long, we don't even notice them anymore. Everyone else might, but to us? It's just how we are.

Sometimes it's defensiveness that flares up in every conflict. Or the need to always be right. Or a quiet resentment we've mistaken for strength.

The psalmist nailed it when he asked, "Who can discern their own errors?" It's a rhetorical question. We *can't*—not fully. That's why he prayed, "Forgive my hidden faults."

Even the greats—David, Martha, Peter—had blind spots. What set them apart wasn't perfection. It was the willingness to be confronted by truth and changed by grace.

Blind spots don't mean you're broken. They just mean you're unfinished.

And the Spirit's job? To help you *see*. Not to shame, but to shape. Not to condemn, but to free.

Anchor Truth

Blind spots may be hidden from you, but they are not hidden from God. He sees you fully and still invites you to grow more whole in him.

Prayer

Lord, open my eyes to what I can't yet see. Give me ears to hear hard truth and the courage to receive it with grace. Shape me into someone who sees clearly, starting with myself.

Invitation

Invite God and someone you trust to speak into one area of your life where you've stopped questioning. What truth might be waiting for you in that blind spot?

The Boundary You Think You Set

The prudent understand where they are going,
but fools deceive themselves.

PROVERBS 14:8

You told yourself you were setting a boundary. No more late-night phone calls. No more stepping back into the emotional cross fire between your parents. No more "just checking in" with someone who keeps hurting you.

But then you answered the text. You returned the call. You let one parent vent about the other. You reengaged because you didn't want to be "cold" or "unkind" or "dramatic."

And it felt noble at first. But now you're knee-deep in the very dynamic you swore you were stepping out of.

The triangle reformed. The confusion crept back in. The boundary you thought you set was more of a line in the sand that the tide rolled right over.

This is what happens when we confuse *intentions* with *integrity*. When we draw boundaries with words but not with actions. When we still need others to think of us as "good" or "available" or "peacekeeping," even if it costs us our clarity.

Proverbs reminds us that the wise understand where they are going, but fools deceive themselves. And that deception can be subtle: *I'm just being kind. I'm just helping out. I'm still holding the boundary . . . kind of.*

But emotional health doesn't grow in "kind of." It grows in clarity. In consistency. In the hard, holy work of sticking to what's necessary even when it's misunderstood.

So if you're tangled up again in what you thought you were out of, you're not weak. You're human. But it's time to pause, reset, and recommit to the boundary you actually meant to keep.

Anchor Truth

A half-kept boundary is a whole new mess. Clarity is kindness—to yourself and to others.

Prayer

God, give me the courage to follow through on the boundaries I set. Help me resist the urge to manage everyone's emotions. Teach me to trust that you honor truth over appearances, and give me wisdom when the lines blur.

Invitation

Is there a boundary you've quietly stepped back from? One that has led to new confusion or emotional drain? Reevaluate not just your words, but also your actions. Reset the boundary with kindness and firmness. And this time, keep it.

Relational Repair After Emotional Rupture

Make allowance for each other's faults, and forgive anyone who offends you. Remember, the Lord forgave you, so you must forgive others.

COLOSSIANS 3:13

It happens in every relationship worth keeping: a rupture. Someone says the wrong thing. You misread a moment. Trust slips. Words sting. Silence grows.

Maybe it's subtle—a comment you can't stop replaying. Or maybe it's a blowup that leaves scorched emotional ground between you.

Emotional safety isn't about avoiding conflict. It's about knowing there's a path back to connection after conflict. In fact, the strongest relationships aren't the ones without friction—they're the ones where repair is possible.

Research has shown that the way two people handle a rupture is more predictive of relationship success than how much they argue. That's good news for anyone who's messed up (read: everyone).

But repair takes courage. It means initiating the awkward, vulnerable conversations. It means naming what hurt, without blaming. It means asking for forgiveness, not just hoping things blow over.

In Scripture, we see relational repair in action when Paul and John Mark reunite. After a sharp disagreement in Acts 15, Paul chose not to travel with John Mark again. But later, in 2 Timothy 4:11, Paul writes, "Bring Mark with you when you come, for he will be helpful to me in my ministry." Somewhere in the background, reconciliation happened. Forgiveness. Trust rebuilt. A rupture mended.

Relational repair is hard. It won't always lead to restoration. And it isn't always safe or wise to reenter every broken relationship. But when both people are willing, healing is holy ground.

Anchor Truth

Repairing a rupture doesn't mean pretending it didn't happen. It means choosing truth and grace over silence and shame. Every act of honest repair creates a deeper kind of emotional safety.

Prayer

God, give me the humility to own my part and the courage to seek repair. Where I've been hurt, help me speak honestly and forgive freely. And where repair isn't possible, help me heal with your peace.

Invitation

Is there a relationship in your life with a lingering rupture? Ask God what one small step of repair could look like—whether it's a conversation, a confession, or simply letting go of resentment.

When the Light Feels Far Away

The light shines in the darkness,
and the darkness can never extinguish it.

JOHN 1:5

Depression doesn't always look like tears. Sometimes it's numbness. Other times it's bone-deep exhaustion. It's losing interest in things you once loved. It's wanting to hide when there's nothing obviously wrong. It's praying but feeling like the heavens are made of concrete.

Depression is sometimes called the "common cold" of emotional health. It's that widespread. More than 280 million people live with depression globally. And that's not just a statistic. That's people you know. That's possibly *you.*

Depression exists on a continuum. Some people experience a passing fog; others are pulled into the undertow for weeks or months at a time. For some, it comes with a trigger—grief, loss, trauma. For others, it's more biochemical. The cause is not always easy to pin down. But the depression is always real. And it's not a failure of faith.

The Bible is full of people who knew the darkness well: David, who cried out from the pit, "How long, O Lord? Will you forget me forever?" (Psalm 13:1, ESV). Elijah, who wanted to die under a tree after great success (1 Kings 19). Job, who cursed the day he was born (Job 3:1). Jeremiah, the "weeping prophet," who said he wished he'd never been born (Jeremiah 20:14-18).

Even in church history, giants of faith battled the shadows—Martin Luther, Charles Spurgeon, Mother Teresa, and C. S. Lewis all confessed seasons of profound emotional darkness.

This isn't about wallowing. It's about remembering: Even when it feels like the light is far away, it's still shining. Jesus stepped into our darkness to remind us we're not stuck there alone.

You may be walking through a shadowed valley, but shadows exist only where there is light. And that light? It's not gone. It may feel faint, but it's still shining on you. Even now.

You're not alone in the dark. The Light is with you, and it's not going out.

Anchor Truth

Darkness doesn't mean God has left you. The light still shines, even when it feels out of reach.

Prayer

God, I don't feel okay. But I'm still reaching for you. Remind me that I'm not alone. That the light is still there, even in this shadow.

Invitation

Take a moment today to write down what your depression feels like, not just what it looks like to others. Bring your unfiltered truth to God. He can handle it.

You Can't Heal What You Won't Name

Search me, O God, and know my heart; test me and know my anxious thoughts. Point out anything in me that offends you, and lead me along the path of everlasting life.

PSALM 139:23-24

Most people are carrying things they've never named. Old pain. Hidden fears. Quiet patterns that sabotage peace. They don't ignore them out of denial. They ignore them out of survival. Because sometimes it's easier to stay busy than to slow down and listen to what's really going on inside.

But here's the truth: You can't heal what you won't face. And you can't face what you won't name.

Self-awareness isn't about navel-gazing. It's about waking up to what's true—internally and emotionally—so you can actually grow with God, not just perform for him.

David's prayer in Psalm 139 is bold: "Search me. Test me. Show me what I can't see on my own." He's not asking for comfort. He's asking for clarity. That's spiritual courage. Because deep down, most of us already know there are things we're avoiding. And self-awareness begins when we stop running and start paying attention.

In therapy, this practice is sometimes called *emotional granularity*—the ability to accurately label what you're feeling instead of just calling it "bad" or "fine." People who develop this skill are more resilient, less reactive, and more in control of their decisions. Why? Because they aren't being hijacked by unnamed emotions. They're responding with intention.

God already knows your inner life. Self-awareness isn't about informing him. It's about inviting him to help you see yourself clearly so you can live with greater freedom, peace, and integrity.

Anchor Truth

Honesty is the first step toward healing.

Prayer

God, show me what I've been afraid to see. Give me the courage to name what's really going on inside me—not to shame myself, but to grow in truth and freedom. Lead me with love.

Invitation

Take five minutes today and ask, "What am I really feeling right now?" Name it. Not "fine," not "busy." Something deeper. That's where growth begins.

When Perfectionism Wears You Out

It is useless for you to work so hard
from early morning until late at night,
anxiously working for food to eat;
for God gives rest to his loved ones.

PSALM 127:2

You might not even realize how tired you are. Not physically, but emotionally. That deep soul-weariness that doesn't go away after a nap or a weekend off. Perfectionism creates a unique kind of exhaustion. It keeps your inner engine running on overdrive.

You're not just doing your best; you're trying to be the best. You're not just being faithful; you're trying to be flawless. And somewhere in the chase, you start to disappear. You smile when you're sad. You say yes when you're drowning. You keep going because stopping feels like failure. And the irony is that the harder you try to hold everything together, the more fragile you become.

God never asked this of you. Psalm 127:2 tells us plainly, "It is useless for you to work so hard . . . anxiously working . . . for God gives rest to his loved ones." Rest isn't a reward for doing everything right—it's a gift. A sign that you're not the source of your own worth.

Emotional exhaustion is often your soul's way of waving a white flag. It's not just fatigue. It's a call to come home. To let go. To remember that being deeply loved has nothing to do with being endlessly productive.

Rest is not weakness. It's resistance against a world (and a mindset) that tells you you're only as good as what you get done.

You weren't created to live on the edge of burnout. You don't have to earn rest. You just have to receive it—and trust that the world keeps spinning even when you stop striving.

Anchor Truth

You are not a machine. Rest is part of your design.

Prayer

God, I'm worn out. I've carried so much for so long. Help me release the need to prove, impress, or overachieve. Lead me into your rest—not just for my body, but for my heart.

Invitation

Give yourself permission to pause today. Take one thing off your list. Say no without guilt. Let your rest be an act of trust.

When Faith Is Blamed for Your Feelings

The LORD is close to the brokenhearted;
he rescues those whose spirits are crushed.

PSALM 34:18

Maybe you've heard it before—maybe from someone in your Bible study, maybe from a sermon, maybe from your own inner critic. "If you had more faith, you wouldn't feel this way." "You just need to pray harder." "This is probably a spiritual attack."

It sounds spiritual. It sounds like wisdom. But for someone already in the pit, those words don't feel like hope. They feel like blame wrapped in Bible-speak.

You already feel low. Already tired. Already wondering if something's wrong with you. And now, on top of the ache, you're told it's your fault for not believing enough.

Let's be clear: Depression is not a failure of faith. There's no question that we live in a spiritual world and that darkness is real. But not every form of suffering is a sign of spiritual warfare. And labeling your depression as a "spiritual attack" can sometimes bypass the real human pain that needs attention.

Too often, Christians see depression as a failure—of faith, of obedience, of spiritual strength. But that's not what Scripture shows. David didn't lack faith when he wept through the night and begged for relief. Elijah wasn't faithless when he curled under a tree and asked God to take his life. Even Paul spoke of despairing "of life itself" (2 Corinthians 1:8, NIV). And Jeremiah? He grieved so deeply he cursed the day he was born.

These weren't spiritually immature people. These were giants of the faith. And God never scolded them for feeling what they felt.

He met them in it. He tended to them. And he still does.

Depression isn't always a spiritual attack. But shame about depression? That just might be.

Anchor Truth

God isn't disappointed by your sadness. You don't have to pretend. He draws near to your crushed spirit. He's already with you in the dark.

Prayer

God, heal the damage left by misguided words. If I've been told that my pain is a spiritual failure, replace that lie with your truth. Meet me in the places that I've been afraid to admit hurt.

Invitation

Have you ever been told that depression is a spiritual attack or failure? How did that shape your response to your pain? Sit with that honestly. Then read Psalm 34:18 aloud and let it interrupt the shame.

The Meaning in the Struggle

Though he brings grief, he also shows compassion because of the greatness of his unfailing love. For he does not enjoy hurting people or causing them sorrow.

LAMENTATIONS 3:32-33

When suffering drags on—especially the kind that sits in your mind and messes with your emotions—it's easy to feel like it's all for nothing. You're not "getting better." You're not "snapping out of it." You're exhausted from the weight of trying to keep it together. And beneath it all is that aching question: *Why?*

Suffering doesn't always come with a clean explanation. But it can come with meaning.

Paul wrote that "suffering produces perseverance; perseverance, character; and character, hope" (Romans 5:3-4, NIV). But that doesn't mean suffering is automatically good. It just means it's not wasted.

Mental health struggles can feel like the loneliest, most misunderstood kind of pain. But when you let God meet you there, your story begins to reshape. It doesn't happen overnight. But over time, you become a person who knows how to sit with pain—your own and others'. You grow softer, wiser, deeper. And that's not a detour from your purpose. It's part of it.

Psychologists talk about *post-traumatic growth*—the idea that people can become stronger, more grateful, more compassionate because of what they've endured. It changes them in ways comfort never could. That doesn't make the pain okay. But it does mean that it doesn't get the last word.

When mental anguish feels like it's erasing your purpose, remember: This season might be writing a deeper one.

So, no, your pain isn't pointless. It's planting something. Something strong. Something sacred.

You may not have chosen this road, but it's shaping you into someone who can walk with wisdom, lead with empathy, and love with depth. Don't wait until you feel better to believe it's working. Meaning is being made, even here. Even now.

Anchor Thought

God never wastes pain. What feels like breaking may be the beginning of becoming.

Prayer

God, I don't want this pain. But I want you to meet me in it. Use what feels unbearable to shape in me what's unshakable. Help me see that even this can be part of something meaningful. I trust you to redeem what I can't understand.

Invitation

Think of one way your pain has quietly shaped your perspective, your empathy, or your character. Write it down as a reminder: This isn't pointless. This is forming something in me.

When the Outside Matches the Inside

People judge by outward appearance,
but the LORD looks at the heart.

1 SAMUEL 16:7

Congruence is when your inner world and outer life are in sync, when your behavior reflects your true beliefs, values, and emotions. For many, that alignment feels foreign because they've spent years perfecting the opposite.

Congruence is a foundational condition for psychological and spiritual health. When we live out of sync with who we really are—when we smile while we're breaking inside or agree while we're silently screaming no—we create emotional dissonance. That internal tug-of-war leaves us depleted, anxious, resentful, and eventually numb.

Incongruence often starts early. Maybe you were rewarded for being "an easy child," "nice," or "strong." Maybe you learned that showing sadness made others uncomfortable. Maybe honesty got you in trouble. So you adapted. Overfunctioned. Smoothed edges. Said the right things. Hid the rest.

But over time, living behind a mask erodes your sense of self. You forget what you really want. You question what's real. You feel disconnected from others—and from God—not because you're unfaithful, but because you're not present as yourself.

Congruence isn't about oversharing or being raw all the time. It's about *integrity*—not just in morality, but in wholeness. It's about closing the gap between who you are and how you show up. It's about honoring your limits. Owning your truth. Letting your yes be yes and your no be no, even if it disappoints someone.

It takes time. And it often starts with small shifts: Noticing when you're people-pleasing out of fear. Saying "I need a minute" instead of faking being okay. Choosing honesty even when it feels awkward.

Congruence doesn't demand perfection. Just truth. And truth is where healing begins.

Anchor Truth

You don't need to be flawless. You need to be honest.

Prayer

God, give me the courage to stop hiding and start living in alignment. Peel back the layers that keep me distant, even from myself.

Invitation

Where in your life are you out of alignment? Notice one place where your outside doesn't match your inside—and ask what a truer step would look like today.

The Spirit as Friend

And I will ask the Father, and he will give you another Advocate, who will never leave you. He is the Holy Spirit.

JOHN 14:16-17

Sometimes the world doesn't feel safe. Sometimes your own mind doesn't feel safe. And sometimes the very people who should've protected your heart have become the reason it's in pieces.

This is where emotional safety becomes more than a psychological need—it becomes a spiritual necessity. And the good news is, you're not alone in searching for it.

Jesus knew what it was like to be misunderstood, betrayed, falsely accused, and abandoned. He also knew that after he left, his followers would need more than instructions—they would need presence. A companion. A *safe* companion. So he gave them (and us) the Holy Spirit. Not as a distant force. As a friend.

The Greek word Jesus uses is *paraklētos*, often translated as *Advocate*, *Helper*, or *Comforter*. At its root, it means "the one who comes alongside." Not to fix you. Not to judge you. To walk with you. To remind you of what's true when you forget. To groan on your behalf when you don't even have the words.

This is the deepest kind of emotional safety: Someone who sees all of you and never flinches. Someone who isn't surprised by your anxiety or shame. Someone who isn't waiting for you to "get it together" before showing up with compassion and strength.

Yes, therapy is a safe place. Trusted friends are a gift. But the Holy Spirit offers something no one else can: 24/7 presence.

No masks needed. No performance required. You can whisper the unfiltered truth, and he stays. You can be at your worst, and he doesn't walk away. When you don't feel safe anywhere else, go to him.

Anchor Truth

The Holy Spirit is more than a concept. He's a companion—a steady, safe presence who will never leave you, even in your mess.

Prayer

Spirit of God, be my refuge. Be my reminder. Be my friend. Teach me how to rest in your presence when I feel scattered, anxious, or alone. I need your nearness—right now.

Invitation

What would you say if you believed the Spirit was really listening? Try sitting in silence today—no performance, no pretending—and say it. Then wait. Let his presence be enough.

Meaning Within Your Limits

Each time he said, "My grace is all you need. My power works best in weakness." So now I am glad to boast about my weaknesses, so that the power of Christ can work through me.

2 CORINTHIANS 12:9

We often equate meaning with mastery. Bigger achievements. Greater strength. Unlimited capacity. But what if that's not the full picture? What if meaning is not found by pushing past your limits—but by embracing them?

Paul understood this deeply. He begged God to remove his "thorn in the flesh"—something painful, persistent, and limiting. But the answer wasn't healing. It was grace. God didn't remove the limitation. He redefined it.

That's hard for us. Especially in a culture that tells us to hustle, stretch, overcome, and optimize. Limits feel like failure. But Scripture tells another story. God's strength shows up best not in our power, but in our need.

Mental health struggles often highlight our limits. Fatigue. Anxiety. Fragile focus. A desire to do more than we can. But limits don't *disqualify* us from a meaningful life—they can *deepen* it. They invite humility. Compassion. Slower rhythms. Deeper trust.

The paradox is that limits can actually lead to more freedom. When you stop trying to be everything, you start becoming more of who you really are. You're not failing because you can't do it all. You're human. And meaning doesn't come from the illusion of perfection, it comes from offering what you can, from where you are.

So if you're feeling held back by what you can't do, remember this: You are not disqualified by your limits, you're refined by them. Some of the most meaningful lives aren't lived in the spotlight of strength, but in the quiet courage of surrender.

Anchor Truth

Your limits are not the edge of your value. They're the doorway to grace. God's power meets you there.

Prayer

God, I don't always like my limits. Sometimes they frustrate me or make me feel like I'm not enough. But help me see them as places where your grace enters in. Teach me to live meaningfully—not by doing more, but by trusting you more.

Invitation

Instead of resenting a limit today, name it. Then ask how it might become an invitation—to rest, to ask for help, or to let go. Your limit might just be your most meaningful place.

Naming Your Strengths

The LORD turned to him and said, "Go with the strength you have. . . . I am sending you!"

JUDGES 6:14

Sometimes the hardest part of building resilience is believing you have any strength at all. Trauma, anxiety, depression, burnout—they all have a way of shrinking your self-image. You stop seeing what's strong in you. You only feel what's broken.

That's exactly where we find Gideon. Hiding in fear. Beating grain in a winepress. Feeling small, overlooked, and underqualified. And yet God calls him "Mighty hero." Not because Gideon looked strong, but because he was *called* strong.

Psychologically, we know that identifying your own strengths—like persistence, compassion, creativity, or insight—is one of the most powerful tools for resilience. It builds *self-efficacy* (the belief that you can handle hard things), which is linked to lower anxiety, greater adaptability, and higher recovery.

But here's the key: You often need someone else—God, a mentor, or a friend—to help you *name* what you can't see in yourself. That's what God did for Gideon. He didn't give him new strength, he helped Gideon recognize the strength he already had.

What if the same is true for you? What if strength is already inside you—buried beneath fear, grief, or shame but ready to rise when it's called out? You don't need superhuman grit. You just need a clearer view of what God already sees in you.

You have more strength than you realize—not because you feel it, but because God placed it in you. And he's not done calling it out.

Anchor Truth

Resilience begins when you stop waiting to feel strong and start trusting the strength that's already within you.

Prayer

God, I don't always feel brave. Sometimes I can't even name one good thing about myself. But you see me clearly. Help me believe in the strength you've already given me. Call it out, and teach me how to use it.

Invitation

Write down three strengths you've used to survive hard things. Ask someone close to you to name a few more. Let their words remind you: You are not weak. You're learning to see your strength.

When You Stuff It

I am silent before you;
I won't say a word, for my punishment is from you.

PSALM 39:9

Some of us don't scream, shout, or throw things when we're angry. We don't raise our voice, we raise our tolerance. We get quiet. We retreat. We tell ourselves it's not worth making a fuss.

But here's the problem: Unspoken anger doesn't stay small. It stores up. It simmers. And over time, it turns into bitterness, emotional numbness, or self-directed shame.

Maybe you grew up in a family where expressing anger wasn't safe. Maybe you learned that anger makes you unlovable or too much. Maybe you've been praised for being chill, agreeable, or accommodating.

So now, every time something hurts, you minimize it. Every time a boundary is crossed, you question whether it really matters. Every time someone disrespects you, you blame yourself for being too sensitive.

But Scripture doesn't say, "Don't feel anger." It says, "Don't let it control you" (see Psalm 4:4). That includes the silent kind of anger. The swallowed kind. The kind that builds like pressure in a sealed jar, until one day it breaks or explodes.

Stuffed anger doesn't make you more spiritual. It just makes you more resentful.

But the antidote isn't aggression. It's honesty. It's learning to name your anger before it morphs into something worse. It's practicing emotional awareness and safe expression—journaling it, praying it, speaking it aloud with someone trustworthy.

Jesus never pretended something didn't matter when it did. He was clear. Calm. And fiercely truthful.

You're allowed to speak up. You're allowed to set limits. You're allowed to say, "That hurt" or "I need something to change." Not to lash out, but to live free.

Anchor Truth

Ignoring anger doesn't make it go away. It just sends it deeper underground.

Prayer

God, I don't want to carry buried anger. Help me unearth what I've stuffed and bring it into your healing light.

Invitation

Think of a time recently when something upset you, but you said nothing. What stopped you from speaking up? What might it look like to give that anger a voice now, in a healthy way?

Your Resilience Is Not Just for You

He comforts us in all our troubles so that we can comfort others.

2 CORINTHIANS 1:4

You've made it through battles others didn't see. You've carried burdens with shaking hands. And somehow you're still standing. That's not just survival—that's a story someone else needs.

Resilience isn't only for you; it's also for the ones who come after you. It's the strength you pass on, the comfort you extend, the steady presence you offer because you *know* what it's like to fall and get back up.

Just look at Barnabas, whose very name means "son of encouragement." He stood beside Paul when others doubted him. Later, he advocated for John Mark—the one who had failed. Barnabas's belief became the bridge that brought others back to purpose.

And then there's Deborah, who judiciously and righteously led a nation. She lived with steadfast integrity when everyone else was choosing evil, and her perseverance ultimately led to Israel's victory over decades-long oppression.

Or Peter, who broke under pressure but didn't stay there. Restored by Jesus, he later became the rock of the early church—offering boldness, compassion, and unwavering faith to countless others.

Post-traumatic growth—the positive change that can follow pain—often includes a greater desire to help others. Your resilience equips you not just to heal, but to help. Not just to recover, but to restore.

Your scars can be someone else's road map. Your endurance can be someone else's hope. You didn't walk through fire just to survive it. You walked through so you could carry light to others still finding their way. Your strength is contagious.

And your story is living proof that hope can rise from hard places—and light still shines through cracked things.

Anchor Truth

Your resilience holds healing not just for you, but for someone else who needs to know it's possible.

Prayer

God, thank you for walking with me through the hard places. Use my story, my strength, even my scars to be a comfort to others. Let my resilience ripple outward and become part of someone else's healing.

Invitation

Who in your life might need a reminder that they're not alone? Reach out. Share part of your story. Let your strength become someone else's safe place.

The Shedding

Throw off your old sinful nature and your former way of life. . . . Instead, let the Spirit renew your thoughts and attitudes. Put on your new nature, created to be like God—truly righteous and holy.

EPHESIANS 4:22-24

At some point, most of us create a version of ourselves we think the world wants. Put together. Polished. Predictable. The one who doesn't ask for much. The one who keeps the peace. The one who outperforms the pain.

Sometimes this persona forms early—built out of necessity, survival, or the need to belong.

Other times it's shaped over years by expectations, disappointments, or someone else's voice lodged in your head like truth.

But the longer you live in that version of yourself—the one curated for applause or protection—the further you drift from your *real* self. And here's the thing: You can't live whole if you're living false.

The fake self might earn you approval, but it won't give you peace. It won't hold up under pressure. It won't sustain you when life gets brutally honest.

Letting go of that constructed identity can feel terrifying. You may ask, "If I stop performing, who will still love me? If I stop pretending, who will still stay?" But the only relationships worth keeping are the ones that love you as you are, not as you perform. And the only life worth living is one aligned with who you were created to be.

In psychological terms, this is called *identity integration*—the process of moving toward congruence. It's when your inner world and outer life finally start telling the same story. And it's a key predictor of emotional health.

Jesus never called people to be impressive. He called them to be whole. To follow him with unfiltered hearts. To live in the light, not behind a mask.

It's time to shed the false self. Not all at once, but one brave layer at a time.

Anchor Truth

You can't be whole and hide at the same time.

Prayer

God, help me unlearn the version of myself I built for survival. Give me courage to live from the person you made me to be—no filter, no mask, no shame.

Invitation

Ask yourself, "What part of me feels performative or self-protective right now? What would it look like to lay that down and live a little more honestly today?"

The Gift of Seeing Someone

Don't look out only for your own interests,
but take an interest in others, too.

PHILIPPIANS 2:4

There's a kind of magic in being seen—not just looked at, but truly seen. It's the feeling that someone is paying attention not just to what you say, but to who you are. David Brooks calls it *illumination*—the generous act of making another person feel known and valued by how deeply you listen, how attentively you notice, and how persistently you stay curious.

To illuminate someone is to make them feel real. It's not about fixing, diagnosing, or even encouraging. It's about offering the full weight of your presence. In a world that rewards loud voices and constant self-expression, it's rare—and deeply powerful—to focus entirely on someone else.

Jesus modeled this often. Think of the bleeding woman in the crowd (Luke 8). She reached for the hem of his garment, hoping to go unnoticed. But Jesus stopped. He looked for her. He made sure she was not just healed, but seen. "Daughter," he said, "your faith has made you well." That word—*daughter*—wasn't just kindness. It was identity. It said, "I see you. You matter."

The irony is that connection grows most when we stop trying to be interesting and start being interested. Make sure you really heard that: Connection happens when we turn our gaze outward instead of inward. When we ask real questions and actually care about the answers.

This is the quiet superpower of connection: Illuminating someone else brightens your own life, too. Because love deepens in the seeing.

Anchor Truth

People don't open up when they feel judged, they open up when they feel seen.

Prayer

God, help me slow down and see the people around me—not as obstacles or afterthoughts, but as image-bearers. Show me how to reflect your love by paying real attention.

Invitation

Choose one person today—a friend, partner, coworker—and ask a question that goes beyond small talk. Then listen like it's holy. Because it is.

Acting on Insight, Not Impulse

A person without self-control
is like a city with broken-down walls.

PROVERBS 25:28

One of the most powerful tools for emotional regulation is so simple it's easy to dismiss: the pause. Just a breath. A moment. A holy hesitation. It doesn't sound like much, but it's everything.

That pause is the difference between snapping and staying grounded. Between saying something you regret and speaking with intention. Between reacting out of woundedness and responding with wisdom.

Most of us don't naturally pause—we react. Especially when we feel threatened or hurt. The amygdala, the brain's alarm system, gets hijacked. Our bodies get flooded with adrenaline. Logic takes a back seat. And suddenly we're acting on impulse, not insight.

But when you train yourself to pause—to take one breath, one beat—you short-circuit the emotional chain reaction. You give your prefrontal cortex (the part of your brain responsible for reasoning and self-control) a chance to weigh in. You give the Spirit room to move.

Jesus modeled this beautifully. When accused, he didn't lash out. When tested, he didn't panic. He paused. He wrote in the dust. He asked a question. He turned the moment over. That pause wasn't passivity; it was power under control.

Learning to pause isn't about stuffing your emotions. It's about stewarding them. It's about creating space between what you feel and what you choose to do with it. That space is where growth happens. That's where wisdom lives.

So the next time you feel the surge—of anger, fear, defensiveness, shame—don't suppress it. Don't act on it. Just pause. Let it rise. Notice it. Name it. And then ask God, "What's the wise way forward?"

Anchor Truth

The pause isn't weakness. It's strength. It's the space where emotion meets maturity and where reaction gives way to redemption.

Prayer

God, teach me to pause before I respond. Slow me down so I can act with love, not just react from pain. Help me to listen, breathe, and walk in step with your Spirit.

Invitation

Pick one moment today to practice the pause. When you feel triggered or tense, breathe deeply, count to five, and ask, "What's the wise response here?" Write down what happens.

When Someone Else Sets the Boundary

So now we can tell who are children of God and who are children of the devil. Anyone who does not live righteously and does not love other believers does not belong to God.

1 JOHN 3:10

Sometimes it's not your boundary that's hard to enforce, it's someone else's boundary that's hard to accept. Maybe they stopped replying as quickly. Maybe they declined your invitation. Maybe they asked for space or silence. Maybe they didn't explain themselves at all. And it stings.

You're left wondering what you did wrong. Was it something you said? Something you didn't say? Should you chase them down and ask for clarity? Or is backing off the right thing, even if it feels like rejection?

When you're on the receiving end of a boundary, especially one that's fuzzy or unspoken, your mind wants to fill in the blanks. You'll be tempted to assume the worst about yourself or about them.

But a healthy response starts by remembering that boundaries aren't always about punishment. Sometimes they're about *preservation*. Of peace. Of healing. Of emotional safety—on either side of the relationship. That doesn't mean the other person is handling it perfectly. But it doesn't mean you're being abandoned, either.

First John reminds us that *love* is the mark of God's people, not perfect understanding. Love gives others room. It doesn't demand constant access. Love can accept a boundary, even one that's painful or unclear, without keeping score or spiraling into self-condemnation.

So what can you do when faced with a difficult boundary? You can honor it. You can examine your own emotional response without judgment. You can pray for wisdom and for the other person. And you can remember that just because someone steps away doesn't mean your worth has stepped down.

God's love never retreats. And his presence doesn't hinge on anyone else's proximity.

Anchor Truth

Receiving someone's boundary is a form of maturity. Loving well includes letting go—without letting shame fill the gap.

Prayer

God, when I feel confused or hurt by someone's boundary, give me your perspective. Teach me to hold space without grasping for control. And help me grow more secure in your unwavering love—even when others create distance.

Invitation

Is there a relationship where someone's boundary has triggered insecurity or confusion in you? Instead of seeking immediate clarity, try offering grace. Let it become an opportunity to deepen your self-awareness and your trust in God.

The Deeper Well

Then I realized that it is good and proper for a [person] to eat and drink, and to find satisfaction in [their] toilsome labor under the sun during the few days of life God has given [them]—for this is [their] lot.

ECCLESIASTES 5:18

You can have everything the world says should make you happy—comfort, success, even applause—and still feel hollow. You can dine on a $200 tasting menu at a Michelin-starred restaurant, wear a perfectly tailored luxury suit or trendy athleisure outfit that screams "put together," and still feel like something essential is missing. Because happiness isn't just about *what* you have or *what* you're doing. It's about *why*.

The deepest kind of happiness isn't found in leisure or luck. It's found in living a life that matters. Meaning is what roots you when your circumstances shift. It's what makes the ordinary sacred and the daily worthwhile. Without it, happiness becomes a moving target. With it, even the mundane starts to shine.

Often seen as the Bible's most honest book about wrestling with purpose, Ecclesiastes offers this simple, almost surprising insight: Meaning is found in embracing your life as it is. Finding satisfaction in your work, your rhythm, your lot. Not in chasing something shinier, but in living with intentionality. With presence. With purpose. It's not about having more. It's about living for something beyond yourself.

So what have you been entrusted with? Who have you been called to love, serve, or shape? What brings you quiet satisfaction, even if no one notices?

The world will keep selling you happiness in sleek packaging—dream vacations, luxury handbags, the perfect home renovation, or the next career milestone. And sure, those things can bring a moment of pleasure. But they don't bring meaning. Not the kind that anchors you when the applause fades or the thrill wears off.

You don't need a different life to feel more alive. You need a deeper *why*. And when you find it—rooted in purpose, steeped in love, and tethered to something greater than yourself—you'll discover a joy no circumstance can steal.

Anchor Truth

Pleasure is fleeting, but meaning endures. Lasting happiness flows from a life anchored in purpose.

Prayer

God, help me look beyond the surface. Give me eyes to see the meaning buried in my everyday life, and let that meaning become a steady source of joy.

Invitation

Where in your life do you feel most aligned with your deeper purpose? What activities, roles, or relationships bring a sense of fulfillment? Press into those places today. They're the well that doesn't run dry.

The Strength to Stand Tall

So be strong and courageous,
all you who put your hope in the LORD!

PSALM 31:24

Humility and confidence are not opposites. You don't have to choose between standing tall or staying grounded. In fact, the healthiest people do both at the same time. True humility isn't thinking less of yourself; it's thinking of yourself accurately. And genuine confidence isn't puffed-up bravado. It's the steady belief that who you are, by God's design, has value and purpose.

Psychologists call this *secure self-esteem*—where your worth isn't built on applause or performance but on something deeper and more stable. That kind of confidence creates space for humility to flourish.

Think of Esther. She wasn't loud or domineering. But when the moment came, she stood with quiet courage in the face of probable death. That's humble confidence. She didn't think she was better than anyone else, but she knew she'd been placed in her position "for just such a time as this" (Esther 4:14).

Or look at Joseph. Betrayed, enslaved, forgotten. And still, when Pharaoh called on him, he didn't shrink back. He named his gifting boldly: "It is not in me; God will give Pharaoh an answer." That's a man who knew his limitations but also his calling.

Humble confidence is the ability to say, "I know who I am. I know what I've been given. And I'm here to serve, not to prove."

It doesn't demand the spotlight. But it's not afraid of it either. It doesn't crumble under criticism or inflate with praise. It stays rooted.

Real confidence doesn't come from pretending to have it all together. It comes from being anchored in the truth that you don't have to.

Anchor Truth

You can be both grounded and bold. True confidence grows from humility.

Prayer

God, help me release the need to prove myself. Remind me of who you've made me to be. Give me quiet courage and humble strength to show up with grace and conviction.

Invitation

Today, show up where you tend to shrink back. Speak honestly. Act boldly. Not for attention, but because you've been given something good to offer.

Lowering Your Defenses

Fools think their own way is right,
but the wise listen to others.

PROVERBS 12:15

You're in a conversation, and someone gives you feedback. It's not even that harsh, but suddenly you feel your chest tighten, your mind race, your tone sharpen. You're not listening. You're defending. It happens fast. Often without us realizing.

That's the thing about defensiveness: It's sneaky. It doesn't always show up as yelling or snapping. Sometimes it looks like shutting down, overexplaining, deflecting, or silently rehearsing your counterpoints while the other person is still talking.

But here's the deeper truth: Defensiveness isn't just a behavior. It's a form of self-protection. It says, "If I let this in, it will undo me." So instead of receiving, we resist. Instead of growing, we guard.

Clinically, defensiveness is often rooted in shame or insecurity. The fear that we're not good enough, that being wrong makes us unworthy, or that criticism equals rejection. But humility breaks that cycle.

Humility gives you room to hear feedback without it wrecking your identity. It doesn't mean you have to agree with everything that's said. It means you stay open. You listen with curiosity, not combat. You ask questions instead of forming comebacks. You seek to understand even if you don't agree. And you trust that your worth won't crumble just because someone sees a flaw.

In Scripture, wisdom is repeatedly tied to the ability to *listen.* Not to win, but to understand. Not to defend, but to grow. Jesus—who had every right to correct and command—often just listened first. He asked questions. He gave space. He saw hearts. If we're going to walk in his ways, we'll need to soften our edges and open our ears.

Anchor Truth

Defensiveness builds walls. Humility opens doors. And real growth begins when you stop guarding your ego and start listening with grace.

Prayer

God, when I feel attacked, help me slow down. When I want to defend myself, help me listen instead. Give me the humility to hear what's true and the courage to grow from it.

Invitation

Think back to a recent conversation where you felt defensive. What might have been underneath your reaction? This week, practice listening with one goal: understanding—not proving, fixing, or protecting.

The Inner Critic's Megaphone

Even if we feel guilty, God is greater than our feelings, and he knows everything.

1 JOHN 3:20

There's a voice in your head—you know the one. It questions everything. It rewinds every word you said in that meeting. It tells you you're too much, or not enough, or both in the same breath. It demands perfection and then mocks you for trying. That voice is your inner critic.

And for those who struggle with approval seeking, it doesn't whisper. It shouts. It straps on a megaphone and plays highlight reels of every awkward moment, every flaw, every time you didn't measure up. Then it adds, "And this is why you need to try harder. Be better."

Many approval seekers weren't born that way. Somewhere along the line, they internalized a lie that love must be earned, that worth must be proven. And so they hustle. Not just to win others' approval, but to silence the relentless commentary from within.

It's not just "I did something wrong." It becomes "Something is wrong with me." And the more we believe it, the louder that inner voice becomes.

But Scripture offers a beautiful interruption: Even if we feel guilty, God is greater than our feelings. God sees it all—every wound that formed the voice, every time we gave in to its pressure—and still says, "You are mine."

Think of Peter. He blew it in public, denying Jesus three times. The critic in his head must've been brutal. But Jesus didn't scold. He restored. He gave Peter a chance to declare love where fear had taken over. And Peter went on to lead the church—not because he silenced his critic perfectly, but because he trusted a greater voice.

Anchor Truth

You are not the sum of your harshest self-judgments. God's voice is kinder and louder if you let it be.

Prayer

God, sometimes the voice inside my head is merciless. Teach me to notice it without obeying it. Help me hear your voice above the noise.

Invitation

Write down one repeating message your inner critic says. Then write God's truth next to it. Keep it where you'll see it this week, and let the greater voice reshape your self-talk.

The Deep Need for Meaning

Where there is no vision, the people perish.

PROVERBS 29:18 (KJV)

There's a reason the days that feel the worst are the ones that feel the most pointless. You can survive exhaustion. You can push through discomfort. But emptiness? That's soul-level depletion. It's the ache that creeps in when you're checking all the boxes, doing all the things—and still wondering, "What's the point?"

Psychologists have long confirmed what Scripture declared centuries ago: People aren't wired to just exist. We're wired for meaning. We need a sense of *why*—something that anchors our story and gives shape to our suffering. Something that answers the quiet question behind our choices—"Does any of this matter?"

This isn't about platform or prestige. It's not about being important or impressive. It's about knowing that your life—even in its quiet corners—counts.

That's why the Bible doesn't just offer rules; it offers relationship and purpose. From Genesis to Revelation, we meet real people invited into real purpose. Some were kings. Some were nobodies. But all of them found meaning—not by chasing significance, but by aligning with God's vision for their lives.

Meaning fuels hope. It steadies us when everything else is shaky. And the beautiful paradox? Meaning isn't something you *achieve*. It's something you *receive*—when you stop chasing identity built on your own efforts and start walking with the one who gave it to you.

You don't have to change the world. But you do have to care about why you're in it. Because your well-being isn't just tied to how you feel. It's tied to what you're living for. And when you know your life is part of something eternal, even the smallest things take on divine significance.

So don't settle for a life that just looks good on paper. You were made for more than survival. You were made to live on purpose, with purpose. When you chase meaning instead of mere comfort, you'll discover a joy that doesn't depend on your circumstances because it's anchored in something eternal.

Anchor Truth

God created you with purpose—not just to survive, but to live meaningfully. A life aligned with his vision gives you hope, endurance, and emotional strength.

Prayer

God, I don't want to just go through the motions. Help me live with intention. When I feel lost in the fog of routine or uncertainty, remind me that you've made me for more. Anchor me in your purpose and wake me up to the meaning I was made for.

Invitation

Take five minutes today to reflect, What am I living for? *Write down one area of your life where you feel empty, and ask God to show you how it might be infused with deeper meaning.*

The Joy Shift

I have learned how to be content with whatever I have.
I know how to live on almost nothing or with everything.
I have learned the secret of living in every situation. . . . For
I can do everything through Christ, who gives me strength.

PHILIPPIANS 4:11-13

Let's be honest—so much of life is out of our hands. The diagnosis. The detour. The way someone else shows up (or doesn't). We can't always control what happens. But we can choose how we respond.

That's not just a pep talk, it's psychology and theology.

Psychologists call this *cognitive reappraisal*—the ability to reinterpret a situation in a way that shifts your emotional response. Paul, writing from prison, called it "the secret of living in every situation." What's the secret? It's the attitude you bring to what you didn't choose.

Joy doesn't come from fixing everything. It comes from adjusting to what you can't fix without letting it wreck your soul. That kind of joy is fierce. Resilient. Spirit-backed.

Paul wasn't pretending prison was a good time. But he chose contentment. He chose trust. He chose to say, "Christ strengthens me for this."

So the next time life throws something your way—something you didn't ask for, can't undo, and don't know how to handle—pause. Don't just react, reframe. You don't need control to have joy. You need perspective. And the Spirit can help you find it. How? By nudging you to pause before you spiral. By whispering truth louder than your fear.

Joy isn't always loud. Sometimes it's a quiet defiance—a Spirit-born resolve to say, "This may not change, but I can."

Anchor Truth

Joy isn't the product of perfection. It's the result of a Spirit-shaped perspective.

Prayer

God, I can't control everything, but I can choose how I see it. Help me trade bitterness for perspective. Help me shift my focus from what's wrong to what's possible. Teach me the secret Paul knew: Joy is still an option.

Invitation

What's one frustrating thing you can't change right now? Instead of spiraling, ask, "What else could be true here?" That question might just unlock a joy you didn't see coming.

Your Pattern Has a Pulse

Examine yourselves to see if your faith is genuine. Test yourselves.

2 CORINTHIANS 13:5

You don't have to repeat every pattern you've lived. But first you have to see it. Most of us live on emotional autopilot more than we realize. We default to defensiveness when we feel exposed. We avoid hard conversations until disconnection becomes the norm. We numb out when things feel overwhelming. We chase approval to avoid rejection. We say yes to stay liked and call it kindness.

These aren't random behaviors. They're patterns. And patterns always have a pulse.

Paul tells the Corinthian church to examine themselves—not as a form of guilt, but of growth. "Test yourselves." It's not self-shaming. It's self-checking. It's an invitation to wake up, to notice, to ask, "What am I repeating without realizing it?"

Psychologists refer to this kind of reflection as *metacognition*—the ability to think about your thinking. It's what allows you to step outside of your reactions long enough to observe the pattern instead of being ruled by it.

When you're not self-aware, your patterns own you. When you *are* self-aware, you can interrupt the cycle.

You can say, "Oh, this is the part where I usually ghost someone." "This is when I withdraw instead of speaking up." "This is the moment I usually betray myself to keep the peace."

When you name it, you're not trapped in it anymore. That's the beginning of freedom. Not a full fix. Just a quiet shift. A sacred pause. A deeper breath. A better choice.

Anchor Truth

You can't break a pattern you won't name.

Prayer

God, help me notice what I'm repeating without realizing it. Give me eyes to see my own cycles and courage to tell the truth about them. Interrupt what needs to be broken. Restore what needs to be rebuilt.

Invitation

Pay attention today to what feels familiar—especially in moments of tension. Is this part of a pattern? If so, name it. Even that one act of awareness can change your next move.

Is Depression Contagious?

Walk with the wise and become wise;
associate with fools and get in trouble.

PROVERBS 13:20

Depression isn't a virus. But it can spread in subtle ways, especially in close relationships. If you've ever found yourself absorbing the heaviness of someone else's struggle—feeling inexplicably low, anxious, or emotionally drained after being with them—you've experienced what psychologists call *emotional contagion.*

It's the human tendency to "catch" others' emotions through empathy and attunement. And while this is a powerful relational strength, it can also take a toll. This doesn't mean you should distance yourself from someone who's hurting. But it does mean you need to take care. Even Jesus didn't absorb everyone's pain without rhythm, replenishment, prayer, and boundaries.

If *you're* the one struggling, you may feel ashamed of your emotional impact on others. You may even start to isolate, thinking, *I don't want to be a burden.* But that's not healthy either. Isolation only deepens the ache. Depression may be emotionally contagious, but so is hope. So is tenderness. So is asking for help.

The goal isn't to harden yourself or cut people off. It's to stay soft without losing your center. To love others without emptying yourself completely. To recognize when you're being pulled under, and to say, "I need to come up for air."

Because walking alongside someone with depression—or being that someone—requires strength, honesty, and grace. Not perfection. Not martyrdom. Just a willingness to stay wise in how you walk—with others and with yourself.

"Walk with the wise," Proverbs says, "and become wise." That includes surrounding yourself with people who point you toward light, even in the dark. And it means recognizing that emotional health is not a solo act. It's a relational rhythm of mutual care.

You weren't meant to carry every burden alone or become someone else's savior, either. Wisdom walks with compassion *and* clarity. With tenderness *and* truth.

So ask for what you need. And remember: Just as depression can spread, so can hope.

Anchor Truth

Being emotionally present doesn't mean absorbing someone else's pain. You can offer compassion without collapse. You can be supportive without drowning.

Prayer

God, help me love others well without losing myself. Give me wisdom to notice when I'm carrying what isn't mine—and the grace to let it go. Help me ask for support when I need it and offer it with tenderness when I can.

Invitation

Who in your life might need your presence but also your limits? What emotions have you been "catching" without noticing? Reflect on how to hold space without losing your own.

The Power of Being Known

I have loved you even as the Father has loved me. Remain in my love.

JOHN 15:9

There's a reason being known feels so powerful—and so rare. To be truly seen by someone, to have your fears and flaws exposed without fear of rejection, strikes at the core of our need for emotional safety. It's not just a warm fuzzy ideal; it's a psychological necessity.

Research in interpersonal neurobiology and attachment theory shows that being deeply known and accepted by even one person reshapes our nervous system. It helps regulate stress, increases emotional resilience, and lays the groundwork for self-compassion. It shifts the way we see ourselves. It even impacts the way we relate to God.

But this isn't just psychology: It's theology. We were created by a relational God, wired for connection, and formed in love. When someone looks at you and doesn't flinch at your mess, something sacred happens. You feel safe enough to exhale. You begin to heal. You find your way back to yourself.

In the Old Testament, we find this kind of connection in the friendship between Jonathan and David. Jonathan wasn't just loyal; he saw David's heart. He knew who David was under the armor and behind the anointing.

When David was on the run, hunted and disoriented, Jonathan risked everything to find him in the wilderness and "encouraged him to stay strong in his faith in God" (1 Samuel 23:16). That's what emotionally safe relationships do. They meet you in the wilderness and remind you of who you are—and whose you are. They become mirrors of grace.

You don't need to be fully known by everyone. But you were made to be fully known by *someone*.

Don't settle for surface-level connections. You're worthy of relationships that go beneath the polish and pretense, where you can show up as your whole self and still be held with kindness. Those relationships may be few, but they are worth seeking, worth fighting for, and worth waiting on.

Keep showing up. Keep staying open. God's heart is for you to be known and loved in real time, not just in theory.

Anchor Truth

Being known isn't a luxury: It's a lifeline. And it's how God designed you to thrive, both emotionally and spiritually.

Prayer

God, give me the courage to let myself be seen. Lead me to people who are safe. And help me be that kind of presence for someone else.

Invitation

Who in your life really knows you, mess and all? If no one comes to mind, ask God to lead you to someone safe. If someone does, thank them. Let them know what their presence means.

The Pressure to Be Perfect

The LORD is compassionate and merciful,
slow to get angry and filled with unfailing love.

PSALM 103:8

Perfectionism wears many disguises. It can look like excellence. Responsibility. Ambition. Morality. Even spirituality. But underneath, it's often driven by something far more fragile: fear. Fear of not being enough. Fear of failure or rejection. Fear of disappointing others or God.

Perfectionism whispers, "If you just try harder, do better, stay in control—you'll be safe." But instead of peace, it leads to exhaustion. Shame. Self-criticism. Paralysis. It creates a moving target you can never quite reach.

Why do we fall into it? Sometimes it's the way we coped when love felt conditional. Or how we learned to avoid punishment, chaos, or criticism. It may have helped us survive, but it doesn't help us thrive.

And you're not alone. The Bible is full of people who struggled with the pressure to perform: Martha was anxious to get everything "just right" while missing the moment with Jesus. Peter boasted of loyalty, then buckled under pressure. Paul obsessed over religious perfection before discovering grace. Job questioned why suffering came even when he had "done everything right." King Saul tried to manage outcomes and please people, unraveling in the process. Even the Pharisees—the Jewish religious leaders—mistook perfection for holiness and missed the heart of God.

Perfectionism isn't just a personality quirk. It's a form of self-protection. But it keeps us from rest. From joy. From connection. And from grace.

The good news? God never asked you to be flawless. He invites you to be faithful. And his mercy isn't based on performance—it's rooted in love.

So take a breath. You're already fully seen and fully loved. Not because you're perfect, but because you're his.

Anchor Truth

Perfectionism is a heavy burden you were never meant to carry. God's grace makes space for your humanity.

Prayer

God, I confess that I often feel pressure to get everything right. But I'm tired. I want to trade this pressure for your peace. Help me release the lie that I must be perfect to be worthy. Teach me to rest in your love.

Invitation

Notice today when perfectionism tries to take over. When it does, whisper this: "I am loved not for what I do, but for who I am." Then take the next step with grace.

Safe Enough to Pray Honestly

I cried out to the LORD,
and he answered me from his holy mountain.

PSALM 3:4

For some, prayer is a lifeline. For others, it feels like speaking into silence. And for many—maybe you—it's complicated. You've been told to pray "boldly," but your honesty has been met with shame. You've tried to pray consistently, but your own thoughts get in the way. You want to come clean with God, but something in you still wonders, *Is it safe?*

That's a real question. Because if you've ever experienced rejection after vulnerability—if your raw emotions were once punished or dismissed—you've learned to put up walls. And those walls don't suddenly vanish just because you bow your head.

But prayer isn't a performance. It's not about having the right words, tone, or posture. It's about showing up. Not cleaned up. Just real.

David prayed ugly prayers. So did Job. And Hannah. And Jeremiah. And Jesus himself in Gethsemane. None of them held back. They prayed with trembling voices, messy hearts, and zero filters. And they met a God who didn't flinch. That kind of prayer—gutsy, honest, unfiltered—is where emotional safety with God is born.

Because when you bring the parts of you that you're afraid to speak aloud and still feel held by grace, something shifts. You stop bracing and clenching. You start breathing. You realize you're not too much for God. And you never were.

There's freedom in no longer pretending. There's healing in no longer hiding. And there's emotional safety in knowing the Spirit intercedes with sighs too deep for words when yours won't come.

When you feel blank or broken, when you can't string two thoughts together, when all you can do is sit in the quiet—he is already praying for you. You are not alone in the silence. Not abandoned in the ache. When your words run out, heaven leans in.

Anchor Truth

The safest place for your rawest emotions is in the presence of a God who already knows and stays.

Prayer

God, I don't always know how to pray. But I want to stop pretending. Teach me to bring the unedited version of myself to you. Remind me that I'm safe in your presence, even when I'm falling apart.

Invitation

Pray one honest sentence today. Just one. Don't worry about sounding holy. Be human. And let that be enough.

The Lie of "What If"

So don't worry about tomorrow, for tomorrow will bring its own worries. Today's trouble is enough for today.

MATTHEW 6:34

Anxiety loves the future. It feeds on possibility, magnifies uncertainty, and fuels your mind with endless loops of *what if?* What if I lose everything? What if I never feel better? What if this panic never goes away?

The brain, in its attempt to protect you, tries to prepare for worst-case scenarios. But that protective instinct can become a prison, locking you in a cycle of catastrophizing.

Psychologists sometimes call this *future-tripping*—mentally living in tomorrow's fear instead of today's reality. Your nervous system doesn't always know the difference between imagination and reality. So even your thoughts can trigger a physical stress response, making the danger feel real even when it isn't.

Jesus knew this about us. That's why he didn't just say "Don't worry." He acknowledged that life does have trouble, but he asked us to stay rooted in today. Not because the future doesn't matter, but because worrying about it steals the peace we need to face it.

The what-ifs will come. That's normal. But you don't have to chase every one of them down. You don't have to pre-live pain that hasn't happened. You don't have to carry tomorrow's weight on today's shoulders.

What if God is already in the future, holding what you can't control? What if you're allowed to exhale today, even if nothing's fixed yet? What if this very moment is enough?

Here's the truth: "What if" is a signal, not a sentence. It's your brain trying to prepare, but it doesn't define your story.

"What if" is a question anxiety asks, not a verdict on your future. It feels urgent, but it isn't ultimate. And it's rarely kind. You don't have to answer it. You can let it pass because God is already holding the outcome.

Anchor Truth

Anxiety often lives in the future, but God meets us in the present.

Prayer

God, you already know the things I'm worried about, even the ones I haven't said out loud. Remind me that you are already there. Help me come back to this moment. Teach me to trust you with what I cannot control.

Invitation

Focus on one of your repeating what-if thoughts that's been haunting you. Write it down, then add this sentence under it: "Even if that happens, God will still be with me." You're not dismissing the fear; you're anchoring it in truth.

When Grief Lingers

Blessed are those who mourn,
for they will be comforted.

MATTHEW 5:4 (NIV)

Some losses don't leave. Not really. They fade around the edges, maybe. They don't hit as hard every morning. But they still catch you off guard—on birthdays, in smells, in songs, in the laughter of someone who sounds almost like them.

There's this myth that time heals all wounds. But for many, time simply teaches us how to live with a limp. Grief from long ago can still stir in the quiet corners of the soul. And when it does, people often feel ashamed, wondering, *Shouldn't I be past this by now?*

But love doesn't vanish with time. So why should sorrow?

Jesus said, "Blessed are those who mourn." Not those who "mourn quickly." Not those who "move on." Just those who mourn—who give honest voice to their ache, however many years have passed. Even the apostle Paul, years into ministry, wrote with tears about his losses. David sang psalms of sorrow over absences that would never be reversed.

So if grief still visits you years later, that's not weakness. It's testimony. You loved deeply. You remember honestly. And even in the ache, you are being tenderly held by a God who never forgets, never hurries healing, and always meets you in the memory.

Grief is not a sign that you're stuck. It's a sign that something mattered. Someone mattered. You don't have to tidy it up. You don't have to explain it away.

God is not impatient with your sadness. He doesn't call your tears "old news."

So let them fall when they need to. Remember what was good. Name what was lost. And trust that the Comforter isn't finished with you yet.

Anchor Truth

You're not broken for feeling what still aches. Grief that lingers is often love that endures.

Prayer

God, thank you for holding space for my old wounds. For not rushing me through the ache. Help me honor what was lost and open my heart to your ongoing comfort. Remind me that I'm not behind; I'm beloved.

Invitation

If the ache returns today, don't resist it. Light a candle. Say their name. Write a memory. Let the tears fall in your Father's presence. He's still there.

Cultivating a Curious Mind

Put on your new nature, and be renewed as you learn to know your Creator and become like him.

COLOSSIANS 3:10

Some people seem born curious. They ask questions, dig deeper, and follow their wonder like a trail of breadcrumbs. But for others, curiosity doesn't come so easily, especially when it comes to self-reflection or relationships. If that's you, take heart: Curiosity isn't just a personality trait. It's a mindset you can build.

Psychologists call this a *growth orientation*—a belief that you can learn, change, and understand more over time. And research shows that cultivating curiosity not only improves learning, it enhances emotional intelligence, relational satisfaction, and even resilience.

Curious people are less reactive, more empathetic, and better at resolving conflict. Why? Because they pause before assuming. They wonder before judging.

So how do you grow curiosity? Start small. Ask, "What else could be true?" when you feel certain about someone's motives. Instead of labeling emotions as good or bad, ask, "What's this emotion trying to tell me?" Notice the stories you tell yourself and ask, "Where did that story come from? Is it still serving me?"

Cultivating curiosity means replacing shame with compassion. It means learning to be a student of your own soul without grading yourself for every flaw. It also means staying open to mystery.

Curiosity doesn't require all the answers. In fact, it thrives in the tension of the unknown. That's where growth begins. Even Paul, the brilliant theologian and church builder, admitted, "Now we see things imperfectly, like puzzling reflections in a mirror" (1 Corinthians 13:12). He embraced the reality that faith includes questions. So does healing.

Let the Spirit renew your thoughts. Not with more certainty, but with a deeper willingness to explore—your emotions, your habits, your relationships, your blind spots. Growth begins where curiosity takes root.

Anchor Truth

Curiosity can be cultivated. It starts with replacing judgment with wonder and choosing compassion over shame.

Prayer

God, give me a teachable spirit. When I'm tempted to shut down or assume, help me stay open, ask questions, and welcome growth.

Invitation

Choose one area of your life where you've felt stuck. Instead of judging it, explore it. Ask yourself, "What more is there to understand here?" Let that question be your guide today.

What Are You Doing with What You've Been Given?

Well done, my good and faithful servant. You have been faithful in handling this small amount, so now I will give you many more responsibilities. Let's celebrate together!

MATTHEW 25:23

We often look for meaning in what we *don't* have—more time, more talent, more opportunities. But Jesus flips that script. In the parable of the talents, each servant is given something, and the meaning is found not in how much they had, but in what they did with it. One received five bags of silver. Another got two. The last, just one.

But the master's praise wasn't based on quantity; it was based on faithfulness. The first two invested what they had and doubled it. The third buried his gift out of fear. He didn't lose it. He just didn't *live* it.

Here's the hard truth: Meaning doesn't show up fully formed. It's cultivated. It's created through action—through showing up, taking risks, and investing what God has entrusted to you. That includes your skills, your passions, your story, and even your wounds.

Jesus wasn't handing out financial advice here. He was giving us a lens for life. You were never meant to hoard your life in fear. You were meant to multiply it in love. That's where joy is found.

So maybe the question today isn't "What should I be doing with my life?" Maybe it's "What have I already been given—and what am I doing with it?" You don't need to wait for a grand calling or perfect conditions.

Meaning is made in motion, when you stop burying what you've been given and start believing it matters. Even the smallest act of faithfulness can echo with eternal significance. Your life isn't random. It's entrusted. And the Master delights in your courage to invest it well.

Anchor Truth

The search for meaning doesn't begin with having more. It begins with faithfully using what you already have.

Prayer

God, open my eyes to what you've placed in my hands. Teach me to stop comparing and start investing. Give me courage to live with intention, knowing you delight in my small steps of faithfulness.

Invitation

Make a list of three gifts you've been given—resources, relationships, or life experiences. Choose one to invest in more intentionally this week, trusting that meaning grows through movement.

Social Media and the Metrics of Worth

Am I now trying to win the approval of human beings, or of God? . . . If I were still trying to please people, I would not be a servant of Christ.

GALATIANS 1:10 (NIV)

There's a strange little rush that comes when a post gets attention—a dopamine drip of likes, hearts, claps, shares. You know it shouldn't matter, but somehow it does. You tell yourself you're just sharing. Just keeping in touch. But deep down, it's hard not to feel like you're always auditioning. Always performing. Always curating a version of your life that's just a little shinier than it really is.

Social media has changed the currency of worth. We measure value in views. We equate affirmation with acceptance. And we learn to self-censor in exchange for hearts that flash on a screen but do little for the ache beneath our ribs.

Here's the clinical reality: Studies have linked social media engagement with rising rates of anxiety, depression, and disordered self-esteem, especially among younger users. That's not just correlation. When your sense of self becomes intertwined with public feedback loops, you stop asking the deeper questions: *Am I loved? Known? Growing? Honest?* And instead you start asking, *How did it perform?*

But Paul pushes back with clarity and force: "If I were still trying to please people, I would not be a servant of Christ." That's the hinge. You can live for the algorithm or you can live for truth. You can chase approval or you can rest in your identity. But it's nearly impossible to do both at once.

And maybe the most important truth? God's affection for you is not performance-based. You are already seen. Already cherished. Already enough. Even when the post gets no engagement. Even when you're unseen. Even when you stop hustling to be liked.

Anchor Truth

Your worth isn't measured in metrics. You're already loved—before the first like and long after the last one fades.

Prayer

God, it's hard not to care about how I'm perceived. I want to be liked, admired, seen. But I don't want to lose myself chasing it. Anchor me in what's real and eternal.

Invitation

Take a one-day break from social media. Pay attention to what surfaces: insecurity, boredom, peace, relief. Let it show you where your soul is looking for something deeper than likes.

What If It Turns Out Beautiful?

I pray that God, the source of hope, will fill you completely with joy and peace because you trust in him.

ROMANS 15:13

Children rarely ask, "But what if it all falls apart?" They ask, "Can we do it again?" "Will it be awesome?" "Can I try?" They imagine the best. Expect the good. And they're not afraid to say it out loud.

But somewhere along the way, many of us unlearned that posture. We call it growing up. We stop hoping out loud because we are tired of being let down. But what if childlike hope isn't something to outgrow, but something to reclaim?

That doesn't mean pretending everything is fine. It means letting yourself believe again—in something good, something true, something beautiful that's still possible. Romans 15 calls God the source of hope, the one who fills us with joy and peace because we trust. Not because life is predictable. But because God is trustworthy.

Psychologists say that hope requires two ingredients: a goal and the belief that you can get there. It's not just dreaming. It's choosing to move toward light, even when you've seen the dark. And sometimes the path back to hope starts with a question: What if it turns out beautiful? What if your healing takes root? What if this ache becomes a new strength? What if joy really *can* come in the morning?

Let yourself ask those questions again—not because you're childish, but because you're brave. And if hope feels awkward at first—like putting on clothes that used to fit—keep trying. It's not too late to live like good things are still ahead.

Anchor Truth

Childlike hope isn't weakness. It's holy defiance in a broken world.

Prayer

God, awaken my hope again. Help me look ahead with joy, not fear. And teach me to expect your goodness without apology.

Invitation

Ask yourself, "What would change today if I approached it with childlike hope instead of guarded cynicism?" Try one act, one word, or one choice that reflects that shift.

The Loneliness of Pain No One Sees

I look for someone to come and help me, but no one gives me a passing thought! No one will help me; no one cares a bit what happens to me. They I pray to you, O LORD. I say, "You are my place of refuge. You are all I really want in life."

PSALM 142:4-5

One of the hardest parts of trauma isn't just the moment that broke you. It's what comes after. The silence. The loneliness. The ache of carrying something no one else can see. People around you move on. Or they never noticed anything in the first place.

You might hear things like "Just let it go." "You're too sensitive." "That was a long time ago." But what they don't see is how much it still lives in you. And how exhausting it is to keep pretending you're okay.

This is a kind of grief that doesn't get flowers. A kind of pain that hides in plain sight.

David knew something of this kind of ache. In Psalm 142, he said, "No one gives me a passing thought!" His soul was unraveling, and he felt invisible. Alone. Forgotten. But even in that desolate space, he cried out to God as his refuge—not just from enemies, but from despair.

You may feel like no one gets what you're going through. And honestly, some people won't. But that doesn't mean your pain isn't real. And it doesn't mean God has left you to carry it alone.

The God who meets Hagar in the wilderness, the God who weeps at Lazarus's tomb, the God who sweats blood in Gethsemane—he is not indifferent to your suffering.

When no one else sees your pain, God does. When no one knows what to say, he stays.

Anchor Truth

You may feel unseen by others, but you are never invisible to God. Your sorrow is known, and you are not alone.

Prayer

God, sometimes it feels like no one really understands what I'm going through. Help me believe that you see me, even when others don't. Be my refuge when I feel invisible.

Invitation

Today, when you feel misunderstood or unseen, speak this to your soul: "God sees me here. God stays with me here. I don't have to carry this alone."

When Guilt Is the Driver, You Crash

It is for freedom that Christ has set us free.

GALATIANS 5:1 (NIV)

Guilt might get you moving, but it won't get you very far. At least not without damage on the way. You might tell yourself, "I need to do better." "I have to get it right this time." "I can't let anyone down." That pressure *feels* like progress—until it doesn't.

Psychologists have long warned that guilt-motivated behavior often leads to burnout, resentment, or relapse. Why? Because guilt focuses on avoiding punishment, not building purpose. It says, "I messed up, so I have to fix myself to feel worthy again."

Guilt is rooted in fear: Fear of failure. Fear of rejection. Fear of being "too much" or "not enough." And the research is clear: Lasting change doesn't grow well in soil fertilized by guilt and shame.

The gospel offers a radically different starting point. Not guilt. Not fear. But grace.

Galatians 5:1 is Paul's mic drop: "It is for freedom that Christ has set us free." Freedom from guilt-as-a-goalkeeper. Freedom from trying to outrun your flaws. Freedom from living on edge, afraid of letting God or others down. That kind of fear-based motivation might produce short-term compliance, but it never creates long-term transformation.

What does? Love. Hope. Purpose. The kind of fuel that doesn't run out when you mess up. The kind that runs deeper the more you understand it.

So if you've been chasing spiritual or emotional growth just to make up for your mistakes—stop. You don't need to hustle to be whole. You're already loved. Start there.

Anchor Truth

Guilt is a terrible engine for growth. Real change flows from grace, not pressure. And Jesus invites you to start from freedom, not fear.

Prayer

God, I confess I've been trying to fix myself out of guilt. Help me let go of that weight and move forward with your grace as my fuel.

Invitation

Take one step today—not out of guilt, but from a place of love. Do something life-giving to remind yourself that you're already enough in Christ.

When Your Work Feels Meaningless

And whatever you do or say, do it as a representative of the Lord Jesus, giving thanks through him to God the Father.

COLOSSIANS 3:17

Maybe you love your work—if so, pause and give thanks. What a gift, to rise each day with passion for what you do. This one, though, is for those who don't.

For the person who feels stuck in a job that pays the bills but drains the soul. For the one clocking in and counting down. For the stay-at-home parent wondering if anyone sees. For the caregiver worn thin. For the burned-out, the overqualified, the overlooked. Many people quietly carry this kind of weariness, unsure if their efforts matter. It's a slow kind of soul erosion.

But the truth is, meaning isn't reserved for people in glamorous roles or dream jobs. Meaning is made, not found. And it begins when you shift from asking, "Do I love this?" to "Can I love through this?"

Scripture doesn't romanticize work. It acknowledges its toil (Genesis 3:19), yet also affirms its dignity. Paul reminds us that even in ordinary tasks, we're "serving the Lord Christ" (Colossians 3:24, ESV). When you fold a shirt, send a message, sweep a floor, or fill out a form, you're participating in something bigger—especially when love, care, or integrity is behind it.

What about the mental health connection? Research shows that meaningful work—even in small doses—fuels motivation, resilience, and emotional strength. And meaning doesn't require a dream job. It grows when you know your *why*.

You might not be able to change your job tomorrow. But you can reclaim the meaning in what you're doing today. Shift your focus from task to impact. From job to journey. From performance to purpose.

Our well-being is deeply tied to a sense of purpose. You don't have to stay in a meaningless place forever, but while you're there, you can invite meaning in. Through love. Through intention. Through remembering who you really serve.

Anchor Truth

When your work becomes an offering, even the routine becomes rich.

Prayer

God, I admit—sometimes my work feels dry and lifeless. Help me see it through your eyes. Infuse my tasks with purpose. Let me remember that small things, done with love, can make an eternal difference.

Invitation

Today, take one ordinary task and give it a purpose. Pray as you do it. Bless someone quietly through it. Then watch how meaning starts to return.

Learning to Get Back Up—Again

You intended to harm me, but God intended it all for good.

GENESIS 50:20

Resilience isn't about a dramatic comeback. It's about getting back up again. And again. And again. Not once. Not perfectly. Just faithfully.

Joseph knew what it meant to be knocked down—by betrayal, by lies, by injustice. He was sold by his brothers. Thrown in a pit. Imprisoned for something he didn't do. Forgotten by the people he helped. And yet, he got back up. Not because life got easier, but because grace held him every time he fell.

Resilience doesn't mean the hits don't hurt. It means you don't let the hurt be the end of your story. And clinically speaking, one of the most important aspects of resilience is what psychologists call *psychological recovery capital*—the ability to draw from inner and outer resources when you've been knocked down. That might look like faith. Support. Purpose. Or simply remembering that this won't last forever.

Joseph could've let bitterness become his identity. Instead, he stayed open. He interpreted dreams. He led in prison. He served with excellence. And when the time came, he forgave with grace: "You intended to harm me, but God intended it all for good." That's resilience—not rewriting the story, but redeeming it.

You don't need to bounce back with strength you don't feel. Just rise, one inch at a time, with the strength you have. Even if it's shaky. Even if you're still healing.

Falling doesn't disqualify you from growing. Getting back up, even slowly, is what builds resilience.

Anchor Truth

Resilience isn't about never falling. It's about trusting that every rise, no matter how messy, is part of your healing.

Prayer

God, I've been knocked down more than once. And sometimes I wonder if I have what it takes to get back up again. But I believe you're with me in the rising. Strengthen my heart, and help me take the next step forward.

Invitation

Look back on a time you got back up after something hard. It may have taken weeks or years, but you did it. Let that memory remind you that falling didn't stop you then, and it won't stop you now.

The Armor That Keeps You Lonely

People who conceal their sins will not prosper,
but if they confess and turn from them,
they will receive mercy.

PROVERBS 28:13

Sometimes what protects you also isolates you. Maybe you learned early on to keep it light. Stay agreeable. Be competent. Be needed. You offer surface-level honesty while keeping the deeper stuff under wraps. People like you. They say you're steady, selfless, funny, strong. But deep down, you're not sure if anyone truly knows you—or if they'd still love you if they did.

We all wear emotional armor. And usually there's a good reason for it. That armor helped us get through a hard season. Or a traumatic relationship. Or a childhood where emotions weren't safe. Maybe it started as wisdom. But over time, it became a wall.

It's called *protective masking*—a coping strategy rooted in fear. It allows you to function, but not flourish. It makes you likable, but not fully loved. Because here's the hard truth: You can't receive real connection while hiding behind a persona.

The ancient wisdom of Proverbs points to this when it says that those who conceal won't prosper—not because they're morally failing, but because they're relationally blocked.

Healing, mercy, and connection begin the moment we get honest. And that starts by choosing someone—just one person, even—who is safe enough to see you. You don't have to spill everything to everyone. Vulnerability isn't about recklessness. It's about brave, intentional honesty with people who've earned your trust.

It's also about telling the truth to God. Sometimes the first step in dropping your guard is admitting to him what you've been pretending not to feel.

Anchor Truth

The parts of you that you're most tempted to hide may be the ones most in need of love.

Prayer

God, I'm tired of the act. Show me where I've been hiding. Help me take a small, brave step toward deeper connection—with you and with others.

Invitation

What's one mask you tend to wear in relationships? Name it. This week, risk lowering it, just a little, with someone safe.

Falling Leaders, Failing Confidence

Don't put your confidence in powerful people;
there is no help for you there.

PSALM 146:3

You never expected to see the headlines. Or scroll past the screenshots. Or hear the audio clips, the leaked emails, the teary online confessions. You never expected to watch someone you admired unravel in real time—in front of the whole internet.

When a spiritual leader falls—morally, financially, sexually, spiritually—it shakes more than just the person involved. It can send an entire community into confusion and grief. And for you? It may have left a crack in your faith you didn't know how to name.

You trusted them. You looked up to them. Maybe you even shaped your view of God around their voice. So when they lied, manipulated, abused their power—your confidence in everything started to falter.

This kind of disillusionment is a form of *betrayal trauma*—when your trust is violated by someone who represents safety and moral authority. In spiritual settings, the impact cuts even deeper because leaders are often viewed not just as people, but as spiritual symbols. So when they fall, it doesn't feel like just they failed—it can feel like God did.

Psalm 146 offers a blunt but freeing reminder: "Don't put your confidence in powerful people." That doesn't mean you should trust no one. It means human leaders, no matter how gifted, are still human. Capable of getting it wrong. Capable of causing harm. Capable of needing grace and accountability, just like the rest of us.

If a leader's failure has made your faith feel unstable, you're not overreacting. You're grieving. And that grief deserves space.

But please know this: Their actions don't undo your experience with God. They may have misrepresented him, but they are not him.

It's okay to step back. To ask hard questions. To reevaluate everything. Just don't confuse a shattered pedestal with a shattered faith. They're not the same.

Anchor Truth

Spiritual leaders may fall, but God never will. Their behavior still impacts us, but we can put our confidence in God himself.

Prayer

God, I'm disillusioned. I trusted someone who claimed to speak for you, and now I don't know what to do with the anger, the hurt, and the doubt that followed. Help me separate their voice from yours. Show me who you are beyond what they did.

Invitation

Has someone's failure caused you to question your faith? Write down one way that person shaped your view of God—for better or worse. Then whisper, "They are not God. And God is not them."

The Grief You Didn't Know You Were Carrying

The Spirit of the Sovereign LORD is on me, because the LORD has anointed me to proclaim good news to the poor. He has sent me to bind up the brokenhearted, to proclaim freedom for the captives and release from darkness for the prisoners.

ISAIAH 61:1 (NIV)

Grief isn't just about funerals. It's also about the job you didn't get. The friendship that faded. The marriage that didn't turn out the way you imagined. The body that's aging. The child who pulled away. The life you thought you'd be living by now.

Grief is the ache of absence, the emotional echo of something lost. Sometimes it's loud and obvious. Sometimes it's a quiet hollow you can't quite name. Either way, it hurts.

Grief is a natural, normal, and necessary response to loss—any loss. Not just death. Divorce, infertility, a move across the country, a betrayal, the finality of "used to be," even aging itself—all can stir sorrow. And yet, because these kinds of grief don't often come with casseroles and sympathy cards, we tend to minimize them.

We call ourselves "too sensitive" or "dramatic" or "ungrateful." We shove it down and keep going. But unacknowledged grief doesn't disappear. It just hardens. And over time, that quiet sorrow can shape how we show up in the world—with guardedness, cynicism, anxiety, or even chronic exhaustion.

The truth is, you don't have to earn your grief by losing everything. You're allowed to grieve what didn't go the way you hoped. You're allowed to name what hurts, even if others don't see it. Because God sees it.

He's not only close to the shattered-hearted. He's near the quietly aching, too. The ones who smile in public but feel hollow in private. The ones who keep showing up while carrying silent losses.

The point is that God doesn't show up only at gravesides. He shows up in the everyday aches. In the what-ifs. In the not-yets. In the things that could've been. You don't have to keep carrying it alone. Grief is a sign of what you've loved, and love is never wasted.

Let God meet you in what you've lost. Because that's exactly where healing begins.

Anchor Truth

Grief comes in many forms, but so does God's comfort.

Prayer

God, I've lost some things I didn't even give myself permission to mourn. Help me name what I've buried. Thank you for being close, even when I pretend I'm fine. I'm done pretending. Meet me in the ache.

Invitation

What "small" grief have you minimized? Say it out loud or write it down today. God is not asking you to get over it. He's inviting you to bring it into the light.

What Are Healthy Boundaries and Why Do They Matter?

Guard your heart above all else,
for it determines the course of your life.

PROVERBS 4:23

We hear a lot about setting boundaries, but what are they, really? Healthy boundaries are limits we set to protect what matters most: our mental health, emotional peace, and sacred relationships. They help us define where we end and someone else begins. They tell the world, "This is what I will allow. This is what I won't. This is who I am—and who I'm not."

But let's be honest: Boundary-setting can feel uncomfortable. Especially if you're used to keeping the peace, over-giving, or letting guilt call the shots. You might wonder if it's selfish to say no. Or unkind to protect your time, energy, or emotional space.

It's not. It's wisdom.

The Bible doesn't use the word *boundaries* in this way, but the concept is laced into the fabric of Scripture. God created borders—between day and night, land and sea. Jesus stepped away from crowds to rest, said no to premature expectations, and didn't allow guilt or manipulation to drive his decisions.

In psychological terms, boundaries are essential to emotional regulation and relational health. People without them tend to feel overwhelmed, resentful, used—or completely shut down. People with rigid boundaries can become isolated.

But healthy boundaries? They create safety and connection without sacrificing selfhood. Boundaries aren't about pushing people away. They're about letting people in with clarity. And when you guard your heart—not with walls, but with wisdom—you stop living on autopilot or under obligation.

You start living from intention. With peace. With purpose.

Anchor Truth

Boundaries are a form of self-respect. They protect what's sacred so love can flourish in a healthy way.

Prayer

God, help me recognize where I've let others override my limits or where I've lost myself trying to please them. Give me the courage to guard my heart, not with fear but with clarity. Teach me to love others without losing myself.

Invitation

What area of your life feels out of control right now? It might be a sign that a boundary is needed. Ask God to show you one step you can take to guard your heart and restore your peace.

Progress, Not Perfection

And I am certain that God, who began the good work within you, will continue his work until it is finally finished.

PHILIPPIANS 1:6

Perfectionism demands instant results. No room for error. No margin for failure. It says, "You should be further along by now." But God doesn't say that.

God starts with the long view. He begins a good work and then continues it. Which means you're in process, not on trial. You're becoming, not failing. In clinical terms, this is the shift from a *fixed mindset* to a *growth mindset.*

Instead of seeing failure as proof of inadequacy, a growth mindset sees it as part of progress. Research shows that this mental shift improves long-term mental health. And here's the spiritual parallel: Grace doesn't demand perfection. It invites transformation. Slowly. Steadily. Patiently. Like a potter with clay or a gardener with seed.

Perfectionism says, "Get it right the first time." God says, "Let's work this out together."

The early followers of Jesus didn't "arrive" overnight. Peter sank. Thomas doubted. Paul had to grow out of his self-righteousness. They all stumbled forward. But God kept working with them and in them.

You can release the shame of not being "done" yet. God is not rushing you toward some invisible standard. He is forming you, layer by layer, through both victories and setbacks. And he won't stop halfway.

You're allowed to be in progress. That's how God works—with grace, with time, and with you.

Anchor Truth

God's not waiting for perfection. He's celebrating your progress.

Prayer

God, I often feel like I should be further along. But you're not in a hurry with me. You're faithful to finish what you start. Help me trust the process and see growth, even when it's slow.

Invitation

Reflect on one area where you've grown, even if imperfectly. Celebrate the step, not just the outcome. Then remind yourself, "Progress is proof that God is still at work in me."

Living Under the Gray Sky

The light shines in the darkness,
and the darkness can never extinguish it.

JOHN 1:5

Not all depression storms in like a hurricane. Sometimes it drizzles quietly for years. It's called *persistent depressive disorder*—a chronic, low-grade depression that lingers like a gray sky you can't escape.

You may still go to work, care for your family, check all the boxes. But inside, you feel flat. Empty. Tired. The colors of life seem muted. And maybe you've started to think this is just how life is. Just how *you* are. But it's not.

You were created for joy—not constant euphoria, but the quiet, sacred kind that returns again and again, like the sun breaking through clouds.

Many biblical figures show signs of persistent struggle. Consider Jeremiah, often called the "weeping prophet." His calling was marked by sorrow, rejection, and long, lonely faithfulness. Or Naomi, who renamed herself Mara (meaning "bitter") after enduring loss upon loss. They didn't fake joy. They lived in the ache. But they didn't walk it alone.

Your low mood isn't a moral failure. It's a signal—one worth listening to. Persistent depression is treatable. There is no trophy for toughing it out. There is no shame in reaching for help.

Healing may be slow. But it's possible. And it begins when you stop calling darkness your home. Remember this: Even if you can't see the light right now, it's still shining. The clouds don't cancel the sun. They only obscure it for a time.

God has not gone silent. Joy is not extinct. You are not stuck forever. Keep going. Even a small step toward light counts as sacred ground. Because the light *does* shine in the darkness, and the darkness can never extinguish it.

Anchor Truth

Long-standing sadness doesn't mean you're beyond hope. Healing is possible, even if it takes time.

Prayer

God, I've forgotten what light feels like. Restore the flicker inside me. Help me believe that life can be more than just getting through.

Invitation

Have you been feeling low for a long time? Don't dismiss it. Talk to a counselor, a doctor, a trusted friend. There's help for this kind of heaviness.

Quiet Doesn't Mean Insecure

Better to be patient than powerful;
better to have self-control than to conquer a city.

PROVERBS 16:32

If you've ever been told you're "too quiet" or been asked, "Why don't you speak up more?" you may have wondered if something is wrong with you. Maybe you've even started to believe that being quieter means being less confident or less worthy.

But here's the truth: Being an introvert isn't a flaw. It's not a weakness. It's not a sign of insecurity. It's a personality trait, one wired into your nervous system and temperament.

Introverts often gain energy through solitude, prefer depth over small talk, and think before they speak. That's not shameful. It's wise.

In a world that often praises loud personalities, introversion can get misinterpreted as insecurity. But silence doesn't always mean fear. Stillness doesn't always mean weakness.

Some of the strongest people in Scripture and history were deeply introspective. Think of Mary, the mother of Jesus. After the shepherds' visit, Luke tells us, "Mary treasured up all these things and pondered them in her heart" (Luke 2:19, NIV). She wasn't leading the room. She was quietly absorbing the moment, and yet she was favored by God.

Research tells us that introversion is distinct from social anxiety or low self-worth. The key difference is that introverts may *enjoy* people, but they need alone time to recharge. Those with insecurity or social fear may *dread* interaction altogether due to fear of judgment or rejection. Or they become adept at posing.

There's freedom in embracing your God-given wiring. You don't have to apologize for being reserved. You don't have to fake loudness to prove you're okay.

The world doesn't need more noise. It needs more depth. More presence. More patience. More thoughtful voices who speak not to be heard, but to say something worth hearing. And maybe that's you.

Anchor Truth

Your quiet nature is not a defect to fix. It's a design to honor. God delights in the whole of who you are—including your calm, reflective, steady self.

Prayer

God, thank you for wiring me the way you did. Help me stop comparing myself to louder voices or faster movers. Remind me that I can live fully, speak truthfully, and love deeply—even when I do it quietly.

Invitation

Instead of trying to "fix" your quietness, start to see it as a gift. Notice how your introversion allows you to listen deeply, notice details, and create space for others. You don't need to become louder to be valuable, just more at home in your own skin.

Let Go, For Real

Sin is no longer your master, for you no longer live under the requirements of the law. Instead, you live under the freedom of God's grace.

ROMANS 6:14

You've promised yourself before, "This is the last time." You delete the app. Dump the bottle. Block the site. You clench your fists. Dig in your heels. And try harder. And for a while, it works—until it doesn't.

That's the exhausting cycle of *white-knuckling*—gripping harder and harder, trying to force your way into freedom. But all that tension, all that effort? It's unsustainable.

Eventually your fingers cramp. Your willpower cracks. And the guilt rolls back in like a tide. White-knuckling feels like control. But it's actually just fear in disguise.

Addiction recovery—whether from substances, screens, control, or approval—isn't about strength. It's about surrender—not giving up, but giving over. The gospel doesn't say, "Be strong enough to beat this." It says, "You live in freedom."

God's power shows up not in your clenched fists, but in your open hands. Surrender means admitting, "I can't do this alone. I need help." It means trusting that grace is more effective than grit. It means accepting that your healing might take longer than you'd like—and that's okay.

There's nothing weak about asking for support. Or seeing a counselor. Or joining a group. That's not failure. It's wisdom.

Surrender isn't passive. It's brave. It's having the courage to stop pretending you can save yourself. It's loosening your grip so you can finally exhale.

Anchor Truth

Your strength won't save you. Grace will.

Prayer

God, I've been trying to muscle my way through this, but I'm tired. Help me loosen my grip and trust that you're with me, not disappointed in me.

Invitation

Where are you still white-knuckling your healing? Identify one area where you could trade willpower for support and take one concrete step today.

Don't Wait to Feel Ready

Be strong and courageous! Do not be afraid or discouraged. For the LORD your God is with you wherever you go.

JOSHUA 1:9

Readiness is a mirage. It looks real from a distance, but try to get close, and it keeps moving just out of reach. You think, *I'll start when I feel more confident. I'll speak up when I'm less anxious. I'll make the change when I'm stronger.*

But what if those feelings never show up? What if courage isn't the prerequisite but the companion to the first shaky step?

When God commissioned Joshua to lead, he didn't wait until Joshua felt ready. In fact, God told him to be strong and courageous, which implies that he wasn't. He was probably terrified. And still, the command was to go.

Readiness isn't about how you feel. It's about how you move. We call it *activation energy*, the mental resistance you feel just before starting something hard. That resistance doesn't mean you're not ready. It just means you're human. Most people wait to act until their fear goes away. But people with agency act while the fear is still there.

That first step might feel awkward. You might second-guess yourself. That's normal. But don't let discomfort convince you that delay is more faithful than action. You can be afraid and still be moving in the right direction.

You don't need to feel ready. You need to remember who's with you. And move anyway.

Anchor Truth

Courage doesn't mean you're ready. It means you're willing.

Prayer

God, I often wait until I feel strong or certain before I act. But you never asked for that. You asked for trust. Walk with me as I step into things I don't feel ready for. Remind me that I'm not doing this alone.

Invitation

What's one action you've been putting off while waiting to "feel ready"? Name it. Then do a first step—messy, small, or unsure. Just move.

Be the Safe Place

Live in harmony with each other. Don't be too proud to enjoy the company of ordinary people. And don't think you know it all!

ROMANS 12:16

Everyone's carrying something. A private ache. A story they've edited down to sound less painful. A shame they've named a dozen different things to keep it at arm's length. And most people are just trying to figure out: *Is it safe to be real with you?*

That's the power you hold: You can be the person who offers safety or the reason someone retreats. Emotional safety isn't just something you receive. It's something you give. And it may be the greatest gift your presence offers.

Being someone's emotionally safe friend doesn't mean you have all the answers. It means you listen without hijacking the conversation with your own story. You don't flinch at their feelings, even the big ones. You don't slap on spiritual platitudes to patch their pain. You don't rush them. Or fix them. Or advise them when they just need to be heard.

It means you honor their trust like it's something sacred. You show up gently, consistently, humbly.

Romans 12:16 gives us a beautiful picture of what that looks like: Live in harmony, stay humble, don't act superior. That's emotional safety in a sentence.

People open up when they sense you're not judging them, comparing them, or trying to one-up their vulnerability. They soften when they see that you're not playing the expert, but are instead walking beside them as a fellow traveler.

If you've ever had someone be that kind of friend to you, you know how healing it is. And if you haven't—you know how much it hurts not to have it.

So let's be the friend we've longed for. Because when you become a refuge for someone else, you just might discover healing of your own.

Anchor Truth

You don't have to be a therapist or have all the answers. You just have to show up with empathy, humility, and a heart that says, "You're safe here."

Prayer

Jesus, make me the kind of friend who helps others breathe easier. Help me to listen well, speak gently, and offer the kind of presence that reflects your love.

Invitation

Think of someone who might need emotional safety right now, perhaps a person who's going through something they haven't fully named. Reach out—not with advice, but with presence. Let them know they're not alone.

Your Emotions Aren't the Enemy

Be angry, and do not sin.
Meditate within your heart on your bed, and be still.

PSALM 4:4 (NKJV)

A lot of us grew up with the message that emotions are dangerous. That anger is sinful. That sadness is weakness. That fear is a lack of faith. So we stuffed it. Smoothed it over. Called it "trusting God."

But buried emotions don't disappear. They just go underground. And eventually they show up somewhere else—in your body, your relationships, your decisions, your mental health.

The truth is, your emotions aren't your enemy. They're messengers. Signals. Alerts from your inner world that something needs attention, not avoidance.

Psalm 4:4 gives permission for anger but also puts it in its place: "Be angry, and do not sin." That's the line. Feel it, but don't let it drive. Reflect on it. Sit with it overnight if needed. Don't react. Respond.

Self-awareness means learning how to listen to your emotions without letting them hijack you. It's not about suppressing your feelings—it's about *regulating* them. Naming them. Understanding where they come from. Choosing how you want to act in light of them.

This is core to emotional intelligence. In clinical terms, it's the foundation of *affect labeling*—the ability to name a feeling as you're experiencing it. When you label your emotions accurately, your brain actually calms down. You regain perspective. You reclaim agency.

God doesn't shame you for feeling. He's not asking you to be numb or detached. He's inviting you to pay attention—to get honest about what's under the surface and bring it into the light.

Anchor Truth

Your emotions aren't a problem to fix. They're a signal to notice.

Prayer

God, help me stop judging myself for what I feel. Teach me to listen without reacting, to name emotions without fear, and to bring them to you honestly. You can handle all of it. Help me believe that.

Invitation

When you feel something rise today—frustration, hurt, joy, shame—pause. Ask, "What is this feeling trying to tell me?" Don't push it away. Get curious.

Safe to Be Seen

Therefore encourage one another and build each other up, just as in fact you are doing.

1 THESSALONIANS 5:11 (NIV)

Let's be honest: Emotional safety isn't just a nice idea, it's oxygen for the soul. Without it, relationships choke. And we do too.

Emotional safety means you can be fully human without paying a price for it. It means you don't have to calculate your tone or edit your truth. You don't have to trade authenticity for acceptance. When safety's present, you can let your guard down because you know you won't be punished for being real.

But when it's missing? People pretend. They perform. They avoid. Marriages become cold or combative. Friendships turn surface-level. Families orbit around one unspoken rule: *Don't upset the system*. Churches become stages instead of sanctuaries. And spiritual growth stalls.

When you're not safe, you stop showing up. Not just physically—but emotionally, mentally, spiritually. You wear a mask, play the part, and wonder why you still feel so alone.

Some people have never experienced true emotional safety. Is that you? Maybe you grew up walking on eggshells. Maybe your vulnerability was mocked. Maybe your pain was ignored, your needs dismissed. So now, even when someone offers safety, you flinch. You've been trained to hide.

But listen closely: Jesus doesn't shame you for that. He sees your bracing. He understands your fear. And he's not asking you to fake it. He's offering you safety. Not safety from discomfort, but safety in love. Not immunity from pain, but protection from abandonment.

Jesus was the safest person to ever walk the planet. He didn't minimize people's pain. He didn't weaponize their weaknesses. He looked them in the eye and called them by name. He told the truth with tenderness. And he offered grace before they got their act together.

That's the kind of safety your soul craves. And that's the kind Jesus still offers today.

Anchor Truth

Emotional safety isn't about softening the truth. It's about speaking it with love, grounded in grace. Jesus is your safest place.

Prayer

Jesus, I've learned to hide parts of myself out of fear. Meet me in those places. Show me what it means to feel safe in your presence. Teach me how to offer that kind of safety to others and to myself.

Invitation

Where in your life have you been wearing emotional armor? Ask Jesus to meet you there. Let him show you what it feels like to be fully seen and still loved.

The Body Carries Memories

Honor God with your body.

1 CORINTHIANS 6:20

You may be years removed from what happened. You may have talked it through. Prayed it through. Worked hard to move forward.

But then your heart races out of nowhere. Your chest tightens. Your stomach sinks. You freeze. Or lash out. Or completely shut down. And it makes no sense—except that it does.

Because the body remembers. Long after trauma passes, your nervous system still scans for danger. Still sounds the alarm. Still tries to protect you, even if it doesn't need to anymore. This isn't overreaction. It's survival wiring that got stuck in the "on" position.

Your body isn't betraying you. It's trying to keep you alive. It's been faithful to you, even in its fear.

That's why healing from trauma isn't just about thinking differently; it's also about feeling safe in your skin again. Learning to breathe, to ground, to soothe. To speak to your body with the same compassion God offers your soul.

Paul wrote, "Honor God with your body." That includes listening to it. Caring for it. Treating it not as a burden, but as a sacred place that has carried you through more than anyone knows.

Jesus honored bodies. He touched lepers. He healed with his hands. He sweat, wept, bled. And he didn't just save your soul—he came to restore your whole being.

You don't have to hate your body for remembering. You can thank it for surviving and invite it into the healing too.

Anchor Truth

Your body is not the enemy. It's a survivor. God sees it. Loves it. And is redeeming it, one breath at a time.

Prayer

God, I don't always feel safe inside myself. My body carries memories I didn't choose. Help me show it kindness, not blame. Teach me to care for it, to listen to it, and to trust that healing can happen here too.

Invitation

Take a moment to breathe deeply while you place a hand over your heart. Say this aloud: "Thank you, body, for keeping me alive. God, help me make peace with the place where I live."

Faith After Trauma—Can I Still Believe?

Lord, I believe; help my unbelief!

MARK 9:24 (NKJV)

You used to believe more easily. Prayers came naturally. Worship felt real. Scripture brought comfort. But trauma changes things. It shakes the ground beneath your faith. You may wonder now, *Where was God? Why didn't he stop it? Can I trust him again? What does faith even look like after this?*

These aren't signs of spiritual failure. They're signs of honest wrestling.

Trauma doesn't just wound the body or emotions. It impacts what we believe about God, safety, justice, love, and even ourselves. When your world breaks, it's hard to know how to relate to the one who's supposed to hold it all together.

If you've found yourself questioning your faith after trauma, you're not backsliding—you're healing. Faith that's never tested may feel pure, but faith that walks through the fire and still whispers, "Help me" is something sacred.

In Mark 9, a desperate father brings his suffering child to Jesus and says, "Lord, I believe; help my unbelief!" And Jesus doesn't rebuke him. He meets him there. He honors the tension.

God can handle your doubts. Your questions. Your silence. He's not fragile. He doesn't love you less for struggling to trust him again. In fact, he draws near to the brokenhearted, and that includes hearts broken by what they can't explain.

You don't need perfect faith to be held by a perfect God. You just need to keep reaching, even with trembling hands.

Anchor Truth

Faith after trauma may look different, but it's still faith. God meets you in the middle of belief and doubt.

Prayer

God, I don't always know how to believe anymore. I miss the clarity I used to have. But I want to believe again. Help me trust you in a new way—honest, messy, but real.

Invitation

If you're struggling with faith, name one thing you can still believe—no matter how small. Start there. Let that flicker be enough for today.

Self-Directed Anger

Why am I discouraged? Why is my heart so sad?
I will put my hope in God!

PSALM 42:5

Not all anger explodes outward. Some of it turns inward—quiet, corrosive, and sharp. This kind of anger doesn't yell at others, it punishes *you*. You replay the mistake. You scold yourself in your mind. You call yourself names you'd never say to someone else. And you wear the guilt like penance, hoping it'll earn you back some peace.

This is *self-directed anger*—when the critic in your head sounds louder than compassion. It tells you that you're not doing enough, not trying hard enough, not good enough. And it often masquerades as humility. But it's not humility. It's hostility turned inward.

You may have been raised to believe that being hard on yourself is "virtuous." That self-punishment is how you grow. That shame is the path to holiness. But that's not the voice of God. That's the voice of fear.

Even David, the psalmist, had to speak back to his own soul: "Why are you so downcast?" He didn't berate himself. He got curious. He paused to name the ache. And then he pointed his heart gently back toward hope.

If you're caught in a loop of self-directed anger, here's the truth: You don't have to be your own enemy. You can be your own witness. Your own advocate. You can learn to hold your regret without turning it into a weapon. That doesn't mean excusing harmful choices. It means refusing to believe that punishment is the only path to change.

Compassion fuels transformation more than condemnation ever could.

Anchor Truth

Beating yourself up is not the same as taking responsibility.

Prayer

God, I'm so quick to turn my anger against myself. Teach me to speak to my soul the way you do—with truth, but also tenderness.

Invitation

Next time you catch yourself spiraling in self-criticism, pause. Ask, "Would I say this to someone I love?" If not, try again—with more grace.

When the Inner Critic Gets Loud

Even if we feel guilty, God is greater than our feelings, and he knows everything.

1 JOHN 3:20

There's a voice that lives in the mind of many of us from time to time, but especially in the mind of a perfectionist. It sounds like your own, but it's not kind. It says things like "That wasn't good enough." "You should've known better." "You always mess things up." "Everyone else is doing it better." "Why can't you get it right?" That's your inner critic, and it's ruthless.

This voice doesn't motivate. It shames. And instead of pushing you forward, it keeps you trapped—afraid to try, afraid to rest, afraid to be seen.

You might think it's the voice of God, because it sounds moral, demanding, and serious. But here's the truth: It isn't. God convicts to restore. The inner critic condemns to control.

And the voice of God is *always* rooted in love, even when it's firm. He may correct, but he never berates. He may challenge, but he never shames. "God is greater than our feelings," John reminds us. When your guilt gets loud, his grace gets louder.

Think of Peter. He failed spectacularly, denying Jesus three times. The inner critic could've destroyed him. But Jesus didn't meet him with a lecture. He met him with breakfast and a question: "Do you love me?" That's the voice of grace.

If your inner critic is stealing your joy, your courage, or your sense of identity, it's time to replace it with truth. God's voice may be convicting, but it is always compassionate.

You don't have to obey the voice that tears you down. Tune your heart to the voice that builds you up.

Anchor Truth

Your inner critic isn't your conscience, and it isn't God. His voice is kinder, wiser, and always laced with grace.

Prayer

God, sometimes I confuse your voice with my own harsh thoughts. Help me tell the difference. Quiet the critic in my mind and help me hear your truth instead—rooted in grace, not shame.

Invitation

Pay attention today when the inner critic speaks. Then pause and ask, "Is this how God would speak to me?" If not, replace it with truth. Memorize 1 John 3:20 and let it become your new inner voice.

More than the Screen

I will not be mastered by anything.

1 CORINTHIANS 6:12 (NIV)

Let's talk about pornography. Not to shock or shame. But to name something real—something many wrestle with but rarely bring into the light.

For some, it's a compulsion. For others, it's occasional. For many, it's complicated. And for nearly all, it's a source of quiet struggle.

Porn promises connection but delivers isolation. It offers pleasure but often leaves behind shame, numbness, and guilt. It becomes a substitute for real intimacy, real presence, real emotion.

But here's the truth no one talks about enough: You don't have to be addicted for it to affect you. It might not rule your life, but it might still be rewiring it.

Neuroscience reveals that repetitive exposure to porn reshapes your brain's reward system, dulls natural desire, and trains you to dissociate emotion from intimacy. It doesn't just impact your habits. It shapes your lens. It distorts what bodies are for, what connection means, and what love looks like.

This isn't about moral panic. This is about freedom. Paul's words are striking: "I will not be mastered by anything." Not because pleasure is bad—but because being mastered by anything strips you of agency, presence, and peace.

So if you find yourself clicking in moments of loneliness or stress—numbing instead of engaging—know that you're invited into more. More than managing the shame. More than pretending you're fine. More than numbing yourself to the ache.

You're invited into real connection. Real healing. Real freedom. It starts by being honest. And refusing to be mastered.

Anchor Truth

What numbs you will eventually control you unless you bring it into the light.

Prayer

God, I want more than quick escapes; I want real healing. Help me face what I've been hiding and trust that you meet me with grace, not shame.

Invitation

Notice what draws you toward the screen. Is it stress? Boredom? Loneliness? Be curious, not condemning. Then bring that need to God, not just the behavior.

When the Past Keeps Following You

Forget the former things; do not dwell on the past. See, I am doing a new thing!

ISAIAH 43:18-19 (NIV)

You've moved on, at least on paper. The event is behind you. The person is gone. The crisis has passed. But it still follows you. In the quiet. In the flash of a sound. In the way you flinch. In the moments when your heart races and you can't explain why.

This is one of the cruelest parts of trauma: It doesn't stay in the past. It lives in your body, in your brain, in your relationships. Long after the moment ends, the effects echo.

You wonder, *Why can't I just get over it?* But trauma doesn't respond to willpower. It's not just a memory. It's a wound. And it takes time, care, and often professional support to begin healing.

You're not weak for still feeling it. You're human.

God knows this about you. That's why when he says, "Forget the former things," he doesn't mean ignore them or pretend they didn't happen. He means, "Don't dwell there. Don't stay stuck in the place where you were hurt." God is doing something new—not in spite of your pain, but through it.

Think of Joseph—betrayed, trafficked by his own brothers, falsely accused, forgotten in prison. His trauma didn't vanish overnight. But years later, when he saw his brothers again, he said, "You meant to harm me, but God intended it all for good."

That's not denial. That's redemption. Your past may still visit you, but it doesn't get to define you. God is not finished with your story.

Anchor Truth

Your trauma has shaped you, but it has not sealed your future.

Prayer

God, sometimes I feel stuck in moments that should be behind me. Help me be gentle with myself. And help me believe that the past is not the only thing shaping me—you are.

Invitation

When the past shows up today—in a thought, a feeling, a reaction—pause and breathe. Instead of judging yourself, whisper this: "God is doing something new, even here."

When Sleep Won't Come

In peace I will lie down and sleep,
for you alone, O LORD, will keep me safe.

PSALM 4:8

There's something about the dark that makes everything feel louder. The thoughts you kept at bay during the day come rushing in. The fears get sharper. The silence feels suffocating. And sleep, something so natural, suddenly feels impossible.

You've tried the routine. You've adjusted the lights. Maybe you've even prayed. But still, your mind won't slow down. Your heart won't settle. Your body won't rest.

And then comes the shame. You think, *Why can't I just let go? Why am I like this? Why does my body feel wired when I'm utterly exhausted?*

Here's why: When you finally lie down, your brain loses the noise of the day—but not the noise inside. Without distractions, your nervous system has space to process what it's been suppressing. And if anxiety is lingering under the surface, it often surges when the world goes quiet.

The clinical term for this is *hyperarousal*—a heightened state of alertness that makes it difficult to relax, fall asleep, or feel safe, even when there's no actual danger. Your brain is still operating in fight-or-flight mode, as if there's danger, even though you're lying in bed.

That's not your fault. That's not a failure of faith or discipline. That's how anxiety works. It doesn't clock out at bedtime. In fact, it works the night shift. Your body is still in protection mode. Your brain is trying to stay alert. It thinks you need to stay ready, just in case.

But here's what's also true: You don't have to be fully calm to be fully loved. And you don't have to be asleep to be held. In Psalm 4, David doesn't fall asleep because everything is fixed. He falls asleep because he trusts that he's not alone. That's what peace is—not the absence of struggle, but the presence of God within it.

So if you're staring at the ceiling again tonight, you're not failing. You're not forgotten. You're just tired—and that matters to God. Let the shame go. Keep breathing.

Anchor Truth

God is not waiting for you to calm down before he draws near. He meets you in the restless hours too.

Prayer

God, I want to rest, but I can't seem to let go. My thoughts keep circling, my body won't settle, and I feel like I'm losing control. Remind me that you are here, even now, and that I'm not alone in this night. Let your presence be my comfort and my calm. I surrender what I can't control and trust you to hold me.

Invitation

Write down one thing that's keeping you awake—just one. Then place the paper next to your bed, or even under your pillow, as a symbolic gesture of handing it to God. Let your bed be a place of surrender, not anxiety.

Gratitude for the People Who Shaped You

I thank my God every time I remember you.

PHILIPPIANS 1:3 (NIV)

Some people leave fingerprints on your soul. A teacher who believed in you. A friend who stood by you when everyone else bailed. A mentor who called something out of you that you didn't yet see. A parent, a pastor, a teammate, a stranger—you didn't get here on your own.

And maybe you've never stopped long enough to say thanks. Psychologists call it *relational gratitude*, and it's a key predictor of emotional well-being. Naming the people who have shaped you increases your empathy, deepens your sense of connection, and even improves physical health outcomes.

In other words, it changes you. That's not surprising when you look at Paul. He wrote, "I thank my God every time I remember you" while sitting in a Roman prison. This man had been beaten, betrayed, shipwrecked, and misunderstood. But when he wrote to the believers in Philippi, it wasn't with bitterness. It was with warmth, affection, and overflowing gratitude. He remembered their generosity, their partnership in the gospel, their loyalty. His words weren't perfunctory. They were saturated with emotion.

It's as if gratitude were the antidote to isolation. Paul didn't ignore his pain, but he didn't let it eclipse the people who had loved him well. He held their names close. He prayed with joy. And somehow, even from a dark, dank prison cell, he found light through the lens of memory.

Maybe you've done the same—whispered thanks for a grandmother's quiet faith, a friend's steady presence, or even a boss who challenged you to grow. Maybe you've never said it out loud, but you know who helped shape your soul. And maybe today's the day to remember that you've shaped someone else.

You may never see the full ripple effect of your love, your time, your faithfulness, but someone is thanking God when they remember *you*. Your presence has mattered more than you know.

Anchor Truth

Gratitude grows deeper when it has a name and a face.

Prayer

God, thank you for the people whose lives have touched mine with their time, their resources, their intentionality. Help me love others well, even though I may never know the impact I leave.

Invitation

Whose name came to mind when you read this? Write down their name. Whisper a prayer. Maybe even reach out and let them know. Because gratitude grows roots when it's expressed. And healing happens on both ends.

Resurrection, Virgin Birth, and Other Mysteries

God chose the foolish things of the world to shame the wise.
1 CORINTHIANS 1:27

Let's be honest: Some of the Bible is hard to believe. A virgin gives birth. A man walks on water. The dead come back to life. You're not trying to be difficult—you're just trying to be *honest.* And the more you engage your intellect, the harder it becomes to nod along as if these aren't wildly implausible claims.

From a psychological standpoint, what you may be experiencing is a disruption in your need for *cognitive closure*—the human desire for logical consistency and understandable explanations. It's a natural instinct. We want things to make sense, to be verifiable, to fit the rules of reality we've come to rely on.

But Christianity isn't built on what's logical. It's built on what's miraculous. And that's where the tension lies.

Some of us were taught that if we question any miracle, we're questioning everything. That faith is an all-or-nothing contract, and if one detail doesn't add up, the whole thing collapses. But that's not how faith works. You're allowed to struggle with mystery. You're allowed to hold questions in one hand and hope in the other.

Even the earliest disciples had doubts. Some stood face-to-face with the risen Jesus and *still* weren't sure what to believe. And yet, God doesn't seem threatened by it.

Maybe faith doesn't mean convincing yourself that everything makes sense. Maybe faith means staying curious even when it doesn't. Maybe it's choosing trust where certainty stops. And leaving room for the possibility that mystery might hold more truth than you can see right now.

Anchor Truth

God can handle your darkest doubts, even the parts of your faith that feel hardest to believe.

Prayer

God, I want to believe, but some things still feel impossible. Help me bring those doubts into the light instead of hiding them. Let mystery be a place where I meet you, not a reason to run.

Invitation

Write down the parts of your faith that feel hardest to believe. What scares you about naming those things?

Hungry for More

Can a mother forget her nursing child?
Can she feel no love for the child she has borne?
But even if that were possible, I would not forget you!
See, I have written your name on the palms of my hands.

ISAIAH 49:15-16

Attachment wounds are the hidden bruises left behind when love was inconsistent, unsafe, or unavailable. Maybe someone important let you down. Or walked away. Or simply couldn't offer the security your heart needed.

Those unmet needs don't vanish with time. They go underground, often reappearing as relational hunger—the aching desire to be seen, known, chosen, cherished. It's why some people chase relationships that never feel secure. Or keep walls high even when they crave connection. It's why you can feel empty in a crowd or desperate after a text goes unanswered.

These aren't character flaws. They're the echoes of an attachment system trying to make sense of old pain. But here's the good news: What formed in relationship can be healed in relationship. And that includes your relationship with God.

God doesn't shame your hunger. He meets it. Not always in the timing or form you expect, but always with presence.

Isaiah doesn't say God might forget you. He says it's unthinkable. And when you've been shaped by absence, that kind of unwavering presence is radical healing.

Healing begins when you stop blaming yourself for the ache and start bringing it to the one who's not afraid of it.

God is not distant. He's not withholding. He's not disappointed that you still long for more. He *is* the more your soul was made for.

Anchor Truth

The ache in your heart is not a flaw to fix. It's a signal pointing you back to the only love that truly satisfies.

Prayer

God, I've been carrying hunger I didn't fully understand. Help me to name the pain and trust that you won't turn away from it. Teach me how to let you in and slowly, safely, let others in too.

Invitation

Take ten minutes to reflect on any early wounds that might still be shaping how you seek (or avoid) connection today. Write a letter to God about that ache—honestly, without censoring. And let it be the beginning of healing.

The Strength to Bend, Not Break

Wherever you go, I will go; wherever you live, I will live. Your people will be my people, and your God will be my God.

RUTH 1:16

We often mistake resilience for rigidity—gritting our teeth, holding the line, pushing forward no matter the cost. But the truth is, resilience isn't about being unshakable. It's about being able to bend. Adapt. Adjust. Recalibrate. It's about remaining connected to your purpose even when the path keeps shifting. And that kind of flexibility? That's strength.

Ruth is a picture of that strength. She loses her husband, her home, and her cultural identity all at once—and yet she chooses loyalty. Movement. Forward motion. Not because it's easy, but because it's right. She says to Naomi, "Wherever you go, I will go."

Her resilience isn't loud, but it's relentless. It bends with grief, but it doesn't snap.

Clinical research shows that *emotional flexibility*—being able to adapt how we respond to stress—is a key predictor of long-term resilience. It's not denying emotions, but learning to shift perspective, stay grounded, and choose response over reaction.

Resilient people don't just endure; they adjust. They stop when needed. Cry when needed. Pivot when needed. And then they keep going

If life has knocked you sideways, this is your reminder: You're allowed to bend. You're allowed to change direction. That's not giving up. It's growing up. It's wisdom. It's survival. And it's holy.

You don't have to power through in a straight line. You just have to stay rooted enough to bend.

Anchor Truth

Resilience means that bending is not the same as breaking.

Prayer

God, I've tried to stay strong by staying rigid. But I see now that real strength means adapting, not pretending. Help me be like Ruth—anchored by love, open to change, willing to keep walking forward.

Invitation

Today, identify one area in your life where you've had to adapt. Name it as resilience, not failure. Let it remind you that the ability to bend is part of your strength.

When You Hate the Way It Feels—But Still Go Back

As a dog returns to its vomit,
so a fool repeats his foolishness.

PROVERBS 26:11

This is not the most comforting verse. But it is brutally honest. There's something wild about the fact that you can hate the consequences of a behavior and still crave the behavior. You can despise the way it leaves you feeling—numb, ashamed, disconnected—and still do it again.

That's not weakness. That's addiction.

Psychologically, this is called *ambivalence*—the push and pull of wanting both relief and release from the same behavior. The craving and the regret. It's the war between your survival brain (which just wants to feel better now) and your higher brain (which knows this won't help in the long run). In recovery work, naming that ambivalence is a powerful first step toward change.

You're not crazy for repeating what hurts. Your brain is wired to return to what gave relief, even if it brought pain too. And God sees it—not with contempt, but with compassion. Jesus didn't recoil from broken patterns, he walked straight toward them. He sat with people stuck in their own loops. He offered them truth, but never without tenderness.

Today, don't pretend you're fine. Don't shame yourself for the tug-of-war you feel inside. Instead, admit it. Confess the loop. And ask God to help you stay present through the craving rather than escape it.

That space between urge and action—that's the holy ground of transformation. You can interrupt the loop.

Anchor Truth

You can't change what you won't admit. But once you name it, grace can meet you there.

Prayer

God, I don't want to keep going back to what breaks me. Help me stay present in the tension. Meet me there.

Invitation

Next time the urge comes, pause. Don't fight it, just feel it. Breathe. Notice the craving without reacting. You're practicing freedom, one pause at a time.

The Next Right Thing Is Enough

The LORD gives his people strength.
The LORD blesses them with peace.

PSALM 29:11

When life feels big, do something small. That's not a cop-out. It's wisdom. Because agency isn't about controlling everything. It's about doing the next right thing with courage and clarity.

We often get overwhelmed not by the actual work of healing or growing, but by the idea that we have to get it all right, all at once. That kind of pressure isn't holy—it's paralyzing.

But you don't have to overhaul your life today. You just have to take one step. One honest move. One act of integrity, or kindness, or courage. Then tomorrow you do it again.

That's how real change happens. Not through grand gestures, but through consistent, soul-aligned choices.

The clinical term for this is *behavioral activation*—a practice often used to treat depression and emotional paralysis. You start small. You act before you feel ready. You take a step even when your brain says it won't matter. And slowly, momentum builds. Agency returns. Hope cracks through.

Spiritually, it's no different. God often strengthens us *in* motion, not before it. Psalm 29 says he gives strength and peace—not once everything is settled, but as we step into the storm.

You don't need to have it all figured out. You just need to do the next right thing. That's enough. And that's agency.

Anchor Truth

You don't need a five-year plan. You need one faithful step.

Prayer

God, when everything feels like too much, help me take a breath and focus on the one thing I can do. Give me strength in motion and peace in the process. Thank you that I don't have to fix everything. I just have to follow you.

Invitation

What's your next right thing today? Not the perfect thing. Not the impressive thing. Just the right thing. Do it. Let that be enough.

The Fear of Being Replaced

You are a chosen people, a royal priesthood, a holy nation, God's special possession.

1 PETER 2:9 (NIV)

Jealousy doesn't just show up on social media. Sometimes it shows up in real life: At the group dinner you weren't invited to. When someone else becomes "their person." When the text thread gets quiet. When you realize you're not their go-to anymore.

It's not about attention. It's about belonging. And the fear that maybe you've been replaced.

That's the raw side of jealousy. It's not just envy over success—it's the ache of being left out. The sting of relational shift. The silent question: *Was I ever really wanted? Or just convenient?*

In 1 Corinthians 13:4, Paul's famous words about love say that love "is not jealous." But that doesn't mean you won't feel jealous. It just means love doesn't act from a place of jealousy. Love doesn't lash out. It doesn't compete. It doesn't turn cold to punish.

But it does pay attention to what's going on underneath. Because underneath jealousy in relationships is often *attachment pain*—a reaction to perceived rejection, abandonment, or loss of connection. You feel like something is slipping away, and your mind scrambles to protect you from it.

That doesn't make you needy. It makes you human. And you don't have to pretend you're unaffected.

But you don't have to let the fear of being replaced push you into bitterness, comparison, or withdrawal. Sometimes self-awareness sounds like *This hurts more than I expected. And that's okay.* Because naming the ache is how you start healing it.

Anchor Truth

Jealousy in relationships often signals a deeper longing to feel chosen.

Prayer

God, when I feel replaced or left out, remind me that I matter to you. Help me stay soft even when my instinct is to pull away. Teach me to respond with love, not fear.

Invitation

If jealousy shows up today in a relationship, don't ignore it. Ask, "What deeper fear is being stirred here?" Talk to God about that—not just the moment, but the meaning underneath it.

When Affirmation Becomes Addiction

They loved human praise more than the praise of God.

JOHN 12:43

Affirmation feels good—of course it does. Your brain is wired for it. Each "Like," compliment, or nod of approval gives a little hit of dopamine, reinforcing the belief that you're okay—as long as other people think so.

The problem is, that need can become insatiable. It's built on what social scientists call a *variable reward schedule*—the same system that keeps you hooked on slot machines or checking your phone. You never know when the next dose of affirmation is coming, so you keep chasing it. And over time, the hunger for approval becomes addictive.

But there's an even deeper danger: When affirmation becomes your primary and unquenchable fuel, you'll bend and twist yourself in whatever direction it takes to get it. You start crafting a version of yourself for consumption, not connection. And worse, you may lose touch with your God-given identity beneath all that performance.

Jesus also dealt with people who were addicted to affirmation. John 12:43 describes leaders who believed in him but stayed silent because they feared losing their status. They were more drawn to human praise than divine calling. You don't have to live like that.

It's not easy to detox from affirmation addiction. But healing starts when you begin noticing the moments you perform, exaggerate, or withhold just to win favor.

Pay attention. And instead of reaching for validation, reach inward. Reach upward. The truest you doesn't need applause to be real.

Anchor Truth

Affirmation is a gift, not a god.

Prayer

God, I confess how easily I seek approval to feel secure. Help me find my worth in your unwavering love, not in someone else's reaction. Teach me to live from identity, not for it.

Invitation

Pause the next time you're tempted to earn applause. Ask yourself, "Would I still do this if no one noticed?" That question just might lead you back to freedom.

The Risk (and Reward) of Going Deep

The purposes of a person's heart are deep waters, but one who has insight draws them out.

PROVERBS 20:5 (NIV)

Most of us live on the surface—scheduling, scrolling, smiling politely. We share highlights. We mention stress. We joke. We deflect. And it's fine, until it isn't. Because no matter how many texts you send or how much small talk you make, surface-level relationships can't sustain your soul.

Deep connection—where you feel known, heard, understood—is a core human need. It's not optional for flourishing. But beware: Going deep is risky. To go deep is to let yourself be seen, not just curated. It means saying things like "I've been struggling." "I'm not sure what I believe right now." "I feel lonely, even in this room."

Connection means choosing vulnerability over performance. And it's scary, because depth requires mutual risk. It means trusting that the other person will hold your truth with care and offering them the same in return. Being shallow won't heal you. Pretending won't connect you. And emotional safety doesn't grow without brave honesty.

Jesus didn't stay on the surface. He wept in front of his friends. He asked hard questions. He broke bread with people others avoided. And when his disciples wanted to follow, he made it clear: "Come and die" (see Luke 9:23). Not exactly small talk.

The reward for depth isn't just catharsis. It's communion. It's discovering, maybe for the first time, that you're not alone. That your messy, complicated self is worth loving—and capable of loving others just as bravely.

Anchor Truth

Going deep might feel risky, but it's where the real healing begins.

Prayer

God, I want relationships that go beyond the surface. Give me the courage to share truthfully and listen tenderly. Help me find people who will meet me there—and help me be that person for others.

Invitation

Think of one relationship you want to deepen. Initiate a conversation where you share something real. It doesn't have to be huge, just honest. Then watch what happens.

When Their Life Feels Like an Accusation

A peaceful heart leads to a healthy body;
jealousy is like cancer in the bones.

PROVERBS 14:30

You weren't planning to feel jealous. But you're scrolling through someone else's vacation, announcement, relationship, promotion, house, body, marriage, platform—and suddenly, their joy feels like your failure.

You're not angry at them exactly. You just feel like you're losing some invisible competition you didn't sign up for. Like someone else's "more" makes your "enough" disappear. That's the quiet violence of jealousy.

It's not always loud. It's not always obvious. But it erodes your peace—slowly, persistently—until you can't celebrate others without secretly grieving yourself.

Proverbs says jealousy is like cancer in the bones. Not just unpleasant, but destructive. It eats away at peace. Because underneath jealousy is a lie: If they have it, I can't. And underneath that is often a deeper ache: *Why not me? What's wrong with me? Doesn't anyone see me?*

Here's where jealousy and resentment start to overlap. When jealousy festers, it turns into resentment—not just of others, but of God. You stop saying it out loud, but somewhere inside, you're asking, "Why are you blessing them and not me? Why do I always feel behind?"

But here's the deeper truth: Someone else's joy is not a threat to you. Their success doesn't shrink your worth. Their story doesn't cancel yours. God isn't stingy. He hasn't forgotten you. He hasn't missed the ache behind your smile.

And you don't have to pretend you're not feeling what you're feeling. But you can choose not to let it grow unchecked. How? By naming it without shame. By confessing it instead of hiding it. By bringing it to God before it hardens into resentment.

Anchor Truth

Jealousy doesn't mean you're bad. It means you're hurting.

Prayer

God, I don't want to live in quiet comparison. When I feel the sting of jealousy, help me trace it, not shame it. And remind me that you see me, too. You haven't overlooked my story.

Invitation

Pay attention today: When someone else gets good news, what rises in you? Don't judge it. Just name it. That's the beginning of healing.

Grace Changes Everything

God saved you by his grace when you believed. And you can't take credit for this; it is a gift from God.

EPHESIANS 2:8

Grace isn't fair. If it were, it wouldn't be grace. Grace doesn't wait until you've proven yourself. It doesn't hang in the balance, waiting for you to clean up your mess. Grace shows up in the wreckage. It kneels in the dirt. It lifts your chin and says, "I still choose you."

That's why grace is so offensive to guilt. Guilt thrives on repayment—on punishment and shame.

Grace doesn't play by those rules. Grace takes the ledger, the one where you've been tracking your failures and missteps, and rips it in half.

And that's hard for some of us to swallow. Because we've spent our whole lives earning—our worth, our belonging, our rest. We think grace is for the really broken people. Or we believe we've used ours up. Or we offer it to others but secretly disqualify ourselves.

But Scripture says grace is a gift. Not a paycheck. Not a reward. Not a bonus for good behavior. A gift.

And the most radical part? It doesn't stop with you. When you receive grace deeply—really receive it in the parts of you that are still shadowed by guilt—it changes how you treat other people too. You stop weaponizing their flaws. You release your grip on resentment. You offer compassion without keeping score.

You become a person of grace because you've tasted the power of it yourself. Not because you earned it. But because you were loved enough to be offered it anyway.

Anchor Truth

Grace is not something you achieve. It's something you receive. And when you do, it reshapes how you see yourself and everyone else.

Prayer

God, I've tried to earn what can only be given. Soften my heart to accept your grace. And let it spill into how I love others—with open hands and an unoffended heart.

Invitation

Where are you still trying to prove yourself? Name it. Then imagine God meeting you there—not with judgment, but with the kind of grace that rewrites everything.

Carrying, Not Absorbing

Share each other's burdens, and in this way obey the law of Christ.

GALATIANS 6:2

You're not cold. You're not selfish. You just can't be everyone's emotional sponge. It's one thing to carry someone's burden. It's another to absorb their anxiety, their grief, or their anger until it lives inside your own nervous system like it belongs to you.

This is where emotional boundaries become essential. You can listen to someone's pain without becoming responsible for fixing it. You can care deeply without being consumed completely. You can empathize without internalizing.

It's the difference between support and enmeshment. Healthy emotional boundaries allow you to show up with compassion and maintain your own emotional clarity. They help you distinguish between what others are feeling and what is yours to carry.

Even Jesus didn't take on every emotional storm around him. He wept with others. He was moved with compassion. But he also withdrew, stayed grounded, and responded with calm strength.

Galatians 6:2 tells us to share burdens, not shoulder them solo. "Sharing" means mutuality, not martyrdom. It means walking alongside someone, not drowning with them. If your heart feels overloaded, it's okay to pause and ask, "Am I helping or absorbing? Am I being present or disappearing?"

You're not called to lose yourself in someone else's chaos. You're called to love them wisely—from a place of strength, not emotional depletion.

Anchor Truth

Emotional boundaries aren't walls. They're doors that let compassion in without letting your peace leak out.

Prayer

God, teach me to care without collapsing. Help me love others well without losing my own emotional footing. Show me how to be present with people's pain while remaining anchored in your peace.

Invitation

Notice one relationship where you tend to absorb emotions that aren't yours. Practice separating your feelings from theirs today. Let empathy move you to support them, not to self-erasure.

The Role of Hope in Resilience

Though he slay me, yet will I hope in him.

JOB 13:15 (NIV)

Hope isn't wishful thinking. It's not toxic positivity or pretending everything's fine. Hope is the anchor that keeps you from drifting when life unravels.

In clinical terms, hope is a major predictor of resilience. It strengthens the brain's ability to problem-solve, regulate emotion, and persevere. And it's not based on circumstance. It's based on belief. Hope says, "There's more than this moment. This pain is real, but it's not final."

Just ask Job, who lost nearly everything—his family, his health, his sense of safety. And yet, in one of the rawest declarations of faith in all of Scripture, he said, "Though he slay me, yet will I hope in him." He didn't deny the devastation. He just refused to believe it was the end.

Or look at Paul, who endured beatings, imprisonment, betrayal, and exhaustion. Still he wrote, "We are pressed on every side by troubles, but we are not crushed. We are perplexed, but not driven to despair" (2 Corinthians 4:8). Why? Because he held onto hope. Hope in redemption. Hope in resurrection. Hope that this story—*your* story—isn't over.

Hope doesn't erase the pain, but it gives you strength to keep walking through it. And that's what resilience looks like—believing, even in the dark, that light is coming.

Hope is not weakness. Hope is grit. Hope is holy defiance in the face of despair.

Anchor Truth

Resilience is fueled by hope—the quiet conviction that God is still writing your story, even when the page feels blank.

Prayer

God, I need hope. Not hype. Not platitudes. Just the kind of hope that holds me steady when life feels fragile. Remind me that you are not finished. Anchor me in your goodness, even when I can't see it yet.

Invitation

Where do you need hope right now? Write a simple sentence of belief: "Even here, I trust that God is working." Repeat it to yourself when the waves rise. Let hope become your anchor.

Gratitude in the Grind

Work willingly at whatever you do, as though you were working for the Lord rather than for people.

COLOSSIANS 3:23

Doing the dishes. Fixing spreadsheets. Folding laundry. Reviewing work email threads that go on and on. Sometimes it's hard to feel thankful in the thick of life's most mundane tasks. The grind can dull our sense of purpose. But that's where gratitude has the power to wake us up.

Brother Lawrence, a seventeenth-century monastery cook, famously found peace and joy in his assigned kitchen chores. He called it "the practice of the presence of God." He met God in the chores no one else wanted.

Gratitude in the grind is letting your spirit whisper "Thank you" even when your hands are wringing out the mop. And Scripture agrees. Colossians 3:23 isn't just about working hard; it's about working with intention. With heart. With a posture of thanks because God meets us in the mundane.

Need a biblical example? Look at Ruth. Her story, found in the Old Testament book that bears her name, begins in grief. She ends up in Bethlehem with nothing. No family, no security, no plan—just her mother-in-law and their shared pain.

So Ruth heads to the fields to pick up grain left behind by the harvesters (Ruth 2:2)—a humble, backbreaking task reserved for the poor and overlooked. And right there—in the ordinary, exhausting task—God meets her.

He provides not just food, but a future. Ruth, the foreign widow with dirt on her hands, eventually became the great-grandmother of King David—and part of the lineage of Jesus.

That's the mystery of gratitude. It doesn't always shout. It often whispers through small choices. It shows up in mundane faithfulness. And somehow it turns the dusty corners of our lives into places where divine things unfold.

When you give thanks in the grind, you're not just surviving it—you're sanctifying it.

Anchor Truth

Gratitude in the mundane trains your soul to see meaning where others only see monotony.

Prayer

God, meet me in the middle of my ordinary. Remind me that no act is too small to carry significance when it's done with you in mind. Turn my sighs into thank-yous.

Invitation

This week, practice grateful awareness in something boring—laundry, dishes, emails. Say, "Thank you, God, for this moment to be present." It might just change the atmosphere of your day.

Signs You're Standing Strong

So we can say with confidence, "The LORD is my helper, so I will have no fear. What can mere people do to me?"

HEBREWS 13:6

You may not realize it at first, but there comes a point when you look back and notice that the grip of insecurity isn't squeezing quite as tightly anymore. A secure sense of self-worth doesn't always show up loud or proud. In fact, it's often quiet and steady—less about proving something and more about no longer needing to.

So what are the signs? Psychologically speaking, you're growing in self-worth when: You're able to take feedback without collapsing into self-doubt. You can say no without spiraling into guilt. You don't twist yourself to match every room you walk into. You cheer for others without making it about you. You own your mistakes without needing to defend your worth. You're honest about your strengths and weaknesses—without apology. You feel at peace in your own skin, even when others don't "get" you.

It's not perfection. It's a groundedness that says, "I know who I am—and whose I am."

You see it in Joseph, who went from the pit to the palace and still wept with compassion for his brothers. You see it in Esther, who stood before the king not with bravado, but with brave resolve. You see it in Barnabas, the encourager, who didn't need the spotlight to shine. You see it in Mary of Bethany, who broke the jar of perfume without explaining herself. You see it in Paul, who learned to be content in plenty or in lack because his worth wasn't riding on either.

These weren't flawless people. But they were free. And so are you, more than you might realize.

Anchor Truth

Real self-worth is built on truth, not image. It doesn't need applause to feel secure, and it doesn't collapse under criticism. It stands firm in the unshakable love of God.

Prayer

God, help me recognize the places where I've grown. Help me celebrate the quiet confidence you're forming in me. Let my security come not from the world's approval, but from your unwavering grace. And when I doubt myself, remind me of who I am in you.

Invitation

Take a moment today to list a few ways you've grown in confidence, clarity, or peace. Then thank God for each one. This is your evidence that you're stronger than you think.

Betting on God (Pascal's Wager)

And it is impossible to please God without faith. Anyone who wants to come to him must believe that God exists and that he rewards those who sincerely seek him.

HEBREWS 11:6

You may not be sure what you believe about God. But here's something most of us don't admit: You're already betting your life on something.

Blaise Pascal, a seventeenth-century mathematician, philosopher, and devout Christian, once wrote that belief in God is not about certainty. It's about the wager. He said we're all placing a bet. If you wager that God is real and live like it, you lose very little if you're wrong. But if you wager that God isn't real and you're wrong, you risk losing everything.

At first glance, it sounds like a cosmic insurance policy. But Pascal's wager isn't a cheap trick to scare people into faith. It's an argument for humility. For honest doubt. For seeing belief not as blind, but as a thoughtful risk.

And here's what's interesting: Psychologists often note that most of us are already making unconscious wagers every day. On people, relationships, outcomes, meaning. We call it *decision-based cognition*—the idea that what we choose to lean toward shapes what we believe over time.

So maybe the question isn't "Is God provable?" Maybe it's "What kind of life does your doubt lead you toward?" Is it colder? More closed off? Or is it more curious? More awake?

Faith doesn't always feel rational. But neither does despair. And you're going to build your life on something. Even in your doubt, you already are.

Anchor Truth

Your faith shapes your character. Whatever you bet your life on, it will shape the future version of you.

Prayer

God, I don't always know how to believe. But I do know I want my life to lean toward you. Help me choose trust, even when I'm not sure. Help me take the risk that love is real.

Invitation

Today, act as if God is real—not to fake belief, but to see what shifts in you when you do. Watch how even a small wager changes the way you move through the day.

Gratitude in Chains

I thank my God every time I remember you.

PHILIPPIANS 1:3 (NIV)

Paul didn't write Philippians from a cozy study with a warm drink and a view of the ocean. He wrote it from prison—likely cold, hungry, alone, and unsure whether he'd ever be free again. And yet his letter brims with gratitude. Not forced optimism. Not "it's fine" fakery. Real, unshakable, soul-deep thanks.

How? Because Paul didn't tie gratitude to comfort. He tied it to connection. To the people who had stood by him. To the faith that anchored him. To the God who hadn't let go.

There's something sacred about choosing thankfulness when your circumstances don't warrant it. Paul could've gone bitter. Cynical. But instead, he chose to focus on what hadn't been taken from him—his mission, his memory of God's goodness, his love for people. And that changed everything. Gratitude didn't deny Paul's suffering. It reframed it. Gave it meaning. Grounded him in hope. Even in chains, he was free.

You might not be sitting in a jail cell, but maybe you're stuck in a season that feels like confinement. Maybe joy feels distant. Gratitude feels like a luxury.

Paul's life reminds us that gratitude isn't a bonus for when life feels good. It's a battle stance when life doesn't. Because when you choose to be thankful in hard places, you're not ignoring pain. You're defying it. You're declaring that your spirit is not up for grabs.

When we stop practicing gratitude, we quietly start building our own prison walls—brick by brick. Resentment. Entitlement. Bitterness. Comparison. Before long, we're trapped in a cell of our own making, surrounded not by chains but by the weight of what we think we lack.

Gratitude doesn't just lift our spirits. It unlocks the door. It reminds us that freedom isn't always a change in our circumstances—sometimes it's a change in our perspective.

Paul's chains didn't define him. And yours don't have to define you, either. Gratitude is your jailbreak.

Anchor Truth

Gratitude isn't reserved for the easy seasons. It's a rebellion against despair, a reclaiming of perspective, and a declaration that hope is still on the table.

Prayer

God, help me find thanks not just when life is good, but also when it's hard. Teach me to see through the fog, to remember who you are and what still matters.

Invitation

Write a thank-you note to someone who's helped you stay grounded. Or jot down three things you're grateful for today, especially if life feels heavy. Gratitude might not change your situation, but it can change how you carry it.

Meaning and Mortality

So teach us to number our days,
that we may gain a heart of wisdom.

PSALM 90:12 (NJKV)

Death has a way of clarifying life. Not in a morbid way, but in a motivating way. When we come face-to-face with the brevity of life, we often gain clarity about what actually matters: relationships over accomplishments, purpose over performance, depth over distraction.

Have you ever heard of *terror management theory*? It sounds, well, terrifying, doesn't it? The theory proposes that much of human behavior is subconsciously shaped by our awareness of death. It's not that we walk around thinking about dying all the time, but we do seek to construct lives that feel meaningful enough to push back the fear of impermanence.

Whether we're aware of it or not, we're all trying to build legacies, relationships, or routines that matter. Scripture doesn't avoid this reality. It embraces it. Moses' prayer in Psalm 90 invites us to "number our days" so that we might live wisely. That's not about being obsessed with how much time we have left. It's about becoming intentional with the time we have now.

People who reflect on their mortality—even just briefly—tend to live with greater purpose. They're more generous, more forgiving, more focused on what lasts. And those who anchor their meaning in Christ aren't just living for legacy. They're living for eternity.

So the question isn't "Will I die?" It's "What will I live for while I'm here?" Because in the end, all of us are terminal. But when we live with meaning, we're also eternal.

So when you face your mortality, you just might find more of your meaning. Not in what you own, but in how you love. Not in how long you live, but in what you live for. Live like your days are numbered, because that's how you make them count.

Anchor Truth

You won't live forever on this earth. But what you do with your life can echo in eternity.

Prayer

God, teach me to number my days—not with fear, but with wisdom. Help me live each one with meaning, anchored in you. Remind me of what matters, and give me the courage to live like I believe it.

Invitation

Take five minutes today to write your own "meaning manifesto." What will matter most at the end of your life, and how can you live more fully in that direction today?

When Weakness Tells the Truth

What a wretched man I am! Who will rescue me from this body that is subject to death? Thanks be to God, who delivers me through Jesus Christ our Lord!

ROMANS 7:24-25 (NIV)

Most of us were taught—explicitly or not—that weakness should be hidden. That showing struggle makes us look fragile. That honesty might make you less trustworthy, less respectable, less spiritual.

But Paul didn't buy that. He once relied on pedigree and performance. He once boasted of being blameless under the law. He once tried to control truth by force.

But after meeting Jesus, Paul stopped trying to curate a flawless image. He began to tell the truth about himself, even when it bruised his reputation. He owned his past. Acknowledged his limitations. Named the "thorn" he couldn't fix. And boasted—not in victory, but in need.

In psychological terms, Paul was modeling *authenticity* and *vulnerability*—crucial traits of mental and emotional health. When we hide weakness, we reinforce shame. When we name it, we disarm it.

But that shift isn't easy. It means telling the truth about ourselves even when it costs us clout. It means resisting the pressure to pose or perform. And it means trusting that grace flows most freely when ego gets out of the way.

Paul's life shows that wholeness isn't about image management. It's about integration. Your story, your wounds, your imperfections—they're not liabilities to hide. They're portals to connection, to healing, to the power of Christ showing up where you end.

And if you've spent years proving, performing, or pretending, hear this: You don't have to keep the mask on. You're allowed to be a work in progress. You're allowed to speak from the middle, not just the other side.

Anchor Truth

You don't need to impress anyone with strength. God's power moves through your honesty.

Prayer

God, help me to stop pretending I'm fine when I'm not. Give me the courage to be real and the grace to believe I'm still loved.

Invitation

Where have you been holding back the truth of your experience? Choose one person you trust and share something real, even if it feels small.

When You Swallow It

So don't go to bed angry, because anger gives a foothold to the devil.

EPHESIANS 4:26-27 (NLT, ADAPTED)

Swallowed anger doesn't disappear. It just metastasizes. You might not lash out. You might never raise your voice. People may even call you calm. But your body knows the truth.

That tight jaw? That clenched stomach? That passive-aggressive jab you slipped into a text? That's anger, dressed up and repressed.

Some of us were conditioned early: "Good people don't get mad." So instead of expressing anger, we learned to eat it. Numb it. Spiritualize it. Smile through it. And then we wonder why our hearts feel heavy and our relationships feel fake.

Psychologically, this is known as *repressed affect*—when you don't just avoid anger, you deny it entirely. You stop recognizing it in yourself.

But unexpressed anger doesn't stay dormant. It festers. It warps into anxiety. Depression. Chronic resentment. Or that familiar phrase: "I don't even know why I'm so irritable."

Your soul knows. Your soul is tired of pretending nothing's wrong. It's tired of bypassing truth for the sake of keeping peace. And it's tired of bleeding silently so no one else has to feel uncomfortable.

You don't need to yell to be angry. You don't need to explode to be breaking. Stuffed anger is still anger. It's just turned inward, and that's where it does the most damage.

So what do you do? You name it. You get curious, not condemning. You stop saying "I'm fine" when you're not. You start recognizing where your boundaries were crossed, where your needs were ignored, where your voice went missing.

And then—this part is key—you learn how to express anger safely. Honestly. Without shame. You tell the truth in love, starting with yourself.

Because peacekeeping is not the same as peacemaking. And God is not impressed by your ability to pretend everything's okay.

Anchor Truth

Stuffed anger doesn't make you holy. It just makes you heavy.

Prayer

God, I've buried my anger so deep I barely recognize it anymore. Help me name it. Help me release it. And help me stop mistaking silence for peace.

Invitation

Ask yourself, "When did I first learn that expressing anger wasn't safe or acceptable? What would it look like to tell the truth now, with kindness and clarity?"

Breathing Through the Spiral

When anxiety was great within me, your consolation brought me joy.

PSALM 94:19 (NIV)

Anxiety doesn't always come as a wave. It often spirals in slowly, thought by thought. It begins with something small: a late reply, a sudden shift in tone, an unfinished task. Then your brain begins to build a story around it: *What if something's wrong? What if I messed up? What if I can't fix it?* Before long, you're stuck in a loop of what-ifs.

This is called *cognitive distortion*—a psychological pattern where our thoughts become exaggerated, negative, or disconnected from reality. When anxiety kicks in, the brain's alarm system (the amygdala) takes over, often hijacking logic and amplifying fear. Your nervous system can't tell the difference between imagined threat and real danger, so it reacts as if it's under attack. It's not weakness. It's wiring.

And yet God draws close to us not only when our theology is intact, but also when our minds are spiraling. "The LORD is close to the brokenhearted," David writes in Psalm 34:18. Not to the perfectly calm, but to the ones who feel crushed. That includes those brokenhearted by trauma, yes, but also those whose mental health leaves them weary, flooded, and overwhelmed.

Anxiety in Christian spaces can feel especially isolating. You might feel like you're performing peace while hiding your pain. But God isn't looking for a perfect performance. He rescues those who can barely hold it together.

One of the most effective ways to interrupt an anxiety spiral is to pause and breathe deeply. This isn't just spiritual. It's physiological. Deep breathing activates the *parasympathetic nervous system*—your body's internal brake pedal. It brings you back to the present through *interoception*—the awareness of internal cues like breath and heartbeat.

Slow breathing tells your brain that you're safe. It slows your heart rate. It quiets the spiral. It's a form of nonjudgmental awareness—a way of saying, "This moment is hard, and I'm still okay." It's a small act of surrender, a way to say, "I don't have to fix this all right now. I just need to breathe and let God be close."

You don't have to spiral your way out of the spiral. You can breathe your way into God's presence.

Anchor Truth

God draws near in my spiral, not after it ends.

Prayer

God, I feel stuck in my head. My thoughts are racing, and I don't know how to make them stop. Help me slow down. Help me breathe. Help me feel your nearness—not just when I'm calm, but especially when I'm not.

Invitation

Practice square breathing: Inhale for four counts, hold for four, exhale for four, hold for four. Repeat this for one minute. As you breathe out, whisper, "You are near."

Family Ties, Tangled Lines

Honor your father and mother.

EXODUS 20:12

Family of origin boundaries are some of the most complicated to navigate. Why? Because they're the first lines ever drawn in our lives—and often the most blurred.

You grow up needing your parents, relying on their approval, craving their love. Then one day you're supposed to become your own person—independent, confident, separate. But those old emotional cords don't sever easily.

Maybe you've tried setting boundaries with a parent who calls daily to unload their stress. Or perhaps you've said no to a family gathering because it's emotionally toxic, only to be met with guilt trips and passive-aggressive silence. You may have distanced yourself from a sibling who brings chaos, only to second-guess yourself every holiday.

Boundaries in families can feel like betrayal. But they're actually an act of maturity and, paradoxically, sometimes even an act of honor. To "honor" doesn't mean to obey everything, absorb dysfunction, or ignore damage. It means treating people with dignity and truth. Sometimes the most honoring thing you can do is say, "I love you, but I can't do this in the same way anymore."

Jesus himself redrew family lines. He asked, "Who is my mother? Who are my brothers?" (Matthew 12:48), not to dishonor Mary and his siblings, but to show that emotional and spiritual health sometimes require redefining roles.

You can love someone deeply and still say, "This isn't working for me." That's not rebellion. It's responsibility.

Anchor Truth

Boundaries with family aren't about rejection. They're about restoration—of your peace, your health, and your ability to love freely without resentment.

Prayer

God, help me navigate the messy, meaningful relationships in my family. Give me courage to speak the truth in love and wisdom to know when to hold close and when to create space. Heal what's been tangled, and give me grace for what may never change.

Invitation

Take some time to name where your family dynamics feel draining or unsafe. What would it look like to honor your family and your emotional health? You don't necessarily need to cut people out, but you may need to step back to breathe.

The Joy of Anticipation

Be joyful in hope, patient in affliction, faithful in prayer.

ROMANS 12:12 (NIV)

There's a quiet kind of happiness that doesn't scream or sparkle. It's the kind that lives in waiting rooms and countdowns, in hopeful glances at calendars and whispered prayers at midnight. It's the joy of anticipation.

Anticipation is underrated. In fact, research reveals that simply looking forward to something can boost your mood as much as—or even more than—the event itself.

Planning a vacation, preparing for a reunion, counting down to a goal—these future-oriented moments activate the brain's reward centers and increase dopamine, the feel-good neurotransmitter. You don't have to be there yet to feel joy.

Scripture makes this plain. Romans 12:12 doesn't promise joy in the arrival, it calls us to joy in the hoping. This is a gritty kind of gladness—one that doesn't demand instant gratification but chooses to anchor the soul in what *will be*, even when what *is* feels uncertain.

Think of Abraham. God gave him a promise, but the fulfillment took years. Still, he lived in hope. Or Simeon, who waited a lifetime to see the Messiah—and found deep joy in simply holding baby Jesus in his arms. Their joy was born in anticipation, not resolution.

Anticipation doesn't require certainty—it just needs a spark of belief that something good is ahead. And that spark can light up even the darkest days. Maybe that's the secret: Happiness isn't just what you feel when everything finally comes together. It's what rises in you when you choose to believe that something beautiful is on its way.

Even now—before the breakthrough, before the answer, before the celebration—there's joy to be found in the simple act of hoping. Keep looking forward. Joy is already meeting you there.

Anchor Truth

Joy isn't found only in the moment. It grows in the waiting.

Prayer

God, thank you for the gift of anticipation. Help me hold hope with open hands and find joy in the journey, not just the destination. Teach me to trust that what you're preparing is worth the wait.

Invitation

This week, give yourself something to look forward to. It doesn't have to be grand. Maybe it's a walk, a phone call, a small project, or even time set aside to dream. Let hope stretch your heart toward joy.

Pre-Deciding Your Response

Sensible people control their temper;
they earn respect by overlooking wrongs.

PROVERBS 19:11

Most emotional reactions don't start in the moment. They start in the mindset you bring into the moment. That's why one of the most powerful tools in emotional regulation is pre-deciding your response.

Think of it like this: Emotional regulation isn't just a skill. It's a strategy. It's making small, intentional choices about how you want to show up, especially in moments that test your patience, pride, or peace.

You already know your vulnerable spots. The topics that make you tense. The people who tend to provoke you. The situations that bring out your worst.

What if, instead of hoping you'll handle it well, you actually trained for it? Athletes do this. First responders do this. Even Jesus did this, spending time in solitude and prayer before facing the cross. He didn't improvise his responses under pressure. He prepared for them.

You can too. Make it simple. Create if-then plans: *If I feel dismissed, I'll take a deep breath. If I feel rage rising, I'll take a walk instead of firing off a text. If I feel anger, I'll name it, not aim it.*

These micro-decisions build macro stability. They aren't manipulative scripts; they're anchors. They free you from the tyranny of your impulses and help you live out your values, even when emotions run high. Proverbs 19:11 calls this wisdom.

The ability to regulate anger isn't weakness. It's strength. It's what earns respect—not for being passive, but for being principled.

Anchor Truth

Pre-deciding your emotional response isn't pretending. It's preparing. It's the quiet strength of choosing who you want to be, even before you're tested.

Prayer

God, help me respond with wisdom and grace. Give me the presence of mind to pause and the courage to act from peace, not pressure.

Invitation

Think of one predictable emotional trigger in your life. How can you pre-decide your response in a way that aligns with your values? Write it down and rehearse it.

You're Not Their Savior

I planted the seed, Apollos watered it, but God has been making it grow.

1 CORINTHIANS 3:6 (NIV)

You care deeply. That's not the problem. The problem is when your care turns into control. When their healing becomes your responsibility. When you believe that if you just say the right thing, do the right thing, love the right way—they'll finally get it. Finally change. Finally be okay.

That's not compassion. That's savior syndrome. Codependency convinces you that you must be the one to fix it. To keep them from falling apart. To be the bridge between their pain and their peace. But you are not the bridge. And you are not the Savior. You are a person—a loved, limited, and human person.

Paul makes it clear in his letter to the Corinthians: We can plant, we can water, but only God makes things grow. Translation? You're not in charge of outcomes. You're not responsible for someone else's recovery, clarity, or change. You can support. You can speak truth. You can show up in love. But you cannot—and should not—try to save.

There is a subtle pride that comes with trying to be everything for someone. It can feel noble. But underneath, it's often fear—fear of abandonment, fear of failure, fear of not being needed. The truth is, trying to be someone's savior only ends in exhaustion for you and resentment for them.

Real love doesn't mean rescuing. It means releasing. It means offering what you can and letting God be God. It means trusting that growth, healing, and transformation are divine responsibilities, not yours to manage.

So take the pressure off. You don't have to carry someone else's soul on your back. Plant. Water. Love. And then let go.

Anchor Truth

You are not responsible for saving anyone. You are responsible for showing up in love and trusting God to do the rest.

Prayer

God, help me surrender the weight I've been carrying for others. Teach me to love without trying to fix, and to trust that you care more deeply than I ever could.

Invitation

Where have you been overstepping in someone's life, trying to rescue or repair? What would it look like to hand that back to God? Let today be a day of release.

When They Break the Rules and Still Win

The LORD is good to everyone.
He showers compassion on all his creation.

PSALM 145:9

You did things the right way. You played fair. Stayed patient. Took the high road. You waited your turn. Someone else ignored all of that and got the life you've been working for.

Jealousy hits hard when someone "breaks the rules" and still comes out ahead. When they cut corners, take shortcuts, live louder, or leapfrog their way into blessings you thought were earned through quiet faithfulness. It can make you question everything: *Why am I even trying? Does integrity matter? Is God even paying attention?*

And underneath those questions, something deeper simmers: *If they get rewarded for doing less, what does that say about me?* That's where jealousy turns into spiritual confusion. Because it doesn't just feel unfair. It feels personal. It feels like their win is your loss. Like God is rewarding recklessness and ignoring righteousness.

But Psalm 145 says something that's both comforting and unsettling: "God is good to everyone." Not just the polished. Not just the disciplined. Not just the ones who color inside the lines. Everyone. Because that's who he is—compassionate, generous, and wildly unfair in the most grace-filled way.

That's the scandal of grace. It doesn't follow formulas. It doesn't reward effort proportionally. It's not a system to master. It's a mystery to receive.

And when jealousy whispers, "Why them?" Grace answers, "Because I'm good to them. And I'm still good to you."

Anchor Truth

Grace doesn't always feel fair, but it is always good.

Prayer

God, when I feel bitter about someone else's blessing, meet me there. Remind me that your grace is bigger than my fairness and that it hasn't passed me by.

Invitation

Notice today when someone's success triggers comparison or frustration. Pause and ask, "What rule do I feel they broke? And why does that sting?" Let God speak grace over you, not just over them.

When Moving Your Body Moves Your Mind

Strengthen the weak hands, and make firm the feeble knees. Say to those who are fearful-hearted, "Be strong, do not fear! Behold, your God will come."'

ISAIAH 35:3-4 (NKJV)

There's something sacred about movement, especially when you least feel like it. Depression has a way of making everything heavy: your limbs, your thoughts, your will. Even getting out of bed can feel like scaling a mountain with lead in your bones. So the idea of going for a walk? Laughable. And yet, often necessary.

Modern research backs this up. Movement—especially rhythmic, moderate movement like walking—can significantly improve mood and lessen depressive symptoms. Not because it's a cure-all, but because it gently reawakens a body and brain gone numb. It tells your nervous system, "You're still here. You're still alive. Let's keep going."

Long before research caught on, Scripture hinted at this very truth. In Isaiah 35, the prophet calls for weak hands to be strengthened, feeble knees to be made firm. This isn't just a metaphor. It's a call to embodied hope.

When despair takes hold, hope sometimes looks like just standing up. Taking one step. Then another. The Psalms are filled with this same kind of embodied language: "I walk in the land of the living." "I rise early and cry out for help." "My soul clings to you; your right hand upholds me."

Jesus himself met people in their paralysis—literal and emotional—and invited movement: "Take up your mat and walk." "Stretch out your hand." "Come, follow me."

God doesn't shame you for lying still. But he does lovingly call you back to motion—not for performance, but for restoration. When you move, even a little, you are cooperating with grace.

Anchor Truth

You don't have to feel like moving your body for it to help. Movement can be an act of faith—a stubborn, quiet protest against despair.

Prayer

God, give me the strength for small movements today. Remind me that even slow, weary steps count. Help me rise, one moment at a time.

Invitation

Go outside if you can. Take a walk, even if it's short. Feel your feet touch the ground. And whisper thanks for a body that still carries you forward.

When "Humble" Is Just Insecure

So we can say with confidence, "The LORD is my helper, so I will have no fear. What can mere people do to me?"

HEBREWS 13:6

You know the type—you might *be* the type—that says, "Oh, I don't want to be a bother." "Are you *sure* you don't mind?" "Sorry—just ignore me. I'm probably overstepping." It sounds like humility. It sounds polite. But dig deeper and it often isn't humility at all—it's insecurity dressed up in soft tones and self-effacement.

Humility is grounded. Insecurity is wobbly. Humility says, "I know who I am—and I'm okay being small in the grand scheme." Insecurity says, "I'm not sure I deserve space here at all."

There's a difference between healthy self-awareness and chronic self-doubt. Real humility doesn't require shrinking yourself to make others more comfortable. It doesn't require a constant apology for existing. In fact, true humility honors the image of God in you enough to say, "I can take up space, and so can you."

If you're always asking for permission to have needs or chronically apologizing for your presence, it's time to check what's fueling that pattern. It might be a fear of rejection, a wound from your past, or a belief that your worth hinges on staying small and agreeable. That's not humility; it's quiet shame.

And here's the truth: You don't have to keep tiptoeing through life, afraid to ask for a seat at the table. God has *already* invited you. There's room for your needs. For your voice. For your presence.

Real humility isn't thinking less of yourself. It's thinking of yourself rightly. You can be secure and humble at the same time.

Anchor Truth

True humility isn't insecurity. It's quiet confidence in who God says you are—nothing more and nothing less.

Prayer

God, help me recognize when I'm calling insecurity "humility." Teach me to walk with confidence that honors both you and the worth you've placed in me. Help me speak, ask, and show up without shrinking.

Invitation

Today, pay attention to when you unnecessarily apologize or defer. Instead of defaulting to self-doubt, try this: Pause, breathe, and show up as someone already welcomed. Because you are.

When Childhood Loss Still Lingers

He heals the brokenhearted and bandages their wounds.

PSALM 147:3

Not every childhood wound came from something dramatic. Some came from what didn't happen: No one ever asked how you felt. Affection was rare or conditional. Maybe you had to grow up too fast or maybe no one really saw you at all. It isn't always neglect or abuse.

Sometimes it's subtle: A parent too distracted to connect. A sibling who got all the attention. The slow ache of not being protected, celebrated, or comforted. These are losses. Real ones.

And even if you've long since outgrown the space where they happened, the impact often stays. You might feel it in how you apologize for having needs. Or how you avoid conflict at all costs. You might overachieve, overfunction, or overextend—trying to prove something to someone who's no longer watching. Or you may simply feel stuck, haunted by a sadness you can't quite name.

Unprocessed grief from our earliest years doesn't just disappear. It hides in our habits. It echoes through relationships. And it often resurfaces when we're ready to heal.

God's heart has always been tender toward the brokenhearted. Even the child version of you. *Especially* the child version of you.

Grieving childhood loss isn't about assigning blame. It's about honoring your story. Giving yourself permission to feel what was buried. To lament what was missing. And to let God into the places you learned to survive alone.

It might be scary. But it's not too late to heal those hurts. That little kid inside you deserves compassion. And your adult self deserves freedom.

Anchor Truth

You can't rewrite the past. But you can name what hurt, grieve what was lost, and let God tend to what still aches.

Prayer

God, help me grieve what I didn't know I was allowed to grieve. Shine your light into the hidden corners of my past. Heal the parts of me that still carry old wounds. And help me move forward with tenderness for the child I was.

Invitation

What part of your story still feels unfinished or unacknowledged? Take time to journal, reflect, or talk to someone safe. Grieving your younger self may be the most grown-up thing you ever do.

When Faith Becomes a Hiding Place

The LORD is close to the brokenhearted;
he rescues those whose spirits are crushed.

PSALM 34:18

Sometimes the most sophisticated form of avoidance wears a halo. You say you're "trusting God," but really you're avoiding the hard conversation. You say, "God's got this," but really, you're terrified to face the pain beneath the pattern. You quote Scripture, but you never actually deal with the truth behind your compulsion.

That's called *spiritual bypassing*—using faith to avoid rather than engage healing. Instead of facing the wound, we plaster a verse over it. Instead of sitting in grief, we fast-forward to glory. We pretend that praying harder will erase the craving or the shame that comes when we give in again. And here's the danger: It feels holy. But it keeps us stuck.

Spiritual bypassing disconnects us from our bodies, our emotions, our story. It trains us to mistrust our pain instead of listening to it. And in the name of "surrender," we white-knuckle through our healing, never getting honest about what we actually need.

But here's what Scripture really says: "God is close to the brokenhearted." Not the polished. Not the performative. The crushed. The cracked open.

Your weakness doesn't repel him. It invites him.

Healing from addiction is sacred work. It's not faithless to go to therapy. It's not weak to join a support group. It's not unspiritual to name your trauma. Pretending you don't struggle doesn't make you holy. It makes you hidden.

You don't have to choose between Jesus and honesty. He is the truth. And he meets you exactly where you are, no verse required.

Anchor Truth

Faith is never an excuse to avoid the truth.

Prayer

God, I've tried to shortcut healing by hiding behind spiritual language. Give me the courage to be honest—with you and with myself.

Invitation

What's one faith phrase you use to mask pain? ("God's got it," "I'm fine," "It's all in his hands.") What might it sound like to tell the truth instead?

Self-Awareness Is Not the Goal

Let your roots grow down into him, and let your lives be built on him. Then your faith will grow strong in the truth you were taught.

COLOSSIANS 2:7

You can know your Enneagram number, your attachment style, your trauma history, your love language, and your emotional patterns—and still miss the point. Because self-awareness, for all its value, is not the goal. It's the starting point.

The point isn't just to understand yourself. It's to become someone who's rooted in truth, moved by love, and grounded enough to live with integrity when life gets loud.

Paul's prayer in Colossians is about being rooted in Christ—not just in your thoughts or feelings. He writes about faith growing strong through truth, but not truth for truth's sake. Truth that forms you. Truth that builds your life into something sturdy. Steady. Meaningful.

That's what self-awareness is for. Not self-obsession. Not circling your own story on repeat. But clear-eyed, humble honesty that allows real growth.

In psychological terms, self-awareness that isn't paired with action can become *rumination*—looping thoughts that don't lead to change. You see your issues, but you stay stuck in them. You talk about your patterns, but nothing shifts. It's insight without transformation.

So let this be your reminder: You don't have to be fully healed to move forward. But you do need to stay honest. Not perfectly. But consistently. And always with grace.

Self-awareness is not the end of the story. But it's a really good place to begin writing a better one.

Anchor Truth

Self-awareness is a tool, not a destination.

Prayer

God, thank you for the ways you've helped me see myself more clearly. Now give me the courage to live that truth—not for my ego, but for your glory. Let my awareness lead to love, wisdom, and real change.

Invitation

Look back over the last several days. What have you learned about yourself? Now ask, "What do I want to do with that insight?" Choose one small step that puts that awareness into action.

When Guilt Isn't Yours to Carry

Give all your worries and cares to God, for he cares about you.

1 PETER 5:7

Some guilt you carry isn't even yours. It was handed to you—subtly or straight up—by someone else. Maybe it was a parent who expected you to be the emotional glue. A church leader who confused control for conviction. A partner who made you feel responsible for their emotions. A friend who left, but you're still picking up the pieces of their disappointment.

Sometimes guilt doesn't come from doing something wrong. It comes from someone else needing you to feel wrong—to stay small, compliant, or overly responsible. That's not God. That's manipulation. And it creates a false moral weight you were never meant to bear.

Jesus confronted that kind of toxic guilt often. The religious leaders loaded people down with shame in the name of righteousness. But Jesus called it out: "They crush people with unbearable religious demands and never lift a finger to ease the burden" (Matthew 23:4). He lifted the burden instead.

If you're walking around with shame that doesn't belong to you; if you feel heavy and condemned but can't name the sin; if your guilt sounds more like anxiety than conviction—it might be time to ask, "Whose voice is this?" Because condemnation is *never* the voice of Christ. Even when you're in the wrong, his correction comes with clarity, not confusion—hope, not despair.

So take a breath. Drop the guilt that never belonged to you. And stand tall in the grace that sets you free.

Anchor Truth

Jesus never shames you into growth. He frees you into grace. Not all guilt is holy. And not all of it is yours to keep.

Prayer

Jesus, help me recognize the guilt that isn't mine to carry. Give me discernment to reject condemnation and courage to walk in your freedom instead.

Invitation

Think back: Is there a voice—past or present—that makes you feel wrong for just being human? Invite Jesus into that memory and let him lift what was never yours to carry.

The Power Pair

We refuse to wear masks and play games. We don't maneuver and manipulate behind the scenes. And we don't twist God's Word to suit ourselves. Rather, we keep everything we do and say out in the open.

2 CORINTHIANS 4:2 (MSG)

Authenticity and vulnerability go together like breath and lungs—separate in concept, inseparable in function. Authenticity is the commitment to be real. Vulnerability is the courage to reveal what that realness includes.

You can't have one without the other, not fully. Authenticity without vulnerability becomes performance. Vulnerability without authenticity becomes manipulation.

Social science confirms it again and again: People who live with both—those who are congruent (whose inner life and outer world are in sync) and emotionally open—report higher life satisfaction, stronger relationships, better physical health, and lower rates of anxiety and depression.

Why? Because hiding is exhausting. Living in constant self-protection keeps you in survival mode. Your nervous system is always scanning for threats: *Will I be rejected if they really see me?* And that kind of chronic vigilance chips away at your well-being.

But when you dare to show up as your full self—not just curated, but honest and open—you stop hustling for worthiness. You start living like someone who is already loved. That's not just psychology. That's theology.

Jesus didn't mask up. He wept. He bled. He got angry. He asked for help. He was the most authentic human to ever live—and the most vulnerable. He didn't just tell the truth. He embodied it.

Paul echoed this in his letters, constantly pulling back the curtain on his own struggles—not for pity, but to create connection and model integrity.

And it's your invitation too. Not to overshare or spill to everyone, but to live honestly. To choose truth over image. Wholeness over approval. Healing over hiding.

Anchor Truth

Authenticity says, "This is who I am." Vulnerability adds, "And I'll let you see it."

Prayer

God, help me stop pretending. Give me the wisdom to live truthfully and the strength to be seen. I want to walk in the freedom you offer—unmasked and unafraid.

Invitation

Ask yourself today, "Where am I showing up honestly? And where am I holding back?" Choose one space to practice this power pair—authenticity and vulnerability—side by side.

Truth Over Comfort

Instead, we will speak the truth in love, growing in every way more and more like Christ.

EPHESIANS 4:15

Telling the truth can be terrifying. Not the easy kind of truth, like "I prefer vanilla over chocolate." The kind of truth that shakes things up: "I'm not okay." "That hurt me." "I need to change." "I'm not who you think I am."

Truth-telling is costly. It can disrupt harmony, disappoint others, or even threaten relationships. But staying silent—out of fear of rocking the boat—can cost even more. It costs your integrity. Your growth. Your inner peace.

That's why Paul links truth-telling to spiritual maturity in Ephesians 4. Speaking the truth in love isn't just a communication strategy. It's a path to becoming more like Christ. Because Jesus didn't just embody love. He also embodied truth. He disrupted systems, challenged hypocrisy, confronted sin, and revealed grace. And he did it with compassion, but never at the expense of honesty.

Some truths aren't dramatic or confrontational. They're internal. They sound like "I'm exhausted." "I'm carrying resentment." "I need help." Naming those things out loud—whether to a therapist, a trusted friend, or in prayer—is an act of courage. And it's where transformation begins.

Psychologically, truth-telling reduces anxiety. The brain expends enormous energy trying to suppress, distort, or deny what's real. But naming reality—especially in safe, loving spaces—activates healing. It relieves internal tension. It aligns your inner world with your outer one. And that congruence brings clarity, connection, and peace.

Of course, truth without love becomes cruelty. But love without truth becomes manipulation. Growth comes when you learn to hold both: courageous truth, delivered with compassion.

Anchor Truth

Truth-telling is one of the boldest things you can do—and one of the most loving. It's not about being blunt; it's about being real.

Prayer

God, give me the courage to speak the truth—with love, with grace, and without fear. Let truth be the path that leads me closer to you and to others.

Invitation

What truth are you holding back—internally or relationally? Ask God for the right moment, the right words, and the right heart to speak it. Then take one brave step.

When Grief Gets Buried

I weep with sorrow;
encourage me by your word.

PSALM 119:28

You didn't mean to bury it, but you had to keep going. The funeral ended. The world moved on. The pain didn't. So you shoved it down. You told yourself you were fine. And maybe for a while it looked like you were.

But buried grief doesn't die. It waits. It seeps into your muscles, settles in your chest, hijacks your mood, tightens your shoulders, clouds your thinking. It disguises itself as fatigue. Or frustration. Or apathy. Sometimes even faith.

Some of us were taught that grief is something to push through quickly. That expressing sorrow might look like weakness. That spiritual maturity means moving on.

But the psalmist gives us a better way: "I weep with sorrow; encourage me by your word." He doesn't pretend. He doesn't hide. He names his pain. And he seeks solace, not in distraction, but in the presence of God.

Buried grief often needs to be unearthed gently—with compassion, not shame. Sometimes that happens in prayer. Sometimes in tears you didn't expect while folding laundry. Sometimes in counseling. Sometimes with a trusted friend who can hold space without rushing your process.

Don't underestimate the toll unacknowledged sorrow takes on your mental, emotional, and even physical health. Research in trauma recovery and emotional regulation confirms what Scripture has always hinted at: Unexpressed pain doesn't vanish—it festers.

Grief isn't your enemy—avoidance is. And honesty is holy. God doesn't rebuke you for sorrow. He meets you in it. Because healing doesn't happen where grief is denied. It happens where it's heard.

Anchor Truth

Grief that's buried doesn't disappear—it waits for safe release. And God invites you to bring it into the light.

Prayer

God, I've pushed past some pain I didn't want to feel. Help me unearth it—not to wallow, but to heal. Give me the courage to sit with sorrow, the grace to receive comfort, and the safety to let you meet me there.

Invitation

Is there grief you've buried to survive? Speak it aloud today, even in a whisper. Let your sorrow be seen. Let your healing begin.

Holy Questions

Call to me and I will answer you and tell you great and unsearchable things you do not know.

JEREMIAH 33:3 (NIV)

Some people were taught that having questions means you lack faith. But in Scripture, questions are often the birthplace of faith. Moses questioned his calling. David questioned God's timing. Job questioned his suffering. Mary questioned the angel's announcement. Even Jesus, in his agony, asked, "Why?"

Healthy spirituality isn't built on having all the answers. It's built on a willingness to keep asking. To stay open. To stay curious.

Theologian Frederick Buechner once said that doubts are the "ants in the pants" of faith. They keep it awake and moving. When we ask real questions, it means we're engaged, not indifferent. It means we want to grow.

Psychologically speaking, curiosity activates the brain's reward system. It signals a desire to learn, to explore, to make meaning. That's true in classrooms, and it's true in the soul. Spiritual curiosity is the opposite of complacency. It's the spark that keeps your relationship with God from going stale.

When we stop asking, we risk drifting into shallow belief systems built on borrowed conviction. But when we stay curious—about Scripture, about our pain, about God's voice in our lives—we cultivate a faith that is alive, honest, and grounded.

God isn't threatened by your curiosity. He welcomes it. He's not looking for robotic agreement. He's looking for relationship. And relationship thrives in dialogue.

So bring your questions. Let them sharpen you. Let them deepen you. Let them lead you closer to the one who says, "Call to me."

Anchor Truth

Real faith makes room for questions. When you stop being curious, you stop growing. Keep asking. God isn't scared of your questions.

Prayer

God, give me the courage to bring my honest questions to you, not just the neat ones. Help me trust that in seeking, I will find.

Invitation

What's one spiritual question you've been sitting on or stuffing down? Write it out. Pray it honestly. Then stay open to how God might begin answering—not always with certainty, but with presence.

The Myth of "I'll Be Happy When . . ."

Those who love money will never have enough. How meaningless to think that wealth brings true happiness!

ECCLESIASTES 5:10

You've thought it to yourself. Maybe not aloud, but it's there: *I'll be happy when I lose the weight . . . when I get married . . . when I have kids . . . when the kids move out . . . when I get the promotion . . . when I retire . . .*

But here's the problem with chasing happiness down the timeline: *When* never really arrives. As soon as you reach one milestone, the next one moves the goalpost. It's a treadmill of deferred joy—exhausting, deceptive, and endless.

Psychologists call this the *arrival fallacy*—the false belief that future achievement or change will bring lasting happiness. Studies show that while a new circumstance might bring a short-term emotional boost, it rarely results in long-term satisfaction. Why? Because our minds adapt quickly, and we shift our focus to the next thing.

The writer of Ecclesiastes saw this thousands of years ago. He watched people pursue wealth, pleasure, power—and called it meaningless when it became the basis for fulfillment. It's not that those things are inherently wrong, but they're leaky containers for the kind of joy our souls crave.

So what's the alternative? Live now. Be here. Find gratitude and joy in this moment, not just the next. God isn't waiting until your life improves to love you or bless you. He's in the room with you now, just as it is.

Your soul doesn't need a new chapter to begin rejoicing. It just needs a new lens—one that sees beauty in the mundane, purpose in the waiting, and grace woven through even the messiest parts of your now. Joy isn't postponed. It's present.

Anchor Truth

Joy delayed is often joy denied. Happiness isn't waiting in the next season—it's hiding in this one.

Prayer

God, help me stop chasing the next thing as the source of my joy. Open my eyes to what you're doing now—in the small, the overlooked, the ordinary. Teach me to rejoice without conditions.

Invitation

What have you been telling yourself you need before you can be happy? Try flipping the script. Ask yourself, "How can I begin experiencing joy even here?"

Is God Disappointed in Me?

The LORD is compassionate and merciful,
slow to get angry and filled with unfailing love.

PSALM 103:8

You haven't prayed in weeks. Or months. Or maybe you still do, but it feels half-hearted, more like reaching than believing.

Even the short prayers on these pages might feel strange, like borrowed words from someone more certain than you. That's okay. You don't have to feel every word. Sometimes prayer is just choosing not to close the door.

And underneath it all, this quiet fear has crept in: *God must be disappointed in me.* You didn't mean to wander. You didn't plan to unravel. But now that you're here—tired, unsure, ashamed—you can't help but wonder if God feels far because he's pulling away.

It's known as *self-reproach*—the tendency to turn disappointment inward, assuming that your failure, your distance, your doubt has made you unworthy of love. In faith spaces, this often gets spiritualized: *If I were a better Christian, I wouldn't feel this way. If I had more faith, I wouldn't be struggling.*

But the character of God tells a different story. Psalm 103 says God is "compassionate and merciful, slow to get angry and filled with unfailing love." That's not a God who's pacing the floor, arms crossed, waiting for you to get your act together. That's a God who runs toward prodigals. Who welcomes questions. Who knows your story in full and stays anyway.

Disappointment assumes you've failed a test. Grace assumes you're still growing.

If you've projected your own frustration onto God, it's okay. You're not the first. But you don't have to stay stuck there. God isn't measuring your worth by your spiritual performance. He's not waiting for a perfect prayer. He's already near. Already kind. Already loving. Even now, even here.

Anchor Truth

God looks at his children with compassion, not disappointment. He longs to be close to you today.

Prayer

God, I've been avoiding you—not because I don't care, but because I've been afraid that I've let you down. Help me believe you're not disappointed. Teach me to see myself through your compassion, not my shame.

Invitation

Write this where you'll see it today: God is not disappointed in me. God is compassionate toward me. *Repeat it every time self-judgment creeps in.*

When It Sounds Like Self-Loathing

We are merely moving shadows,
and all our busy rushing ends in nothing.
We heap up wealth, not knowing who will spend it.

PSALM 39:6

Jealousy doesn't always sound like "I want what they have." Sometimes it sounds like "What's wrong with me?" That's the sneaky thing about comparison. It turns your eyes outward but then weaponizes what you see against yourself.

You scroll past someone else's highlight reel, and suddenly your own life feels flat. You hear about someone else's opportunity and immediately question your value. You start wondering, *Shouldn't I be further along by now? Why can't I get it together?* That's not ambition. That's shame in disguise. And left unchecked, it turns into quiet bitterness—not just toward others, but toward yourself.

Psalm 39 reminds us that all the hustling, achieving, and performing we do to feel "enough" can still end in emptiness. Why? Because worth was never meant to be earned through comparison. And peace was never meant to come from measuring up.

Jealousy often exposes where your identity is leaking. It reveals where you've tied your value to visibility, achievement, or approval—and where that foundation is cracking under pressure.

In psychological terms, this overlaps with *social comparison theory*—the way we measure ourselves against others to gauge our standing. But here's the thing: You were never designed to be measured. You were meant to be loved.

God is not handing out identity based on performance. He isn't keeping score. He's not holding you up against anyone else's timeline or talent. And you don't have to either.

Anchor Truth

Jealousy often masks shame, and shame always lies about your worth.

Prayer

God, help me stop using other people's lives as a mirror for my own value. When jealousy turns inward, meet me with compassion. Remind me who I am before the comparison.

Invitation

When you feel jealousy today, ask, "What am I believing about myself in this moment?" Then ask God what's actually true. Write that version down.

What's Good About Loneliness?

But the LORD was with Joseph in the prison and showed him his faithful love.

GENESIS 39:21

Nobody signs up for loneliness. It's not something we chase. It's something we endure. But what if, beneath the ache of isolation, there's something sacred? What if loneliness—unwelcome as it is—can actually give us something, not just take something away?

Ask Joseph. Betrayed by his brothers, sold into slavery, falsely accused, and thrown into prison, he knew what it meant to be alone. Not just alone in body, but dismissed, misunderstood, and cut off from everything familiar. Loneliness wasn't a moment for Joseph. It was a season.

And yet, it was in the silence of that prison that something deeper took root: Joseph's trust. His resilience. His identity. Scripture doesn't say Joseph felt God's presence. It says God was with him. Even when no one else was.

There's a clarity that can come through loneliness. A stripping away of noise, distraction, and approval seeking. In loneliness, you learn what it means to be okay with you. You stop asking every room, every relationship, every response to validate your worth. You start discovering that God's presence is not just a comfort. It's your anchor.

Psychologically, solitude (which is different from isolation) is a wellspring of creativity, self-reflection, and emotional regulation. When embraced intentionally, it can become a catalyst for growth—spiritually and mentally.

That's the paradox: Loneliness, while painful, can purify. It can force you to confront what you've been avoiding. And if you let it, it can open your heart to deeper connection—with God, with yourself, and eventually with others.

You don't have to like loneliness to let it do its work.

Anchor Truth

Loneliness can either shrivel your soul or shape it. The difference is whether you let it lead you toward God or away from him.

Prayer

God, I don't want to feel alone, but I trust that even in this space, you're doing something in me. Help me to stay open, not bitter. Help me to grow, not shrink. And most of all, remind me that you're near.

Invitation

Instead of resisting your loneliness today, try asking it a question: "What are you here to teach me?" Write down what you sense. Even pain can be a prophet.

Choice Isn't a Luxury

Today I have given you the choice between life and death, between blessings and curses. . . . Oh, that you would choose life, so that you and your descendants might live!

DEUTERONOMY 30:19

Some people talk about choice like it's a luxury. Like it only belongs to the confident, the educated, the emotionally stable. But Scripture is clear: Choice is a birthright.

In Deuteronomy, Moses speaks to an entire people who have spent years wandering in the wilderness. They're tired, traumatized, uncertain about their future—and even they are given a choice.

"Choose life," he pleads. Not because it's easy. Not because it's obvious. But because it's still possible.

That's agency. Not having all the answers, but still having a vote. Still showing up. Still believing your decisions matter, even when the road behind you is full of detours.

But here's the hard part: Agency is scary. Because the moment you realize you have a choice is the moment you have to own your next step. Blaming stops working. Numbing stops working. Passivity stops working. And that's when some people pull back—not because they're lazy, but because they're afraid of what ownership might cost.

It's okay to feel that fear. But don't let it fool you into thinking your choices don't count.

In trauma work, one of the most important turning points is helping someone discover that they're not just reacting anymore—they're responding. They're back in the driver's seat, even if the road is rough.

You might feel like your options are limited. And maybe they are. But even a small, soul-aligned choice has power. That's how agency grows—one "yes" at a time.

Anchor Truth

Choice isn't something you earn. It's something you exercise.

Prayer

God, I don't want to live numb or passive. Even when I feel tired or unsure, remind me that I'm still capable of choosing. Help me choose life—not just survival, but real, soul-deep living.

Invitation

Pay attention to a small moment today when you'd normally check out or go along with the flow. Pause. Ask, "What would 'choosing life' look like right here?" Then go do it.

The Pose Is Exhausting

Beware of the yeast of the Pharisees—their hypocrisy. The time is coming when everything that is covered up will be revealed, and all that is secret will be made known to all.

LUKE 12:1-2

It starts subtly. You adjust how you speak in one room, soften your opinions in another. You laugh a little louder than you feel, nod when you disagree, stay quiet when you should speak up.

You're not lying, but you're not fully there, either. You're posing. Posing isn't always fake—it's often fear. Fear of being too much. Or not enough. Fear that if you brought your full self to the table, you'd lose your seat. So you edit. You hustle. You craft a more palatable version of yourself.

And the worst part? It almost works. You might get praise. You might fit in. But it's not you being accepted. It's your pose.

This is *incongruence*—a split between your outward expression and your inner experience. Over time, that disconnection creates anxiety, depression, and burnout. You start to lose track of who you are. You feel like an imposter in your own skin.

It's easy to live that life. Chasing status. Outperforming others. Maintaining appearances. But Jesus confronts us with truth—and with grace. We can drop the mask of hypocrisy, stop performing for human approval, and start living from divine acceptance. This frees us to be bold, honest, and whole.

You don't have to keep shape-shifting to earn love or belonging. You don't have to protect others from your truth.

God doesn't bless the version of you that you're pretending to be. He meets you right where you are and invites that person to come alive.

Anchor Truth

You don't need to perform to be loved. You are already seen and safe in Christ.

Prayer

God, I'm tired of pretending. Give me the courage to live from my true self, not my polished one.

Invitation

Notice where you're tempted to pose today. Instead of defaulting to your usual mask, pause. Breathe. Then choose one small act of authenticity.

When Love Becomes a Tangle

Don't copy the behavior and customs of this world, but let God transform you into a new person by changing the way you think.

ROMANS 12:2

Some families confuse closeness with control. They expect loyalty without limits, unity without individuality, and love without boundaries.

If you've ever felt guilty for having your own thoughts, needs, or dreams—especially when they conflict with "what the family does"—you might know what enmeshment feels like.

Enmeshment isn't about affection. It's about entanglement. It's when emotional boundaries are so blurred that someone else's anxiety becomes your emergency. Their disappointment becomes your failure. Their unspoken expectations become your silent burden.

You grow up learning to suppress your voice to keep the peace. To caretake instead of connect. To stay small so others won't feel threatened. And if you start to step away, even for good reasons, you feel selfish.

You're not being selfish; you're healing.

God doesn't call us to be clones of our parents or carbon copies of a family legacy. He calls us to be transformed—to be *renewed* in how we think, choose, and live.

Yes, honor your family. But don't lose yourself in them.

Even Jesus had to draw lines. When his mother and brothers tried to rein him in, he said plainly, "Anyone who does the will of my Father in heaven is my brother and sister and mother!" (Matthew 12:50). Translation? Even healthy love has boundaries.

And you're allowed to grow, even if your growth makes others uncomfortable.

Anchor Truth

Real love doesn't erase identity. It makes space for it. God calls you to honor others but not abandon yourself in the process.

Prayer

God, I've been tangled in expectations for too long. Help me love my family without losing my voice. Show me how to set healthy boundaries that honor you and bring healing, not hiding.

Invitation

Take one small step toward healthy boundaries today. That might mean saying no without guilt, making your own decision, or acknowledging what's yours—and what's not. Healing starts with clarity.

The Weight You're Carrying

I acknowledged my sin to you, and I did not cover my iniquity; I said, "I will confess my transgressions to the LORD," and you forgave the iniquity of my sin.

PSALM 32:5 (ESV)

You might feel it when you think back to something you did—or didn't do—and your stomach flips. You might feel it lying awake at night, rerunning the same tape. You failed. You let someone down. Maybe yourself. That's guilt. But sometimes it grows into something worse: Shame.

Guilt says, "I messed up." Shame says, "I *am* messed up." While guilt is about your actions, shame attacks your identity. And the enemy of your soul loves nothing more than to keep you tangled up in both.

You were never meant to carry this weight alone. And you were never meant to be *defined* by your lowest moment.

David felt this weight. Psalm 32 pulls back the curtain on his soul. He said staying silent about his guilt made him feel like his bones were rotting from the inside out. That's what guilt does when it festers: It eats away at you.

But the moment David opened his heart, just a little, everything shifted. Grace rushed in. Forgiveness met him. The weight lifted.

You don't have to hustle for that kind of mercy. You don't have to bleed for it, beg for it, or prove you deserve it. And that relentless voice in your head—the one that calls you a failure, a disappointment, too far gone? That's not the voice of God. That's shame talking.

The Spirit doesn't drag you through the mud. He lifts your chin. He tells the truth, but with tenderness. Because conviction heals while shame corrodes.

You get to decide who gets the microphone.

Anchor Truth

God never shames you into change. His conviction is clear but always compassionate—meant to free you, not chain you.

Prayer

God, sometimes I don't even know why I feel so heavy. Show me what I'm carrying that's not mine. Help me bring my guilt—and even my shame—into your light. Remind me that I am more than my worst moments. I am loved. I am seen. And I am yours.

Invitation

Take a deep breath. Say this out loud if you need to: "I am not my shame. I am not my past. I am not beyond grace."

A Lighter Way to Carry Life

The eyes of the LORD watch over those who do right;
his ears are open to their cries for help.

PSALM 34:15

Some people seem wired for lightness. They bounce back quickly. See the bright side. Expect good things. If that's not you, it's okay.

Maybe you tend to scan for problems. Maybe your reflex is to brace, not believe. Maybe the optimism of others makes you roll your eyes.

Here's the good news: Optimism isn't just a personality trait. It's a mental habit, and it can be cultivated over time.

Research shows that optimistic people don't live in a fantasy. They're not immune to grief, loss, or fear. But they're more likely to bounce back from hardship. Build healthier relationships. Cope with stress in constructive ways. Persevere toward their goals. Experience lower rates of depression and anxiety.

Why? Because their mindset changes how they respond to life. They don't just see the light at the end of the tunnel. They move toward it.

Scripture echoes this again and again. Not just "Think happy thoughts," but "Trust in a good God." Psalm 34 reminds us: God sees. God hears. God is near. And when you believe that—when your core lens is trust instead of fear—life becomes lighter. Not easier, but lighter.

If pessimism is your default, start small. Catch yourself when you spiral toward the worst-case scenario. Ask, "Is there another way to see this?" And even if your mood doesn't change immediately, your awareness will. And that's where transformation begins.

Hope isn't pretending. It's partnering with the truth that God is still at work, even when you don't see it yet.

Anchor Truth

Optimism lifts what fear tries to weigh down and makes space for joy.

Prayer

God, shift my perspective. When I default to fear or doubt, help me choose the lighter path of trust.

Invitation

Today, notice your inner commentary. Is it bracing or believing? Write down one scenario in your life where you can begin practicing a more hopeful interpretation.

The Lie It Tells

You will know the truth, and the truth will set you free.

JOHN 8:32

Addiction always tells a story. It whispers promises: relief, escape, comfort, reward. And for a moment, it delivers. That's the hook. But behind every addictive pattern is a lie. And the lie is always the same: "This is the only thing that works."

The substance, the screen, the scroll, the binge, the click, the fix. They show up like a savior, offering what feels like control in a moment when you feel powerless. But what they really create is a cycle of dependence. Of shame. Of disconnection.

It's a strategy the brain adopts to avoid pain or to numb emotion. It works temporarily. And that's what makes it dangerous. But Jesus offers a different path. Not one of cold discipline or guilt, but of truth. Not punishment, but freedom.

Truth doesn't always feel good at first. In fact, it often stings. But it breaks the illusion. The truth is, you are not beyond healing. You are not the sum of your worst habit. You do not need to stay stuck in the loop.

And you don't have to do it alone. Healing happens best in connection—with God and with others who know what it means to struggle and stay.

That first step? Start naming the lie, the one your addiction tells you when no one's watching. Drag it into the light. It can't survive there. Because the truth—the real, liberating, uncomfortable truth—is that you were made for freedom. And you're allowed to want it.

Anchor Truth

Freedom starts with naming the lie.

Prayer

God, I've believed some lies. But you are truth. Help me stop pretending and start healing.

Invitation

Write down the one lie your addiction tells you. Say it out loud. Then write down one truth that gently pushes back. Tape it to your mirror if you need to.

The Trap of Entitlement

You must have the same attitude that Christ Jesus had. Though he was God, he did not think of equality with God as something to cling to.

PHILIPPIANS 2:5-6

Entitlement whispers, "You deserve better." At first, it sounds like justice. But give it time, and it turns sour. You work hard, love well, give generously—and yet life doesn't pay out like a vending machine.

So the story starts to creep in: *This isn't fair. I've earned more than this. I shouldn't have to deal with that.* It's a slippery slope. Because entitlement wears a dozen disguises: Bitterness in marriage. Anger at coworkers. Resentment toward God. And underneath it all, a belief that says, "I'm owed."

Here's the thing: Entitlement isn't always loud. Sometimes it hides in self-pity or silent comparison. Sometimes it dresses up like confidence or boundaries. But it's not contentment. And it's not joy.

Jesus had every right to claim status, power, and glory. But he didn't cling to any of it. He let go—willingly. That's not weakness. That's the deepest kind of strength.

Entitlement binds you. Gratitude breaks the chains.

Want more peace? Loosen your grip on what you think you're owed. Want more joy? Let go of keeping score. You're not here to prove your worth. You're here to live loved—and love freely.

Anchor Truth

Entitlement drains your soul. Gratitude fills it. Jesus didn't demand what he deserved—he chose what we needed. That's your model for real freedom.

Prayer

God, help me recognize when entitlement creeps in. Remind me that I'm not owed anything, but I've been given everything in you. Teach me to live openhanded and grateful.

Invitation

Where are you quietly keeping score? In your marriage? Your work? Your faith? Write down one area where you feel "owed." Then write one unexpected gift in that same area. Gratitude flips the script. Let it.

Resilience Doesn't Mean You Don't Feel

I cry out in anguish, but I cannot find peace. My heart is broken.

JEREMIAH 8:18-21 (PARAPHRASE)

Somewhere along the way, you might have picked up this idea that strong people don't cry. They don't complain. They keep calm. Push through. Stay steady.

But real resilience is not the absence of emotion—it's the willingness to feel it and keep going anyway.

Just look at Jeremiah. He was called by God. Faithful. Courageous. But also heartbroken, exhausted, and overwhelmed. His writings echo with raw sorrow: "My grief is beyond healing; my heart is broken." He's been nicknamed the "weeping prophet," not because he was weak, but because he let himself feel.

That's strength. That's resilience.

Clinical psychology backs this up: Emotional suppression is linked to higher anxiety, burnout, and even physical illness. In contrast, people who allow themselves to experience and process their emotions—through journaling, talking, praying, or crying—tend to recover faster and build deeper emotional resilience.

Resilient people don't numb out. They don't shove everything down. They grieve. They name their fears. They admit when it's too much. And like Jeremiah, they still show up. They still speak truth. They still walk with God.

Feelings don't make you fragile. They make you honest, and honesty is a building block of strength. You don't have to fake fine. Feel what you feel, and know that even your tears can be part of your healing.

Anchor Truth

Resilience means giving yourself permission to feel and trusting that God can handle it all.

Prayer

God, sometimes I think I need to stay strong by staying silent. But you don't ask me to hold it all in. You invite me to pour it out. Thank you for receiving every tear, every ache, every unspoken prayer.

Invitation

Let yourself feel something today without judgment. Cry if you need to. Journal it. Pray it out. Or simply sit in silence and say, "This matters. God sees me." That's not weakness, that's healing.

Gratitude and Mental Health

Fix your thoughts on what is true, and honorable, and right, and pure, and lovely, and admirable. Think about things that are excellent and worthy of praise.

PHILIPPIANS 4:8

Let's be real: When your brain feels like it's wading through mud, the last thing you want to hear is "Just be grateful." Gratitude doesn't cure depression. It doesn't erase anxiety. It's not a spiritual Band-Aid you slap onto deep emotional wounds. But it is powerful.

Research has shown again and again that consistent, genuine expressions of gratitude can rewire the brain. Gratitude strengthens neural pathways linked to optimism, calm, and resilience. Gratitude activates the prefrontal cortex, the part of your brain that helps you regulate emotions and make healthy decisions.

One study even found that people who wrote down three things they were grateful for each day showed better sleep, improved mood, and lower levels of stress and depression over time.

This isn't about toxic positivity. This is about retraining your mind to see what's still good when everything feels hard. Not because you're ignoring the pain, but because you're fighting to keep it from swallowing you whole.

Paul wasn't writing to people while he was on vacation when he penned Philippians 4:8. He was in prison. Shackled. Cold. Uncertain about tomorrow. And still he pointed toward beauty. He reminded believers to fix their thoughts not on fear, not on what's missing—but on what remains lovely, true, and worthy of praise.

That's not denial. That's defiance. That's resilience.

Gratitude isn't a mood. It's a muscle, and you strengthen it every time you stop and say, "Okay, this part of life is hard—but that sunrise, that kind text, that cup of coffee, that breath? That's still good."

And don't forget this: Gratitude is a tool of spiritual warfare. Every time you thank God in the middle of the mess, you're pushing back the darkness. You're declaring that despair doesn't get the final word. That hope still breathes. That light still shines.

Anchor Truth

Gratitude won't erase the pain, but it can anchor you in the storm. It grounds your heart when your mind is spiraling.

Prayer

God, train my eyes to see beauty, even when my mind is tired and my heart is heavy. Help me hold on to what is still good, still worthy, still true.

Invitation

If you're in a tough spot, try this: Write down just one thing you're grateful for today. Don't pressure yourself to feel it. Just notice it. Name it. Let that be enough.

What Do You Really Need?

You do not have because you do not ask God.

JAMES 4:2 (NIV)

You say you need rest, but what kind of rest? A nap? A weekend away? A conversation where you don't have to perform? You say you need support, but what does that look like? A mentor? A therapist? Someone who simply listens without fixing? You say you need healing, but from what, specifically? From resentment? From shame? From a childhood that still echoes in your adulthood?

It's one thing to say you're running on empty. It's another to know what kind of fuel you're actually missing. Most people don't pause long enough to ask themselves, "What do I really need right now?"

The answers are often buried under years of people-pleasing, spiritual bypassing, and emotional fog. Sometimes it's easier to say "I'm fine" than to dig beneath the surface and risk discovering unmet needs we were taught to ignore. But clarity is kindness.

Jesus didn't shy away from asking people pointed questions: "What do you want me to do for you? Do you want to get well?" He didn't assume. He invited specificity, because transformation starts with honest self-awareness.

If you're feeling numb, irritable, or burned out, start here: Name your need. Maybe it's permission. Maybe it's space. Maybe it's reconnection with your own heart. Whatever it is, put language to it. Whisper it to God. Write it down. Speak it to a trusted friend.

You're not too much for having needs. And healing often begins with one brave sentence: "I think I need . . ." But that's only the beginning.

James reminds us that unmet needs aren't always about lack—they're often about silence. "You do not have because you do not ask God." Not because God is stingy, but because you've learned to silence yourself before you ever speak. You've rehearsed the self-sufficiency script. You've whispered your longings into pillows, not into prayer.

But God invites your voice. Your needs aren't too trivial, too tangled, or too late. Ask. Not just generally—specifically. Honestly. Go ahead. Say it out loud: "I think I need . . ." God is already listening.

Anchor Truth

You can't move toward healing if you don't name what's hurting or what's missing. Specificity is a spiritual act of courage.

Prayer

God, I've gotten good at ignoring my needs. Help me slow down long enough to hear them. Give me the clarity to name them and the courage to believe you care.

Invitation

Take five minutes today and answer this question without censoring yourself: "What do I really need right now?" Be specific. Be honest. Don't spiritualize it. Just name it.

Gratitude in the Middle of the Mess

Be thankful in all circumstances, for this is God's will for you who belong to Christ Jesus.

1 THESSALONIANS 5:18

This verse can frustrate. Be thankful in all circumstances? What about the messy ones? The confusing ones? The painful ones?

Turns out, Paul wasn't telling us to fake it. He wasn't calling for toxic positivity or a synthetic smile. He was offering a spiritual survival strategy. Because when life feels like it's unraveling, gratitude is the thread that helps hold us together. Not gratitude for the mess. That's not what Paul said. But gratitude in the mess. Right there in the thick of it.

The kind of gratitude that says, "This is hard—but God is still here." "This hurts—but I'm not abandoned." "This doesn't make sense—but I'll keep looking for the good."

And you know what? Gratitude doesn't change your situation, but it will change you. It softens cynicism. It steadies you in chaos. It keeps your heart open when it wants to shut down.

Paul wrote those words knowing pain firsthand. Beaten, shipwrecked, imprisoned. And still thankful.

Because he had learned that gratitude is a lifeline to joy. Not a denial of suffering, but a defiant choice to keep hope alive within it.

Gratitude in hard times is a holy refusal to let darkness have the last word.

Anchor Truth

Gratitude doesn't just look forward in hope. It looks back in recognition. And that backward glance often carries the healing we didn't know we needed.

Prayer

God, thank you for the people who poured into me, especially when I couldn't see what you were shaping. Help me honor them in memory and action. And show me how to do the same for someone else today.

Invitation

Think of one person who has impacted your life in a meaningful way, then tell them. A text, a letter, a call. Be specific. Let your gratitude be heard while it can still be received.

When You've Been Ghosted

Even if my father and mother abandon me,
the LORD will hold me close.

PSALM 27:10

No goodbye. No explanation. Just silence. Being ghosted messes with your mind. It's not just that someone disappeared. It's the confusion they leave behind. You replay every interaction, searching for clues. *Did I say too much? Not enough? Did I miss something?* And the worst part is, you may never get an answer.

Psychologists call this *ambiguous loss*—a grief without closure. It's real, and it hurts. You feel rejected, abandoned, unworthy, and angry that it still bothers you. But here's what's also true: Their disappearance is not a reflection of your value. It's a reflection of their inability or unwillingness to engage honestly.

Even Jesus experienced sudden abandonment. One minute the crowds were cheering; the next, they vanished. His disciples scattered. But his identity didn't shatter. Because he wasn't anchored to their approval. He was anchored to the Father's love. You can be too.

Yes, being ghosted stings. But your worth isn't erased just because someone walked away. And you don't need their response to move forward. You need healing, not their explanation. You need truth, not their validation. You don't have to chase what vanished.

God hasn't ghosted you. He sees you. Hears you. Holds you. And his presence is more faithful than any flaky friend, flaky date, or disengaged churchgoer who couldn't be bothered to offer closure.

Anchor Truth

Silence from others doesn't mean silence from God. He remains present, even when people disappear.

Prayer

God, I hate the confusion of being left without answers. Heal what still hurts. Remind me that I don't need someone's reply to have peace. You haven't ghosted me, and you never will.

Invitation

Instead of replaying what went wrong, release it. Write a letter you'll never send. Say what you need to say. Then give it to God and take back your power.

You're Not Crazy—You're Curious

It is the glory of God to conceal a matter;
to search out a matter is the glory of kings.

PROVERBS 25:2 (NIV)

You're not trying to rebel. You're not on a mission to deconstruct everything. You're just, well, curious. And for some reason, that's made people nervous.

Maybe you've been told you're "overthinking it," "too analytical," or "just going through a phase." But what if your questions aren't a sign of spiritual drift? What if they're evidence of *spiritual depth*?

Curiosity is a sign of health, not heresy. Curiosity is a vital part of how the brain and soul develop. From a psychological perspective, it's linked to *intrinsic motivation*—choosing to do something simply because you enjoy doing it—and *epistemic drive*—a five-dollar word identifying the internal desire to explore, learn, and make sense of the world.

Curiosity is often a marker of meaning and resilience. It means you're not shutting down or giving up—you're leaning in. You want your faith to grow, not calcify.

Spiritually, it's how many of the greatest faith discoveries have been made. The prophets asked hard questions. The disciples misunderstood constantly. Even Jesus responded to questions with more questions. Proverbs 25:2 reminds us that searching things out is a sacred act. God is not diminished by our desire to explore. In fact, he welcomes it.

Unfortunately, religious environments can sometimes make curiosity feel dangerous. Why? It threatens the illusion of control. It challenges group norms.

In some Christian spaces, curiosity is seen as a threat. It disrupts certainty. It asks people to say, "I don't know," when they've built systems around having answers. But curiosity is not the enemy of faith. It's often the doorway to a more personal faith—one that isn't borrowed, but owned.

So if you find yourself asking, "Am I crazy for wondering this?" the answer is no. You're not crazy. You're awake. And God is not afraid of awakened minds that hold curious questions.

Anchor Truth

God does not condemn curiosity. Ask questions and share them with him.

Prayer

God, thank you for giving me a mind that seeks, wonders, and wrestles. Help me remember that curiosity is not rebellion. It's a reflection of how you made me. Teach me to explore with both humility and hope.

Invitation

Today, name one spiritual question you've been turning over in your head. Write it down—not to solve it, but to honor the part of you that still wants to understand.

The Ache to Be Liked

Our purpose is to please God, not people. He alone examines the motives of our hearts.

1 THESSALONIANS 2:4

Let's be honest: We all want to be liked. It's built into us. From our earliest moments, we learned that being approved of felt like safety—smiles, nods, gold stars, pats on the head. Belonging meant survival.

Disapproval felt like danger. And while we grow up, that reflex doesn't always grow out of us. You know the signs: Replaying a conversation to see if you came off okay. Smiling through discomfort to avoid tension. Editing yourself so you won't rock the boat. Apologizing for having needs.

This isn't just about insecurity; it's about wiring. Psychologists call it *social conformity bias*—our natural tendency to adjust ourselves to avoid rejection and gain approval. It's primal. It's powerful. And it can quietly take over your life.

The ache to be liked isn't evil. It means you care about connection. But when it becomes the compass that guides your choices, you start to drift from your truest self. You become a chameleon. And in the process, you stop trusting that who you are—flaws, edges, and all—is already enough.

Even Jesus wasn't liked by everyone. That didn't stop him from healing on the Sabbath, flipping tables, or calling out hypocrisy. He knew who he was. He had clarity. And that clarity gave him courage. Paul echoed the same truth: "Our purpose is to please God, not people."

If your days are shaped by the hope that everyone will approve, you'll bend yourself out of shape trying to meet their ever-shifting expectations. And still you'll come up empty.

Anchor Truth

Your worth isn't up for debate. You don't have to be liked by others to be loved by God.

Prayer

God, help me see where I'm chasing approval instead of resting in your affection. Remind me that being liked isn't the same as being whole. Give me the courage to live from your delight, not from others' opinions.

Invitation

Notice today when you're tempted to adjust yourself to gain approval. Pause. Ask, "Is this about connection or control?" Let that moment be a turning point toward deeper honesty.

The Shame of Loneliness

Those who look to him for help will be radiant with joy;
no shadow of shame will darken their faces.

PSALM 34:5

Loneliness can feel like failure. Like you did something wrong. Like you're not interesting enough or lovable enough or worthy enough for someone to stick around.

That's the shame of loneliness, and it runs deeper than the ache of being alone. Because it tells you the problem isn't your circumstances, it's you. This isn't just emotional—it's neurological.

Studies show that the parts of the brain activated by physical pain are also activated when we feel excluded or disconnected. But unlike physical pain, the wounds of loneliness can get wrapped in shame, convincing you to stay silent. To pretend you're fine. To isolate more, not less.

But here's the truth: Loneliness is part of being human. Even the most connected people hit seasons where they feel unknown, uninvited, or invisible.

In the Bible, Hagar fled into the wilderness after being mistreated, and it was there, in the middle of her isolation, that God met her. She called him *El-roi*—"the God who sees me."

The shame of loneliness begins to lift when you realize that God sees you too. You don't have to hide your ache. You don't have to hustle to prove your worth. You don't have to pretend you're not struggling just to fit in.

God isn't embarrassed by your emptiness. He's drawn to it. And even when it feels like no one else notices, he does. Not with pity but with love. With nearness. With a reminder that your loneliness doesn't define your identity or diminish your value.

You are not alone in your loneliness.

Anchor Truth

Loneliness doesn't make you less. It makes you human. And God meets you there, without shame.

Prayer

God, sometimes I feel like being lonely means I've failed somehow. Help me see the difference between shame and sorrow. Remind me that you're not disappointed in my ache. You meet me in it. And you call me seen.

Invitation

If you've been pretending you're fine, pause and speak honestly with God. Shame thrives in secrecy, but freedom grows when you get real.

Resilience Through Relationships

Two people are better off than one, for they can help each other succeed. If one person falls, the other can reach out and help.

ECCLESIASTES 4:9-10

Resilience doesn't grow in isolation. In fact, some of the most resilient people in Scripture weren't strong because they stood alone but because they stayed connected. They leaned on community. They received help. They refused to walk through fire without someone by their side.

Think of David and Jonathan. Their friendship was more than affection; it was protection. When Saul turned on David, it was Jonathan's loyalty that gave David the strength to keep running toward his calling.

Or Elijah, who collapsed under the weight of despair in 1 Kings 19. God didn't just send food—he eventually brought Elisha, someone to walk with him, learn from him, and stand beside him. That companionship was part of God's healing.

And then there's Mary—a spiritual giant, yes—but also deeply human. She stayed for three months with Elizabeth, whose presence brought her comfort and joy in the early months of her unexpected pregnancy.

These stories echo what modern psychology confirms: Relational connection is a critical factor in resilience. Supportive relationships—whether through friends, family, mentors, or community—can lower stress, increase emotional regulation, and improve recovery from trauma.

You weren't meant to muscle through life alone. You need people who will speak truth when your mind spirals. People who will sit in the pain without trying to fix it. People who will walk with you when you don't have strength to stand.

That's not weakness. It's wisdom. It's God's design. Resilience isn't just about holding on. Sometimes it's about letting someone hold you.

Anchor Truth

God uses relationships to restore, strengthen, and sustain us.

Prayer

God, I confess that it's hard to need people. Sometimes I think being strong means doing it all myself. But you made me for connection. Help me lean into the support you've placed around me. Give me the courage to reach out and the grace to receive help from others.

Invitation

Who has helped carry you through a hard time? Take a moment today to thank them. And if you need support now, take one step toward finding it: Send a message, make a call, open up. It might be the beginning of new strength.

The Psychology of Resentment

Don't sin by letting anger control you. Don't let the sun go down while you are still angry, for anger gives a foothold to the devil.

EPHESIANS 4:26-27

Resentment is a slow, simmering anger that never quite cools. Psychologists often call it a form of *ruminative anger*—a pattern of stewing over past offenses, real or perceived, without moving toward resolution. It's like emotional Velcro: Everything sticks, nothing releases. Over time, it doesn't affect only your relationships. It starts to rewire your emotional baseline.

Research shows that chronic resentment elevates cortisol levels, increases risk of depression, impairs immune function, and even disrupts sleep. Clinically speaking, it's toxic. Spiritually speaking, it's bondage.

We often confuse resentment with strength. We think holding on keeps us safe, maybe even moral. But it doesn't protect; it paralyzes. It keeps us stuck in a loop of blame and bitterness, reinforcing the idea that someone else's behavior has more control over our emotional life than we do. And the worst part? We think we're punishing them, but we're really punishing ourselves.

Paul's words are jarringly practical: Don't let anger fester. Don't give it a bed to sleep in. Why? Because it invites sabotage. Not always externally, but internally. It gives darkness a foothold where light is trying to break through.

That doesn't mean you pretend nothing happened. Healthy boundaries, honest confrontation, and grief are all part of healing. But resentment isn't a healing process; it's a holding pattern.

If you want to move forward, you have to let go—not of truth or justice, but of the idea that clinging to your pain will somehow even the score. It won't.

Anchor Truth

Resentment pretends it's power, but peace is the real power. And peace begins the moment you stop rehearsing the offense and start reclaiming your heart.

Prayer

God, I've carried things too long. I've let my mind and body absorb the weight of what others did. Help me release resentment—not in denial, but in trust. Heal the wound, quiet the echo, and help me make space for peace again.

Invitation

Talk to a counselor, trusted friend, or mentor about the resentment you've buried. Ask yourself, "What need was violated? What would healing look like now?" Then take one brave step toward that healing.

Anger in the Mirror

Why worry about a speck in your friend's eye when you have a log in your own?

MATTHEW 7:3

Have you ever noticed how the things that irritate you most in other people are often the very things you haven't dealt with in yourself? That coworker who always has to be right. The friend who's constantly late. The partner who doesn't listen. The relative who flies off the handle.

Sure, their behavior may be frustrating. But sometimes, if you're honest, the anger feels outsized. Disproportionate. Like it's pressing on something tender inside you. And often it is.

Psychologists call this *projection*—when we unconsciously off-load parts of ourselves onto others. It's easier to criticize someone else's flaws than face our own insecurities or pain. It's safer to blame than to feel.

Jesus spoke to this when he said, "Take the log out of your own eye." That's not a call to perfection. It's a call to humility. A reminder that sometimes our anger at others is a mirror, not a spotlight.

You might be angry at someone for being unreliable because deep down you're ashamed of your own inconsistency. You might get irritated by someone's emotional neediness because you've disowned your own. You might despise someone's arrogance because it taps into a part of you that feels invisible or insecure.

This doesn't mean your anger is invalid. But it does mean it might be instructive. Before confronting someone else, pause to ask, "Why does this bother me so much?" "What part of me is being poked?" "Am I seeing them clearly—or seeing myself, distorted through the lens of my past?"

Anger in the mirror can sting. But it's also sacred. It's your soul saying, "Hey, there's something in here that needs tending." Not judgment, just healing.

Anchor Truth

Anger can be a mirror. What you see in others might be what's unresolved in you.

Prayer

God, help me look honestly at myself. When I'm tempted to lash out, slow me down. Teach me to let anger lead me—not into blame, but into deeper healing.

Invitation

Think of someone who triggers you often. Write down what you dislike about their behavior. Then ask yourself, "Is there any part of me that's afraid I'm the same?" Be honest and gentle with yourself.

Stay in Your Lane

Let us run with endurance the race God has set before us.

HEBREWS 12:1

Jealousy will make you forget your own race. You start looking sideways—at their pace, their path, their results—and before long, you're not running your race anymore. You're just reacting to theirs.

The writer of Hebrews says that God has set before each of us a race. Singular. Personal. Custom-built. But comparison convinces you there's only one lane that counts. The visible one. The fast one. The shiny one.

So instead of endurance, you live in envy. Instead of joy, you grind. And instead of calling, you chase someone else's life and wonder why it doesn't fit.

Jealousy warps calling. It takes your eyes off of what God has actually entrusted to you and glues them to what he's entrusted to someone else.

In psychology, it's called *external validation dependency*—the belief that success, identity, or worth is only real when it's acknowledged by others. But here's the problem: If you need someone else to applaud your race before you believe in it, you'll never run it with freedom.

God didn't call you to keep up with someone else. He called you to be faithful in your lane—even if it's slower, quieter, or looks completely different from theirs. And even if no one's clapping.

Your peace isn't in outrunning someone else; it's in returning to what's yours.

Anchor Truth

Comparison always distracts you from your calling.

Prayer

God, I keep looking sideways. Bring my eyes back to what you've set in front of me. Help me run my race with endurance, not envy.

Invitation

What's one area today where comparison is stealing your focus? Call it out. Then ask, "What's actually mine to run, build, or carry right now?" Run in that lane.

The Humility That Heals

Always be humble and gentle. Be patient with each other, making allowance for each other's faults because of your love.

EPHESIANS 4:2

Some fights don't explode. They simmer with silent tension. Unspoken resentment. That thing you both know is there but pretend isn't. And before you know it, you're miles apart with no idea how to close the distance.

That's when humility becomes more than a virtue. It becomes a lifeline. Not the false kind that says, "I'm always the problem"—that's insecurity. And not the polished kind that apologizes just to keep the peace—that's manipulation.

Real humility is something else entirely. It's strong enough to own your part and soft enough to see the other person's pain. Humility says, "I might not see everything clearly. I could be wrong. Let's work through this instead of proving who's right."

That posture can melt defensiveness. It deactivates blame. It creates a climate where honesty can breathe. And in relationships that matter, that kind of humility is oxygen.

Think of Abigail in 1 Samuel 25. Her husband, Nabal, was reckless and rude—almost costing his entire household their lives. But Abigail steps in with humility and courage. She takes responsibility not for the offense, but for the reconciliation. She kneels before David and speaks wisdom wrapped in grace. And her humility defuses the rage and saves lives.

Humility doesn't always mean resolution, but it *always* opens the door for it. It doesn't guarantee restoration, but it makes healing possible.

So if your relationship is strained? If there's tension or silence or something you both keep tiptoeing around? Start here: with a heart posture that says, "I'm willing to listen. I'm open to grow." That kind of humility isn't weakness. It's strength in its most powerful form.

Anchor Truth

Humility builds bridges that pride would burn. It's the first step toward healing.

Prayer

God, give me the strength to go first—to listen, to own what's mine, to release what's not. Soften my heart with humility and help me love even when it's hard.

Invitation

Reach out to someone where tension lingers. You don't need all the answers. Just start with a posture of humility and let God work through that open door.

Courage Isn't the Absence of Fear

This is my command—be strong and courageous! Do not be afraid or discouraged. For the LORD your God is with you wherever you go.

JOSHUA 1:9

Courage is often misunderstood. We picture it in action-movie moments—charging into danger, slaying giants, leaping without looking. But real courage is quieter than that. It often looks like shaking hands, a lump in your throat, and still taking the next step. It's fear walking forward.

The Bible is full of trembling people who were told to be courageous. Not because they felt ready. Not because the danger was gone. But because God was with them. That's the key. Courage isn't a feeling, it's a decision. And it often arrives dressed in weakness.

Psychologists describe courage not as fearlessness but as the willingness to act in the presence of fear. That's a critical shift. Fear doesn't mean you've failed. It means you're human. In fact, if you're never afraid, you're probably not living close enough to the edge of growth.

Research shows that courage contributes to mental wellness by increasing resilience, improving confidence, and helping us live in alignment with our values. Courage isn't just heroic, it's healthy.

When God tells Joshua to "be strong and courageous," it's not a pep talk. It's a prescription for what to do *because* fear is part of the path.

Fear isn't a sign you're doing something wrong. It might be a signal you're stepping into something right. You may be facing a situation that makes your hands sweat: a hard conversation, a medical test, a new season, a decision with no guarantees. You don't have to wait for fear to vanish to begin. Start while you're afraid. Shake if you have to. That's real courage.

Anchor Truth

Courage isn't the absence of fear. It's moving forward with it, knowing God is near.

Prayer

God, I don't want fear to make my decisions for me. Help me be brave—not because I feel bold, but because I know you're beside me. Strengthen me for the next step.

Invitation

What fear are you carrying today? Name it. Then take one courageous step, however small, toward what matters most.

The Losses We're Told Not to Grieve

You keep track of all my sorrows.
You have collected all my tears in your bottle.
You have recorded each one in your book.

PSALM 56:8

It wasn't a death. No funeral. No flowers. No casseroles. Just the silent ache of something that slipped away. A friendship that faded. A job that drained you until you quit. A dream that dissolved. A season of life you didn't realize was over until it was. And yet, it hurt.

But you felt like you shouldn't be hurting. Maybe you told yourself, "Other people have it worse." Or "I should be over this by now." Or "This doesn't count as real grief." But it does. Because loss is loss. And your soul knows it, even if no one else sees it.

These "minor" losses aren't minor to your nervous system. Psychology calls it *disenfranchised grief*—grief that doesn't get acknowledged or validated by others. But research shows it carries real emotional weight, and left unprocessed, it can contribute to anxiety, depression, or even physical symptoms like exhaustion and chronic pain.

God doesn't measure your sorrow by public rituals or societal approval. He sees your heartbreak, even when you don't feel socially "allowed" to have one. Psalm 56 paints a picture of this attentiveness: "You have collected all my tears in your bottle," David says. All of them. Not just the ones that make it to an obituary.

In Scripture, we see this kind of grief in action too. Naomi mourned not only the loss of her sons and husband, but the loss of her entire identity as a provider and matriarch. Hannah grieved the ache of infertility before any promise was fulfilled. Even Paul mourned being separated from communities he loved.

Grief isn't just for the catastrophic. It's for the cumulative. The quiet. The in-between. And it deserves your attention, not your dismissal. Because God is not only close to those who wail at gravesides. He's near to those who cry in the car after work, who miss what they used to be, who feel something invisible slipping away.

Anchor Truth

Your grief doesn't have to be big to be sacred. If it draws tears, God draws near.

Prayer

God, I've tried to downplay the weight of some losses. But you don't minimize my pain. You meet me in it. Help me to grieve what's been lost, even if no one else notices. And restore me with your tender presence.

Invitation

Name one loss you've brushed aside as "not a big deal." Write it down. Say it aloud. Let it matter, because healing begins with honesty.

God Is Not Mad at You

The LORD your God is with you, he is mighty to save. He will take great delight in you; he will quiet you with his love, he will rejoice over you with singing.

ZEPHANIAH 3:17 (NIV)

Maybe you've heard the voice before—the one inside your head that sounds suspiciously like God, but is cruel. The one that doesn't correct; it condemns. That doesn't restore; it shames. That doesn't offer grace; it dangles guilt like a leash. This voice doesn't sound like Jesus. But for many, it's what faith has come to feel like.

Shame-based theology teaches you that God's default posture is disappointment. That you're fundamentally flawed and must spend your life proving otherwise. It uses Scripture as a spotlight on your failures instead of a lamp to guide you toward healing. It thrives in performance-based religion where love feels earned and losing security is always one mistake away.

No wonder it distorts your self-worth. Shame attacks identity. It convinces you that your flaws define you and that your standing with God is always at risk.

But Zephaniah 3:17 paints a radically different picture. God is not waiting for you to mess up. He is rejoicing over you. Quieting your inner storm with his love. Singing over you with joy. Not when you improve. Now.

The cross was not a transaction to appease an angry God. It was a rescue mission driven by love. Jesus didn't die because you were disgusting; he died because you are deeply desired.

Healing from shame-based theology means untangling God's voice from the voice of fear, control, and condemnation. It means returning to the Jesus who wept with sinners, welcomed outsiders, and bent down in the dirt to lift the fallen.

You don't have to live as though God merely tolerates you. He delights in you.

Anchor Truth

God isn't waiting for you to clean up before he'll love you. He rejoices over you now—with singing, not shaming.

Prayer

God, I've mistaken shame for truth. I've believed you were disappointed in me. Let your love quiet my fears. Let your song drown out my shame. Help me walk in the freedom of being fully known and still fully loved.

Invitation

Write Zephaniah 3:17 somewhere you'll see it often. Let it confront the voice of shame. When your thoughts spiral into unworthiness, pause and imagine the sound of God singing over you. That's the soundtrack of grace.

We're All Addicted to Something

I don't really understand myself, for I want to do what is right, but I don't do it. Instead, I do what I hate.

ROMANS 7:15

Not everyone struggles with substance misuse. But most of us wrestle with something we turn to in moments of overwhelm, fear, loneliness, or pain. It might be caffeine or carbs. Screens or social media. Shopping or scrolling. It might be success, perfectionism, or constant productivity. Or maybe it's approval, the exhausting need to be liked.

Addiction, in its broadest sense, is anything you use compulsively to escape discomfort or regulate your emotional state—even if it harms you long-term.

So yes, in some way, most of us know what it means to feel powerless over something that started as a comfort and became a cage. It doesn't mean we're all broken beyond repair; it means we're human. We live in a world that rewards distraction, numbing, and hustle. And we all want something that works.

Even Paul, who wrote much of the New Testament, admitted, "I do what I hate." If that's not a universal experience, what is?

Awareness is the first step. Not shame. Not self-loathing. Just honest awareness. What do you run to when life feels too heavy? What do you reach for when you feel invisible, rejected, or out of control?

Sometimes our patterns are inherited. Sometimes they're learned. Sometimes they're survival. But whatever their origin, they don't have to write the whole story.

When we stop pretending we have it all together, something beautiful happens: We make room for healing. For grace. For growth.

You don't have to wait for rock bottom. You just have to be honest.

Anchor Truth

Healing begins with honest awareness, not shame.

Prayer

God, I don't want to keep numbing what you want to heal. Give me courage to face what I'd rather avoid.

Invitation

Notice what you reach for when you're anxious, bored, or overwhelmed. Then ask yourself, "What am I really needing underneath that impulse?"

When Helping Becomes Hurting

Rescue those who are unjustly sentenced to die;
save them as they stagger to their death.
Don't excuse yourself by saying, "Look, we didn't know."
For God understands all hearts.

PROVERBS 24:11-12

At first glance, this verse seems to advocate for total rescue at all costs. And sometimes that's exactly what love requires. But codependency often masquerades as rescue, when it's really about control. Helping becomes hurting when your support robs someone of their own strength.

That's the paradox of codependency. It looks like self-sacrifice, but it's often rooted in fear that if you don't hold it all together, everything (and everyone) will fall apart.

Just look at Martha in Luke 10. She wasn't rescuing her sister Mary from death, but she was certainly trying to rescue their household from disorder and Jesus from perceived social embarrassment. Her anxiety pushed her into overfunctioning. And when Mary didn't match that level of urgency, Martha snapped.

"Lord, don't you care?" she demanded. That's how it often sounds: *I care more than everyone else. Why won't they carry their weight?*

Codependency creates relational imbalance. You end up resenting the very people you're trying to help because deep down, you're not helping. You're managing.

Yes, God calls us to intervene when others are staggering toward destruction. But there's a difference between intervening and interfering. You can offer a hand without dragging someone across the finish line. You can walk beside them without shouldering their entire path.

When love demands action, do it from a place of clarity, not compulsion. When help is needed, give it freely, but don't make it your identity.

Anchor Truth

True compassion walks alongside others, not ahead of them dragging their weight. Love empowers. It doesn't enable.

Prayer

God, show me where I've confused love with control. Give me courage to help wisely and humility to know when to let go.

Invitation

Take inventory: Where are you stepping in out of anxiety instead of love? Is there someone you're "rescuing" out of fear rather than wisdom? What would it look like to trust them and God more today?

Unsafe Systems, Spiritual Wounds

What sorrow awaits you teachers of religious law and you Pharisees. Hypocrites! For you are careful to tithe . . . but you ignore the more important aspects of the law—justice, mercy, and faith.

MATTHEW 23:23

Some of the deepest emotional wounds don't come from strangers. They come from systems that were supposed to be safe—churches, families, schools. Maybe you tried to speak up and were shut down. Maybe you were taught to obey but never encouraged to question. Maybe your doubts were labeled rebellion. Maybe your depression was called a lack of faith. Or maybe your honesty was treated like betrayal.

This is what happens in *unsafe systems*—places where power is protected more than people. Where image matters more than integrity. Where the loudest voices are often the least empathetic.

If you've experienced this, you're not crazy. And you're not alone. These are spiritual wounds. They're real. And they can take longer to heal than we like to admit.

Jesus called it out. He saw the spiritual gatekeepers using rules to control people. He saw the shame-based systems. He saw the crushing weight of religious performance. And he didn't stay quiet. He challenged hypocrisy. He offered rest to the weary and burdened, not more hoops to jump through.

Emotional safety shouldn't be a bonus in spiritual communities. It should be a *baseline*. It's what allows people to bring their full selves before God and others without fear of punishment or exclusion.

If you've been spiritually wounded, hear this: God isn't the one who hurt you. He isn't threatened by your questions. He doesn't need your performance. He wants your heart. Your honesty. Your healing.

And if you've been part of unsafe systems in the past, there's grace for that too. You can unlearn the old patterns. You can help create safer spaces. You can choose mercy over management.

Anchor Truth

God doesn't need you to pretend. He invites your pain, your honesty, your full self. Unsafe systems are a distortion of his heart, but Jesus came to set it right.

Prayer

God, for every place where I was told to sit down, be quiet, or smile through the pain, bring healing. Rewire the parts of me that equated control with love. Teach me to rest in your grace, and help me help others do the same.

Invitation

Have you confused the voice of an unsafe system with the voice of God? Ask him to help you separate the two. Begin to listen again—not for guilt or fear, but for grace.

Where You Might Need a Boundary

Wise choices will watch over you. Understanding will keep you safe.

PROVERBS 2:11

Boundaries aren't just big emotional walls. They're more like doors with locks, hinges, and a doorbell. They allow in what's good—and keep out what's harmful. But where exactly do you need them?

Here are common areas where people often need to set (or strengthen) boundaries:

Your time—Do you feel constantly overcommitted? Say yes too quickly? You may need limits on your availability. *No* is not a four-letter word.

Your energy—Who and what drains you? Healthy boundaries protect your mental and emotional fuel tank.

Your money—Are you loaning, spending, or giving in ways that hurt you? You're allowed to say, "I can't do that right now."

Your values—Do you find yourself compromising to avoid conflict? Boundaries guard your integrity.

Your body—From physical affection to personal space, your body deserves respect. Boundaries reinforce that.

Your conversations—You don't have to engage in gossip, arguments, or shaming. You can step away or say, "I'm not comfortable with this."

Your digital life—Do you feel invaded by texts, emails, or social media? Set screen time limits, mute toxic accounts, and reclaim your peace.

Your schedule—Sabbath is a boundary. Rest is sacred. God modeled it first.

Even Jesus withdrew from crowds, said no to certain requests, and prioritized solitude. Not because he didn't care, but because he did. You don't set boundaries to punish others. You set them to protect what's precious, including your peace.

Read that verse from Proverbs again. It reminds us: Wise choices *watch over you*. They stand guard when you're tempted to overextend, overexplain, or overaccommodate. Understanding what drains you and what restores you isn't weakness. It's the Spirit's way of keeping you safe.

So start small, but start today. Let wisdom do its work. Let understanding lead the way. You're not being selfish when you set boundaries. You're being protected.

Anchor Truth

Every boundary you set is a declaration that your heart, mind, time, and body are worth guarding.

Prayer

God, show me the places in my life that need stronger boundaries. Help me say yes to what brings life and no to what depletes it. Teach me to protect what you've entrusted to me.

Invitation

Pick one area from the list. Where have you been stretched too thin or been too silent? This week, set one small boundary—and follow through.

When Perfectionism Puts Things Off

If you wait for perfect conditions, you will never get anything done.

ECCLESIASTES 11:4 (TLB)

Procrastination doesn't always come from laziness. In fact, for many perfectionists, it's just the opposite: You care *so much* about getting it right that you can't bear the thought of getting it wrong. You delay writing the email, making the decision, starting the project—not because you don't want to do it, but because you don't want to mess it up. It has to be flawless or it's a failure. And that pressure creates paralysis.

Sound familiar? Perfectionism and procrastination often travel together, hand in hand. One says, "This has to be amazing." The other whispers, "And since it probably won't be, let's just wait."

Together, they keep you stuck—overthinking, second-guessing, avoiding. And the longer you delay, the heavier it feels. The more afraid you are to begin.

But Ecclesiastes gives a simple truth: "If you wait for perfect conditions, you will never get anything done." That applies to external situations and also to your internal ones.

If you wait until you *feel* confident, qualified, or ready, you may never start at all.

The good news? God doesn't call you to perfect action. He just calls you to faithful action. A mustard seed of movement is enough. And often the confidence you crave only shows up after you've begun.

So take the first step. Even if it's small. Even if it's messy.

Progress isn't the enemy of perfection, it's the antidote. You don't have to finish it all today. But you do need to begin.

Anchor Truth

You don't need perfect conditions to move forward. Start small. God honors steps, not just outcomes.

Prayer

God, you know how overwhelmed I get when I want to do things "just right." Help me to release that pressure today. Give me the courage to begin, even imperfectly. Meet me in the doing, not just the planning.

Invitation

Choose one thing you've been putting off or avoiding—not because it's hard, but because it feels high-stakes. Break it down. Start small. Let grace carry you, not perfection.

When You're Afraid to Disappoint

I trust in God, so why should I be afraid?
What can mere mortals do to me?

PSALM 56:11

You said yes again. Even though you didn't want to. Even though you didn't have the time, energy, or desire. Why? Because the thought of letting them down felt worse than the cost of overextending yourself—again.

That's not generosity. That's fear in disguise. The fear of disappointing others is one of the most socially acceptable addictions out there. It disguises itself as being "nice" or "servant-hearted." But beneath the surface is something more tangled: a fear of rejection, abandonment, or being seen as selfish.

In clinical terms, this often stems from *enmeshment*—a lack of healthy emotional boundaries. Maybe you grew up with a parent who made you responsible for their emotions. Maybe you were taught that love had to be earned by keeping others happy. Now, as an adult, "no" feels like betrayal. And you carry guilt that was never yours to hold.

Scripture cuts through the noise: "Fearing people is a trap." It doesn't just make you anxious; it distorts your identity. You begin to equate your worth with your usefulness. You measure your goodness by how pleased people are with you.

But what if your job isn't to keep everyone happy? What if disappointing someone is the necessary discomfort of growing into the person God actually created you to be?

Jesus disappointed people all the time. The rich young ruler walked away sad. Jesus' hometown turned on him. His own disciples didn't always understand his decisions. But Jesus didn't apologize for living in alignment with his mission. He loved well, but he didn't bend to everyone's expectations.

You won't become a jerk by learning to disappoint people. You'll become honest. Grounded. Free.

Anchor Truth

You were not made to manage everyone's feelings. You were made to live in truth and love.

Prayer

God, I confess that I've been trying to earn peace by avoiding disappointment. Teach me to be okay with letting others down when I need to stay aligned with you. Help me find safety in your approval, not theirs.

Invitation

This week, notice where you're tempted to say yes out of guilt. Practice a small, holy "no." Then breathe through the fear and see what freedom feels like on the other side.

The Weight of Hyper-Responsibility

Give your burdens to the LORD, and he will take care of you.
He will not permit the godly to slip and fall.

PSALM 55:22

Somewhere along the way, you might have picked up a quiet, relentless belief that if anything goes wrong, it's probably your fault. This is the heart of hyper-responsibility. It's not just about doing your part. It's about doing everyone's part. It's cleaning up the mess, preventing the crisis, managing the emotions, anticipating the needs, and trying to hold it all together—just in case no one else will. And it's exhausting.

Perfectionism doesn't always look like obsessing over results. Sometimes it looks like taking on emotional, relational, and even spiritual burdens that were never yours to carry. Not because you're trying to be controlling, but because deep down, you fear what will happen if you let go.

Maybe you grew up in a chaotic home where you had to be the stable one. Or maybe you were praised for always being responsible, and it became your identity. Or maybe you just genuinely care, and over time that care turned into constant vigilance.

But Jesus never said, "Hold everything together." He said, "Come to me, all of you who are weary and carry heavy burdens, and I will give you rest." That includes you.

Even Moses struggled with this. When the burden of leading became too heavy, he tried to carry it all himself—until God stepped in and redistributed the weight (Numbers 11). Moses had to *learn* to let others help.

Hyper-responsibility may feel noble, but it can be a silent source of anxiety, burnout, and resentment. You are not the glue holding the world together. That role is already taken. You can care deeply and still let go. You can be responsible without being responsible for everything.

Anchor Truth

Your worth isn't measured by how much you manage. It's rooted in who you belong to.

Prayer

God, I feel the pull to take on more than I should. Forgive me when I confuse overfunctioning for faithfulness. Help me trust you enough to release what was never mine to carry. Teach me to rest.

Invitation

Notice one place where you're carrying more than your share—at home, at work, or in a relationship. Name it. Then surrender it to God. You weren't made to hold it all.

Why the Bible Won't Stop Talking About Gratitude

Give thanks to the LORD, for he is good!
His faithful love endures forever.

PSALM 136:1

Gratitude isn't a sidenote in Scripture. It's a major theme. A rhythm. A refrain. It's found on the lips of kings and prophets, written into law, etched into prayers, and sung in psalms.

In fact, the Bible mentions giving thanks or expressing gratitude over 150 times. And that doesn't even include words like *praise*, *bless*, *rejoice*, or *remember*, which often flow from the same posture of the heart. Why does Scripture keep circling back to it?

Because gratitude isn't just polite; it's powerful. It shifts your posture from scarcity to sufficiency. From fear to faith. From striving to surrender. And it roots you in the truth that you are not the source of your own life—God is. Gratitude reorients you, again and again, to the God who provides manna in the desert, peace in the storm, and joy in the morning.

The Bible is relentless about gratitude because humans are forgetful. We drift. We default to complaint. We rewrite the story to make ourselves the hero. But thanksgiving keeps us grounded in the reality that every breath, every blessing, every bit of grace we've received is a gift, not a given.

That's why Psalm 136 repeats the same refrain twenty-six times: *His faithful love endures forever.* Not because the writer ran out of things to say, but because we need to hear it again and again until it sinks in.

After all, when life is hard, gratitude is usually the first thing to go. And when we lose gratitude, we lose perspective. We forget who God is, what he's done, and how he's shown up before.

Repetition isn't just poetic. It's protective. It keeps our hearts soft, our memories sharp, and our faith rooted in something deeper than our circumstances. Gratitude is how we keep the story straight.

Anchor Truth

Gratitude is a spiritual discipline, not because God needs it, but because we do. It anchors us in truth and awakens us to grace.

Prayer

God, don't let me become numb to your goodness. Train my heart to remember—to recognize your hand and give thanks, not just when it's easy, but especially when it's not.

Invitation

Today, notice how often you grumble or take credit. Then interrupt it. Even if it feels small or forced, say thank you to God. It's not a throwaway. It's the start of rewiring your heart.

Holding On When the Outcome Is Unclear

Who knows if perhaps you were made queen for just such a time as this?

ESTHER 4:14

One of the hardest parts of resilience is not knowing how the story ends. You're still in the thick of it. No resolution. No clarity. No promises that this chapter will wrap up neatly.

That's where Esther stood. A young woman thrust into power she didn't ask for, carrying a burden that would likely cost her life. When Mordecai urged her to speak up for her people, he didn't promise success. He just said, "Who knows?" And Esther went anyway. Not because she was sure, but because she was faithful. That's resilience.

Or take Habakkuk—a prophet pleading with God over injustice while he watched his nation crumble. He didn't get clean answers. He got a vision and a choice: Wait, trust, and keep walking. His prayer ends not with certainty, but surrender: "Yet I will rejoice in the LORD! . . . The Sovereign LORD is my strength!" (Habakkuk 3:18-19).

Clinically, this ability to tolerate uncertainty is known as *distress tolerance*—and it's a core skill in resilience. It doesn't mean you like the unknown. It means you learn to stay grounded, even when your mind screams for guarantees.

Resilient people don't need all the answers to keep showing up. They move forward with faith, not because they know what's next, but because they trust the one who walks with them.

You don't have to know the outcome to keep holding on. Courage isn't clarity. It's commitment.

Anchor Truth

Resilience means trusting God not just in the victory, but in the waiting, the wondering, the in-between.

Prayer

God, I wish I knew how this would end. I want closure, clarity, something solid to hold on to. But for now, I hold on to you. Be my strength when answers don't come. Help me trust that you're still working, especially in the unknown.

Invitation

Is there an area of your life where the outcome is still unclear? Whisper this prayer today: "Even without answers, I choose to trust." Let that small act of faith strengthen your resilience.

When You Feel Guilty for Feeling Good

To all who mourn in Israel, he will give a crown of beauty for ashes, a joyous blessing instead of mourning, festive praise instead of despair.

ISAIAH 61:3

You laugh at a joke. You dance a little in the kitchen. You catch yourself enjoying the moment, and then it hits—that sick, subtle twist in your gut. *Should I really feel this happy right now?*

Maybe someone you love is still in pain. Maybe you're still grieving. Maybe life isn't "fixed" yet. And something inside says, "Who are you to feel joy?"

That's guilt talking. But not the holy kind. Not the kind that convicts and heals. This is the false guilt that shames you into believing you don't deserve relief. It whispers, "If you really cared, you wouldn't be smiling right now."

But guilt is not the guardian of your love. It's not proof that you care. Pain and joy can live side by side. Grief and gratitude often do.

You can still be healing and laugh at a movie. You can still be carrying sorrow and notice how good the sun feels on your face. You can still miss someone deeply and celebrate a birthday.

That's not betrayal. That's being human.

Jesus himself wept for Lazarus, then raised him. He felt the agony of the cross, but still broke bread and shared joy with friends. We are invited into that same paradox—where joy does not erase sorrow, but meets it with meaning.

So when the joy comes, let it. You're not leaving your pain behind. You're honoring your humanity. And you're giving God room to turn ashes into beauty—bit by bit, moment by moment.

Anchor Truth

Guilt says joy is inappropriate. Grace says it's healing. You are allowed to feel good again, even while you're still healing.

Prayer

God, help me receive joy without shame. I don't want to shut out what is good just because all isn't perfect. Let your grace make space for celebration in my life again.

Invitation

What moment of joy have you recently shut down or talked yourself out of? Revisit it. Let it breathe. And say, "This, too, is a gift."

Praying Through the Ache

I am sick at heart. How long, O LORD, until you restore me? . . . I am worn out from sobbing.

PSALM 6:3, 6

Grief doesn't come with tidy prayers. Sometimes it shows up as silence. Other times as sobbing. Or a whispered, "God, I don't even know what to say." But prayer in grief was never meant to sound polished. It's meant to be real.

And David—the shepherd, the warrior, the king, the poet—showed us how. His psalms are raw with sorrow and longing. He didn't hide his sadness or edit his questions. He wrote things like, "How long, O Lord?" "Why have you forgotten me?" "I am worn out from sobbing."

David didn't wait to feel better to talk to God. He prayed through the ache, not after it. And it didn't make his pain vanish—but it did give him presence. God's presence.

Grief isolates. It pulls us inward, numbs us, disconnects us. Prayer reconnects. Not always with answers. But with the God who sees it all, holds it all, and doesn't flinch when we fall apart.

From a clinical lens, psychologists say naming our emotions—out loud, in writing, or in prayer—helps metabolize grief. In other words, when we name it, we can begin to move through it.

That's what David did. And that's what prayer can be. A sacred space to name what hurts. To feel the loss without fixing it. To grieve in the presence of the God who doesn't walk away. Even Jesus, in the garden of Gethsemane, wept and prayed in anguish. If the Son of God didn't bypass grief in prayer, neither should we.

So if all you have today is a groan, a sigh, or a single word, let it rise. He hears. He's close. And he never tires of your truth.

Anchor Truth

Prayer doesn't require clarity. It requires honesty. God is near to the brokenhearted, even when all you can offer is pain.

Prayer

God, I don't have all the right words. I don't even know how to talk about this ache. But I want to trust that you are near. So I bring my sorrow to you. Not neatly. Not quietly. Just honestly. And I ask you to hold me through it.

Invitation

Today, write a psalm of your own. Don't worry about making it pretty. Let it be messy, fragmented, tearstained, angry, confused—whatever is true. Then offer it to God. Just as David did.

When Life Feels Too Heavy

We were crushed and overwhelmed beyond our ability to endure, and we thought we would never live through it. In fact, we expected to die. But as a result, we stopped relying on ourselves and learned to rely only on God.

2 CORINTHIANS 1:8-9

Let's say it plainly: Suicidal thoughts are more common than we talk about in church.

Even the apostle Paul, a man who wrote much of the New Testament, struggled with the desire to give up. In his own words, he was "crushed," "overwhelmed," and felt he couldn't make it. He "expected to die." This is a picture of a man at the end of himself.

Paul didn't mask his pain with platitudes. He didn't pretend everything was fine. He wrote it down so we would see that even faithful, devoted people can hit a wall so hard they don't see a way through.

That moment didn't make Paul weak. It made him authentic. Real. Honest. And it became a turning point. He said it was there—when he had nothing left—that he learned to rely on God in a new way. Not as a Band-Aid or bypass, but as a lifeline. A source of strength when his had run dry.

Suicidal thoughts don't always mean someone wants to die. Often it means they want the pain to stop and can't see another way to make it stop.

If that's you—if you've felt that weight—hear this: You are not alone and there is a way out. You are not beyond help. You are not weak. You are not forsaken. You are not a failure of faith.

God does not recoil from your darkest thoughts. He draws near.

Like Paul, your pain is not the end of the story. It can be the beginning of a deeper reliance, a richer mercy, a more honest kind of hope.

Anchor Truth

Despair is not the absence of God. It may be the very place he meets you most tenderly.

Prayer

God, when I am crushed and overwhelmed, hold me. When I see no way out, be my strength. Thank you for staying near, even when I've thought I couldn't keep going. Help me rely on you more than myself.

Invitation

If you've ever felt like Paul—so crushed you didn't know if you could survive—talk to someone today. A counselor. A friend. A pastor. God often works through people to remind us that we're not alone. Let someone be that reminder for you.

The Cost of Empathy

Clothe yourselves with tenderhearted mercy, kindness, humility, gentleness, and patience.

COLOSSIANS 3:12

Empathy is more than a buzzword. It's one of the rarest and most sacred gifts we can offer another person. But let's get one thing clear: It's not the same as sympathy.

Sympathy says, "I feel bad for you." Empathy says, "I feel this with you."

And it's not the same as analysis, either. Analysis stays at a distance: "Here's what's happening."

Empathy enters in: "I imagine that hurts." Empathy costs more than either of those options. It requires that we slow down, turn off the fixer mode, and step into someone else's emotional world without flinching.

That's not easy. Because it requires us to risk feeling something, maybe something uncomfortable. And it means we can't stay detached. We can't just throw a verse at it or offer a shiny solution.

Neuroscience shows us that empathy lights up the same parts of the empathizer's brain as the person experiencing the emotion. In other words, to empathize is to borrow someone's pain, even for a moment. This is why it's so rare. And why it's so healing.

Scripture is full of empathy—not just commands to show it, but actual demonstrations. Jesus weeping at a tomb he was about to empty. The father running to embrace the prodigal before hearing an apology. Paul urging the church to "be happy with those who are happy, and weep with those who weep" (Romans 12:15).

This is the heart of connection: not solving, not sermonizing, but sitting with.

Anchor Truth

Empathy is love in motion. It's costly, risky, and exactly what we're made for.

Prayer

God, give me the courage to feel with others, not just for them. Grow my capacity for empathy. Help me pause my judgments, my need to fix, and just be present, like you are with me.

Invitation

Think of someone in your life who's struggling. Instead of offering advice, ask, "What has this been like for you?" Then listen—fully. Hold space. Let your presence do the work.

Naming the Feeling

Elijah was afraid and fled for his life. . . . He sat down under a solitary broom tree and prayed that he might die.

1 KINGS 19:3-4

You can't manage what you don't understand. And most of us were never taught to name our emotions.

Instead, we use vague catchalls like "I'm stressed," "I'm fine," or "I'm just tired." But beneath those broad brushstrokes is something more specific—and much more powerful: frustration, sadness, disappointment, fear, envy, hurt, shame, even joy.

Research shows that *affect labeling*—simply *naming* your emotion—begins to calm your nervous system. It activates the brain's regulatory systems. In other words, language tames emotion. It's what David models in the Psalms—naming his anguish, his rage, his despair, and his joy.

And it's what Elijah did after his dramatic showdown with the prophets of Baal. Overwhelmed by fear, exhaustion, and despair, he tells God, "I have had enough. Take my life." That's emotional honesty in raw form.

Elijah doesn't bottle it up or pretend to be okay. He names his despair. And God doesn't rebuke him. Instead, God responds with care: rest, nourishment, and a whisper—not a lecture.

This moment models how identifying and expressing our emotions—even the darkest ones—can be a turning point toward restoration. Elijah's story shows that naming the feeling doesn't make us weak; it makes space for God to meet us there.

Giving your feelings words gives them boundaries. Because unspoken emotions don't disappear. They just leak out in sideways behavior: passive aggression, sarcasm, shutting down, snapping at the wrong person at the wrong time.

If you want to learn to regulate your emotions, start with awareness. Don't push the feelings away. Pull them into the light.

Ask yourself, "What am I really feeling?" "Where am I feeling it in my body?" "What might this emotion be pointing me toward?" Be honest, even if the answer feels messy or inconvenient. Emotional regulation starts with emotional honesty.

Anchor Truth

Emotions lose their grip when we give them a name. Awareness is the first step toward healthy regulation.

Prayer

God, help me tell the truth about what I feel. Not to be dramatic, but to be clear. Not to wallow, but to walk in wisdom. Show me how to listen to my emotions without letting them take over.

Invitation

Today, when you feel something stir, pause and name it. Go beyond "mad" or "sad." Try to pinpoint the emotion underneath. Write it down. It doesn't have to be pretty, just true.

The Guilt That Ends in Isolation

Godly sorrow brings repentance that leads to salvation and leaves no regret, but worldly sorrow brings death.

2 CORINTHIANS 7:10 (NIV)

Judas Iscariot. The very name carries the weight of betrayal, the sting of regret, the shadow of a man who couldn't see past his guilt to grace. Judas didn't hate Jesus. He hated himself.

That's what makes his story so tragic. Judas felt the full weight of guilt. He even tried to give the money back. But he never came back to Jesus. Instead, he went off alone. And despair met him there.

Contrast that with Peter, who also betrayed Jesus. Three denials. Public shame. Deep remorse. But Peter didn't stay in the shadows. He let himself be found. And that made all the difference.

Paul calls it "worldly sorrow" when guilt leads to regret without hope. When shame becomes the loudest voice in the room. When you feel disqualified from grace. When your guilt tells you, "You've gone too far. You don't get to come back."

Judas believed that voice. Peter didn't.

It's not that Peter was better. It's that Peter trusted something bigger than his guilt. He let his sorrow bring him *to* Jesus, not *away* from him.

There's a kind of grief that isolates, condemns, and suffocates. And there's a kind that cracks your heart open just wide enough for grace to get in.

If guilt has pushed you toward hiding, pretending, or punishing yourself—stop. Come back. Come back like Peter, don't go away like Judas. Let yourself be found, even in your worst moment.

Because the grace that was big enough for Peter is big enough for you, too.

Anchor Truth

Guilt doesn't have to end in isolation. Let it become the doorway back to Jesus, not the reason you stay away.

Prayer

Jesus, when I feel like I've failed beyond repair, remind me that grace doesn't have a cutoff point. Help me run toward you, not away.

Invitation

Ask yourself, "Is guilt pulling me into shame or drawing me back to God?" If it's the former, let today be the day you shift directions. Let grace interrupt the spiral.

Boundaries, Not Blowups

A person without self-control
is like a city with broken-down walls.

PROVERBS 25:28

It's easy to assume you have an "anger problem" when what you really have is a boundary problem. You keep saying yes when you mean no. You stay quiet to keep the peace. You absorb too much. You stretch too thin.

Until one day, you snap. Not because you're irrational, but because your limits have been ignored for too long, even by you.

Anger doesn't always show up as yelling or slamming doors. Sometimes it simmers. Sometimes it leaks out in sarcasm, coldness, or passive resistance. But the root is the same: Something in you wasn't protected. A line wasn't drawn. And now your internal world is in revolt.

Boundaries aren't mean. They're not a sign of selfishness or immaturity. Boundaries are the preemptive act of love that prevents blowups later. When your "no" is consistent, your resentment doesn't have to be. When your needs are acknowledged, your reactions don't have to explode.

Proverbs says a person without self-control is like a city with broken walls. That doesn't mean you need to become guarded or rigid. It means you need structure—a healthy sense of where you end and others begin. Without it, everything seeps in. And your anger becomes the emergency brake you didn't pull soon enough.

The truth is, most people don't get taught how to set boundaries. Especially if you grew up in a family where peace was kept at any cost, where feelings were hidden, or where saying no felt like betrayal. But healing begins with giving yourself permission to honor your limits.

So ask yourself, "Where am I feeling chronically drained or resentful?" "What am I tolerating that's quietly tearing me up?" "What boundary would help me stay kind without becoming bitter?"

Anger isn't always the problem. Sometimes it's the last alarm before something inside you breaks.

Anchor Truth

Strong boundaries protect your peace. Weak ones provoke your anger.

Prayer

God, give me the courage to set boundaries before I explode. Help me love others without losing myself.

Invitation

Pick one relationship where resentment has been building. Ask yourself, "What's one small boundary I can practice this week—not to punish the other person, but to protect my peace?"

The Mirror in the Middle

If we claim to be without sin, we deceive ourselves and the truth is not in us.

1 JOHN 1:8 (NIV)

There's a sobering truth about relationships: They rarely rise above the emotional health of the people in them. That includes you.

We tend to focus on what's happening in a relationship—who said what, who didn't show up, who always shuts down. But sometimes the most important issue isn't the relationship itself. It's *us*. The unhealed parts we drag in. The patterns we haven't confronted. The fears that still get the final vote.

The evidence? It's called *emotional reactivity*—when your response to someone isn't really about what just happened but about unresolved stuff under the surface. A partner's silence suddenly feels like abandonment. A friend's correction sounds like rejection. It's not always rational. But it is revealing.

Of course, this goes both ways. Sometimes it's their wounds that poison the connection. Their inability to take responsibility. Their chronic avoidance. Their anger disguised as sarcasm. Relationships take two people, but that doesn't mean both are equally ready, honest, or emotionally safe.

This is why self-awareness is not a luxury; it's a relational necessity. The more attuned you are to your own triggers, coping strategies, and blind spots, the more clarity and calm you can bring to your connections. And the more willing you are to see others as they really are—not just how you wish they were—the healthier your relational boundaries become.

So if you're in a relationship that keeps cycling through dysfunction, start with this hard but hopeful question: What part of this is about *the relationship*—and what part is about *me*? And what might be about *them*?

Healing starts where honesty begins.

Anchor Truth

The health of your relationships is often a reflection of your own health.

Prayer

God, help me see clearly—not just what's wrong between us, but what's wounded within me. Show me what's mine to heal, and give me courage to do the work.

Invitation

Take five minutes to reflect on a relationship that feels hard right now. Jot down what you know is true about your part in it and what you're still unsure about. Let it lead you to clarity, not shame.

When Helping You Is Hurting Me

Carry each other's burdens, and in this way you will fulfill the law of Christ.

GALATIANS 6:2 (NIV)

There's a fine line between compassion and collapse. And sometimes the very thing that feels "Christian" is what's quietly crushing you.

Maybe you've been the one who always picks up the phone. The one who shows up, who says yes, who stays up late talking someone off an emotional ledge. You pray with them. Walk with them. Worry about them. And slowly, imperceptibly, you begin to lose yourself in their pain.

You start carrying what was never yours to carry alone. This is where compassion fatigue and burnout thrives—in the quiet erosion of boundaries, in the gradual forgetting of your own needs, in the belief that love means never saying "I can't."

Galatians 6:2 calls us to bear each other's burdens, but just three verses later, Paul reminds us that "we are each responsible for our own conduct." In other words: Help, yes. But don't lose yourself trying to rescue someone who refuses to stand.

Helping someone doesn't mean saving them. You are not their Messiah. Even Jesus let people walk away (Matthew 19:22).

The lie of overfunctioning with compassion is this: *If I stop, they'll fall apart. If I don't give, I'm failing them. If I set limits, I'm selfish.*

But the truth is this: When helping someone chronically hurts you, it's no longer help. It's harm in a saintly disguise. Sometimes the most loving thing you can say is, "I care about you deeply. But I need to step back." Not because you're abandoning them, but because staying too close is keeping both of you stuck.

Stepping back doesn't mean you've stopped loving. It means you're choosing a healthier kind of love, one that honors both their growth and your limits. That's not cold. That's clarity.

Anchor Truth

Compassion is not codependence. You are allowed—called, even—to love others without losing yourself in the process.

Prayer

God, help me love others wisely and well. Give me the courage to set boundaries without guilt and the discernment to know when my care is becoming self-erasure.

Invitation

Who in your life might you be over-helping? What would it look like to set a healthy boundary—not out of anger or rejection, but out of wisdom and love?

You're Not Broken

We are pressed on every side by troubles, but we are not crushed. We are perplexed, but not driven to despair.

2 CORINTHIANS 4:8

Anxiety can make you feel like something's wrong with you. Like you're too fragile. Too reactive. Too *much*. Or maybe just too exhausted to keep pretending you're okay.

You look around and wonder why others seem to handle life better. Why they can relax, laugh, sleep, trust. Why they don't shake, freeze, overthink, or unravel like you do. And quietly, you ask yourself, "What's wrong with me?"

This kind of thinking is common during nervous system overload. Especially when you're in a state of *hyperarousal*—where everything feels too loud, too fast, or too much. In those moments, anxiety often distorts identity, making you believe that how you feel is who you are.

But listen closely: There's a difference between being overwhelmed and being broken. Your nervous system may be overextended. Your mind may be weary. Your emotions may be raw. But none of that makes you defective.

Paul knew what it felt like to be overwhelmed. To be *pressed, perplexed, struck down*. But he also knew this: Being pressed isn't the same as being crushed.

You may be bent, but you are not beyond repair. You may feel weak, but you are not worthless. You may be struggling, but you are still being held.

In clinical work, we often say, "Name it to tame it." Recognizing that your body is in survival mode helps you respond with compassion, not criticism. And that's how healing begins.

You are not broken. You are becoming. You are healing, even if it's happening slowly. And God is not waiting for a better version of you. He's with you in this one.

Anchor Truth

You may feel like you're falling apart, but God sees someone worth holding together.

Prayer

God, some days I wonder if I'm too far gone—too anxious, too messy, too much to handle. But you don't call me broken. You call me beloved. Help me see myself through your eyes. Remind me that healing is allowed to be slow and that I am never beyond your care.

Invitation

Take a walk or sit somewhere quiet. As you breathe, repeat this phrase slowly: "I don't have to be finished to be faithful." Let it settle into your bones. Let it interrupt the pressure. Let it make space for grace.

When Numb Feels Safer than Sad

I weep with sorrow;
encourage me by your word.

PSALM 119:28

You'd think the worst part of depression would be the sadness. But for many people, it's the nothingness. No tears. No joy. No spark. Just numb. It's like being stuck behind glass, watching life unfold but feeling disconnected from all of it. The people, the beauty, the faith that once moved you? Muted. Distant. Out of reach.

This isn't laziness. It's not ingratitude. It's a psychological and physiological response that the brain defaults to when everything inside feels too heavy to hold. The numbness isn't apathy. It's armor. Sometimes feeling nothing is the only way to survive feeling everything.

In clinical terms, this is called *anhedonia*—a big word for the inability to feel pleasure. It's a core symptom of depression. And it can leave you questioning your spiritual health, your relationships, even your identity.

You may wonder, *Why don't I feel close to God? Why can't I cry anymore? Where did I go?* Even David, a man after God's own heart, wrote words that feel eerily familiar to anyone who's been numb: "I weep with sorrow; encourage me by your word" (Psalm 119:28).

David's honesty with God was part of his healing. He didn't fake joy. He didn't muscle through with a smile. He brought his depleted soul to God and asked for help. And you can do the same.

There is no shame in spiritual numbness. There is no condemnation in emotional exhaustion. There is only an invitation to let God meet you in the nothing. To trust that your feelings will return, slowly, tenderly, as healing takes root. Even now, beneath the numb, your soul is still alive. Still longing. Still reaching for light.

Anchor Truth

Numbness is not the absence of faith. It's often the nervous system's response to pain. Bring even that to God. He can hold what you can't feel.

Prayer

God, I'm tired of feeling nothing. I want to feel close to you again. Meet me in this in-between place where I feel disconnected from myself and from you. Speak life where there's silence.

Invitation

If tears don't come, that's okay. But can you offer God one honest sentence? Write it down. Whisper it. Let it be your first step toward healing.

Rebuilding from the Inside Out

For we are God's masterpiece. He has created us anew in Christ Jesus, so we can do the good things he planned for us long ago.

EPHESIANS 2:10

When your self-worth has been eroded—by harsh words, emotional wounds, repeated rejection, or years of self-doubt—it doesn't rebuild overnight. Especially when your inner critic still has the loudest voice in the room.

But here's what's true: Self-worth isn't something you earn. It's something you uncover. You were born with it. That doesn't mean healing is instant. Insecurity is like a sinkhole beneath your feet. It makes everything feel unstable.

Rebuilding your sense of worth takes new foundations. New patterns of thinking. And, often, new relationships that reflect the truth about who you are.

In therapy, this process is called *reparenting*—learning to nurture and affirm yourself in ways you may never have received. It means replacing automatic self-judgment with curiosity and compassion. It means naming your needs instead of shaming yourself for having them. It means becoming a safe place for your own soul.

And biblically? It means returning again and again to the one who already calls you *chosen, beloved, redeemed,* and *whole*. Not because of what you've done, but because of who he is and what he's done for you.

Rebuilding self-worth also means letting go of the measuring sticks. You don't need to prove yourself through achievement, appearance, productivity, or popularity.

God didn't call you his masterpiece because you nailed it. He called you that because he made you. And craftsmanship is never careless. Even when you feel broken, you are not worthless. Even when you feel unsure, you are not unwanted. Even when you feel behind, you are not beyond repair.

You may not feel like much today, but feelings aren't facts. God's fingerprints are all over your design. You were crafted with care, called by name, and counted worthy—not because of what you've done, but because of who he is.

Anchor Truth

You are already enough, not because of your performance, but because of your position in Christ. He called you his masterpiece before you ever got a thing right.

Prayer

God, I've been living from a shaky sense of who I am. Help me rebuild from the truth of who you say I am. Show me where I've been too harsh with myself. Teach me how to speak to myself with grace. Remind me daily: I am loved. I am yours.

Invitation

Name one message you've believed about yourself that isn't true. Then write down the truth God says about you instead. Post it somewhere you'll see it every day. You're not rebuilding alone. God is in it with you. And he knows exactly what he's building.

The Exhaustion of Performing

These people honor me with their lips,
but their hearts are far from me.

MATTHEW 15:8

You know what it feels like: You walk into the room and become someone else. You laugh at things that don't feel funny. You agree when something in you disagrees. You overfunction so no one thinks you're weak. You smile so hard your jaw aches. And when it's over, you feel hollow. Spent. A little less *you* than you were before.

Approval seeking is more than people-pleasing. It's performance. It's the quiet (or frantic) belief that if you can just be impressive enough, charming enough, agreeable enough—you'll finally feel okay.

It's an exhausting way to live. And for some, it's the only way they know. Some call it *impression management.* But let's not pretty it up. It's soul-deep fatigue. And it's often driven by an ancient aching belief that if people really knew us, they wouldn't love us. So we present the curated version. We do the dance. And we never quite feel safe.

Jesus saw this in the religious leaders of his day. They knew how to perform the part. Outward devotion, perfect appearances, public approval. But their hearts were distant, hidden behind the performance. "These people honor me with their lips," Jesus said, "but their hearts are far from me."

It still happens today. Just swap the robes and scrolls for filters and platforms.

Here's the truth: Performance may earn you applause, but it won't earn you peace. It creates fans, not friends. You might win approval, but you lose yourself.

God isn't interested in your polished self. He wants the real one. The messy one. The anxious one. The one behind the grin. You don't have to prove yourself to be embraced. You just have to show up.

Anchor Truth

You weren't made to perform. You were made to be seen, known, and loved without pretense.

Prayer

God, I'm tired of the mask. I want to stop performing. Help me drop the act and trust that I am loved—not for what I do, but for who I am in you.

Invitation

What's one place where you feel the need to perform? Today, take one small risk to be more real—just 5 percent more honest, more human. Let grace meet you there.

How to Say It with Grace

Live wisely among those who are not believers, and make the most of every opportunity. Let your conversation be gracious and attractive so that you will have the right response for everyone.

COLOSSIANS 4:5-6

You finally decide to set a boundary, but now what? How do you say it without sounding defensive? How do you speak the truth without blowing up the relationship?

That's where Paul's wisdom becomes gold: "Let your conversation be gracious and attractive so that you will have the right response for everyone."

Boundaries aren't just about what you say; they're about how you say it. You can be clear without being cruel. Firm without being harsh. Direct without being cold.

Try starting with a posture of ownership: "I've realized I need to limit my availability on weekends so I can recharge." "I love you, but I'm not in a place to have that conversation right now." "I care about our relationship, which is why I need to be honest about what I can and can't do."

Notice the pattern? It's honest, kind, and rooted in self-respect—not blame, shame, or guilt.

When Paul told the Colossians to live wisely and speak with grace, he wasn't just giving them etiquette tips. He was showing them how to build peace without becoming a doormat.

Grace doesn't mean saying yes to everything. It means saying the *right* yes and the *necessary* no—with truth and love intertwined.

Not everyone will respond well. That's not your job.

Your job is to speak with clarity and kindness. That's what makes the boundary not just wise, but holy.

Anchor Truth

God honors boundaries that are communicated with grace and courage. Truth and love are not opposites. They are partners in peace.

Prayer

God, help me speak with wisdom and kindness. Give me the words and the courage to honor both my limits and the people I care about. Teach me to say hard things with grace.

Invitation

Write out one boundary you've struggled to communicate. Now rewrite it using gracious, honest language, keeping Colossians 4:5-6 in mind. Practice saying it aloud to yourself. Let wisdom shape your words.

The Scroll Isn't Making You Safer

Be careful how you live. Don't live like fools, but like those who are wise. Make the most of every opportunity in these evil days.

EPHESIANS 5:15-16

You don't mean to lose forty-five minutes. You just pick up your phone for a second, and suddenly you're halfway down a rabbit hole of bad news, filtered faces, hot takes, and everyone's perfect vacation.

It's not just distraction. It's a habit. One that often masks something deeper.

Doomscrolling isn't just about being uninformed or addicted to your screen. It's often about *emotional avoidance*. You feel overwhelmed, so you reach for control by absorbing more information. You feel disconnected, so you swipe for hits of stimulation. You feel anxious, so you dive into global chaos, like somehow being aware will make you immune. But it doesn't bring peace. It just adds noise.

Paul's words to the Ephesians are like a splash of cold water: "Be careful how you live." Pay attention. Be intentional. Don't drift through your days like you're not being shaped by what you consume. Because you are. Always.

Doomscrolling is a type of *maladaptive coping*—a behavior that helps you temporarily escape discomfort but ultimately deepens it. You don't feel better after doomscrolling. You feel fried. Foggy. Disoriented. And sometimes, ashamed.

And yet, the cycle repeats. Because in the moment, it feels like it might help. Maybe the next post will calm your anxiety. Maybe the next article will give you clarity. Maybe just a few more minutes will distract you from the ache.

But it never quite works, does it? Instead of grounding you, it leaves you more disconnected from your thoughts, your body, your values, and often from God.

You're allowed to set your phone down. You're allowed to opt out of the algorithm's anxiety. You're allowed to reclaim your peace—not because you're ignoring the world, but because you want to be present to it with wisdom, not worry.

Anchor Truth

Numbing your mind doesn't heal your heart.

Prayer

God, I want to live awake and wise, not distracted and drained. Help me pay attention to the habits that are stealing my peace. Give me the courage to be present with myself and with you.

Invitation

The next time you feel the pull to scroll, pause. Ask, "What am I actually feeling right now?" You don't have to run from it. Name it. Then choose something better.

Safe in the Storm

Then [Jesus] got up and rebuked the wind and waves, and suddenly there was a great calm.

MATTHEW 8:26

Close your eyes for a moment and picture it: The boat is small. The sky has turned. The wind is howling louder than your thoughts. Waves slap against the side of the vessel, spraying cold water across your face. Your hands grip the edge, knuckles white. Every creak of the wood sounds like it might be the last. You glance over, and Jesus is asleep.

That's how anxiety feels, right? Like you're drowning while the only one who can save you seems silent.

That moment touches one of anxiety's deepest fears: *perceived abandonment.* Your nervous system senses danger, and the silence of God can feel like a lack of care, even though it isn't.

Your heart races. Your breath shortens. Everything feels out of control. The storm outside starts to mirror the one inside. And it's hard not to wonder, *Why isn't God doing something?*

But here's the truth tucked into that stormy night: Jesus wasn't panicked by what panicked the disciples. He wasn't indifferent. He was at peace. And when the time came, he stood and spoke calm into chaos. Not because the disciples had the right words. Not because they proved their faith. But because he loved them.

That's what psychologists call *co-regulation*—the calming effect of a steady presence in the middle of panic. Jesus brought peace not just to the storm, but to the disciples' overwhelmed bodies and minds.

The presence of a storm doesn't mean the absence of God. And the presence of peace doesn't mean the storm is over. Sometimes peace is what God gives in the storm, not after it.

So if the waves are rising, if your grip is slipping, if your mind is screaming while others seem to sleep, know this: You are not alone in the chaos. Jesus is in the boat. He sees you. And he's not going anywhere. He's got you.

Anchor Truth

Peace isn't always the absence of chaos. Sometimes it's the nearness of Jesus in the middle of it.

Prayer

God, I feel like I'm being tossed around by fear, stress, and uncertainty. The storm feels big, and you feel quiet. But I'm holding on to the truth that you haven't left me. Help me remember that your presence is my safety. Speak calm into the chaos inside me.

Invitation

Pick a simple phrase to be your "storm anchor"—something you can repeat when anxiety builds: Jesus is here. I am not alone. *Write it down. Keep it where you can see it. Let it interrupt the waves when they rise.*

Detachment Isn't Cold—It's Courageous

This I declare about the LORD: He alone is my refuge, my place of safety; he is my God, and I trust him.

PSALM 91:2

Detachment gets a bad rap. It sounds heartless. Harsh. Like giving up. But healthy detachment is anything but that.

In codependent relationships, we often think love means enmeshment. We confuse control with compassion. We believe peace comes from keeping everyone else happy—even if it costs us our identity, sanity, and health.

So we rescue. We fix. We manage. We tiptoe. We shrink. And we burn out. That's where detachment becomes sacred.

Detachment means we no longer need to control how others feel or what they do in order to be okay. It means we can stop white-knuckling their sobriety, their approval, or their mood. It means we can love others without losing ourselves.

Scripture never calls us to abandon love, but it does call us to avoid the trap of fear-based people-pleasing. "Fearing people," Proverbs 29:25 says, "is a dangerous trap."

If you've lived in a codependent dynamic, you know the trap well. You're constantly scanning for signs of disapproval, dreading conflict, making excuses for someone's behavior, or sacrificing your peace to preserve theirs. That's not love. That's bondage.

Jesus modeled a kind of holy detachment. He cared deeply, but he didn't carry everyone's reactions like a cross on his back. He could walk away from the crowds. He could say "no." He could disappoint others without losing his center. That's not apathy. That's strength.

You're not selfish for setting a boundary. You're not cruel for stepping out of the caretaker role. You're not heartless for letting consequences unfold. Sometimes the most loving thing you can do is detach—with grace and grit—and trust God with what you can't control.

Anchor Truth

Detachment isn't about walking away from love. It's about walking away from the illusion that someone else's choices are your responsibility.

Prayer

God, help me know where my responsibilities end and someone else's begin. Give me the courage to detach with love and the wisdom to know what's mine to carry and what's not.

Invitation

Is there a relationship where you've been over-functioning? What would it look like to detach in a way that honors both you and them? Write down one small act of healthy detachment you can take this week.

When Loneliness Pushes You Toward God

LORD, hear my prayer! Listen to my plea!
Don't turn away from me in my time of distress. . . .
I lie awake, lonely as a solitary bird on the roof.

PSALM 102:1-2, 7

We usually treat loneliness like a problem to fix. We try to fill the silence with noise, the void with distraction, and the ache with activity. And when none of that works, we assume something is wrong with us or with God.

But what if loneliness isn't just a burden to carry? What if it's also a doorway? A quiet nudge that says, "There's more."

The psalmist didn't gloss over his loneliness. He named it. And he brought it to God—not as a complaint, but as a cry for grace. The prayer in Psalm 102 is both vulnerable and sacred. Because sometimes loneliness is the very place where your soul becomes most open to encounter.

When no one else is around to affirm you, you're invited to anchor yourself in who God says you are. When no one checks in, you're reminded that he never sleeps or slumbers. When your phone is silent, heaven is still listening. This isn't spiritualizing pain. It's seeing purpose in it.

Clinical research shows that emotional suffering can either pull us into despair or press us into growth. When loneliness becomes a catalyst—not for self-pity, but for deeper connection with God—it shapes something in you that comfort never could.

You don't have to *like* loneliness to let it lead you. Just be honest. Let the ache turn into a prayer. Let the silence become a space for divine whisper. Let your longing guide you—not into shame or panic, but toward the one who knows you fully and loves you completely.

Anchor Truth

Loneliness is not a punishment. It's a place where God can meet you more intimately than ever before.

Prayer

God, I don't want to feel this way, but I trust you'll meet me here. Help me not to numb the ache, but to follow it back to you. Let my loneliness become sacred space.

Invitation

Don't run from the quiet today. Sit with it. Breathe in God's presence. Whisper the words, "I'm not alone. You are here."

The Happiness of Adding Value

Encourage one another and build each other up, just as in fact you are doing.

1 THESSALONIANS 5:11 (NIV)

Happiness isn't just found in the moments you receive something. It's often found in the moments you give. Not the performative kind of giving, but the real kind. The kind that says, "I see you. I believe in you. You matter."

It's called *prosocial behavior*—any action intended to help others. And study upon study shows that people who regularly offer encouragement, support, or practical help to others report higher levels of life satisfaction. Why? Because adding value to someone else adds value to your own life as well.

Think about Barnabas in the book of Acts. His name literally means "son of encouragement." While others doubted Paul's transformation, Barnabas saw potential. He vouched for him, walked with him, and helped launch one of the most influential ministries in history. He didn't have to take center stage to feel joy. His happiness came from helping Paul step into his calling.

You don't have to preach sermons or write books. You just have to show up with your presence, your words, your belief in someone's potential. Send the text. Speak the encouragement. Open the door for someone else to shine.

You'll feel lighter when you stop trying to *impress* others and start trying to *bless* them. Because the happiness you're chasing often hides in the encouragement you give away. It's tucked into the text you almost didn't send. The compliment you hesitated to say.

Joy multiplies when it moves. So go ahead: Be the reason someone feels seen today. And watch what it does to your own heart.

Anchor Truth

You don't need a platform to make a difference. Even quiet acts of kindness echo in eternity and in your own soul.

Prayer

God, help me see the people around me who need a word of encouragement or a reminder of their worth. Fill me with the kind of joy that comes not from being noticed, but from noticing others.

Invitation

Who is one person you could affirm today? Tell them something specific you admire or appreciate about them. It just might lift you both.

The Quiet Kind of Brave

So let's not get tired of doing what is good. At just the right time we will reap a harvest of blessing if we don't give up.

GALATIANS 6:9

Some forms of courage roar. Others whisper. It takes courage to speak truth to power. But it also takes courage to show up, again and again, for the slow work of becoming whole. It takes courage to forgive someone who never apologized. To love someone who's hard to love. To show up for counseling when your progress feels invisible. To do the next right thing when you're weary to your bones.

This is the quiet kind of bravery—the kind that doesn't get applause or attention but still changes everything.

Our culture celebrates big moments. But most growth happens in the small ones. In the unseen. In the not-yet. And that requires a steady kind of courage—the grit to stay faithful to your values, even when it's boring, thankless, or slow.

Paul's words in Galatians aren't glamorous, but they're solid gold for anyone who's tempted to give up. Don't grow tired of doing good, he says. Keep going. Even when the fruit hasn't come yet. Even when it feels like no one notices. Even when you have to borrow hope from someone else just to take the next step.

Jesus honored this quiet kind of bravery too. The widow who gave her last coin. The woman who touched the edge of his robe in hope. The friends who lowered a paralyzed man through a roof. None of them made headlines. But they made history in the Kingdom of God.

So if you're walking through a season that demands more courage than you thought you had, take heart: You're braver than you feel. Keep going.

Anchor Truth

Courage isn't always loud or flashy. Sometimes it's just staying faithful, especially when no one sees except God.

Prayer

God, give me the strength to show up even when I'm tired. Help me trust that the good I do in faith is never wasted.

Invitation

What quiet act of courage are you being asked to keep showing up for? Write it down. Then recommit to it, one day at a time.

Praying Through Loneliness

Turn to me and have mercy,
for I am alone and in deep distress.

PSALM 25:16

Loneliness is more than just the absence of people. It's the ache of feeling unseen, untouched, uncared for—even when others are around. And when that ache settles in, prayer can feel like shouting into an empty room.

But that's not what David did. He didn't fake cheer. He didn't polish his prayers. He cried out from the raw places: "I am alone and in deep distress."

Real prayer doesn't start with the right words. It starts with honest ones. When you're lonely, the temptation is to turn inward—to ruminate, self-blame, or shut down. But the invitation of Scripture is to turn upward. To bring your isolation into communion. To let your groans become your prayers, even when they don't sound "spiritual."

Prayer doesn't always change your circumstances. But it changes your experience of them. It reminds you that your loneliness is never total. That even when you're in the valley, you're not invisible. That you don't have to figure it out or fix it first. You just have to show up.

The very act of praying when you feel most alone is an act of resistance against despair. It's you declaring, "I still believe you're listening." And God is.

Prayer may not always bring immediate answers, but it always brings presence. That's what David discovered. And Elijah. And Hagar in the wilderness. And every soul since who has whispered into the silence and somehow felt heard.

Your lonely place can become sacred ground. Not because it feels good, but because God meets you there in ways you wouldn't know otherwise. When you pray through your loneliness, you're not denying your pain, you're inviting God into it. And sometimes that's the moment the loneliness shifts. Not because the room fills with people, but because your heart remembers who's already with you.

Anchor Truth

Loneliness may isolate you from people, but it never separates you from God. Prayer opens the door to the Presence that never left.

Prayer

God, I feel alone. And some days I don't know what to say. But I'm here. I'm opening the door. Meet me in the silence. Sit with me in the ache. Remind me I'm not abandoned.

Invitation

Loneliness often grows in silence. Today, take one small step toward connection. Send a simple message, respond instead of scrolling past, or let someone know you're thinking of them. You don't need a deep conversation, just a thread of contact.

What Is This Jealousy Trying to Tell Me?

Worship and serve him with your whole heart and a willing mind. For the LORD sees every heart and knows every plan and thought.

1 CHRONICLES 28:9

Not all jealousy is ugly. Some of it is revealing. It's your soul's way of waving a flag and saying, "Pay attention. There's something important here." You scroll past someone's announcement and feel the twinge. You hear about their opportunity, and something inside you tightens. Not because you hate them—but because you want something too.

Jealousy doesn't always mean you're petty. It might mean you're paying attention for the first time in a long time.

David's prayer in Psalm 139 isn't just about confession. It's about curiosity. "Search me, God. Show me what I'm not seeing." That's a posture of humility. Not self-shame, not denial, but honest inquiry.

In therapy, jealousy is sometimes reframed as a *signal emotion*—a sign that there's a longing underneath. Maybe a value you've neglected. A hope you buried. A path you secretly wanted but didn't pursue.

Instead of stuffing jealousy down or judging yourself for it, what if you let it teach you? You might discover that you miss writing. Or a leadership role. Or a sense of creativity you once had.

You might realize your envy of someone's family isn't about them. It's about a deeper ache for connection in your own life. That doesn't mean everything you envy is part of your calling. But it *does* mean it's worth asking, "What am I longing for that I haven't named yet?"

Let your jealousy guide you, not define you. Let it open a conversation with God, not shut you down.

Anchor Truth

Jealousy can be a window into what your soul needs.

Prayer

God, instead of hiding my jealousy, I'm bringing it to you. Help me see what it might be pointing to. Show me what I've buried, ignored, or longed for in silence.

Invitation

When you feel jealousy stir in your heart today, pause and ask, "What is this really about?" Instead of shaming yourself, get curious. Then ask God what's yours to pursue and what's not.

Against the Grain

Don't look out only for your own interests, but take an interest in others, too.

PHILIPPIANS 2:4

Let's be honest: Listening to someone—really listening to them—is hard. It means putting our own thoughts on hold. It goes against the grain. Against the default settings of our nervous system. Against the habits we've spent a lifetime rehearsing.

You're in a conversation, and while the other person is talking, your brain is racing ahead. You're forming a response, analyzing their story, figuring out how it relates to you, or just silently waiting for your turn.

Maybe you don't say it out loud, but the inner monologue runs something like this: *How do I look right now? How can I steer this back to what I want to talk about? What do they think of me?*

That's not a flaw in your character. It's part of being human. Our brains are wired for self-preservation. But love—real connection—asks for something more. It asks us to pause our agenda. To release the need to control the moment. To put our ego in the back seat.

Psychologists call it *decentering*—the ability to momentarily step outside your own mental framework to consider another person's perspective. It's a skill, but also a spiritual discipline. Because it mirrors what Christ did for us.

Philippians 2 says that Jesus, "though he was God, did not think of equality with God as something to cling to. Instead, he gave up his divine privileges" (2:6-7). That's self-giving love. That's presence.

And when we ask, the Spirit helps us do what doesn't come naturally—calm the self-focus, quiet the inner chatter, and attune to another soul. Not forever. Not at the expense of our boundaries. But just long enough to communicate, "I see you. I hear you. You matter."

Anchor Truth

It's holy work to set aside your own agenda long enough to really see another person.

Prayer

God, you know how quickly I default to me—my needs, my worries, my words. Teach me to listen with humility. Help me set aside my agenda long enough to care deeply for someone else.

Invitation

In your next conversation, practice decentering. When you feel the urge to respond or redirect, take a breath. Stay with the other person's story. Ask one more question. Let love lead.

Living in the Present Tense

Be still, and know that I am God!
PSALM 46:10

Anxiety pulls you out of the present. It hijacks your attention, sending your mind spinning into imagined futures and worst-case scenarios. This is what psychologists call *anticipatory anxiety*—the fear of what might happen, often fueled by uncertainty and a deep desire to stay one step ahead of danger.

You find yourself pacing, planning, scanning for threats. Your body locks into fight-or-flight mode, even if there's nothing around you that's truly unsafe. It feels like staying busy or staying worried is the only way to stay in control.

But here's what's clinically and spiritually true: You can't experience peace in a moment you're not in. God doesn't meet you in the future you're trying to predict. He meets you in the present you're trying to escape. This one. Right here.

That doesn't mean you have to love what today holds. Or ignore your responsibilities.

It just means this: Your nervous system can only regulate in the now. Peace lives in the present, never in the spiral of what-ifs.

When we ruminate or catastrophize, our amygdala (the brain's fear center) stays activated, creating a loop of stress and disconnection. But when we ground ourselves in the moment—through breath, body awareness, or quiet trust—we shift into the *parasympathetic state*—rest, calm, connection.

This is what stillness actually is. Not passivity. Not checking out. Stillness is presence. It's choosing to return to your body, your breath, your God.

He's here. Not in yesterday's regret. Not in tomorrow's pressure. Here, in this heartbeat. This minute. This breath.

And yes, that may feel messy. Unfinished. Uncertain. But it's real. And healing only happens in reality—not in imagined futures or revised pasts.

God keeps bringing you back to now. Not to trap you, but to anchor you. To remind you that you're not alone in this moment. And that's where peace begins.

Anchor Truth

God's presence is found in the now. Peace begins when we stop running ahead of grace.

Prayer

God, I confess I'm rarely present. My mind lives in the future, trying to control what hasn't happened yet. But you are not "out there," waiting for me to arrive. You are here. Right now. Teach me to stop, to breathe, to notice. Remind me that this moment, even if it's messy, is the one you're in.

Invitation

Pause for sixty seconds. Look around. Name five things you can see. Four you can touch. Three you can hear. Two you can smell. One you can taste (or imagine tasting). This isn't a trick. It's a return—to your body, to the present, and to the God who is with you in it.

Built for Hope

So be strong and courageous,
all you who put your hope in the LORD!

PSALM 31:24

Optimism isn't wishful thinking. It's not toxic positivity or pretending everything's okay. It's a mindset—a practiced, powerful lens that literally rewires your brain. And it's not fluff. It's science.

Studies show that optimism is strongly linked to an increased quality of life. Lower levels of depression and anxiety. Better cardiovascular health. Improved immune response. Stronger recovery from illness or surgery. Greater resilience in times of stress and trauma.

One study from the University of Illinois even found that people who score high on measures of optimism are 76 percent more likely to report their overall mental health as "excellent."

Why? Because optimism is about how your brain explains adversity. Psychologist Martin Seligman calls it *explanatory style*—the way you interpret life's setbacks.

Optimists tend to believe that problems are temporary ("This won't last forever"), specific ("This doesn't define everything"), and external ("This isn't entirely my fault"). Pessimists, on the other hand, see adversity as permanent ("It'll never get better"), pervasive ("It's completely ruined now"), and personal ("It's all my fault"). And that inner narrative shapes everything.

Here's the good news: Optimism can be learned. You can practice catching your internal narrative and reframing it. You can challenge the belief that things will "always be this way." You can consciously seek out gratitude, possibility, and forward motion.

And spiritually, optimism becomes even more powerful. Because it's not grounded in your circumstances—it's grounded in God's character.

Psalm 31 reminds us, "Put your hope in the Lord. Be strong. Be courageous." Not because life is easy, but because God is faithful. That's what makes biblical optimism resilient. It doesn't deny the storm. It trusts in an anchor.

Anchor Truth

Optimism is a mindset you can build, and it builds you right back.

Prayer

God, help me see life through your lens. Grow in me a resilient hope that changes how I think, feel, and live.

Invitation

When you hit a frustrating moment today, ask yourself: "Is this really permanent? Is it truly pervasive? Is it all on me?" Then reframe it and breathe in some space.

The Chameleon Life

I know, my God, that you examine our hearts and rejoice when you find integrity there.

1 CHRONICLES 29:17

Some of us walk into a room and lose ourselves. We scan for cues. *What do others want from me? What version of me will they accept?* And like a chameleon, we adjust. We shift opinions mid-sentence to avoid conflict. We mirror the energy of whoever we're with. We say yes when everything in us is screaming no.

It's a subtle kind of survival. But over time, it fractures your sense of identity. You're constantly shape-shifting, managing other people's impressions. And the question that simmers underneath it all is this: *If they knew the real me, would they stay?*

Psychologists call this *self-monitoring*—modifying your behavior depending on the situation. A little of it is normal, even healthy. We all adapt somewhat to different social settings. But when self-monitoring becomes chronic, it's no longer about connection. It's about control. It's about maintaining the mask so no one sees what you fear might be rejected.

But here's the paradox: The more you perform for others, the more disconnected you become—from them and from yourself. Real intimacy can't form without authenticity. The approval you gain from performance feels hollow because it is.

God wants us to have clarity and know who we are—and who we serve. Our aim isn't other people's applause, it's alignment. Living for the approval of others puts you at odds with your truest calling. You can't walk in freedom and keep everyone happy at the same time.

Anchor Truth

Authenticity will always cost you something. But so will pretending. Choose the cost that leads to peace.

Prayer

God, I've spent too long trying to be what others expect. Give me the courage to stop shape-shifting and start standing in the identity you've given me.

Invitation

Pay attention to when you feel the urge to "adjust" yourself in conversation. Pause and ask, "Is this truly me, or am I performing?" Try holding your ground and letting your real self show up.

Do It Afraid

So be strong and courageous! Do not be afraid and do not panic before them. For the LORD your God will personally go ahead of you. He will neither fail you nor abandon you.

DEUTERONOMY 31:6

Fear doesn't disqualify you from courage. It's often the sign you're headed somewhere that matters. When God tells Joshua to "be strong and courageous," it's not because Joshua feels brave. It's because he's terrified. He's stepping into leadership, following in the shadow of Moses, and heading into unknown territory. It's a moment loaded with pressure and risk.

And God doesn't tell him to *feel* courageous. He tells him to *choose* courage. That's the pivot point: Courage is not a feeling; it's a decision.

You might feel shaky. Your voice might crack. Your hands might sweat. You might want to bolt. But courage says, "Do it anyway." It comes down to facing the very thing you fear to prove to your brain that fear isn't the end of the story.

Over time, what once triggered panic begins to lose its grip. You stretch your capacity. You expand your window of tolerance. And you begin to realize that you're braver than you thought.

Courage doesn't mean you'll get it perfect. It means you'll show up. To the conversation you've been avoiding. To the stage you never thought you'd be on. To the healing you've been afraid to start.

Some people wait for fear to disappear before they move. But fear doesn't vanish. It shifts. It morphs into regret if you let it make your decisions for you. But when you choose courage, even with trembling hands, you grow. You grow spiritually. You grow psychologically. You grow into someone more whole.

Anchor Truth

Courage isn't the absence of fear. It's the willingness to act in spite of it. You don't have to wait to feel brave. Just start.

Prayer

God, I'm scared, but I don't want to be ruled by fear. Walk with me into the unknown. Help me choose faith over paralysis.

Invitation

What are you postponing out of fear? Identify one next step you can take this week, even if your heart's racing. Do it afraid.

What Resilience Really Is (and Isn't)

But those who trust in the LORD will find new strength.
They will soar high on wings like eagles.
They will run and not grow weary.
They will walk and not faint.

ISAIAH 40:31

You've heard the word *resilient* before. Maybe people have even called you that, like it's a badge of honor. But maybe it hasn't felt like one. Maybe it's felt like survival. Like holding your breath. Like staying upright because you had no other choice.

Here's the truth: Resilience isn't about being tough. It's about getting back up. It's not the absence of pain, but the presence of recovery. It's not about always bouncing back. It's about slowly, courageously growing forward.

Psychologists know resilience not as a trait you're born with, but a skill you can build. It's the ability to adapt under stress, to regulate your emotions, to stay connected to meaning and hope even when life feels heavy. And most importantly, it doesn't require perfection. It just requires movement.

In Scripture, the prophet Isaiah describes resilience in the raw terms of human endurance: "run and not grow weary"; "walk and not faint." He's naming the exhaustion and the pain—and also the strength.

Resilience is both/and. Bruised and breathing. Struggling and still here.

You don't have to power through with a fake smile. You don't have to ignore your pain to be resilient. In fact, the most resilient people are often the ones who feel deeply and keep going anyway.

Today, we begin a journey of reclaiming what resilience really looks like. Not endless strength. Not numbing out. But leaning in—with honesty, grace, and hope. You're not weak because you feel the weight. You're resilient because you keep showing up.

Anchor Truth

Resilience isn't the absence of struggle. It's the courage to keep moving through it, one honest step at a time.

Prayer

God, I've confused resilience with pretending to be okay. But I want to learn what it really means to be strong in you. Help me build strength that bends, not breaks. Show me how to rise—not by force, but by faith.

Invitation

Reflect today on what resilience has looked like in your life—real, messy, imperfect resilience. Write down one way you've kept going. Let that remind you: Resilience lives here too.

When You Can't Just "Move On"

Then Jesus wept. The people who were standing nearby said, "See how much he loved him!"

JOHN 11:35-36

They meant well. They told you to stay strong. To "move on." To "let it go." Maybe they thought those words would lift you. Instead, they landed like bricks. Because grief isn't a switch you flip. It's not a project you complete. It's not something you "get over."

Grief is a process. A slow, clumsy, sacred one. It loops and spirals. It surprises you in grocery store aisles. It shows up in birthdays, in songs, in the seat across from you that stays empty.

When someone says, "move on," they usually mean "don't make me uncomfortable." But grief isn't about their comfort. It's about your healing. And healing doesn't mean forgetting.

It means learning to live with the love that still lingers in the absence. It means giving yourself permission to feel *everything*—the ache, the anger, the tenderness, the tears. And it means remembering this: You are not broken because you still hurt. You are brave for still loving.

Jesus never rushed the grieving. He didn't meet Mary and Martha at Lazarus's tomb with a quick fix or empty clichés. He wept. He stood with them in their sorrow before he ever spoke of resurrection.

Grief doesn't need a shortcut. It needs a companion. And Jesus offers exactly that—not from a distance, but with tears in his eyes and tenderness in his voice. He enters the ache. He honors the loss. He dignifies the sorrow.

You don't have to pretend you're okay. You don't have to hurry toward healing.

The savior who stood outside a tomb and wept is the same one who stands beside you now. Let that be your comfort: You're not grieving alone. You're grieving with God.

Anchor Truth

Grief doesn't have a timeline. God doesn't rush your healing. He meets you in it.

Prayer

God, I'm tired of pretending I'm fine. Help me not to rush past the pain or hide it. Sit with me in this space. Give me the courage to grieve fully and to trust that you're holding every piece of my heart.

Invitation

What part of your grief have you been trying to "move on" from too quickly? Today, give yourself the grace to pause there. God isn't asking you to be done. He's asking to be near.

Humble Confidence

But blessed are those who trust in the LORD
and have made the LORD their hope and confidence.

JEREMIAH 17:7

Some people walk into a room and demand attention. Others shrink into the corners, hoping not to be noticed. But then there's a third kind—the ones who carry themselves with quiet strength.

You can feel their presence, not because it's loud, but because it's solid. That's humble confidence. It's not arrogance. It's not bravado. It's not self-deprecation, either. It's knowing who you are and whose you are—and letting that be enough.

Humble confidence isn't about proving anything. It's about *being rooted*—anchored in something (or Someone) stronger than your insecurities, your résumé, or your reputation. It says, "I don't have to puff myself up or tear myself down. I can stand here, open-handed, and let my life speak for itself."

Jesus modeled this. He washed feet and didn't flinch at the cross. He served and still spoke with authority. He welcomed children and silenced storms. No ego. No insecurity. Just presence, power, and peace.

In psychological terms, this is *secure identity*. In biblical terms, it's abiding in the vine (John 15:1-11).

You don't need applause to feel valuable or invisibility to feel holy. You simply need to stay connected to the one who defines your worth.

If you've been equating humility with passivity or confidence with pride, it's time to rewrite the narrative. You can be both humble and bold. Gentle and grounded. You can speak the truth without arrogance and lead courageously, without ego.

You don't need to *announce* your confidence. You just need to *embody* it.

Anchor Truth

You were made to live with humble confidence—rooted in God's love, unshaken by the need to impress or disappear.

Prayer

God, teach me to carry myself the way Jesus did, with strength that serves and confidence that rests in you. Help me walk into each moment grounded in grace and courage.

Invitation

Today, walk into every room like you belong, because in Christ, you do. Let humility and confidence hold hands as you speak, serve, and show up with love.

You Can Still Come Home

So he returned home to his father. And while he was still a long way off, his father saw him coming. Filled with love and compassion, he ran to his son.

LUKE 15:20

He wanted out. Freedom. Fun. Control. He didn't want limits or expectations. He wanted pleasure, immediacy, indulgence. And for a while, it worked. Until it didn't.

Jesus' story of the prodigal son—the crash-and-burn kind—isn't just about rebellion. It's about the spiral: the binge, the burnout, and the bottom. The slow unraveling that happens when desire runs untethered. When we chase something to fill the void and find ourselves emptier than before.

Scripture doesn't say the self-sabotaging prodigal was addicted, but let's be honest: The pattern is there. A compulsive escape. Numbing the ache. A fast crash. And then shame so thick it nearly kept him from turning back.

He rehearsed a speech. He lowered his expectations. He braced for rejection. That's what addiction does: It convinces you that you're disqualified from grace. That you're only welcome if you clean yourself up first.

But Jesus flips that script. While the son was still a long way off, the father ran. Not with scolding or suspicion, but with compassion. No tests. No probation. Just embrace. Celebration. Restoration.

You don't have to earn your way back to God. You don't have to detox your soul before you're seen. If all you have is a limp and a whisper of repentance, that's enough.

This story doesn't minimize the damage of compulsive choices. But it refuses to let shame have the final word. That's what grace does. It meets you in the mess and calls you *beloved* anyway.

Anchor Truth

Your failures don't forfeit your Father's love. You can always come home.

Prayer

God, I've wandered. I've wasted. I've believed the lie that I'm too far gone. Thank you for running toward me before I even reach the door.

Invitation

What speech have you been rehearsing for God? One soaked in shame? Take a breath. You don't need it. Just start walking home.

You Are Not Your Panic

When you go through deep waters, I will be with you.
When you go through rivers of difficulty, you will not drown.

ISAIAH 43:2

Panic attacks don't ask permission. They hijack your body, override your thoughts, and convince you that something is terribly wrong, even when you're safe. Your heart races. Your chest tightens. Your hands tremble. You feel dizzy, detached, or like you might die.

That sense of detachment is called *depersonalization*—when your mind temporarily disconnects from your body or surroundings. It's common during panic, and deeply unsettling, but not dangerous. The worst part? It feels like no one else can see it happening.

If that sounds familiar, you're not alone. And more importantly, you are not your panic. Your panic is a moment, not your whole story. It's a storm in your body, not a flaw in your faith. It's a signal, not your identity.

Clinically, panic is your body in survival mode—your *sympathetic nervous system* firing as if there's incredible danger, even when there isn't. It's often triggered by accumulated stress or unresolved emotional tension.

Panic is your nervous system stuck in overdrive. It's not weakness. It's not sin. And it's not the full truth of who you are.

God doesn't wait until the panic subsides to be near. He comes close when your heart is racing. He stays when you feel like running. He rescues not because you've performed peace, but because he sees your pain.

This is part of what psychologists call *distress tolerance*—the ability to stay grounded in the middle of discomfort. And it's what faith invites: not escaping the deep waters, but remembering you're not alone in them.

You may feel out of control in those moments, but you are not unsafe. And you are not out of reach.

Anchor Truth

Panic may feel overwhelming, but it doesn't define your identity or your worth.

Prayer

God, you know the fear that rises without warning and how hard it is to ride the waves of panic. Remind me that I am not broken. That even when my body betrays me, your love holds steady. Help me not to shame myself for what I cannot control. Teach me to trust that you're with me in the chaos.

Invitation

Create a simple grounding kit for when panic strikes. It could include a calming verse, a note to yourself, a comforting scent (like lavender), or a small object you can touch to stay anchored in the present. You don't need to fix the panic. Just remind yourself you're safe and seen.

When Optimism Feels Out of Reach

Even when I walk through the darkest valley, I will not be afraid, for you are close beside me.

PSALM 23:4

Optimism gets a bad reputation sometimes. Especially when it's packaged as clichés: "Everything happens for a reason." "Good vibes only." "God's got this!"

While those may come from well-meaning people, they can land like a slap to the soul—especially if you're grieving, barely hanging on, or just exhausted from trying to stay positive. Forced or toxic positivity isn't optimism.

It's spiritual bypassing dressed up in bumper-sticker theology.

Real optimism makes room for sorrow. It doesn't deny the valley. It just says, "This valley isn't forever." It's the belief that even here, even now, God has not abandoned you. Your story isn't stuck. The end of your rope is not the end of your future.

Psychologists who study resilience note that the most hopeful people are often the most realistic. They don't pretend bad things won't happen. They just refuse to let those things have the final word.

Their optimism is practiced, not automatic. It's a posture of *learned hopefulness*—rooted in daily choices to stay open, to look up, and to believe in a future beyond their current pain.

David didn't write Psalm 23 in a palace. He wrote it as a man who'd lived through rejection, betrayal, and danger. His optimism wasn't naive. It was tested. And it still rang out: "I will not be afraid, for you are close beside me."

That's the kind of optimism worth holding on to. Not fluffy. Not forced. But fierce. The kind you whisper when everything else feels loud.

Anchor Truth

Real optimism doesn't silence your fear. It speaks a louder truth beside it.

Prayer

God, I don't need perfect circumstances to believe in your goodness. Help me lean in to hope even when my heart feels tired.

Invitation

What kind of "positivity" have you been forcing or faking? Today, let go of the pressure to pretend. Instead, name one small thing that helps you remember that this moment is not the end.

Cooling Down the Inner Storm

Control your temper,
for anger labels you a fool.

ECCLESIASTES 7:9

Ever had a moment where something small set off a big internal storm? A sideways comment. A minor disappointment. A look that landed wrong. Suddenly your emotions are on fire and you're not sure whether to shut down, lash out, or escape.

That's the moment emotional regulation steps in—not to shut the storm down, but to keep it from flooding the streets. Emotional regulation is the art of noticing your internal temperature and knowing how to turn down the heat.

While you might justify it ("I'm just passionate" or "They pushed me too far"), Scripture is blunt: Lose your temper and you wear the fool's label. Not because you got angry, but because you let it run you. This verse isn't scolding you for feeling big feelings. It's inviting you to pause before those feelings become your identity.

We all know what unregulated anger can do. It damages relationships, distorts judgment, and deepens regret. But here's the hope: You can learn to slow the storm. Not by pretending you're fine, but by interrupting the automatic cycle.

Here's what the research says: When we pause to name what we're feeling—"I'm frustrated," "I feel disrespected," "I'm scared"—we engage the part of our brain responsible for reason and decision-making. That pause gives us space to choose how we respond rather than reacting out of instinct or ego.

It's not just neuroscience—it's wisdom. The book of Proverbs echoes this truth again and again: Patience is power. Restraint is strength. Slow is wise.

And Jesus? He modeled this kind of emotional mastery again and again. He wept. He got angry. He grew tired. But he didn't let his emotions own him. He named them, made space for them, and responded in alignment with his purpose. He calmed external storms, and he knew how to quiet the ones inside, too.

Anchor Truth

Anger is part of being human. But left unchecked, it clouds your judgment and damages your witness. The ability to slow the storm inside you is a mark of emotional strength, not weakness.

Prayer

God, when emotions surge and I want to lash out, help me breathe. Help me recognize what I'm feeling and respond from a place of wisdom instead of impulse. Teach me to calm the storm before it speaks for me.

Invitation

Think of a recent moment when you felt the storm rise. What would it have looked like to pause for just ten seconds? What did you need in that moment—connection, clarity, compassion? Practice that pause today.

When Sorrow Settles In

He was despised and rejected—
a man of sorrows, acquainted with deepest grief.

ISAIAH 53:3

Grief is not a detour from life. It is life for a time. Psychologists describe grief as a natural emotional response to loss. And while the stages of grief—denial, anger, bargaining, depression, and acceptance—are often quoted, real grief doesn't follow clean lines.

It loops. It spirals. It lingers. Sometimes it fades into the background. Other times it hijacks the whole day.

But here's the truth: You are not malfunctioning because you're grieving. You're responding like a human being with a heart that remembers, that longs, that loved.

In fact, unprocessed sorrow can lodge itself in the body. Studies have linked prolonged, unacknowledged grief to fatigue, weakened immunity, disrupted sleep, and increased anxiety or depression. That weight in your chest? It's not just in your head. It's real, and it's worthy of care.

The Bible doesn't deny sorrow. It gives it voice. Isaiah 53 describes Jesus as "a man of sorrows, acquainted with deepest grief." He's not just a God who observes suffering from afar, but one who knows it intimately. If grief was part of his story, why wouldn't it be part of ours?

Grief isn't a sign of weak faith. It's a sign that something mattered. That *someone* or *something* mattered.

And here's what the clinical world affirms and Scripture echoes: Naming your sorrow is one of the first steps toward healing. Suppressing it prolongs the pain. But bringing it into the light—through conversation, counseling, community, or prayer—releases its grip.

You don't have to rush it. There's no expiration date on sadness. But you do deserve space to feel it. And even here, in the heaviness, you are not forgotten. Grief may bend you, but it doesn't break your story. There's still beauty ahead.

One breath, one prayer, one honest step at a time.

Anchor Truth

Grief isn't the absence of faith. It's the presence of love that has lost something real.

Prayer

God, sometimes the sorrow settles in so deeply I wonder if it will ever lift. But you were no stranger to grief. So hold me in mine. Help me name it, feel it, and slowly heal with your presence beside me.

Invitation

What loss, big or small, have you tried to move on from too quickly? Try giving it space today. Say it out loud. Write it down. Let it be known. Healing begins where honesty lives.

Hannah and the Loneliness No One Saw

I am a woman who is deeply troubled. . . . I have been praying here out of my great anguish and grief.

1 SAMUEL 1:15-16 (NIV)

Some loneliness is loud. But some is silent, even invisible.

Hannah's ache didn't show on the outside. She had a husband who loved her. A home. A place in the community. But her heart ached with an unmet longing—a child she couldn't have. And to make matters worse, she was surrounded by reminders of what she lacked, from Peninnah's taunts to the confused assumptions of Eli the priest.

It's possible to be surrounded by people and still feel painfully alone. Hannah didn't hide from her pain. She brought it to God. Raw. Unfiltered. She didn't tidy up her grief before stepping into the Temple. She just came as she was—anguished and honest.

And that's where the shift began. Her story reminds us that transformation doesn't always start with external change. It begins inside—with surrender, with prayer, with showing up before God when we feel most forgotten.

After pouring out her soul, the Bible says Hannah went on her way and was "no longer downcast" (1 Samuel 1:18, NIV). The miracle of conception came later. But her countenance lifted before her circumstances did. Why? Because something had shifted in her spirit.

She had been seen. She had been heard. And she dared to hope again. Hannah's story doesn't end with her holding a baby; it continues with her becoming a woman who gives back to God in trust.

Her loneliness had carved out a deeper capacity in her for faith, sacrifice, and love. She didn't just become a mother. She became a spiritual mentor to a prophet.

If you feel isolated by your longing, like no one sees the ache behind your smile, remember Hannah. God met her in her hidden place. And he can meet you in yours, too.

Anchor Truth

Loneliness doesn't mean you're unloved or unnoticed. Like Hannah, you can be misread by others and still be deeply known by God.

Prayer

God, meet me in the moments when I feel invisible or misunderstood. I pour out my heart to you, just like Hannah did. Let me walk away from this moment with a lifted face, not because my circumstances have changed, but because I know you've heard me.

Invitation

Are there places you've been holding back in prayer—maybe because it felt like no one would understand? Try praying like Hannah today: honestly, vulnerably, and without editing. God is listening.

The Power of Perspective

I am doing a great work and I cannot come down.

NEHEMIAH 6:3 (ESV)

Resilience isn't just about what happens to you. It's about how you *see* what happens. That's the power of perspective. The ability to reframe, refocus, and stay rooted when life tries to pull you off course.

Psychologists call this *cognitive flexibility*—the ability to shift your mindset without losing your meaning. And it's one of the strongest predictors of lasting resilience.

In Scripture, Nehemiah gives us a master class in perspective. Tasked with rebuilding Jerusalem's broken walls, he faced nonstop opposition—mockery, distraction, sabotage, and fear. People tried to lure him away from the work. But Nehemiah's answer? "I am doing a great work and I cannot come down." That's perspective.

He could've spiraled. He could've doubted. He could've backed down. But instead, he remembered what he was doing—and why.

Resilient people don't pretend things aren't hard. But they do look for meaning inside the mess. They zoom out when life closes in. They ask, "What is still true?" "What matters most?" "What am I building, even here?"

You may not be rebuilding a wall, but you're rebuilding a life, a heart, a sense of safety and hope. And that is a great work. So when discouragement tries to distract you, don't come down.

Resilience grows when you fight to see the whole picture, not just the pain. Not just the fear. But the deeper purpose that's still unfolding.

Anchor Truth

You can't always control your circumstances, but you can choose your focus.

Prayer

God, when everything feels urgent or overwhelming, help me see clearly. Remind me what matters most. Give me the perspective to keep going—not in denial, but with determination.

Invitation

Today, finish this sentence: "I am doing a great work, and I will not come down because . . ." Let that truth ground you. Post it where you can see it. Come back to it when life pulls hard.

You Still Have a Say

The LORD directs the steps of the godly.
He delights in every detail of their lives.

PSALM 37:23

Some days life steamrolls you. Plans fall apart. People disappoint. Your emotions run the show. And before you know it, you're just reacting, shutting down, or coasting—hoping the day ends quietly. It's easy to believe the lie, *I don't have a say in this.* But you do.

Maybe not in everything. You can't control other people. You can't erase what's already happened. You can't snap your fingers and fix what hurts. But you still have *agency*—the ability to choose how you respond, how you carry yourself, and how you move forward.

In psychology, there's a term for what happens when life beats that belief out of you: *learned helplessness.* When enough hard things stack up, your brain starts to shut down your sense of choice. You stop looking for options. You assume you're stuck. You tell yourself, "This is just the way it is now."

That mindset is heavy, and it's dangerous. Because the moment you stop believing you have a say is the moment you stop living on purpose.

Even in faith circles, we sometimes reinforce this passivity without meaning to. We say things like "Let go and let God" or "God's got it." And while there's truth there, this mindset can twist into resignation if we forget that Scripture actually shows a God who works *with* us. A God who delights in our movement. Who gave us minds to think, hands to act, and hearts to decide.

Psalm 37 doesn't say God delights only when you're certain. Or successful. Or calm. It says he directs your steps and delights in the details. Period. That includes the wobbly ones. The late ones. The scared-but-brave ones.

So today, when the stress builds or the doubts creep in, stop and ask, "What's still mine to choose?" Then do that. Even if it's just one thing.

That's agency. That's strength. That's how moving forward begins.

Anchor Truth

You don't have to control everything to move forward.

Prayer

God, I'm tired of feeling stuck. Show me where I've stopped believing I have a say. Help me remember that agency isn't arrogance. It's part of your design. Give me the clarity to see my choices and the courage to take one step.

Invitation

When you hit a wall today—emotionally, mentally, relationally—pause. Ask yourself, "What do I still get to choose here?" Start there. Take one step. Don't wait for permission.

The Strength of Being Small

Now Moses was very humble—more humble than any other person on earth.

NUMBERS 12:3

If there's anyone you'd expect to walk with swagger, it would be Moses. Burning bush? Check. Parting the Red Sea? Check. Delivering plagues, leading a nation, receiving the Ten Commandments? Check, check, check.

And yet, Numbers says he was the most humble man on earth. Not *used to be*. Not *became over time*. Right in the thick of miracles, Moses was marked by humility.

But here's what's easy to miss: Moses didn't start that way. When God first called him, Moses hesitated. He offered excuses. He questioned his worth and asked for someone else to take the job.

That wasn't humility. That was insecurity dressed in sheep's clothing.

True humility came later—not from minimizing himself, but from seeing more of God. Moses spent time in the Tent of Meeting, face-to-face with the Lord (Exodus 33:7-11). After meeting God on Mount Sinai, he came down with his face glowing. He didn't need to cling to his role or his reputation because he knew the one who gave him both.

His humility wasn't about thinking less of himself. It was about thinking of himself less.

That's the shift. Insecurity asks, "Am I enough?" Humility says, "God is enough."

And that's where your strength is. Not in loud declarations or quiet apologies for existing, but in the deep confidence that comes from walking closely with the one who called you.

Anchor Truth

True humility isn't self-doubt. It's God trust.

Prayer

God, when I feel small, remind me that you are big. Let my humility come not from fear, but from knowing you walk with me, speak through me, and shine beyond me.

Invitation

Spend a few moments today reflecting on Moses' journey from excuses to courage. Where are you still minimizing yourself? Ask God to fill that space with holy confidence.

Give What You Crave

The generous will prosper;
those who refresh others will themselves be refreshed.

PROVERBS 11:25

When you're lonely, the natural instinct is to pull inward. You hope someone will see the ache in your eyes, send the invitation, initiate the conversation. And when no one does, the silence confirms the lie that you don't matter. But what if the way out of loneliness isn't waiting to be seen, but choosing to see?

That may sound counterintuitive, maybe even unfair. Why should you have to give what you're not getting? Because, paradoxically, the act of reaching out rewires your heart.

Neuroscience confirms that social circuits in the brain can be reignited when you shift your attention outward, even in small ways: Asking a coworker how their weekend went. Texting a friend to say you're thinking of them. Holding space for someone else's hard day.

It doesn't take much. But it does take movement. And that movement, no matter how small, begins to break the grip of isolation.

Ruth did this. She had every reason to shut down after the death of her husband. Instead, she clung to Naomi. Her faithful presence—her decision to serve—became the very path that led to her healing and restoration. She gave what she likely longed for most: connection.

And the same can be true for you. When you offer kindness in the middle of your ache, you not only bless someone else—you remind your own soul, "I still have something to give. I am not invisible. I am still connected."

Loneliness may whisper that you're empty. But giving to others is proof that you're not.

Anchor Truth

God made you for connection, and when you refresh others, he promises to refresh you.

Prayer

God, you know how I long to be seen. Help me choose to see others today. Remind me that I still matter, that I can still give, even when I feel alone. Let my small acts of kindness be seeds of healing, for me and for others.

Invitation

Reach out today. Text someone encouragement, ask a question, send a simple note. It doesn't have to be big. Just start. Watch how it softens the silence.

The Pause That Protects

Everyone should be quick to listen, slow to speak and slow to become angry, because human anger does not produce the righteousness that God desires.

JAMES 1:19-20 (NIV)

There's a moment, often just a few seconds long, between stimulus and response. Someone rolls their eyes. A text hits a nerve. You feel disrespected, dismissed, or blindsided. Your body tenses. Your mind races. Your gut screams, "Say something. Do something. Let 'em have it!"

And in that moment, you have a choice: React or regulate. Emotional regulation doesn't mean you ignore what's happening. It means you interrupt the autopilot. You create space between what's done to you and what you do next.

That space is everything. It's the difference between escalation and peace, between burning a bridge and building one. It starts with noticing. Feel the heat rising in your chest? The clench in your jaw?

That's your nervous system gearing up for a fight, flight, or freeze response. Your amygdala—your brain's emotional alarm system—is lighting up like a Christmas tree. It wants to react fast. But speed rarely serves you well here.

What helps? A pause. A breath. A step away. Naming what you're feeling. Reminding yourself, "I don't have to act on this feeling right now."

This pause doesn't make you passive. It makes you powerful. Because now you're responding with intention, not impulse. You're staying grounded in your values. You're protecting your peace.

Jesus did this constantly. He was interrupted, insulted, and misunderstood. But he didn't react with defensiveness or rage. He knew when to speak and when to stay silent. When to confront and when to walk away. His self-control wasn't weakness. It was strength under control.

You don't have to master this overnight. Just try pausing once today when your emotions flare. One holy pause. One deep breath. That's where transformation begins.

Anchor Truth

Reacting is automatic. Responding is intentional. And every time you pause instead of exploding, you reclaim your peace and your power.

Prayer

God, help me notice the moments when I'm about to react in ways that don't reflect who I want to be. Teach me to pause, breathe, and respond with wisdom and love.

Invitation

Today, when something triggers a strong emotional reaction, stop and take three full breaths before saying or doing anything. Let that be the space where the Spirit meets you.

When Emotions Drive the Bus

But the fruit of the Spirit is . . . self-control.

GALATIANS 5:22-23 (NIV)

Have you ever been hijacked by your own emotions? Like one minute you're calm and the next you're snapping at someone you love, drowning in shame, or spiraling into anxiety? That's what it feels like when emotions take the driver's seat and you're stuck in the back, white-knuckling your way through the wreckage.

This is where emotional regulation steps in. It's not about faking calm or bottling things up. It's about learning how to stay in the driver's seat. Emotional regulation is the ability to respond to emotions in a way that is wise, grounded, and aligned with your values—even when everything in you wants to blow up, break down, or shut off.

This isn't just pop psychology. Study after study has shown that emotional regulation is foundational to mental health, resilience, and satisfying relationships. It's linked to lower anxiety, stronger immune function, and better decision-making. And spiritually? It's the soil where patience, peace, and true self-control grow.

But here's the best part: This is a skill you can learn. It starts with self-awareness. Noticing when you're getting hijacked. Paying attention to what's happening in your body—tight jaw, racing heart, clenched fists.

Then, instead of reacting on impulse, you create a pause. You breathe. You name what you're feeling. And then you choose your next step *on purpose.*

The world doesn't teach us this. Many of us were raised to either blow up or shut down. Some of us never saw anyone model what it looks like to stay steady in a storm.

But Scripture calls us to it. Jesus didn't stuff his emotions. He wept, he flipped tables, he withdrew to pray—but he never lost the plot. His emotions served his mission. They didn't derail it. Yours can do that too. But only if you stop letting your feelings run the show.

Anchor Truth

Emotional regulation doesn't mean feeling less. It means handling what you feel with wisdom, courage, and grace. It's not natural. But it's learnable. And it's life-changing.

Prayer

God, I'm tired of being ruled by emotions I don't always understand. Teach me to slow down, notice what I'm feeling, and respond in a way that reflects your Spirit at work in me.

Invitation

When was the last time your emotions took the wheel and drove you somewhere you didn't want to go? Replay that moment and imagine hitting pause. What might have changed? Keep that vision in your pocket for the next storm.

When the Calendar Hurts

[There is] a time to cry and a time to laugh.
A time to grieve and a time to dance.

ECCLESIASTES 3:4

It sneaks up on you. The date on the calendar. The song on the radio. The season turning in the air. Even if your mind forgets, your body remembers. That was the day you got the diagnosis. The anniversary of the funeral. The birthday that's now an ache instead of a celebration. Or the quiet reminder of what could have been.

It's called *anniversary grief*—a natural resurfacing of sorrow on meaningful dates. It's not a setback. It's not regression. It's the emotional echo of something (or someone) that mattered.

And it's okay to feel it. We're not meant to move on as if nothing happened. We're meant to move forward, carrying the love and memory, without denying the pain.

Grief isn't tidy. It doesn't follow the rules. But Scripture never says it should. Instead, it tells us there's a time to grieve. And sometimes the calendar sets that time for us.

David wept when his son died. Jacob grieved Joseph for years, even believing he was dead. And Job's friends got it right at first, when they sat beside him in silence for seven days, honoring his sorrow without trying to fix it.

You don't need to "be strong" on hard anniversaries. You don't have to brush it off or spiritualize your way past it.

Light a candle. Take a walk. Say their name. Or just let the tears fall and know God doesn't flinch.

Time doesn't erase loss. But it can soften the edges. And in each tender return to grief, you just might find a little more healing.

Anchor Truth

God doesn't expect you to forget. He promises to be with you, especially on the days that still hurt.

Prayer

God, you see what this day means to me. You know the ache beneath the surface. Be near in this tender space. Help me honor the grief without being overwhelmed by it. And let your love steady me in the waves.

Invitation

Are there calendar dates that still bring pain? Don't ignore them. Instead, mark them with intention. Create a ritual of remembrance, reach out to someone who understands, or simply give yourself grace to feel what you feel.

Courage in the Middle of the Mess

I restore the crushed spirit of the humble
and revive the courage of those with repentant hearts.

ISAIAH 57:15

Courage is the choice to move forward while fear is still buzzing in your chest. Most people assume courage is a dramatic, heroic act. But in real life, it usually looks like something much quieter: getting out of bed when anxiety tells you to hide, making a phone call you've been avoiding, or being honest when silence feels safer.

Psychologically, courage is the willingness to tolerate discomfort for the sake of something meaningful. It's choosing values over avoidance. It's taking a step—not because certainty has arrived, but because hiding is shrinking your life.

Fear activates your threat system. It tells your brain to freeze, flee, or fight. But courage activates something else entirely: agency. It pulls you back into reality, where you can choose, respond, and act. Courage doesn't make fear disappear, but it keeps fear from being the one who decides.

Some of the bravest people in Scripture weren't confident; they were terrified. Gideon was anxious. Elijah felt hopeless. Jeremiah wanted to quit. Esther approached a fickle king with her life on the line. Even Paul admitted he came to the Corinthians "in weakness—timid and trembling" (1 Corinthians 2:3). Their courage wasn't confidence. It was trust. Not trust in themselves, but trust that God was with them in the trembling.

You don't need loud bravery today. You just need honest bravery. One small step that says, "Fear doesn't get the final say." God never demands you to be fearless. He asks you to remember you're not alone.

Anchor Truth

Courage isn't feeling strong. It's choosing what matters, even when fear tags along.

Prayer

God, you know the fear that grips me. You know the places where I hold back, hesitate, or hide. Give me the courage to take the next small step. Not because I feel brave, but because I trust you in my trembling. Strengthen my heart and steady my mind.

Invitation

Do one small thing today that fear has been talking you out of. Name it, take the step, and afterward ask yourself, "What changed when I moved with courage instead of waiting for confidence?"

Sad or Depressed? Knowing the Difference

The human spirit can endure a sick body,
but who can bear a crushed spirit?

PROVERBS 18:14

Sadness is part of being human. Depression is something else entirely.

Sadness has a reason—grief, disappointment, heartache. It comes in waves. It softens over time. It responds to comfort, a good conversation, a walk outside, a reminder of hope.

Depression doesn't follow the same rules. You can't always explain it. You can't "cheer up" out of it. You can't will yourself to move. You wake up with a weight you can't name, and it follows you like a shadow—silent, heavy, relentless.

Sadness is a passing guest. Depression often feels like an uninvited roommate who won't leave. This distinction matters. Because too many people have been told they're "just being dramatic" or "need to pray more."

But depression is not a character flaw. It's not a lack of faith. It's not weakness. It's a real and diagnosable mental health condition—one that affects how you think, feel, and function.

Proverbs 18:14 puts it plainly: "The human spirit can endure a sick body, but who can bear a crushed spirit?" When your inner world collapses, it's more painful than a broken bone. More excruciating than physical pain. And just like physical illness, it deserves care—sometimes professional help, sometimes medication, always compassion.

Jesus wept in sadness. Elijah collapsed under depression. Paul despaired of life itself.

Scripture makes space for both emotions. One doesn't cancel out the other. But knowing the difference can help you seek the right kind of support.

If you're sad, let yourself feel it. Grieve it. Name it. If you're depressed, don't minimize it. Don't ignore it. Get help.

You are not failing if joy doesn't come easily right now. You're human. And healing rarely follows a straight line. But light still finds its way through the cracks. Give it time.

Anchor Truth

Sadness is a feeling. Depression is a condition. Both matter—but only one requires clinical care and deeper support. Know the difference. And seek help when you need it.

Prayer

God, give me clarity about what I'm feeling. Help me name it honestly. And give me the courage to get help when I need it. I trust you to walk with me through the shadows.

Invitation

Do you wonder if what you're feeling might be depression? Take an honest inventory today—your sleep, energy, appetite, emotions, motivation. If it's more than sadness, don't keep walking alone. Reach out.

Expect Something Good

Yet I am confident I will see the LORD's goodness while I am here in the land of the living.

PSALM 27:13

Some people brace for disappointment like that's being responsible. Keep your expectations low, they say, and you won't get hurt. But there's a cost to living like that. Because when you're always anticipating the worst, you stop noticing the good right in front of you.

Optimism doesn't mean you won't face heartbreak. It means you don't let heartbreak be the only voice in the room.

David wrote Psalm 27 in a season of chaos and fear. He wasn't living in some spiritual highlight reel. And yet he wrote, "I am confident I will see the LORD's goodness." Not just someday. Not just in heaven. "Here in the land of the living."

That's what hopeful expectancy looks like. It dares to believe that goodness is not behind you or beyond you—but available, even here. Even now.

Psychologists call this *anticipatory joy*—the practice of looking forward to something good. And it matters. Why? Because your brain starts releasing feel-good chemicals like dopamine even before the good thing arrives. Hope actually prepares your body to receive joy.

So go ahead: Expect something good. Plan a small joy. Hold space for something better. Write it down if you have to. Speak it over your day. Not because you're naive. But because your soul needs light to walk toward.

If you've lived your life waiting for the next letdown, this might feel risky. It might even feel foolish. But it's not foolish to believe in a good God. It's faith.

Anchor Truth

God's goodness isn't just for later. It's for here. And it's for you.

Prayer

God, I want to expect your goodness again. Help me loosen my grip on fear, and open my hands to hope.

Invitation

Name one thing, big or small, that you're looking forward to. If nothing comes to mind, create something. Put joy on the calendar. Let your heart practice expectancy.

Grace for the Overthinking Soul

You will keep in perfect peace all who trust in you,
all whose thoughts are fixed on you!

ISAIAH 26:3

If overthinking were an Olympic sport, you'd have medals by now, right? You replay conversations long after they've ended. You analyze every word, every silence, every look. You prepare for things that might never happen. And still, your mind refuses to rest.

This is more than just mental noise; it's a form of *rumination*—your brain's attempt to resolve perceived threats by running the same loops over and over again.

Overthinking can feel like control, like preparation, even like responsibility. But underneath? It's often just fear dressed up in logic. You're afraid of making a mistake. Afraid of being misunderstood. Afraid of missing something important.

These fears activate your brain's internal alarm system: the amygdala, the part of your brain that detects threats and triggers your fight-or-flight response. This keeps you in a constant state of hyperalertness, even when there's no real danger.

And while your mind spins and respins, you start to wonder, *Why can't I stop thinking? What's wrong with me?* Nothing. You're not broken. You're just tired. Your brain is trying to protect you, but it's forgotten how to pause.

This is where self-compassion becomes powerful. Naming the pattern without judgment is the first step toward interrupting it. Isaiah 26:3 reminds us that peace doesn't come from figuring it all out. It comes from where we fix our focus.

You can't always stop the spirals. But you can shift your attention. You can interrupt the loop with grace instead of guilt. You can whisper truth into the overthinking mind that thinks it has to hold the universe together.

God isn't asking you to think your way to peace. He's offering peace even when your thoughts haven't settled.

Anchor Truth

God gives grace to overthinkers, too, and peace isn't earned by having a quiet mind.

Prayer

God, you know how loud it gets in my head. How hard it is to stop spinning through what-ifs and if-onlys. I want peace, but I often feel stuck in analysis. Help me release the need to have everything figured out. Teach me to fix my thoughts on you, even when they wander. Thank you for giving grace to my restless mind.

Invitation

Pick one overthought thought—just one. Instead of solving it, write this next to it: God, I give you this loop. Help me release what I can't resolve. *Let it be the start of peace.*

You Are Not Stuck with Old Scripts

Throw off your old sinful nature and your former way of life, which is corrupted by lust and deception. Instead, let the Spirit renew your thoughts and attitudes.

EPHESIANS 4:22-23

Some beliefs don't come from God. They come from childhood wounds. Tense dinner tables. Relational trauma. Unspoken rules you absorbed before you even had language for them.

Be quiet. Don't need too much. Don't rock the boat. You're too sensitive. You're not enough. You're too much.

We're all carrying *personal scripts*—quiet, powerful lies that shape how we move through the world. And unless we name them, we follow them. Automatically. Repeatedly. Even when they make us small.

But here's the good news: You can rewrite the script. That's part of agency.

Paul's language in Ephesians is bold. Throw off the old. "Let the Spirit renew your thoughts and attitudes." That word translated "renew" (Greek: *ananeoō*) carries the idea of total renovation—not just tidying up a thought or softening an edge, but overhauling the entire structure. Rebuilding your mind from the inside out.

In therapy, we call it *cognitive restructuring*—a tool used to challenge and replace unhelpful beliefs. It takes practice. And it's rarely instant. But over time, those old, inherited scripts start to lose their grip.

You stop running the same patterns. You start noticing the lies for what they are. And, slowly, you begin to live out of truth, not trauma.

Agency means you get to participate in that process. You're not doomed to repeat the past. You're not stuck with someone else's story. You can name the old script and write a new one.

Anchor Truth

The story you inherited isn't the story you have to live.

Prayer

God, help me see what I've been carrying without even realizing it. Give me the courage to name the scripts that no longer serve truth or love. And as I let them go, renew my mind one thought at a time.

Invitation

What's one old message you still believe about yourself? Write it down. Now write a better, truer one beside it. Start practicing that version today.

It's Not a Sin to Be Angry

Jesus made a whip from some ropes and chased them all out of the Temple. He drove out the sheep and cattle, scattered the money changers' coins over the floor, and turned over their tables.

JOHN 2:15

You've probably heard it taught—or at least implied—that good Christians shouldn't get angry. That if your faith is strong enough, your tone will always be gentle, your heart calm, your attitude cheerful. But here's the truth: Anger isn't inherently sinful.

Scripture says, "Be angry, and do not sin" (Ephesians 4:26, NKJV). That's a permission slip—not to explode, but to feel. To acknowledge what's real. To stop pretending everything is fine when it's not.

Jesus got angry. He flipped tables. He called out hypocrisy. He wept at injustice. His anger wasn't reactive or petty, but it was real. And it was rooted in love. When guided by compassion, anger can fuel change, name truth, and defend what's good.

The trouble comes when we stuff it down or let it fly unchecked.

Some of us pretend not to be angry at all. We swallow our frustration. We "keep the peace." But unacknowledged anger doesn't disappear: It ferments. It resurfaces as resentment, sarcasm, detachment, or self-hatred.

Others of us erupt. We use anger like a blowtorch, scorching the people we love. We don't feel powerful unless we're loud. But that's not healthy anger either. That's control. That's reactivity.

The invitation here isn't to eliminate anger. It's to understand it. To let it rise without letting it rule.

Psychologists call anger a *secondary emotion*—it often masks something deeper, like fear, sadness, or shame. The more curious we get about our anger, the more likely we are to handle it with wisdom instead of regret.

You can be faithful and frustrated. Holy and human. What matters isn't whether you get angry, it's how you respond when you do.

Anchor Truth

Anger isn't the enemy. Avoiding it or obeying it is.

Prayer

God, thank you for showing me that anger has a place. Teach me how to feel it fully, and guide me in using it well.

Invitation

This week, when anger rises, pause before you judge it. Ask, "What's beneath this? What do I need to say, name, or heal?"

Assume Less, Ask More

Sympathize with each other. Love each other as brothers and sisters. Be tenderhearted, and keep a humble attitude.

1 PETER 3:8

It's easy to assume. "She's mad at me." "He doesn't care." "They're just being dramatic."

Assumptions are mental shortcuts. They help us make sense of things quickly, but they often lead us away from truth and connection. Curiosity does the opposite. It slows us down. It asks, "What else might be going on here?" It invites us to seek understanding before drawing conclusions.

Psychologically, it's the difference between *automatic thinking* and *reflective thinking*. Automatic thinking is fast, reactive, and often fueled by past wounds or fears. Reflective thinking—the kind fueled by curiosity—is slower, more intentional, and more generous.

Curiosity can transform a conversation. Instead of reacting to what someone said, you might ask, "What did you mean by that?" "What's behind that response?" "Is there more you want me to know?"

It sounds simple, but these are powerful, connecting questions—especially in moments of tension. They can disarm conflict, surface hidden pain, and rehumanize someone you were about to write off.

Consider the model of Jesus. When others labeled people as sinners, outcasts, or nuisances, Jesus asked questions. He noticed nuances. He saw people in context. His questions weren't traps. They were invitations to be seen, to be honest, to be known.

It's not always easy. Curiosity requires humility. It means admitting we don't know the full story. It means laying down the impulse to be "right" so we can be relational.

Anchor Truth

Assumptions shut people down. Curiosity opens people up. Choose connection over certainty; ask before assuming.

Prayer

God, help me resist the urge to jump to conclusions. Give me the humility to ask, the patience to listen, and the wisdom to understand what's really going on.

Invitation

Think of someone you've been making assumptions about. This week, ask a curious question—not to trap or confront, but to understand. Let the conversation surprise you.

Redeeming Regret

God causes everything to work together for the good of those who love God and are called according to his purpose for them.

ROMANS 8:28

We all have moments we wish we could undo. Words we shouldn't have said, decisions we wish we hadn't made, seasons we'd relive if we could. That's the weight of regret. It lingers, quietly telling us that our story is tainted, our past disqualifying. But here's a powerful truth: Regret doesn't have to be the end of the story. It can become the beginning of deeper meaning.

Regret can lead to growth when it prompts reflection rather than rumination. The goal isn't to rewrite the past. It's to reframe it. Instead of "What if?" try asking, "What now?" Instead of being haunted by your regret, let it become a holy teacher—shaping your values, strengthening your empathy, and clarifying your purpose.

Biblically, we see this in Peter. His denial of Jesus was a gut-wrenching moment of failure. The kind of thing that could have defined him. But it didn't.

Jesus met him again by the fire, on the beach—and didn't rub it in but reframed it: "Feed my sheep," Jesus said (John 21:17). In other words, *Let this regret feed your calling.*

God doesn't erase your past. He transforms it. He weaves it into a bigger story—not despite your regrets, but through them.

You are not disqualified. You are being refined. Your lowest points don't have to be your heaviest burdens. They can become the soil where humility grows, where mercy takes root, and where your purpose gets deeper and more real.

You can't rewrite your past. But you can redeem it. Meaning doesn't erase regret—it transforms it. It takes your "I wish I hadn't" and turns it into "Now I know better." And that wisdom? It's gold.

Let your regrets become the soil where compassion, purpose, and maturity take root. That's how you stop being stuck in the past and start shaping a life that matters.

Anchor Truth

Your past isn't a prison. When surrendered to God, it becomes part of your purpose.

Prayer

God, I give you my regrets. Don't let them define me. Use them to shape me. Help me find meaning in what I'd rather erase. And lead me forward with grace and clarity.

Invitation

Take one regret and talk to God about it honestly. Then ask, "What can I learn from this? How can it shape who I'm becoming?" Let your past pain give birth to present purpose.

Burnout Isn't Just Being Tired

But Jesus often withdrew to lonely places and prayed.

LUKE 5:16 (NIV)

Burnout doesn't feel like being tired. It feels like being done. Done caring. Done trying. Done pretending you're okay. It's waking up with the weight of dread pressing on your chest. It's scrolling instead of praying. It's crying in the car because that's the only place no one's asking anything of you.

Burnout doesn't announce itself with a warning. It sneaks up like erosion—slowly wearing you down while you convince yourself you're "just going through a season." But this isn't seasonal. It's soul-deep depletion.

And here's what makes it tricky: You can burn out while doing good. While parenting. Pastoring. Teaching. Serving. Loving. Even when it's meaningful, the constant output—especially without rest or replenishment—will eventually bankrupt you.

And when you get there, you start feeling numb, irritable, resentful. You don't feel like yourself anymore. Or maybe you don't even remember who "yourself" was.

But hear this: Burnout is not failure. It's a signal. It's your body and soul saying, "Something has to change."

Even Jesus—God in flesh—stepped away. He walked away from crowds, withdrew from pressure, and sought solitude. Not because he was weak, but because he was wise. He knew his limits and honored them. He knew that constant output without rest is unsustainable.

So ask yourself, Is what you're calling *faithfulness* actually just fear of disappointing people? Is what you're labeling *perseverance* really just ignoring your need for rest?

God doesn't need you to be superhuman. He's asking you to be honest. Human. Dependent on him. And willing to admit when you're not okay.

Anchor Truth

Burnout isn't weakness; it's a warning. God doesn't ask you to run on empty. He invites you to rest, refuel, and remember who you are.

Prayer

God, I'm tired in a way that sleep can't fix. Show me where I've ignored my limits, and help me find a rhythm that honors your design for my life and soul.

Invitation

Name one thing that's draining your soul today. Then name one thing that could restore it, even just a little. Make space for that restoration this week.

When Control Takes Over

Trust in the LORD with all your heart;
do not depend on your own understanding.

PROVERBS 3:5

One of perfectionism's favorite disguises is control. If you can plan it, predict it, prevent it—maybe you can protect yourself from disappointment, failure, or pain. It sounds smart. Safe. Even responsible. But underneath, it's fueled by fear.

Control says, "If I let go, everything might fall apart." Faith says, "Even if things fall apart, God will still hold me together." Control convinces us we're being mature, wise, or careful. But often it's our way of avoiding vulnerability. And the cost? Anxiety, disconnection, and an inability to experience joy in the present moment. You're so busy managing outcomes, you miss the grace unfolding right in front of you.

Spiritually, control is exhausting. Because deep down, it places the burden of holding the world together on your shoulders. But that burden was never yours to bear.

Think of Moses. When the people cried out for water, he took matters into his own hands, striking the rock instead of speaking to it as God had instructed (Numbers 20). The result? Consequences, yes—but also a powerful lesson that obedience is about trust, not control.

In therapy, control is often named for what it really is: *a trauma response*. It comes from places where we felt powerless. But healing begins when we surrender—not in defeat, but in faith.

God doesn't invite you to be in control. He invites you to be in relationship. Growth comes not from gripping tighter, but from letting go.

You can't control your way to peace. But you can surrender your way into freedom.

Anchor Truth

Control is a poor substitute for trust. Real peace begins where surrender takes root.

Prayer

God, I confess that I like to control things. It makes me feel safe. But I know it also makes me tired. Teach me to trust you with what I can't predict, prevent, or perfect. Help me release control and rest in your care.

Invitation

Name one area where you're gripping too tightly. Then say aloud, "God, this belongs to you." You don't have to hold it all. That's his job.

You Can Be a Mystery to Yourself

I don't really understand myself, for I want to do what is right, but I don't do it. Instead, I do what I hate.

ROMANS 7:15

There's something oddly comforting about Paul's confession in Romans 7. Here's this bold, brilliant leader of the early church, and he flat-out admits, "I don't get me."

That's self-awareness, too. Not the polished kind. Not the kind that wraps everything in a neat bow. But the kind that says, "Something in me is misfiring, and I'm willing to notice it instead of pretending it's not happening."

We all carry contradictions. You want to be patient, but you snap. You long for connection, but you isolate. You commit to a new habit, then sabotage it by Wednesday. You're not broken. You're human. And self-awareness means creating space for those tensions—without shame.

This dissonance between intention and behavior is common. It can be shaped by subconscious beliefs, trauma patterns, nervous system dysregulation, or even your environment. What matters most is not whether the contradiction exists—it's how honest you're willing to be about it.

Spiritual growth doesn't require perfection. But it does require truth.

So when you find yourself doing the thing you swore you wouldn't, don't collapse into guilt. Get curious. Ask, "What was I really needing in that moment? What was I avoiding? What didn't I see coming?"

Self-awareness doesn't always provide instant answers. Sometimes it just helps you stay in the room with yourself long enough to stop pretending, start learning, and let grace meet you there.

Anchor Truth

Self-awareness isn't about solving yourself. It's about staying honest in the tension.

Prayer

God, I don't always understand myself. But I don't want to run from the confusion. Help me stay open, stay curious, and stay grounded in grace, even when my motives are mixed.

Invitation

When you notice yourself acting in ways that contradict what you value, pause. Ask, "What might be going on beneath the surface?" Don't judge it. Just listen.

You Can't Outsource Your Growth

Work hard to show the results of your salvation, obeying God with deep reverence and fear. For God is working in you, giving you the desire and the power to do what pleases him.

PHILIPPIANS 2:12-13

You can't hire someone to go to the gym for you. You can't delegate your healing. And you can't outsource your growth. There's no substitute for your own participation in the process. Yes, God is at work in you. He gives you the desire and the power. But the next move? That's on you.

Paul's words to the Philippians are a powerful balance: God initiates the change, but you participate in it. He supplies the engine, but you still have to steer.

Some people lean hard on grace and forget effort. Others hustle for worth and forget grace. Agency sits in the middle: It's knowing God is already moving in you and knowing your choices still matter.

This is the difference between *learned dependence* and *empowered responsibility*. Some people grow up believing someone else will always step in, fix the problem, or take the blame. Others believe if they don't fix everything themselves, they're failing. Neither posture is sustainable.

The sweet spot? Owning what's yours while staying deeply connected to the God who's doing the deeper work inside you. Spiritual maturity isn't about being hyper-independent or helplessly passive. It's about cooperating with grace—daily, intentionally, imperfectly.

You won't always feel motivated. You won't always get it right. But every small act of ownership—every time you show up and say, "This part is mine"—you grow. And that growth? No one else can do it for you. But no one can take it from you either.

Anchor Truth

Growth doesn't happen to you. It happens with you.

Prayer

God, I know you're working in me. Give me the courage to work with you—not to earn your love, but to live it out. Help me show up to my own life with reverence, grit, and grace.

Invitation

Name one area where you've been waiting for someone else to change things. What's one small move you can make instead? Take it. Let it count.

Overfunctioning and Underliving

"Martha, Martha," the Lord answered, "you are worried and upset about many things, but few things are needed—or indeed only one."

LUKE 10:41-42 (NIV)

You handle it. You fix it. You make the calls, clean the messes, manage the moods, and smooth the tensions. You do it all, because if you don't, who will? But in doing everything, you may be living almost nothing.

Overfunctioning is the socially acceptable form of drowning. It looks like responsibility, leadership, even devotion. But beneath it often lies anxiety, guilt, and a deep fear of what might happen if you stop performing. Overfunctioning is a coping strategy that says, *If I can just keep all the plates spinning, I won't have to face the chaos or my own emptiness.*

In Luke 10, Jesus gently calls out Martha—not for serving, but for striving. For being consumed by activity and missing the point of connection. Mary chose presence. Martha chose pressure. And Jesus didn't commend the busy one.

Codependency thrives in overfunctioning. You become the one who holds it all together, even when it's costing you your health, peace, and identity. You step in for others at the expense of your own needs.

But here's the secret: The more you overfunction, the more others underfunction. Your constant intervention may be enabling stagnation, not growth. And you? You're quietly burning out.

Jesus' invitation to Martha is the same one he extends to you: *Come sit down.* You don't have to earn your worth through productivity. You don't have to be the emotional glue for everyone else's life. You don't have to outrun your fear of what might fall apart. You were never meant to carry it all.

Anchor Truth

Doing more doesn't always mean loving more. Sometimes the bravest and healthiest choice is to stop overfunctioning and start simply being.

Prayer

Jesus, I've confused responsibility with righteousness. Show me where I'm overfunctioning, and teach me to rest in your presence instead of proving my worth through performance.

Invitation

Where are you taking on more than your share—emotionally, mentally, relationally? Choose one place to step back this week. Not to punish others, but to trust God and to breathe again.

Letting Go of What You Can't Control

Let it be with me just as you say.

LUKE 1:38 (MSG)

If you're wired to plan, protect, or predict, then surrender can feel like failure. But in truth, letting go of what you can't control is one of the most courageous acts of resilience. It doesn't mean giving up. It means releasing what was never yours to carry in the first place.

Moses had to learn this the hard way. Called to lead a people through the wilderness, he faced rebellion, uncertainty, and unrelenting responsibility. Yet he reached a point where he handed his burden back to God, saying, "If you don't personally go with us, don't make us leave this place" (Exodus 33:15). That's resilience—refusing to move forward without God's presence, even if you're supposed to be in charge.

In Genesis, Joseph had no control over his brothers' betrayal, the lies that imprisoned him, or the years of waiting. His story turned not when he fought harder—but when he trusted deeper. He said to those who wronged him, "You intended to harm me, but God intended it all for good" (Genesis 50:20).

And then there's Mary—a young woman facing an unexpected pregnancy, uncertainty, and risk. She didn't ask for guarantees. She simply said, "Let it be with me." That's not weakness. That's brave surrender. That's holy release. That's resilience.

Clinical insight confirms this too. When we release the illusion of control, our anxiety decreases and our capacity for adaptation increases. You may not control what happens. But you can choose how you respond. You can surrender the outcome and still move forward in faith.

Resilience grows when you stop trying to control everything and start trusting the one who already sees the end.

Anchor Truth

Letting go doesn't make you powerless. It sets you free to focus on what matters most.

Prayer

God, I've held tight to things I was never meant to carry. Fear, outcomes, expectations. Help me loosen my grip. Teach me the strength of surrender. I want to walk with trust, not tension.

Invitation

Today, name one thing you cannot control and release it. Pray this simple prayer: "God, it's yours now." Every time you're tempted to grab it back, repeat the release. Let go and lean in.

Holding Opposite Emotions

Don't be quick-tempered,
for anger is the friend of fools.

ECCLESIASTES 7:9

There's a kind of emotional growth that only comes when we stop demanding that our feelings make sense. Because sometimes they won't. You can feel deep love for someone and also intense frustration. You can feel grateful and still be sad. You can trust God yet feel afraid. The human emotional experience isn't linear. It's layered. Complex. Messy.

But for some, this complexity feels threatening. So we do what we've been conditioned to do: suppress one emotion to make room for the one that feels more acceptable. We choose optimism over grief. Anger over sadness. Numbness over fear.

But emotional health isn't about choosing just one feeling. It's about learning to hold opposing emotions without being hijacked by either. This is called *emotional dialectics*—the ability to sit with tension without rushing to resolve it. And it's a sign of maturity. Psychologists have found that those who can tolerate *emotional ambivalence*—who don't need to force a resolution—tend to be more resilient, empathetic, and wise.

Jesus modeled this brilliantly. In the garden of Gethsemane, he was "overwhelmed with sorrow to the point of death," and yet surrendered to the will of his Father (Matthew 26:38, NIV). He wasn't choosing between obedience or anguish—he held them both.

And David, in the Psalms, regularly swung between despair and hope, anger and praise, sometimes within the same breath. That's not instability; it's authenticity.

The invitation here isn't to feel less but to expand your capacity to feel more—without letting emotions run the show. When you learn to say, "I'm feeling joy . . . and I'm feeling fear," you're practicing self-awareness, compassion, and emotional regulation all at once.

Anchor Truth

You don't have to choose between two emotions that seem opposed. Growth comes when you learn to hold both and still move forward with grace and integrity.

Prayer

God, help me grow in my ability to feel without shutting down. Teach me to sit with complexity without rushing to control or fix it. Strengthen me with grace in the tension.

Invitation

Name two emotions you're feeling today that seem to contradict each other. Don't attempt to resolve them. Just notice them. Hold them both and bring them into the presence of God.

You Can't Think Your Way to Meaning

Let's not merely say that we love each other;
let us show the truth by our actions.

1 JOHN 3:18

You can spend hours thinking about your purpose. Reading books. Taking assessments. Journaling. Praying. And all of that can help, but it can't do the whole job. At some point, you have to move.

The paradox of meaning is this: You often won't *feel* it until you *live* it. That's why people who are stuck in cycles of overthinking or depression are often told by therapists to take a small action, even before they feel ready. Because sometimes action generates clarity—not the other way around.

Scripture affirms this too. "Let's not merely say that we love each other," John writes. "Let us show the truth by our actions." Love becomes real through movement. And so does meaning.

Think of the good Samaritan. He didn't sit on the roadside reflecting on the moral implications of human dignity. He *crossed the road*. He knelt down. He lifted. He paid. The point? His purpose wasn't a concept; it was a commitment.

If you're waiting to feel inspired before you act, you may be waiting a long time. But if you take a meaningful step, even a small one, you might just find the spark returning.

Meaning is lived more than it's figured out. Especially when mental health struggles cloud our motivation, action becomes a kind of protest—against paralysis, against apathy, against despair.

So don't wait for the fog to lift before you move. Do the loving thing, the helpful thing, the next right thing. Meaning often doesn't show up in your mind first; it meets you on the move.

Anchor Truth

You don't have to think your way into purpose. Sometimes the deepest meaning comes from doing the next right thing.

Prayer

God, I get stuck in my thoughts so easily, trying to figure everything out before I move. Help me take one small step today toward love, purpose, or service. Use my actions to anchor me in meaning, even when my mind is weary.

Invitation

Do something today that aligns with your values, even if your feelings haven't caught up. Write the note. Wash the dish. Send the text. Love with your hands, and let meaning follow.

Hope Holds the Thread

Let all that I am wait quietly before God,
for my hope is in him.

PSALM 62:5

Optimism is often misunderstood. It's not about having a sunny personality. It's not about pretending everything's fine. And it's definitely not about ignoring the ache in your chest or the questions you can't answer.

Optimism is rooted in hope. Not hype. Not headlines. Not the illusion that life will unfold according to your plans. But in the quiet, often trembling belief that *God is not done yet.*

Hope is what lets you whisper "still" when everything says "stop." Still trusting. Still praying. Still believing there's more than this moment.

It doesn't mean you're always upbeat. But it does mean you keep showing up, with the smallest shred of faith that the thread you're holding will lead somewhere good.

Psalm 62:5 says, "Let all that I am wait quietly before God, for my hope is in him." *All that I am.* Not just the presentable parts. Not just the believer who's full of confidence. But the parts that doubt, ache, wander, and long.

When optimism is hard to access, reach for hope. Optimism looks ahead and assumes the best. Hope holds on even when the outcome is unclear.

Optimism is a posture. Hope is a lifeline. Hope is sturdier. It's been through more. It's seen the valley and stayed anyway. And here's the thing: Hope doesn't guarantee an outcome. But it *does* anchor you in something deeper than your circumstances—something eternal.

This kind of hope has a memory. It remembers how far you've come. It remembers God's faithfulness, even when your feelings can't. And it dares to believe that what's ahead is not an accident but a continuation of grace.

Anchor Truth

Hope isn't hype. It's trust in the God who's not finished.

Prayer

God, when my optimism runs out, let hope rise up. I'm trusting not in an outcome, but in your presence, your mercy, and your love.

Invitation

Think back to one season in your life when hope carried you through. What did it sound like? Feel like? Let that memory remind you: This thread is still strong.

The High Cost of Keeping the Peace

Love must be sincere. Hate what is evil; cling to what is good.

ROMANS 12:9 (NIV)

Psychologists call it *conflict avoidance*. It looks polite on the surface—cooperative, agreeable, adaptable. But underneath, it's often driven by fear—fear of rejection, abandonment, or disapproval. People who lean toward conflict avoidance tend to internalize the belief that if they keep everyone happy, they'll be safe.

So they smooth things over. Swallow their opinions. Put others' comfort above their own clarity. And over time? They disappear.

When peacekeeping becomes a pattern, it doesn't build stronger relationships. It builds fragile ones. Relationships based on silence, not truth. On appeasement, not authenticity. This pattern often starts early. Maybe you learned to avoid opposing opinions in your family. Maybe your worth became tied to being "easy to get along with."

Maybe it just felt safer to nod and smile. But here's the catch: If you can't speak your mind or bring your full self, you're not actually connected. You're just performing.

Jesus didn't perform. He spoke with truth and grace, disrupting social comfort zones and religious traditions in the name of real peace. Not surface harmony. Not fake smiles. But peace built on wholeness, integrity, and love.

Paul echoed this when he challenged the church to think of others while holding fast to the mindset of Christ—not the mindset of martyrdom or self-erasure, but of sacrificial love rooted in authenticity (Philippians 2:4).

Keeping the peace at the expense of your truth isn't maturity. It's a mask. Real love can handle tension. Real relationships can weather honesty. And real peace? It only comes when you're not disappearing to maintain it.

Anchor Truth

You weren't made to disappear. Real peace doesn't require self-erasure.

Prayer

God, help me notice the moments when I trade truth for comfort. Give me the strength to speak with love and the courage to stop shrinking. Teach me to choose connection over performance.

Invitation

Where have you confused peacekeeping with peacemaking? This week, try saying one thing you've been holding back—with gentleness, yes, but also with truth.

Managing the Impression

Watch out! Don't do your good deeds publicly, to be admired by others, for you will lose the reward from your Father in heaven.

MATTHEW 6:1

There's a whole world that lives in your head. A stage. An audience. A spotlight. It's called *impression management*, and we've all done it. Shaping what we say. Editing what we share. Performing what we hope will make us likable, impressive, safe.

We do it on social media. In meetings. At church. Even with people we love. We read the room. We adjust. We ask ourselves, *What version of me will get the best response?* And just like that, we're not living—we're managing.

But the problem is, it's exhausting to be so curated. You start to lose track of who you are when you're not trying to be someone else. You can't be present in your own life when you're constantly monitoring how you're being perceived.

And while managing impressions might feel safe, it comes at a cost. You may gain approval, but you lose connection. You might feel admired, but you're not actually known. You might impress people, but you never feel loved.

Jesus warned us not to fall into this trap. He drew a clear line between performing for people and living for God. One leads to anxiety, burnout, and a fractured identity. The other leads to freedom.

Authenticity isn't reckless transparency or unfiltered chaos. It's about showing up as someone who is whole, honest, and no longer willing to be run by fear or people-pleasing.

God didn't create you to be a brand. You're not a product. You're a person. And the people who truly matter don't need the slick version of you. They just need *you*.

Anchor Truth

You weren't made to impress. You were made to live honestly and be loved fully.

Prayer

God, help me stop editing myself to fit what others expect. I want to live freely, not perfectly. Teach me to root my worth in you, not in applause.

Invitation

Notice today where you're subtly managing impressions. An extra pause before you speak. A spin on your story. Just notice. Then ask, "What would honesty look like right here?"

Unloved, But Not Unseen

When the LORD saw that Leah was unloved, he enabled her to have children.

GENESIS 29:31

Leah knew what it was like to be second choice. Overlooked. Unwanted. Jacob worked seven years for her sister, Rachel. Not for her. And even after Leah became his wife, it was clear where his affection landed—and where it didn't.

Can you imagine living in the shadow of someone else's beauty or charm? Feeling like you have to earn attention just to matter?

That's the heartbreak of low self-worth. It's not always about how *you* see yourself—it's about how others seem to overlook you. Or worse, define you by your comparison to someone else.

But there's a turning point in Leah's story. In Genesis 29, we see her naming her children with hope that her husband will finally love her. But by the time she gives birth to Judah, something shifts. This time, she says, "Now I will praise the LORD" (29:35). Not, "Now Jacob will notice me." Not "Now I'll feel like enough." Just "I will praise the LORD."

Leah's worth stopped hinging on Jacob's attention. She started anchoring her identity in something deeper. And that son, Judah, would become the ancestor of Jesus himself. God saw her. Even when Jacob didn't. Even when the world said she wasn't enough.

There's healing power in that. Because when you feel like the one passed over, the one left out, the one trying too hard to matter—God sees.

And in seeing, he blesses. Not because you earned it, but because you were always loved, always known, always enough.

You may feel overlooked by people, but you are handpicked by God. His eyes never miss your worth, even when others do. Let that truth settle deep: You are not invisible to the one who matters most.

Anchor Truth

You don't have to be someone's favorite to be significant in God's story.

Prayer

God, help me stop chasing approval to feel worthy. Teach me to see myself through your eyes—chosen, seen, and deeply loved.

Invitation

Read Genesis 29 and 30. As you do, make a note of every time the text says God saw, noticed, or heard something. Let that be your reminder: You are never unseen.

When Your Boundary Is Ignored

Don't throw your pearls to pigs! They will trample the pearls, then turn and attack you.

MATTHEW 7:6

You were clear. You were kind. You set a boundary with love. And they bulldozed right over it. Maybe they laughed it off. Maybe they guilt-tripped you. Maybe they said, "You've changed," as if growth was a betrayal. This is one of the most discouraging moments in boundary setting: When your limit is met with dismissal, manipulation, or flat-out defiance.

Jesus gave a vivid metaphor for this: "Don't throw your pearls to pigs!" Translation? Don't offer your most vulnerable, valuable efforts—things like honest communication, emotional safety, and respect for your limits—to people who have no intention of honoring them.

That doesn't mean labeling someone a pig. It means paying attention to the pattern. If someone consistently ignores or steamrolls your boundaries, the problem isn't your delivery. It's their disregard.

So what do you do? You *reaffirm* the boundary. Calmly. Consistently. Without apology. You *follow through* on the consequences you've already communicated. Boundaries without follow-through are just suggestions. And you *adjust* the level of access they have to your life. That's not cruelty; it's stewardship.

Sometimes the most loving thing you can do is take a step back from someone who refuses to respect your no. Not out of spite, but out of wisdom.

You were never meant to sacrifice your mental or emotional health for the comfort of someone who is unwilling to grow. Jesus walked away from people who weren't ready to receive truth. You can too.

Anchor Truth

A boundary is not truly set until you're willing to maintain it when it's tested. Love never demands that you stay in harm's way.

Prayer

God, when my boundaries are pushed or ignored, give me strength to stay rooted. Help me honor what you've taught me about my worth, and show me how to move forward in wisdom and love.

Invitation

Think of one boundary that hasn't been respected. How have you responded so far? What follow-through needs to happen next? Take one step today to reinforce it with clarity and kindness.

When False Humility Masquerades as Virtue

Don't think you are better than you really are. Be honest in your evaluation of yourselves, measuring yourselves by the faith God has given us.

ROMANS 12:3

False humility sounds spiritual. It wears a cloak of modesty, often deflecting praise or insisting, "Oh, it was nothing."

But beneath that well-practiced downplay often lives a deeper struggle: low self-worth.

The problem isn't just underplaying your gifts. It's undervaluing your God-given identity.

Some people mistake insecurity for humility. They believe that thinking poorly of themselves is a sign of godliness. But Scripture doesn't call us to deny our value. It calls us to evaluate ourselves with sober judgment. That means being honest, not harsh.

Take Gideon, for example. When God called him a "mighty hero," Gideon pushed back. "Me? I'm the weakest in my clan. I'm the least in my family." His first instinct was self-doubt, not self-awareness. He was certain God had chosen the wrong person.

But God didn't say, "You're right, let's find someone stronger." Instead, God reminded Gideon who would be with him. True humility isn't about thinking less of yourself; it's about knowing where your strength comes from. It's standing tall not because you're great, but because God is.

False humility often shows up as self-deprecation, people-pleasing, or imposter syndrome. It can even drive burnout because you keep trying to prove your worth by shrinking it. But humility isn't about playing small. It's about playing your part with courage and clarity.

Your gifts were given on purpose. Dimming them doesn't glorify God. It hides the light he put in you.

Anchor Truth

False humility feeds insecurity, not virtue. True humility acknowledges weakness but also accepts worth.

Prayer

God, help me stop confusing low self-worth with humility. Teach me how to honor the strengths you've given me without pride or fear. I want to live grounded in you—neither shrinking back nor puffing up, but walking confidently in truth.

Invitation

Where have you been minimizing your voice, your work, or your worth—not out of reverence, but out of fear? Ask God to help you see yourself through his eyes, and take one bold step today to walk in your true identity.

The High Cost of Hyper-Empathy

Guard your heart above all else,
for it determines the course of your life.

PROVERBS 4:23

Empathy is a love gift. But unchecked, it can become a guilt trap. When your heart is overly attuned to the emotional state of others? When you feel their pain *more* than your own, take on their stress as if it's your responsibility, and abandon your own needs to manage their moods? You're not practicing compassion anymore.

You're enmeshed. You're in hyper-empathy. And that's not noble. It's exhausting.

Hyper-empathy can look like being the go-to listener for a friend who never reciprocates. It can look like dropping everything—every time—for someone who rarely shows up for you. It can feel like a compulsion to fix, to smooth over, to make sure everyone is okay while you're falling apart inside. At its core, this isn't empathy. It's anxiety wearing a kindness mask.

The Bible warns us to guard our hearts, not fling them open indiscriminately. And when Jesus wept with those who were hurting, he never lost himself in their suffering. He didn't carry every burden people tried to hand him. He knew his purpose, and he knew where he ended and others began.

Hyper-empathy often stems from early conditioning. Maybe you grew up reading the room to stay safe. Maybe you learned that peace meant managing everyone else's emotions. Maybe love looked like disappearing so someone else could shine. But what once protected you can become the very thing that now depletes you.

Even the good Samaritan—a model of compassion—helped within limits. He bandaged the wounds, provided shelter, and then moved on with his journey. He didn't move in. He didn't sacrifice his life to fix the other man's. He cared, but he didn't collapse.

Here's the truth: You can be deeply kind without being constantly consumed. You can be generous without being drained. You are not a bottomless well.

Anchor Truth

Empathy is powerful, but without boundaries it will wreck your well-being. Guard your heart. Love others without losing yourself.

Prayer

God, help me show compassion wisely. Teach me how to love without rescuing, to care without carrying what isn't mine.

Invitation

Where in your life is your empathy tipping into exhaustion? Identify one place where you need to set a limit—with grace, not guilt.

Paralyzed by Perfection

That's why I take pleasure in my weaknesses, and in the insults, hardships, persecutions, and troubles that I suffer for Christ. For when I am weak, then I am strong.

2 CORINTHIANS 12:10

You've been so afraid of messing up that you've stopped moving forward at all. You rewrite the email five times. You delay the conversation you know you need to have. You keep polishing the project that's already good enough. You don't want to make a mistake—not because you're arrogant, but because deep down, you're afraid that a misstep means you're unworthy.

That's not excellence. That's perfectionism, and it's a prison made of guilt. Perfectionism whispers, "If I do it flawlessly, I'll finally be enough." But perfectionism is a liar. And guilt often tags along with it. Together, they trap you in a loop of never-good-enough, where every shortcoming feels like a moral failure.

Know this: God's grace doesn't wait for perfect. Paul learned that firsthand. He begged God to remove his weakness. Instead, God offered him something better: a new view of strength. One where weakness wasn't shameful. It was sacred space for grace.

That means your flaws don't disqualify you. In fact, they qualify you for grace. You don't have to get it all right. You just have to get real.

Growth comes not from flawless performance, but from honest dependence on a God who already knows your limits and still delights in you. You were never meant to earn love by getting everything right. The pressure to be perfect will always leave you anxious and empty.

But grace? Grace sets you free to show up as you are, do what you can, and trust that God's strength will meet you in the gaps.

Anchor Truth

You're not called to be perfect. You're called to be present—fully human and deeply loved by a God who works through your weaknesses.

Prayer

God, I confess that I've equated perfection with worth. I've carried guilt over every mistake, delay, and flaw. But you don't require me to be flawless. You invite me to be faithful. Help me rest in your grace instead of chasing a moving target.

Invitation

Today, notice where you're hesitating because of perfectionism. Instead of aiming for flawless, aim for faithful. Let progress, not guilt, be your guide.

When It's Not About Your Worth

He will take great delight in you; in his love he will no longer rebuke you, but will rejoice over you with singing.

ZEPHANIAH 3:17 (NIV)

If your heart races at the thought of speaking in a group or walking into a room alone, you may assume you're struggling with low self-worth. But not all social anxiety stems from insecurity. Sometimes it's just how your nervous system is wired to perceive threats in social settings.

In other words, your shakiness doesn't necessarily mean you're unsure of who you are. It might just mean your brain is on high alert. Social anxiety is often confused with low self-esteem, but the two aren't interchangeable.

People with healthy self-worth can still experience intense anxiety in social environments—especially if they've faced past rejection, trauma, or chronic overstimulation. And conversely, some people with low self-worth appear totally at ease socially because they've developed adaptive behaviors like people-pleasing or performance. Understanding the difference matters. If you mislabel social anxiety as a lack of value, you may end up treating the wrong issue—and missing the compassion you actually need.

Even biblical heroes experienced social overwhelm. Think of Timothy, Paul's protégé. Paul had to encourage him to stop letting his timidity hold him back: "Don't let anyone look down on you because you are young" (1 Timothy 4:12, NIV). Timothy didn't need to boost his confidence. He needed support to step into his calling despite his temperament.

Clinical insight tells us that healing social anxiety often comes through gentle exposure, self-soothing techniques, and learning new patterns. But healing low self-worth? That's a deeper journey into identity, rooted in how you see yourself and how you believe God sees you.

The truth is, your creator already delights in you. He sings over you, not just when you feel strong or socially smooth, but even in your stammering, blushing, trembling self.

Your worth is not up for debate.

Anchor Truth

Social anxiety is a struggle, not an identity. You are deeply loved, even when your nerves tell you otherwise.

Prayer

God, thank you for understanding my fears, even the ones I can't explain. Remind me that my worth is anchored in you, not in how comfortable I feel in a crowd. Help me walk in peace, not pressure.

Invitation

Pay attention to when your discomfort is truly about value and when it's just your nervous system trying to protect you. Consider talking with a counselor or trusted friend about what you're feeling, and take one step toward gentleness with yourself today.

The Berean Instinct

They searched the Scriptures day after day to see if Paul and Silas were teaching the truth.

ACTS 17:11

The Bereans weren't spiritual pushovers. They lived in a small Macedonian town, off the beaten path of Paul's missionary journeys, far from the buzz of Jerusalem or Rome. But when Paul and Silas rolled into their synagogue preaching a message that sounded radical—even risky—they didn't scoff, and they didn't swallow it whole.

Instead, they leaned in. They listened eagerly, but they also investigated. They took Paul's words and lined them up with Scripture, like holding a thread to a plumb line. They opened their scrolls and their minds. And they did it daily. Every. Single. Day.

That's what curiosity with discernment looks like. It's not blind acceptance. Not knee-jerk dismissal. But curiosity with backbone. Having a drive to seek knowledge—to dig deeper, to verify, to connect the dots. It's a kind of mental hunger, but it's not just about gathering facts. It's about making meaning.

The Bereans weren't just curious—they were grounded. Their search was rooted in a desire for truth, not novelty or spiritual sensation. We need more of that today.

Not a suspicious spirit, but a searching one. The Bereans weren't cynical, they were attentive. They didn't blindly accept, nor did they blindly reject. They held teaching up to the light and did the work to discern what aligned with God's heart. That kind of curiosity takes time. It takes spiritual maturity. And it takes courage—because when you search the Scriptures honestly, you sometimes find your assumptions unraveling.

The Bereans remind us that faith isn't about checking your brain at the door. It's about engaging it with humility and hunger. The truth is, anyone can parrot opinions. But it takes spiritual curiosity to test, question, study, and grow. This is what transforms secondhand beliefs into firsthand convictions.

Anchor Truth

Curiosity isn't a threat to your faith. It's the very thing that can make it your own.

Prayer

God, make me a seeker of truth. Give me the patience to explore your Word deeply and the discernment to recognize your voice in it. Let me be bold enough to ask questions and wise enough to pursue answers in your presence.

Invitation

What's one teaching or assumption you've held that you've never really examined? Today, take a Berean approach: Search, study, and ask, "Is this really what God says or just what I've heard?"

You Are Not Beyond Repair

He heals the brokenhearted
and bandages their wounds.

PSALM 147:3

Maybe part of you still wonders, *What if I'm too far gone? What if this broke something in me that can't be fixed?* It's a quiet fear, but a heavy one. You look at other people and think they're whole while you're just surviving. You feel fractured in places no one can see. And deep down, you wonder if healing is for people who haven't been this hurt.

But here's the truth: You are not beyond repair. Not because it didn't hurt. Not because it wasn't real. But because the one who made you holds the blueprint for your healing.

Psalm 147 says that God doesn't ignore the shattered pieces. He heals the brokenhearted and bandages their wounds. That's not quick. That's not clean. That's a process. And it's personal.

God doesn't toss you aside when you're struggling. He moves in closer. He tends to the parts of you that feel beyond hope. He doesn't shame you for being in pieces. He starts putting you back together with gentleness, with time, with love.

You may walk with a proverbial limp. You may carry emotional scars. But restoration doesn't mean going back to who you were. It means becoming someone deeper, braver, softer, stronger. The cracks in you don't cancel your worth. They're just the places where God's healing light can shine through.

You are not too much to heal. Not too damaged to love. Not too far gone to begin again.

There is more story ahead, and God is already there.

Anchor Truth

You are deeply loved, gently held, and slowly being restored.

Prayer

God, some days I wonder if healing is even possible for someone like me. But today, I choose to believe that your grace goes deeper than my wounds. I trust that you are still writing my story and it's not over yet.

Invitation

Speak this aloud today, even if you only halfway believe it: "I am not beyond repair. God is healing what I thought was lost. I am still becoming." Let that truth carry you forward.

When Love Becomes Leverage

Love is patient, love is kind. It does not envy, it does not boast, it is not proud. It does not dishonor others, it is not self-seeking.

1 CORINTHIANS 13:4-5 (NIV)

Love was never meant to be currency. But when you've lived inside codependent patterns, it can be hard to spot the difference between *love* and *leverage*. "If I show up for you, you better show up for me." "If I sacrifice for you, you owe me loyalty." "If I stay silent to keep the peace, I expect your gratitude." It's love with strings attached. And it's not actually love. It's a transaction dressed up as care.

Codependency often turns affection into a bargaining chip. And it happens subtly: You give more than you have, then feel resentful when it's not reciprocated. You bend over backward for someone who is emotionally unavailable, hoping that your effort will finally unlock their tenderness. You suppress your needs to preserve harmony, then silently keep score. It's love used as leverage. And it's exhausting.

Contrast that with the kind of love Paul describes in 1 Corinthians 13—a love that doesn't manipulate, keep score, or serve itself in disguise. That kind of love is self-aware and strong. It doesn't vanish into martyrdom or demand repayment for emotional labor.

But here's the rub: When you've learned to equate love with sacrifice, letting go of this dynamic can feel selfish. It's not. It's sacred. Because true love can only grow in freedom, not under the weight of obligation or emotional debt.

Think of the older brother in Jesus' story of the prodigal son. He did all the "right" things—stayed home, worked hard, remained loyal. But he resented the celebration thrown for his reckless sibling. Why? Because his love came with an invisible contract: *If I do all this, you had better reward me.* When that contract was broken, so was his peace.

When love becomes leverage, everyone loses. You can't manipulate someone into real connection. And you shouldn't have to.

Anchor Truth

Love that demands a return on investment isn't love. It's control. Real love is freely given, without strings or scorekeeping.

Prayer

God, show me where I've confused control with care. Help me love with open hands, not clenched fists. Teach me to give without expectation and to receive without guilt.

Invitation

Reflect on a relationship in which you feel unappreciated or resentful. Ask yourself, "Have I been giving with conditions, even silently?" Write down one way to offer love that's free of expectation or set a boundary that protects your heart from manipulation.

Radical Acceptance Isn't Resignation

I have learned how to be content with whatever I have. I know how to live on almost nothing or with everything. . . . For I can do everything through Christ, who gives me strength.

PHILIPPIANS 4:11-13

There's a difference between *giving up* and *letting go.* Between resignation and acceptance. Between apathy and peace. But if you've been through enough disappointment, it's easy to confuse them. Maybe you've thought, *If I accept this, I'm just giving in.* Or *If I stop trying to change it, that means it wins.* Or even, *If I stop fighting, I'll lose who I am.*

But here's the truth: Agency and acceptance aren't enemies. They're teammates.

In therapy, this is called *radical acceptance*—the ability to fully acknowledge what is, without resistance or denial. Not because you like it. Not because you choose it. But because fighting reality doesn't change it. And accepting reality doesn't mean you're stuck. It means you've stopped wasting energy pretending.

Paul didn't write Philippians from a peaceful mountaintop. He was in prison. And still, he wrote about contentment—not as passivity, but as strength. He wasn't saying, "This is fine." He was saying, "I'm grounded here. I have peace, even here. And from this place, I can still act."

That's the paradox of agency: Sometimes the most powerful move is to stop flailing and get honest. *This is what it is. Now, what's mine to do?*

You're allowed to stop fighting what you can't control. You're allowed to grieve the loss, name the truth, and take a breath. And you're allowed to act—not out of panic, but out of peace.

Anchor Truth

Acceptance is the starting point for meaningful change.

Prayer

God, I've been exhausting myself trying to change what's out of my hands. Help me practice real acceptance—not as surrender, but as strength. Show me what's mine to release and what's still mine to do.

Invitation

Is there something you've been resisting—emotionally, mentally, spiritually? Try naming it today without judgment. Then ask, "What changes when I stop fighting this?" Let peace guide your next move.

Rest Isn't Lazy. It's Life-Giving.

Then Jesus said, "Let's go off by ourselves to a quiet place and rest awhile." He said this because there were so many people coming and going that Jesus and his apostles didn't even have time to eat.

MARK 6:31

There's a kind of fatigue that sleep can't fix. It's the kind that comes from chronically overriding our limits. And it's why we need more than rest—we need rhythms of rest.

Modern psychology calls this *strategic recovery*—a practice of intentionally building periods of renewal into your schedule before you're running on empty. Studies show that without it, our nervous systems remain on high alert, flooding our bodies with cortisol, hijacking emotional regulation, and eventually leading to irritability, disconnection, and burnout.

Rest isn't a break from productivity. It's what makes productivity possible. From the beginning, God set a pattern: six days of creation, one day of rest. Not because he needed it, but because we do.

The Sabbath wasn't a suggestion. It was a rhythm built into the fabric of creation itself. Jesus honored it. Not legalistically, but lovingly. He understood the human need for margin and modeled it, even in the midst of ministry.

Somewhere along the way, we started seeing rest as optional. Worse, we saw it as laziness. We wear exhaustion like a badge of honor and run from stillness as if it's failure. But what if rest is sacred? What if stopping isn't slacking—it's soul work?

Rest is where your spirit exhales. It's where your identity is no longer defined by output. It's where you remember: I'm loved, not for what I do, but for who I am.

Anchor Truth

You weren't created for nonstop output. You were created for rhythm—work and rest, give and receive, pour out and be filled again.

Prayer

God, help me break free from the lie that rest is weakness. Teach me to build rhythms of renewal into my life. Let my rest be an act of trust in you—not guilt, not escape, but sacred surrender.

Invitation

When was the last time you practiced intentional rest? Not collapse, not distraction—but real, nourishing rest. This week, schedule just one hour to unplug and be still. Make it recurring.

More Than Saying Thanks

Let all that I am praise the LORD;
may I never forget the good things he does for me.

PSALM 103:2

Gratitude isn't just a nice attitude. It's a lifeline. It's what keeps us from spiraling into bitterness, from drowning in the constant drip of daily disappointments.

Gratitude is a discipline—a fierce, intentional act of remembering. And it's not always easy. You can be grateful and grieving. You can be thankful and tired. You can be aware of your blessings and still wish some things were different. That's because gratitude doesn't cancel pain. It creates room for joy to coexist with it.

In psychological terms, gratitude acts like a spotlight for the brain. Whatever you point it at, your awareness sharpens. So when you choose to notice what's good—even just one small thing—it shifts your perspective. Your mood changes. Your body relaxes. Your hope flickers back to life. That's not optimism. That's neurobiology. And it's spiritual formation.

David knew this. That's why, in Psalm 103, he says to himself, "Hey, soul, don't forget what God's done. Don't miss the mercy in front of you." Because he understood how forgetful we get in the fog. How fast we drift toward despair.

Gratitude is how we fight back. It grounds us. It opens our eyes. It reminds us of who God is, even when life hasn't gone as planned. And here's the good news: You don't need to feel thankful to practice gratitude. You just need to name one thing worth noticing. Then another. Then another. Over time, those small acknowledgments become a thread strong enough to pull you through.

Gratitude won't make your problems disappear, but it will keep them from defining you. It's not about denying pain, it's about defying despair. Every thank-you whispered in the dark is a declaration that light still shines, that God is still good, and that your story isn't over yet.

Gratitude is how you hold on.

Anchor Truth

Gratitude isn't a feeling you wait for. It's a habit you build. And it can change your heart, your mind, and your life.

Prayer

God, open my eyes to the good I've been walking past. Help me remember what you've done and notice what you're doing now. Teach me to make gratitude a daily act of worship.

Invitation

Think of one good thing in your life that didn't have to be. Name it. Thank God for it. Then write it down somewhere you'll see it again tomorrow.

People-Pleasing vs. God-Pleasing

While [Jesus] was still speaking, a bright cloud covered them, and a voice from the cloud said, "This is my Son, whom I love; with him I am well pleased. Listen to him!"

MATTHEW 17:5 (NIV)

People-pleasing often masquerades as kindness. You're agreeable, flexible, quick to apologize. You anticipate others' needs and shape-shift to meet them. You avoid conflict and keep the peace. But under the surface, there's a gnawing anxiety: *What will they think of me if I say no?*

At its root, people-pleasing is rarely about kindness. It's about fear. Fear of rejection. Fear of disapproval. Fear of being seen as difficult or disappointing. It's the fear of being unworthy unless you're needed or liked. And that fear becomes a snare.

This is a social pattern called *approval dependence*—a way of managing anxiety by aligning yourself with others' expectations. The short-term reward? A sense of security. The long-term cost? Exhaustion. Identity loss. Emotional fragmentation.

Even spiritually, this tendency can get twisted. You might convince yourself that always saying yes is being like Jesus. But Jesus wasn't driven by approval. He disappointed people constantly—the religious leaders, his disciples, his own family. He didn't bend to people's wills; he aligned himself with God's. And that's the difference.

Living to please God doesn't mean becoming harsh or unkind. It means becoming whole. You're no longer fractured by every opinion or request. You're led by discernment, not guilt. You can still be generous, but now it's rooted in conviction, not compulsion.

It might feel scary to let someone down. But disappointing others is sometimes the price of spiritual maturity. The truth is, you can't keep everyone happy and stay healthy.

Something has to give. Let it be the myth that you must be all things to all people.

Anchor Truth

Living for God's approval sets you free from everyone else's expectations.

Prayer

God, I confess how often I've let fear of others dictate my decisions. Help me untangle my worth from their approval. Teach me how to walk in truth and love without losing myself. Give me the courage to live for an audience of one.

Invitation

Today, practice saying a holy "no." Pay attention to where your yes has become automatic. Ask yourself, "Am I doing this out of fear or freedom?" Then choose the decision that leads to peace.

Tiny Wins—Why Healing Is Never Linear

[The Kingdom of God] is like a mustard seed planted in the ground. It is the smallest of all seeds.

MARK 4:31

Healing never moves in a straight line. Some days you feel strong—clear, hopeful, maybe even free. And then something hits. A sound, a memory, a word. And you feel like you're back where you started. You're not.

This is the truth most people won't tell you: Healing is uneven, unpredictable, and often invisible. Progress is measured in inches, not miles. Sometimes in breaths. Sometimes in simply staying. You might not be where you want to be. But you're not where you were. And that matters.

Jesus once said the Kingdom of God is like a mustard seed. It's the smallest of all seeds, but once it's planted, it grows into something far greater. That's how healing works too. It starts small. It takes time. It doesn't look like much at first. But tiny wins, faithfully nurtured, become something beautiful.

Tiny wins look like: Making it through the day without shutting down. Telling someone the truth about what hurts. Taking your meds, showing up to therapy, praying when you don't feel anything. Saying no. Saying yes. Saying *not yet.*

You don't have to impress anyone with your healing. You just have to keep tending to it. Because every little bit counts.

Progress isn't perfection. It's presence. And if you're still here, still trying, still breathing, that's a win.

Anchor Truth

Healing is holy, even when it's slow. The small steps are still sacred.

Prayer

God, I get discouraged when I don't feel better fast. Remind me that growth doesn't have to be dramatic to be real. Help me see the small wins and trust that you're doing something good in me, even when it's quiet.

Invitation

Write down one small win today, something you did that moved you even slightly toward healing. Celebrate it. That's a seed planted. And it matters.

The Fear of Slipping Too Far

If I go up to heaven, you are there;
if I go down to the grave, you are there.

PSALM 139:8

You used to feel close to God. Or at least close to the idea of him. But now everything feels distant. Muted. Faded. And you're scared that this season might never end. Maybe you haven't said it out loud, but it's there: *What if I've gone too far? What if I've questioned too much? What if I can't come back?*

Psychologists call this *catastrophic thinking*—a pattern where the mind jumps to the worst possible conclusion and camps there. It's not just fear. It's fear turned up to full volume, echoing through your thoughts until it feels like the only possible outcome.

And in spiritual life, it sounds like this: "God's done with me. I've lost my faith. I can't undo this." But here's what Scripture says: "If I go up to heaven, you are there; if I go down to the grave, you are there."

There's no height you can climb that makes you more worthy of God. And no depth you can sink that puts you out of his reach.

Yes, this season is hard. Yes, you may be doubting everything. Yes, you may feel numb, lost, or unrecognizable even to yourself. But you're not beyond grace.

You're not outside of mercy. You haven't slipped too far. God doesn't lose track of his children. Even when they wander. Even when they fall. Even when they wonder if they still believe.

If you're worried you've gone too far to be found, take heart. He already knows where you are. And he hasn't moved.

Anchor Truth

No matter how far you feel from God, you are always within his reach.

Prayer

God, sometimes I'm afraid I've gone too far, that I've lost you or that you've lost me. Help me let go of that fear. Help me believe that even in this fog, you haven't left.

Invitation

Place your hand over your heart and say softly, "I am not lost. I am not too far gone. I am still seen by God." Let that be your anchor today.

Naming Your Needs Without Guilt

Your Father knows exactly what you need even before you ask him!

MATTHEW 6:8

Somewhere along the line, you got the message. Maybe it came from church, maybe from family, maybe from the culture around you. But it was clear that your needs were less important than everyone else's.

Be selfless. Be sacrificial. Be strong. What you weren't taught is that always saying "yes" to others can be a quiet way of saying "no" to your own health, your own voice, your own soul.

When the exhaustion catches up to you, when your fuse is short and your prayers feel hollow—you still hesitate to say what you need. You feel the guilt creep in like smoke under a door: *Other people have it worse. Don't be selfish. Tough it out. Be grateful.*

But here's the thing: You were never called to be a martyr of your own well-being. That's not biblical. That's not brave. That's burnout.

Look at Elijah. After his mountaintop moment of triumph, he crashed. He wanted to die. He didn't ask for a pep talk. He didn't need a sermon. What he needed was sleep and food—twice. God didn't lecture him. God met his need. And that care was sacred.

Your need for rest, for help, for space, for healing—it isn't a flaw in your faith. It's part of being human. Tending to your needs—honestly, gently, without shame—is how you stay connected to yourself and in step with the Spirit.

Jesus didn't shame people for being needy. He moved toward them. And if you'll let him, he'll do the same for you. So name the ache. Admit the depletion.

If you've been raised to believe that martyrdom is holiness, it will feel wrong to say, "I need help." But wrong isn't always wrong. Sometimes it's just unfamiliar.

So begin there, with naming what you need. Not just to function, but to flourish. Not out of entitlement. Out of truth.

Anchor Truth

Getting your needs met isn't selfish. It's sacred. And when you do it in step with the Spirit, it's a form of obedience, not indulgence.

Prayer

God, peel back the guilt I've carried about needing anything. Meet me in the honest place where I admit what I lack, and help me receive your care without shame.

Invitation

What need have you been minimizing or ignoring? Say it out loud today. Not to justify it, just to honor it. You're not a machine. You're beloved.

When You Don't Feel Safe in Your Own Mind

You will keep in perfect peace all who trust in you, all whose thoughts are fixed on you!

ISAIAH 26:3

Sometimes the greatest threat to your peace isn't what's happening around you. It's what's happening inside your head. Racing thoughts. Worst-case scenarios. Internal accusations on repeat. The inner critic with a megaphone. The loop of shame or fear or dread that plays without your permission. It's disorienting when your own mind feels like enemy territory.

Mental health professionals often refer to this as *cognitive dysregulation*—when thoughts become chaotic, unanchored, or intrusive. For some, it shows up as anxiety or catastrophic thinking. For others, it's perfectionism or self-loathing. Either way, the result is the same: You feel unsafe within yourself.

And that's where emotional safety must begin. Inside. In the quiet corners of your soul where no one else hears the noise. This is where your faith meets your frontal lobe. Scripture doesn't promise a quiet mind. But it does promise a place to fix your thoughts—on God who steadies what spirals. Isaiah 26:3 offers a lifeline: "You will keep in perfect peace all who trust in you, all whose thoughts are fixed on you!"

This doesn't mean slapping Bible verses over your panic. It means *redirecting* your inner gaze—again and again—to the one who is unshaken when you feel undone. It means learning to name your feelings without becoming them. It means reaching out for help—to a counselor, a doctor, a trusted friend—because emotional safety often grows in community.

David wrestled with his own mind constantly. "Why am I discouraged?" he asks in Psalm 42. "Why is my heart so sad?" But he doesn't stop there. He keeps going: "I will put my hope in God!" (verse 5).

That's emotional safety in action—not pretending to feel peace, but choosing to anchor your thoughts even in the storm.

Anchor Truth

You may not always feel safe in your mind, but you are never alone in the battle. There is peace for the restless. Steadiness for the spiraling. A God who meets you in the mental mess.

Prayer

God, when my thoughts feel wild and heavy, be my calm. Help me fix my mind on what is true, noble, and good. Thank you for being a refuge I can carry within me.

Invitation

If your thoughts have been overwhelming lately, take one small step toward grounding: Breathe slowly, name what you're feeling, and speak one truth aloud. If needed, reach out for support. Healing often begins when we stop hiding the struggle.

Happy for You

*Be happy with those who are happy,
and weep with those who weep.*

ROMANS 12:15

You'd think it would be easy to celebrate someone else's good news. A promotion. A pregnancy. A big win. But sometimes instead of joy, you feel a pang. Jealousy. Insecurity. A low-grade ache that whispers, "Why not me?" That's not because you're mean or broken. It's because you're human.

Social comparison is baked into our wiring. But so is the potential for growth. In fact, mental health research shows that the ability to feel authentic joy for others—what's called *sympathetic joy*—is a key marker of emotional maturity and overall well-being. It doesn't mean you fake it. It means you train your heart toward freedom.

Because when you can celebrate without comparing, you lighten your emotional load. You grow your empathy. And you deepen your connection with others, because few things build trust like someone who's truly glad for your good news.

In Scripture, Elizabeth models this beautifully. When young Mary showed up at her doorstep pregnant with the Messiah, Elizabeth didn't compete. She was experiencing her own miracle pregnancy, but she didn't diminish Mary's joy to protect her own. She celebrated. She blessed Mary. She was genuinely happy for her, and Scripture says she was filled with the Holy Spirit (Luke 1:41-45). That's the fruit of a healthy soul.

So the next time someone else gets the thing you've been praying for, try this: Pause the self-comparison. Look them in the eye. Let your heart crack open with love. And say, "I'm so happy for you."

You'll find yourself freer than you expected. Because joy doesn't run out when it's shared. It multiplies. And every time you choose to cheer someone on, you loosen the grip of comparison and step more fully into the abundance God has for you, too.

Anchor Truth

Genuine joy for someone else expands—rather than shrinks—your capacity for happiness.

Prayer

God, help me celebrate others with sincerity. When envy creeps in, reroute my heart. Fill me with the kind of joy that multiplies, not divides.

Invitation

Who can you celebrate today? Send the text. Speak the words. Let their joy become your joy. That's how wholeness grows.

Saying No Without the Guilt Spiral

Just say a simple, "Yes, I will," or "No, I won't." Anything beyond this is from the evil one.

MATTHEW 5:37

Some people are haunted by the word *no*. Not because they don't want to say it, but because of what they fear will come next. Disappointment. Distance. Maybe even rejection. So they agree to help, volunteer, show up, listen, fix, accommodate. Again. And again. And again. Not from joy, but from guilt.

This is the codependent trap. And it's not love. It's appeasement. It's the reflex to prioritize someone else's comfort over your own convictions. And over time, it erodes your identity, your energy, and your ability to act with integrity.

The Bible gives us pictures of boundary-setting. Moses burned out trying to do everything for everyone—until his father-in-law, Jethro, stepped in. Jethro said, "What you are doing is not good. . . . You will only wear [yourself] out. The work is too heavy for you; you cannot handle it alone" (Exodus 18:17-18, NIV). Moses had to learn to delegate. To say no. To release what wasn't his to carry.

Nehemiah is another bold example. When enemies tried to lure him away from his God-given assignment under the guise of dialogue, he answered, "I am doing a great work and I cannot come down" (Nehemiah 6:3, ESV). No apology. No compromise. Just clarity. He wasn't rude; he was resolute.

Even Paul said *no* to people and places. In Acts 16, he's prevented from preaching in Asia. Later, he parts ways with Barnabas in a sharp disagreement. Paul's path was guided by calling, not codependency.

So here's the uncomfortable truth: Saying no doesn't make you selfish. It makes you responsible. But you are not responsible for everyone. You're responsible *to* live with intention, integrity, and wisdom. That means saying no sometimes, even when it makes others uncomfortable.

You don't need to explain endlessly. You don't need to earn your no. You just need to trust that you are allowed to choose limits without losing love.

Anchor Truth

Saying no isn't unloving. It's often the most honest, courageous thing you can do. You're allowed to disappoint someone else in order to stay aligned with your values.

Prayer

God, give me the courage to say no without shame and the clarity to know when it's time to step back. Help me value honesty over people-pleasing.

Invitation

Where in your life do you feel pressure to say yes when you mean no? Practice saying no with grace and without overexplaining. Let it be enough.

The Cost of Playing It Safe

If you try to hang on to your life, you will lose it. But if you give up your life for my sake, you will save it.

MATTHEW 16:25

Personal growth never happens in the comfort zone. It happens when you step out—into the unknown, into the awkward, into the unfamiliar. Playing it safe may feel smart, even spiritual. But if you never risk, you never grow.

Think of Abraham. God didn't hand him a map. He simply said, "Go to the land I will show you." No details. No timeline. Just go. Leave what's safe. Leave what's familiar. That's the beginning of transformation.

Growth always involves uncertainty. That's why courage is required. Not the kind of courage that slays giants or starts movements, but the quiet courage to take the next faithful step when the outcome is unclear.

Psychologists call this *optimal anxiety*—a sweet spot of discomfort where learning and growth happen. Too little challenge and you stagnate. Too much, and you freeze. But just enough discomfort? That's where transformation begins.

Most people overestimate the safety of the status quo. They think staying put is neutral, but it's not. It has a cost. A shrinking of your world. A numbing of your soul. A life marked by avoidance, not abundance.

Jesus made it plain: If you clutch your life too tightly, you lose it. If you open your hands and let go—if you surrender—you discover a richer, deeper way of being alive.

Abraham's courage didn't just launch a journey. It redefined his identity. He went from wanderer to father of a nation, not because he had a flawless plan, but because he walked in faith, one step at a time.

Most of us wait for clarity before we act. But in God's economy, courage often comes first, and clarity follows. Growth doesn't ask, "Are you ready?" It asks, "Are you willing?" And the truth is, you may never feel ready. But when you stop demanding certainty and start walking in trust, you make space for transformation. You give God something to work with.

Anchor Truth

Comfort may feel safe, but it rarely leads to growth. Courage is the engine of transformation.

Prayer

God, help me trust you more than I trust my comfort. Give me the courage to take the next step, even when the road ahead is unclear.

Invitation

Where is fear keeping you from growing? What's one brave decision you've been avoiding? Write it down. Pray over it. Then take one uncomfortable, faith-filled step forward.

The Secret to Lasting Happiness

I have told you these things so that you will be filled with my joy. Yes, your joy will overflow!

JOHN 15:11

We chase it like it's just around the corner. A better job. A deeper relationship. A few more dollars in the bank. We keep thinking, *Once I get that, I'll finally be happy.* But Jesus didn't say joy comes after the achievement. He said it overflows from something far more accessible and far more lasting: relationship. Not the kind you have to hustle to earn. Not one that depends on how well you perform. But a rooted, abiding, unshakable connection with him.

In John 15, Jesus paints the picture of a vine and its branches. Stay connected to him, he says, and you'll not only bear fruit—you'll be filled with joy. That kind of happiness isn't flimsy. It doesn't shatter when things go wrong. It's not based on what's happening around you but what's alive within you.

This is another place where science and Scripture sing the same tune. Psychology tells us that connection—real, authentic, soul-deep connection—is one of the strongest predictors of enduring happiness. Not stuff. Not status. But being known. Being loved. Belonging.

Jesus knew this all along. He didn't come to give you a quick shot of feel-good. He came to give you joy that doesn't run dry. Joy that sustains, surprises, and overflows—even on your worst days.

And it starts not with striving, but staying—staying close to him. Because the secret to lasting happiness isn't a secret at all. It's a person. And he's not playing hide-and-seek with your happiness. He's already here—closer than your next breath, waiting to meet you in the middle of your mess, not on the other side of it.

You don't have to hustle to earn joy or wait for your life to get easier to experience joy. You just have to stay connected to the one who is joy. Because when you're rooted in him, you're not chasing happiness anymore. You're living it.

Anchor Truth

True and lasting happiness is found not in circumstances but in deep connection with Christ.

Prayer

Jesus, I've looked for happiness in all the usual places. Help me to stay connected to you—the source of real, lasting joy. Fill me with your joy, not just when life feels good, but especially when it doesn't. Teach me what it means to abide in you.

Invitation

Take five minutes today to unplug from your tasks and replug into the Vine. Let your heart lean into his presence. Not to achieve anything, just to be. Let joy begin there.

What Is Codependency, Really?

We must obey God rather than any human authority.

ACTS 5:29

Codependency isn't just about being overly nice. It's not the same thing as being supportive, compassionate, or loyal. It's deeper and more dangerous.

At its core, codependency is a loss of self. It's when your identity becomes so wrapped up in another person's needs, emotions, or approval that you can't find the line between where they end and you begin. Your moods, choices, and sense of worth become tethered to their behavior.

Codependency often comes from early environments where love was conditional. Where approval had to be earned, peace had to be kept, and your feelings didn't have a safe place to land. So you adapted. You became hyperaware of others' emotions and quick to fix, please, or disappear.

It can sound like, "If they're okay, I'm okay"; "I can't say no or I'll hurt them"; "It's my job to keep this relationship alive, no matter the cost." But here's the danger: In trying not to lose the relationship, you end up losing yourself.

Scripture offers sobering examples. Martha, who frantically served while stuffing her resentment—possibly more invested in appearances than connection (Luke 10:38-42). Aaron, who gave in to the people's demand for a golden calf, choosing popularity over integrity (Exodus 32). King Saul, who was so obsessed with the people's opinion that he disobeyed God and unraveled under the weight of insecurity (1 Samuel 15). Each of these moments echoes a truth: When fear of disconnection overrides trust in God, we act out of codependency, not courage.

Healing starts with recognition. It's not about blame; it's about reclaiming. You're allowed to have your own opinions. Your own boundaries. Your own life. And love—real, godly love—never asks you to vanish.

Anchor Truth

Codependency is fear in disguise. But you don't have to live from fear. God calls you to show up as your whole, God-given self, not a shadow version shaped by others' approval.

Prayer

God, help me untangle who I am from who I've been told I have to be. Show me where I've let fear—rather than love—take the lead. Help me stand in truth, even if my voice shakes.

Invitation

Reflect on one area where your sense of self feels blurry or lost in someone else's needs. Write a sentence that starts to reclaim it: I am allowed to . . . *Then breathe into that truth today.*

We Heal in Relationships

Confess your sins to each other and pray for each other so that you may be healed.

JAMES 5:16

Some wounds need witness. You weren't meant to heal alone. Even when your wounds didn't come from a relationship, healing almost always requires one.

And when the wounds do come from others? Even more so. As therapist Adam Young is often quoted, "We are wounded in relationships . . . and we are healed in relationships." It sounds counterintuitive. Trust again? Open up? When relationships were the source of your pain?

But it's not about trusting just anyone. It's about finding someone *safe*. Someone who listens with curiosity, not control. With compassion, not correction.

James, the brother of Jesus, understood this. He led the early church, but he wasn't offering hollow platitudes. His call to "confess your sins to each other and pray for each other" came from a place of lived community.

The early believers depended on each other—not just for bread and teaching, but for *healing*. James knew that restoration didn't come only from vertical confession to God, but from horizontal connection with others.

And it's not just a spiritual principle. It's physiological. Neurobiology shows us that our nervous systems are shaped by relationships. In moments of distress, another person's calm presence can stabilize our inner chaos. When someone truly sees us and stays, our body breathes a little easier. Shame loosens its grip.

Think of Peter. After denying Jesus three times, his shame could've buried him. But Jesus met him, looked him in the eye, and asked three times the tender question that mirrored his failure: "Do you love me?"

And then came purpose: "Feed my sheep" (John 21:17). Peter's healing happened *in relationship*—in a moment of mercy, face-to-face with the one he betrayed.

Anchor Truth

We don't heal by hiding. We heal when we're safely seen.

Prayer

God, I want to heal, but I'm afraid to let others see where I'm still bleeding. Give me the courage to reach out, to be real. And help me offer that same grace to someone else.

Invitation

Reach out to someone you trust. Share one thing you've been keeping in the dark. Let their presence remind you that healing begins where honesty lives.

When You're Afraid to Set the Boundary

Fear of man will prove to be a snare,
but whoever trusts in the LORD is kept safe.

PROVERBS 29:25 (NIV)

You know the boundary needs to be set. But you're scared. Scared they'll get mad. Scared they'll leave. Scared they'll twist it into something it's not. So instead, you say nothing. Or you drop hints and hope they'll read your mind.

But boundaries unspoken are boundaries unkept.

Fear of disapproval is one of the biggest reasons we delay setting boundaries. And it's not a small thing—especially if you were raised in an environment where peace meant compliance and love had conditions. You might still carry the belief that saying no equals rejection. Or that prioritizing your needs means you're selfish.

But here's the truth: Silence doesn't protect relationships. It distorts them. Without clear boundaries, resentment quietly grows, authenticity erodes, and intimacy becomes an act.

Yes, setting a boundary might be awkward. It might ruffle feathers. But you're not doing it to control others. You're doing it to live from a place of clarity and health. And if someone's love for you can't survive a boundary, that's not love. It's control.

The fear of disappointing people is real. But it can't be what governs your decisions. God never asks you to live from a place of people-pleasing. In fact, Proverbs 29:25 reminds us that fearing people's opinions is a trap, but trusting God leads to safety.

So when the fear rises, pause. Breathe. Ask God for courage. And speak with grace and conviction. Not every boundary will be welcomed. But every healthy boundary you set becomes an act of faith. A declaration that your worth is not measured by how little space you take up or how much pain you're willing to carry to keep the peace.

Anchor Truth

Setting a boundary doesn't mean you're letting someone down. It means you're rising up into the life God is inviting you to live.

Prayer

God, I confess I've been afraid. Afraid of rocking the boat. Afraid of being misunderstood. Give me courage to speak the truth in love and trust that you—not other people's opinions—are my anchor.

Invitation

Is there a boundary you've been too afraid to voice? Take one small step toward naming it—first with God, then with someone safe. Clarity is an act of courage, not cruelty.

The Long Game

Let us run with endurance the race God has set before us.

HEBREWS 12:1

It's hard not to compare timelines. They got married at twenty-seven. They bought the house. They published the book. They launched the thing you've been dreaming about—while you're still waiting, still wondering if it will ever happen for you.

There's a quiet kind of jealousy that creeps in when someone else's life seems to be unfolding "on schedule"—especially when yours feels like a delay, a detour, or a dead end. And the messages around you don't help: *Hurry up. Achieve more. Make it look effortless.* So you scroll through someone's highlight reel and wonder if you somehow missed your moment.

But Hebrews reminds us that you're not in a sprint. You're in a race marked out for you. Not someone else's race. Not someone else's timeline.

Psychologists call this marker of maturity *delayed gratification*—the ability to stay focused on long-term goals even when short-term wins look shinier. And it's hard. Especially in a culture built on fast results and instant validation.

But spiritual growth almost never goes viral. It's quiet. It's cumulative. It happens in the unseen hours. The ordinary moments. The small moments of faithfulness that no one claps for.

If you're still in process—good. That means you're still in it. Still showing up. Still choosing endurance over ego. Still becoming. And while others may seem to be ahead of you, they're not you.

God is not late. He's just not in a rush. Because he's forming more than a future. He's forming your soul.

Anchor Truth

You're not behind. You're becoming.

Prayer

God, when I feel like life is passing me by, help me trust your pace. Give me strength to run the long game and peace when others seem to get there first.

Invitation

Name one area where you feel behind. Ask yourself, "What am I learning here that I couldn't have learned if things came easily?" And thank God that the process is part of the purpose.

Triggers, Flashbacks, and Feeling Unsafe Inside Yourself

Don't be afraid, for I am with you. Don't be discouraged, for I am your God. I will strengthen you and help you. I will hold you up with my victorious right hand.

ISAIAH 41:10

Trauma doesn't just live in the past; it echoes into the present. Sometimes it's a sound, a scent, a sentence. A normal moment that turns suddenly not normal. Your body tightens. Your heart races. You feel hijacked—by fear, by memory, by something invisible but overwhelming.

This is what a *trigger* does. It bypasses logic and brings your nervous system straight back to a moment when you weren't safe. You may feel embarrassed or confused, wondering, *Why now? Why this? Why can't I stop it?* But these responses are not weakness. They are your brain's way of trying to protect you.

A *flashback* can feel like time folding in on itself. You know where you are, but part of you is somewhere else, somewhere hard. Somewhere you never wanted to go back to. And then there's this unbearable layer of feeling unsafe inside your own body. You may want to escape your thoughts, your feelings, even your skin. But there's nowhere to run.

Here's what you need to hear: You are not crazy. You are not broken. You are not weak. You are someone whose system is trying to heal from what it wasn't built to endure. And you are not alone.

God doesn't flinch when your trauma surfaces. He doesn't grow impatient with your trembling. He draws near. He strengthens. He stays.

The healing journey may include counseling, grounding techniques, medication, prayer, rest, and a lot of grace. None of those tools make you less faithful. They make you courageous. You may not feel safe inside yourself yet, but you are held by a God who is safe and steady, even when everything else spins.

Anchor Truth

Triggers don't make you weak. They make you human. God is not afraid of what you carry. He will not let you go.

Prayer

God, sometimes I feel hijacked by fear or memories I didn't ask for. Help me be gentle with myself when those moments come. Remind me that I'm not alone and that healing is possible. Let your presence be my safe place.

Invitation

Create a grounding phrase to say when you feel triggered. Something simple, like, "I'm safe right now. I'm not back there. God is with me here." Repeat it when the fear rises. Let it be a lifeline.

Patterns Have a Path

So I say, let the Holy Spirit guide your lives. Then you won't be doing what your sinful nature craves.

GALATIANS 5:16

Addiction isn't just about weakness or willpower. It's about wiring. Every repeated behavior in your life carves a groove in your brain, a well-worn path called a habit loop. It starts with a trigger (stress, boredom, sadness), moves into a behavior (scrolling, eating, drinking, buying), and ends with a reward (numbness, distraction, comfort).

Do that loop enough times and your brain starts to automate it. Eventually, you don't even think. You just reach.

But the good news? Habits are learned—and they can be unlearned. You can build a new loop. One where your triggers don't take you down the same road.

It starts with noticing the pattern. Naming it. Pausing long enough to ask what you're actually needing and whether the reward you're chasing is real or just familiar.

Scripture doesn't just tell us to resist the craving. It invites us into a better story: "Let the Holy Spirit guide your lives." In other words, you're not alone in the battle. You have help. And healing doesn't start by trying harder. It starts by training differently.

Neuroscience confirms what Scripture has long said: What you feed grows stronger. If you train your mind toward truth, hope, and grace, new pathways begin to form. And the more you walk those pathways, the easier they become.

This isn't about becoming perfect. It's about becoming aware and choosing the next right step.

Anchor Truth

Patterns can be rewired. Freedom is possible.

Prayer

God, help me slow down long enough to see the path I'm on, and give me the strength to take one step toward healing today.

Invitation

Notice your next craving or impulse. Pause and ask, "What triggered this? What do I really want right now?" Try substituting a healthier choice, even just once, and pay attention to how it feels.

Busy Can Be a Great Hiding Place

Be still, and know that I am God!

PSALM 46:10

Busyness looks productive. It looks responsible. Motivated. Strong. But sometimes it's just well-disguised avoidance. You stay in motion so you don't have to feel what's lurking underneath. You fill your schedule to quiet the ache you don't want to name. You check things off your list and call it progress—but inside, you're spinning. Because when you slow down, the silence gets loud. And what you haven't dealt with starts to rise.

That's why self-awareness and stillness go hand in hand. You can't get honest with your inner world if you never stop moving. And sometimes the most courageous thing you can do isn't pushing through—it's pausing.

Psalm 46 doesn't say "Be efficient and know" or "Get more done and know." It says, "Be still." Stillness is where the knowing begins—of God, yes, but also of yourself. Not the self you curate for others, but the real one beneath the performance. The one who's carrying things that haven't been named. The one who's aching to breathe.

In psychological terms, chronic busyness can function as an *emotional avoidance strategy*—a way to outrun discomfort. But eventually it catches up. The anxiety. The resentment. The emptiness. The disconnection. You can't outrun your soul forever.

So what if today, instead of filling every minute, you left a little space?

Now, if that idea makes you squirm, you're not alone. For a lot of people, stillness feels awkward, even threatening. You're so used to moving—fixing, managing, producing—that just sitting with yourself feels unnatural. Like silence might expose something you're not sure you want to see.

That's okay. You're not doing it wrong. It just means you've been surviving for a long time.

So don't let hustling become a shield from your own soul. Stillness isn't weakness. It's where truth rises. It's where God meets you without the noise. And it's where you begin to notice what's been waiting to be named.

Anchor Truth

Stillness reveals what busyness hides.

Prayer

God, I confess that I sometimes use activity to cover up what I don't want to feel. Help me stop running long enough to hear you and to hear myself. Meet me in the quiet. I'll try to stay there.

Invitation

Block off ten minutes today without your phone, task list, or noise. Just sit. Not to fix anything. Just to notice what surfaces. That's where awareness begins.

The Hijack

Better to be patient than powerful;
better to have self-control than to conquer a city.

PROVERBS 16:32

You slam the door. Or fire off the text. Or go silent for days. Later, you ask yourself, "What just happened?" It wasn't just the situation. It was the surge. That tidal wave of emotion that took over before your wiser self had a say. You didn't choose your reaction. It chose you. That's what it feels like to be emotionally hijacked.

Neuroscientists call this an *amygdala hijack*—when the emotional center of your brain takes control and overrides the prefrontal cortex (the part responsible for reasoning and reflection). It's primal. Fast. And messy. And unless you've trained yourself otherwise, your brain will always default to what feels like survival: fight, flight, freeze, or fawn.

But emotional regulation is the skill that lets you pause before the storm hits full force. It's what turns reactions into responses. It doesn't mean you ignore your emotions. It means you learn to hold them—to name them, breathe through them, and respond with clarity instead of chaos.

That's not weakness. That's strength. As Proverbs says, self-control is better than conquering a city.

Look at Moses. He was called to lead but was also known for his temper. That one moment when he struck the rock instead of speaking to it cost him his entrance into the Promised Land (Numbers 20). It wasn't just about disobedience. It was about dysregulation. Unchecked emotion can derail even the most sacred of callings.

Emotional regulation *can* be learned. Through prayer, relying on the Spirit, self-awareness, trusted relationships, and even therapeutic tools like mindfulness and cognitive reframing, we can train our nervous system to tolerate discomfort and choose wisely.

It's not always glamorous. But it is transformative.

Anchor Truth

Being ruled by your emotions isn't a personality trait. It's a pattern you can change. God gave you emotions to inform you, not to control you.

Prayer

God, when emotions rise fast and hot, help me not be swept away. Teach me to pause, to breathe, to ask for your wisdom before I act.

Invitation

What emotion tends to hijack you the most—anger, fear, shame, envy? Name it. This week, practice noticing its arrival before it explodes. That's where growth begins.

Healing Takes a Safe Place

Plans succeed through good counsel;
don't go to war without wise advice.

PROVERBS 20:18

Not every wound heals on its own. And not all healing happens in a quiet moment of prayer or on a weekend retreat. Some healing takes place in an office with tissue boxes and clock ticks and a question that makes you exhale through your nose and say, "Huh. I've never thought of it that way."

Therapy isn't weakness. It's wisdom. "The way of fools seems right to them, but the wise listen to advice" (Proverbs 12:15, NIV).

We often carry pain we can't name. Patterns we don't understand. Reactions that don't make sense until someone helps us trace the thread back to where it frayed.

Counselors and therapists—good ones—hold space for that work with gentleness, curiosity, and courage. They help us name what hurts, explore why it formed, and choose how we want to move forward. They offer emotional safety when you feel like a jumbled mess of thoughts and contradictions. They remind you that your story matters and it makes sense, even if it hurts.

Jesus said the truth will set you free, but truth often needs a midwife. Counseling can be that—trained, boundaried, and fiercely committed to your wholeness. It's not a shortcut. It's not self-indulgence. It's courage.

Jesus modeled emotional safety in every encounter. He didn't flinch at trauma. He didn't bypass pain. He looked hurting people in the eyes, asked real questions, told hard truths, and offered hope. He honored their pain with presence. "He heals the brokenhearted and bandages their wounds" (Psalm 147:3).

If you've been on the fence about counseling—or if you've felt ashamed to seek it—know that you're not broken for needing help. You're brave for wanting healing. And therapy might just be the sacred space where your next layer of healing unfolds.

Anchor Truth

Seeking help isn't a sign of weakness. It's a step toward wholeness. Sometimes the safest place to begin your healing journey is in the presence of a skilled, compassionate counselor.

Prayer

God, thank you for those who create safe spaces for healing. Give me the courage to seek wise counsel when I need it, and help me shed the shame that keeps me silent.

Invitation

If you've ever considered seeing a counselor, what's held you back? What would it look like to take a step toward that today? Even researching a therapist can be an act of emotional bravery.

I Did the Work. They Got the Credit.

So let's not get tired of doing what is good. At just the right time we will reap a harvest of blessing if we don't give up.

GALATIANS 6:9

You were faithful. You gave the late nights. The ideas. The emotional labor. You said yes when no one else stepped up. You stayed when others left. And then someone else got the applause. They got the platform. The compliment. The promotion. Or maybe just the gratitude you never heard.

There's a particular ache that comes from being unseen. Especially when someone else gets seen for your work. And that ache can turn into jealousy or resentment faster than you'd like to admit. You might brush it off—*It's not about recognition.* But deep down, it kind of is. It's about being known. Being valued. It's about someone saying, "You matter. I see you."

Jealousy and resentment in these moments aren't about greed. They're about grief. The grief of feeling like your impact is invisible. Like your effort somehow got erased.

But Galatians 6:9 reminds us of something hard to hold: You don't control the harvest. You just keep sowing. Keep loving. Keep showing up. And at the right time—not always the visible time—you will reap a return that can't be taken or misassigned.

In psychology, this taps into the concept of *injustice sensitivity*—the pain that rises when we perceive something as deeply unfair, especially when it hits a place of personal investment.

So what do we do? We tell the truth: *This hurts.* We release what we can't control: *I won't let this resentment shape me.* And we return to our why: *I do this not for applause, but because it's who I am.*

Anchor Truth

Being unseen by people doesn't mean you're unnoticed by God.

Prayer

God, when I feel overlooked or underappreciated, meet me in that quiet pain. Remind me that no act of love or faithfulness is ever wasted with you.

Invitation

If jealousy surfaces today because of recognition someone else received, pause. Name what you wanted and why it mattered. Then ask, "What would it look like to keep showing up anyway?" Not for credit. For character.

Glued to the Glow

"I have the right to do anything"—but I will not be mastered by anything.

1 CORINTHIANS 6:12 (NIV)

You know the glow. That soft, addictive light of a screen that promises connection, entertainment, escape. It's with you when you wake up. It lingers in your hand when you lie in bed. It travels with you to the bathroom, the dinner table, the checkout line. And before you know it, it becomes the last thing you see before sleep.

This isn't a lecture about technology. It's an invitation to ask, "What am I really looking for when I pick up my phone for the eighty-seventh time today?" For many, phone use has crossed the line from convenience to compulsion. It's not just a habit. It's a way to avoid discomfort. Silence. Boredom. Vulnerability. Grief. Even prayer.

Psychologists call it *dopamine chasing*—that little hit of reward you get from notifications, likes, messages, or just the novelty of something new. But over time, that chasing becomes draining. You scroll to relax but end up feeling more tense. You escape to feel better but wind up emotionally foggy and vaguely guilty.

And yet, you go back. Because that's what addiction does: It hijacks your attention, not just your behavior. It convinces you that the momentary relief is worth the long-term disconnection. The glow numbs, but it doesn't satisfy.

You can interrupt the pattern. Not by throwing away your phone (although some boundaries might help), but by noticing your impulses. By asking, "What's really pulling me to check again right now?"

God invites you into presence. Not performance. Not perfection. Just presence. And you won't find it glowing back at you. You'll find it in stillness. In breath. In honesty. In him.

Anchor Truth

Anything that numbs your pain without healing it will eventually own you.

Prayer

God, I keep reaching for distraction instead of reaching for you. Help me notice what I'm avoiding and let you meet me there.

Invitation

Try a one-hour screen fast today. When you feel the urge to reach for your phone, pause and ask, "What am I hoping to feel right now?"

When Hope Slips Through Your Fingers

I cry out to God; yes, I shout. Oh, that God would listen to me! . . . I think of God, and I moan, overwhelmed with longing for his help.

PSALM 77:1, 3

There's a kind of ache that lives deeper than words. It's when you want to want to hope again, but you can't quite reach it.

Depression has a way of draining the color out of life. It doesn't just make you sad. It makes you indifferent. Numb. Like you're walking through smog and everyone else is breathing clear air. And slowly, hope—once a bright beacon—becomes a faint flicker you're not sure you believe in anymore.

It's not just you. That's how the writer of Psalm 77 feels too. He's not sitting in quiet peace, whispering prayers. He's shouting. He's moaning. He's overwhelmed. He thinks of God and instead of comfort, he feels grief.

This is what raw spiritual depression looks like—and it made it into the Bible! God didn't filter it out. He didn't edit the despair into something tidy. Instead, he preserved it as part of Holy Scripture so we would know that even our most hopeless cries belong in his presence.

Hope isn't always a warm feeling in your chest. Sometimes hope is the act of showing up again. Whispering a prayer you're not sure you believe. Opening the Bible when the words blur. Letting someone in when all you want is to shut down.

Sometimes hope is borrowed. Sometimes it's handed to you by someone who's walked through the dark and still holds a candle.

If you've lost your grip on hope, you're not defective. You're depleted. And that's where God often meets people—in the empty places.

Anchor Truth

Losing hope doesn't make you less faithful. It means you're human. And even there, God is not distant. He's listening in the silence.

Prayer

God, I don't feel hope right now. I'm tired of trying. But I believe you're near, even when I can't feel it. Hold me until I can believe again. Don't let go of me.

Invitation

Reread Psalm 77 today. Slowly. Out loud if you can. Let it give voice to what you can't quite say. Let someone else's honesty lead you to your own.

How to Spot Safe People

Rejoice with those who rejoice; mourn with those who mourn.

ROMANS 12:15 (NIV)

There's a certain kind of relief that floods your system when someone really gets you. When they hear what you're saying—and what you're not. When they pick up on your tone, your sigh, the subtle shift in your body language. That relief? That's emotional safety.

And it almost always begins with *attunement*—the practice of being emotionally present with someone. It's tuning in, not just to words, but to feeling. It's the parent who notices their child's forced smile and says, "Hey, are you really okay?" It's the friend who senses your silence isn't peace but pain. It's the spouse who hears disappointment behind your sarcasm and moves toward you instead of away.

Attunement says, "I see you. I hear you. You matter." And when you're on the receiving end of that? It's disarming. Healing. Holy.

Romans 12:15 doesn't say "correct those who mourn" or "fix those who rejoice." It simply invites us to *be with*—to attune, to resonate with others' emotional reality.

In the Bible, we see this kind of presence in Jonathan, the friend of David. When David was on the run and emotionally unraveling, Jonathan didn't tell him to toughen up or quote platitudes. He "helped him find strength in God" (1 Samuel 23:16, NIV). Jonathan entered David's experience with empathy and truth, not judgment or distance.

Attunement isn't about having the right words. It's about having the right posture. A heart that listens. A presence that steadies.

So if you want to know who is emotionally safe in your life, ask yourself, "Do they move toward my pain or away from it?" "Do they validate my emotions or minimize them?" "Do they *really* listen, or just wait for their turn to speak?"

If you don't have someone like that right now, it doesn't mean you're broken or destined to walk alone. It just means you're human. We all need safe people, and sometimes we have to go looking for them. Don't give up. Keep showing up with honesty, and keep asking God for wisdom and discernment. Because emotional safety isn't a luxury. It's a lifeline.

You are worth being deeply known and gently held.

Anchor Truth

Attunement is a sacred act of love. When someone leans in emotionally, without fixing or judging, they create the safety your soul needs to be real.

Prayer

God, help me recognize emotional safety when I see it. Teach me to attune to others with presence and grace, and guide me to relationships where I can be seen and supported.

Invitation

Who in your life has practiced emotional attunement toward you? Take a moment to thank them. And if no one comes to mind, ask God to help you identify someone who could and to help you become that kind of person for others.

No Is a Holy Word

It is useless for you to work so hard
from early morning until late at night,
anxiously working for food to eat;
for God gives rest to his loved ones.

PSALM 127:2

Somewhere along the way, *no* became a dirty word in Christian culture. We confuse kindness with compliance. We confuse love with self-erasure. We confuse faithfulness with burnout. So we say yes—over and over—while our soul quietly frays at the edges.

But the God who calls us to love also calls us to rest. Psalm 127:2 makes it plain: Frantic, boundaryless effort isn't holy. It's anxiety dressed in productivity. And it leaves us brittle and bitter.

Saying no is not rebellion. It's recognition that you are not limitless. You are not the savior. And you are not emotionally available to everyone at all times.

Moses gives us a powerful picture. As the leader of a weary, wandering people, he tried to carry everything on his shoulders—resolving disputes, answering questions, standing in the gap for thousands. But his father-in-law, Jethro, saw the warning signs: "What you are doing is not good," he said bluntly. "You and these people who come to you will only wear yourselves out. . . . The work is too heavy for you; you cannot handle it alone" (Exodus 18:17-18, NIV).

Jethro's advice wasn't just practical. It was sacred. It was an invitation to sanity. To sustainability. To trust. Learning to say no often begins with listening to the voice of wisdom—whether it's from a mentor, a friend, or your own internal compass stirred by the Spirit. Sometimes it's not God who's asking too much of you. It's you. Or it's a system you've come to believe is spiritual.

True love is free. And it flows better when you're not emotionally bankrupt. So practice saying, "No, I can't take that on right now." "No, I need to protect my time this weekend." "No, thank you." Not because you're unkind, but because you're learning to be wise.

Anchor Truth

You were never meant to run on empty. Saying no doesn't make you less loving. It helps your love last.

Prayer

God, I confess that sometimes I say yes because I'm afraid to disappoint. Teach me the wisdom of limits. Help me honor the boundaries that lead to wholeness.

Invitation

Think of one place in your life where a boundary is overdue. What would it look like to say no with grace and courage? Try it this week and notice how your soul responds.

The Courage to Feel

Pour out your heart to him,
for God is our refuge.

PSALM 62:8

Some of the most courageous people aren't climbing mountains or charging into danger—they're sitting quietly in therapy, facing their pain. They're naming feelings they were taught to bury. They're choosing not to numb, distract, or lash out—but to feel. That's courage.

Emotional courage is the willingness to stay present in discomfort. It's letting yourself grieve. It's choosing to process rather than suppress. It's acknowledging your jealousy, your sorrow, your shame without letting it define you or dictate your next move.

Many of us were conditioned to believe that strong people "suck it up" or "move on." We confuse stoicism with strength. But that mindset doesn't heal anything; it just creates emotional constipation. What we resist doesn't dissolve. It festers.

The Psalms are full of emotional courage. David raged, wept, doubted, repented, rejoiced. He didn't hide from God. He brought the full weight of his inner world to the surface. That's what spiritual and emotional maturity look like: honesty without shame.

Research backs this up. Naming your emotions—a practice called *affect labeling*—can reduce their intensity. When you identify and express what you feel, your brain shifts out of survival mode and begins to regulate. But this kind of work requires bravery. Because once you admit what you feel, you're responsible for how you respond.

You don't need to be fearless to face what you feel. You need to be grounded. Anchored in the truth that God is safe. You can be vulnerable with him. You can fall apart with him. And through that brave surrender, healing begins.

Anchor Truth

Courage isn't just about action. It's about honesty. Facing your emotions with God is one of the bravest, most transformative things you can do.

Prayer

God, give me the courage to feel—not just what's comfortable, but what's real. Teach me to pour out my heart to you, trusting that you can hold it all.

Invitation

What have you been trying not to feel? Choose one emotion and write it down. Say it out loud. Bring it into God's presence—not to fix it, but to be honest about it. That's where healing begins.

When Even Breathing Feels Like a Burden

My spirit is crushed, and my life is nearly snuffed out.
The grave is ready to receive me.

JOB 17:1

If you've ever felt like getting out of bed was too much? If you've sat in silence because the words wouldn't come? If you've felt invisible in a world that keeps spinning? You're not alone.

Job knew that place. He didn't just face loss—he sat in the ashes of it. Children gone. Wealth destroyed. Health ravaged. Friends turned into accusers. And in the thick of it, Job said things that sound eerily familiar to anyone who has ever stared into the void of depression.

He said he loathed his life. He wished he had never been born. He described God as feeling distant, even cruel. And yes, he cried out, "My spirit is crushed." And yet he stayed in the conversation. That's the power of the book of Job. It doesn't give us quick answers. It doesn't wrap grief in a bow.

Instead, it gives us permission to speak plainly when we hurt—to rage, lament, weep, and question. Job didn't edit his emotions for theological neatness. He gave God the unfiltered version. And even though he didn't always get the answers he wanted, he got something better: He was heard.

If you're in a season where joy feels unreachable, where hope feels hollow, where your energy is on fumes—don't fake it. But don't shut down, either. Follow Job's lead and stay in the conversation with God. Say what's real.

Because the story of Job isn't about a man who never wavered. It's about a man who wavered toward God.

Anchor Truth

God doesn't wait for you to clean up your feelings before he'll meet you. He draws near to the brokenhearted, even when the words sound more like grief than praise.

Prayer

God, I don't feel okay right now. Help me stay honest with you. Remind me that I don't need polished prayers to be heard—just the courage to keep talking.

Invitation

Read Job 3 or Job 17 today. Don't sanitize your emotions. Name them. Lament if you need to. You're allowed to feel crushed and still be deeply held.

The Braver Choice

Do everything without complaining and arguing, so that no one can criticize you. Live clean, innocent lives as children of God, shining like bright lights in a world full of crooked and perverse people.

PHILIPPIANS 2:14-15

Cynicism is cool. Sarcasm gets the laughs. Complaining connects people faster than honesty ever could. But none of it heals you. Negativity has become a cultural reflex. Scroll your feed. Sit in a break room. Skim the group chat. The world is exhausted and trying to outsnark the pain.

But Paul says something radical in Philippians 2: Don't blend in with the grumbling. Shine. Not by being perfect. Not by pretending. But by resisting the gravitational pull of despair.

Choosing optimism doesn't mean you don't see what's wrong. It means you still choose to believe in what's good. It's not about turning your face from the world's pain. It's about turning your posture toward light anyway.

Optimism is countercultural now. It's not naive. It's rebellious. Because in a world that expects cynicism, hope is the brave choice.

This doesn't mean putting on a happy face when you're hurting. It means being the kind of person who can acknowledge the darkness but still lights a candle. And it's contagious. Studies show that *emotional contagion*—the transfer of mood from person to person—is real. One person's hope, optimism, or calm can shift the atmosphere. You can be that person in a room full of eye rolls and hot takes.

So next time everyone starts spiraling into "What's the point?" Try saying, "But what if it's not over?" Try speaking life instead of piling on. Try being the quiet voice of light. Because someone near you might be desperate for it.

Anchor Truth

In a culture of despair, optimism is rebellion. And you're allowed to shine.

Prayer

God, help me resist the pull of cynicism. Let my words carry light, and let my hope spark something in others.

Invitation

Notice where negativity shows up in your conversations today. Then choose one moment to offer a different tone—a word, a pause, a hope.

When You Stop Feeling

Having lost all sensitivity, they have given themselves over to sensuality so as to indulge in every kind of impurity, with a continual lust for more.

EPHESIANS 4:19 (NIV)

There's a haunting warning in Ephesians 4:19: They have lost all sensitivity. That's not just about sin. It's about becoming emotionally shut down. About reaching a point where you stop feeling.

At first, you're just tired. Then you start pulling back. You become more sarcastic. You zone out when someone shares something painful. You nod, but don't really listen. You're still functioning, still showing up, but your heart's gone flat. You're no longer moved. This is what psychologists call *desensitization*—a survival response to chronic emotional overload. It's the body's way of saying, "This is too much."

The irony? The very people who tend to care the most are the ones most at risk for numbing out. And here's where it gets dangerous: The numbness doesn't just shield you from pain—it blocks joy, wonder, and connection too.

The more you stop feeling, the more you lose your sense of meaning. You start going through the motions. And eventually you wonder why you even cared in the first place.

But this isn't the end of the story. You can feel again. You can recover your emotional resonance—but not by pushing harder. You have to soften. You have to create space to *feel* again, without judgment.

That might mean grief. It might mean anger. It might even mean laughter. But the path back begins with honesty: "I've gone numb. I need help."

That's what Paul longed for the Ephesians to grasp. His words weren't just a warning about apathy. They were a call to wake up. To reconnect with the Spirit. To throw off the calluses that build when you live too long on empty.

When Paul says "having lost all sensitivity," he's describing the opposite of spiritual wholeness. The gospel invites us into a life where we *feel*—where we notice, we respond, we care. That kind of life isn't easy. But it's alive. And it's possible for you, even now.

Anchor Truth

Compassion fatigue doesn't mean you're broken. It means you've been running too long without tending to your own soul. Numbness is a signal, not a sentence.

Prayer

God, I confess I've been emotionally distant, even from myself. I don't want to live shut down. Reawaken what's gone quiet in me. Help me feel again, without fear.

Invitation

Do a pulse check: What emotions have you been avoiding lately? Give yourself ten minutes today to name them and sit with them gently. You don't have to fix anything. Just let yourself feel.

Listening Between the Lines

You must be compassionate, just as your Father is compassionate.

LUKE 6:36

Some people are expert talkers. Fewer are expert listeners. And fewer still can do what transforms a relationship: hear what isn't being said.

People don't always name their emotions directly. Instead, they say things like, "It's been a week." "I'm fine." "I don't want to talk about it."

But beneath the words is a current. Grief. Fear. Anger. Loneliness. Joy. Excitement. Longing. And people who thrive in relationships have learned to listen beneath the surface and reflect it back. Not by fixing. Not by analyzing. But by noticing. Naming. And showing care.

That's *empathy*—the ability to tune into another person's emotional experience and communicate that you get it. It's not projection. It's not mind reading. It's attunement. A leaning-in kind of love. It sounds like "That sounds overwhelming." "I imagine that hurt." "You must be proud." Or sometimes just "Tell me more."

This kind of compassionate emotional reflection builds trust. It tells the other person, *You're not too much. You're worth understanding. You matter.*

Jesus did this again and again. When Mary was weeping at Lazarus's tomb, he didn't offer a quick fix, even though he knew resurrection was coming. He entered her emotion. He wept with her (John 11:33-35). That's presence. That's compassion. That's what love looks like with skin on.

And it's not just for crisis moments. Reflecting emotion in everyday conversations—celebrating good news, noticing someone's anxiety, honoring their disappointment—creates connection that lasts.

People feel safe around someone who truly listens.

Anchor Truth

When you listen for emotion and reflect it with care, you help others feel known, and that's holy ground.

Prayer

God, slow me down so I can hear beyond the noise. Help me notice what others are feeling and respond with compassion and grace. Make me the kind of person others feel safe with.

Invitation

In your next conversation, pay attention not just to words—but tone, pace, body language. Listen for what's underneath. Then name what you notice gently, without trying to fix it.

When Humor Has a Blade

Some people make cutting remarks,
but the words of the wise bring healing.

PROVERBS 12:18

Sarcasm is clever. Sharp. Effortless. And when it lands just right, it can leave a room in stitches. But when it cuts the wrong way? It leaves people bleeding and laughing to cover the sting.

Humor can be holy. It's a gift that lightens heavy loads. But when it's used as a weapon, it gets sneaky. Subtle. Deniable. "Relax, I was just kidding." "Can't you take a joke?" "Don't be so sensitive." That's how sarcasm protects itself. By masking hostility as humor.

This is called *deflective aggression*—a way of expressing anger without taking ownership of it. It's common among people who feel uncomfortable being direct about their emotions, especially anger. So they bury it under irony. Cloak it in banter. Wrap it in wit.

But here's the thing: Sarcasm can erode trust. Especially when it becomes your go-to way of expressing dissatisfaction or disconnection. It creates distance. And it teaches others that getting close might come with a sting.

If you're the one using cutting humor, pause and ask, "What am I really trying to say? Is this about connection or control? Am I covering my own discomfort by making someone else the punch line?"

And if you're on the receiving end, trust your gut. If it feels like a dig, it probably is. Not every jab needs a response, but not every jab should be swallowed, either.

Humor doesn't have to be humorless to be kind. And sarcasm doesn't have to disappear altogether. But it does need to be handled with care, especially when there's pain beneath it.

Because the most courageous thing isn't the perfect comeback. It's speaking the truth with kindness. And letting the people around you know they're safe in your presence.

Anchor Truth

Sharp wit can build a wall or build a bridge. One cuts for protection. The other cuts to heal.

Prayer

God, show me where I use sarcasm to hide or to wound. Help me trade sharpness for sincerity and cleverness for courage.

Invitation

Notice the next time you make a cutting comment. Ask yourself, "What was I really trying to express?" Would honesty, or even silence, have served better?

Tending to the Wound, Not Just the Emotion

Then he lay down and slept under the broom tree. But as he was sleeping, an angel touched him and told him, "Get up and eat!"

1 KINGS 19:5

When Elijah fled into the wilderness, exhausted and afraid, he wasn't just on the run. He was unraveling. This was a man who had just called down fire from heaven, defeated false prophets, and stood boldly for truth. But now? He was done. Emotionally fried. Spiritually hollow. He collapsed under a broom tree and begged God to let him die.

What God did next is stunning. He didn't give Elijah a pep talk. He didn't correct his theology. He didn't even challenge his despair. God sent an angel—with a nap and a snack.

Why? Because the wound beneath the emotion needed tending.

Elijah's fear and hopelessness weren't just irrational mood swings. They were the surface signals of deeper depletion. His soul was malnourished. His nervous system was maxed out. What he needed first was restoration, not rebuke.

Emotional regulation isn't just about managing the feeling; it's about addressing the source. Anger might be masking grief. Anxiety might be fueled by past trauma. A shutdown response might be rooted in years of being unheard. If we treat only the outburst and not the injury, we're just putting emotional Band-Aids on bullet holes.

God invites you to slow down and check in. To ask, *What's really going on underneath this emotion? What is this feeling trying to protect me from? What do I actually need right now—rest? Truth? Help?* Healing starts there.

Like Elijah, you may need to eat. To cry. To rest. To talk to someone who can help you untangle the thread. And when you do, you'll find that God's care runs deeper than your collapse.

Anchor Truth

God doesn't shame your emotion; he tends to your exhaustion. Real regulation begins by naming the wound, not silencing the symptom.

Prayer

God, help me listen to what my emotions are trying to say. Show me the wounds beneath them, and meet me there with your healing.

Invitation

What's one strong emotion you've felt recently? Take time today to ask what deeper need or wound it might be pointing to. Then do one thing to care for that wound, not just to calm the feeling.

Enmeshment vs. Intimacy

Each one should carry their own load.

GALATIANS 6:5 (NIV)

Let's get one thing straight: Closeness isn't the same as connection. What looks like intimacy on the outside can sometimes be enmeshment in disguise. If you've ever felt the pressure to anticipate someone's needs before they voice them, or felt crushed under the weight of their moods, you may be experiencing *identity fusion*, not bonding.

Enmeshment is when the boundaries blur. Your emotions become entangled with theirs. Their crisis becomes your crisis. Their silence becomes your guilt trip. You don't know where they end and you begin. It feels like closeness until you realize you've lost yourself.

Real intimacy, on the other hand, is rooted in freedom and differentiation. It means being deeply known and still respected as an individual. It's saying, "I care for you deeply, but I'm not responsible for your every feeling." That's love with oxygen. That's what we're made for.

The apostle Paul distinguishes between bearing each other's burdens (see Galatians 6:2) and carrying our own load (see Galatians 6:5). The first is compassion; the second is responsibility. Enmeshment confuses the two.

You might have learned enmeshment as a survival strategy. Maybe you grew up tiptoeing around a parent's temper or absorbing their sadness like a sponge. Maybe you believed closeness required compliance. Or maybe your worth was measured by how needed you were.

But love doesn't mean erasing yourself.

Let's take a cue from Ruth and Naomi. Their bond was strong—so strong Ruth famously said, "Where you go, I'll go." But their relationship wasn't about control or guilt or identity fusion. It was a commitment rooted in choice, not obligation. Ruth remained fully herself, even as she remained close. That's intimacy. That's strength.

When you stop confusing enmeshment with intimacy, you make room for healthier, holier connections. Relationships marked by mutual respect, shared responsibility, and sacred space to breathe.

Anchor Truth

Healthy love requires boundaries. You can be close without being consumed. Intimacy flourishes where individuality is honored.

Prayer

God, help me untangle love from enmeshment. Teach me how to hold space for others without losing the space I need to be whole.

Invitation

Think of a relationship where you feel responsible for someone else's emotions. Ask yourself, "Am I showing up in love or disappearing in the name of it?" Write down one small shift you can make to move toward true intimacy.

The Joy of Presence

Better one handful with quietness
than two handfuls with hard work
and chasing the wind.

ECCLESIASTES 4:6

You don't have to chase happiness. You can catch it—right here, right now—if you slow down enough to notice. But let's be honest: That's hard.

We've been conditioned to believe that happiness lives in the next thing. Next goal, next achievement, next vacation, next version of ourselves. But while ambition isn't a bad thing, *chronic striving* can leave you emotionally bankrupt. That's why Scripture gives us this countercultural wisdom: "Better to have one handful with quietness than two handfuls with hard work and chasing the wind."

The point? You can have less and be more content. Because presence is often where joy is hiding.

In psychological terms, this shows up in what researchers call *savoring*—the ability to fully engage with and appreciate a positive experience in the moment. Studies show that people who practice savoring are consistently happier, more resilient, and less anxious. It's not about the size of the experience. It's about the depth of your attention.

Jesus modeled this kind of presence. He paused. He noticed. He ate slow meals with friends. He gave his full attention to people others rushed past. He lived the joy of being even while carrying the weight of doing.

And you? You don't have to outrun your to-do list to tap into joy. You just have to show up for your own life. Because the present moment is where peace is waiting—and where God already is.

Anchor Truth

Joy doesn't come from having it all. It comes from being fully present with what you already have.

Prayer

God, help me release my white-knuckle grip on the chase. Quiet the noise in my mind so I can hear you in the stillness. Teach me to savor the life I'm living, not just dream about the one I'm chasing.

Invitation

Today, resist multitasking for one moment. Pause. Breathe. Look around. Taste the food. Listen to the laughter. Notice the sunlight. And let your soul say, "Thank you."

The Deepest Why

Three things will last forever—faith, hope, and love—and the greatest of these is love.

1 CORINTHIANS 13:13

There's a reason every great story—sacred or secular—comes back to love. It's the thread that binds meaning to our days. You can achieve, accumulate, even amaze, but without love, it's all a hollow echo.

We were made to love deeply and give ourselves away with purpose. That's why even our smallest acts of love—showing up for a friend, speaking truth in gentleness, holding space for someone's grief—can anchor us in something greater than ourselves.

Psychologists have long noted that meaningful relationships are the single greatest predictor of well-being. Not wealth. Not fame. Not even achievement. What gives our lives meaning is love—not just being loved, but *loving others well.*

And here is something beautiful: Love doesn't have to be perfect to be powerful. It doesn't have to be dramatic to be divine. It just has to be real—genuine, consistent, selfless. The people who experience the deepest sense of meaning aren't those with the least struggle, but those who have let love drive their story.

Love gives us courage. Love invites healing. Love reminds us why we matter.

Faith matters. Hope matters. But love is the greatest. Not just in a romantic sense, but in the daily decision to care for others, to reach out, to show up when it's inconvenient. Love creates meaning because it connects us to something larger than ourselves.

If you're feeling adrift, start small. Send a message to someone who's struggling. Offer encouragement. Let someone know they matter. When you love like that—on purpose—you won't just help them. You'll feel more grounded yourself.

Love outlasts achievement, outshines performance, and outlives pain. It gives meaning where there was none. So if you're searching for purpose, don't just look inward. Look outward. Choose to love today.

Anchor Thought

Meaning isn't found in what you do. It's found in how you love, because love always outlives the moment.

Prayer

God, help me see today through the lens of love. Let me live not for applause or approval, but for the joy of giving myself away the way you gave yourself for me. Teach me that even small love brings great meaning.

Invitation

Think of one small, tangible way to express love to someone today. A note. A gesture. A word. Not for what you'll get out of it, but for what you'll grow in it.

Passive-Aggression Isn't Peacemaking

Do all that you can to live in peace with everyone.

ROMANS 12:18

Some people yell. Others sulk. Passive-aggression is anger in disguise. It doesn't shout. It simmers. It leaks out in sarcasm, silent treatments, backhanded compliments, or veiled guilt trips.

And while it may feel safer than open conflict, it still causes damage. In fact, it may be more confusing and more corrosive—because it communicates without clarity and wounds without ownership.

Many of us learned this style young. Maybe we watched adults shut down emotionally, avoid hard conversations, or weaponize politeness. Maybe we were taught that expressing anger directly was rude or disrespectful. So now we try to keep things "peaceful," but what we're really doing is *avoiding truth*.

Passive-aggression masquerades as maturity. It sounds like "No, it's fine," when it's absolutely not. Or "I'm not mad," while we slam a cabinet door and quietly withdraw.

But Scripture doesn't say, "Pretend everything's okay." It says, "Do all that you can to live in peace." And real peace requires real honesty.

Jesus didn't dance around issues. He didn't dodge hard conversations or sugarcoat conflict. He spoke the truth in love. His words were sometimes hard, but they were never manipulative. When we withhold what we really think or feel, we rob others of the chance to understand us. And we rob ourselves of the growth that comes from honest connection.

Avoiding confrontation isn't always kindness. Sometimes it's fear.

God invites you to something better: clear, kind, courageous communication. Not so you can get loud. But so you can live real.

Anchor Truth

Peacekeeping avoids conflict. Peacemaking moves through it with truth and grace.

Prayer

God, help me notice when I'm hiding my anger behind sarcasm or silence. Give me the courage to speak clearly and kindly, even when it's uncomfortable.

Invitation

Today, if you feel yourself slipping into passive-aggressive patterns, pause and ask, "What do I really need to say?" Practice saying it in a way that's honest and honoring.

When You're Just Plain Tired

Those who refresh others will themselves be refreshed.

PROVERBS 11:25

We live in a culture that glorifies exhaustion. We've made burnout a badge of honor and overfunctioning a personality type. But the human body doesn't lie. When you push too long, care too deeply, and give without pause, your nervous system takes the hit.

You may find yourself snapping at the people you love, spacing out in important conversations, or feeling numb when you're supposed to care.

That's not a failure of faith. It's fatigue. You're just tired. Deep-in-your-bones tired. Nothing-left-to-give tired.

Chronic tiredness isn't just about lack of sleep. It's about unrelieved stress. When your *sympathetic nervous system* (what controls the fight-or-flight response) stays activated too long, it floods your body with cortisol and adrenaline. This keeps you alert but slowly fries your emotional circuits. You can't pour out what you haven't replenished. Eventually, your body forces the issue through irritability, forgetfulness, muscle tension, insomnia, or even illness.

Proverbs 11:25 says that "those who refresh others will themselves be refreshed." But many of us skip that second part. We know how to refresh others. We don't know how to let ourselves be refreshed. Or worse, we don't believe we deserve to be.

Let's be clear: Self-care is not selfish. It's stewardship. It's choosing to tend to the life God has entrusted to you—including your body, your boundaries, your breath. It's recognizing that fatigue doesn't need just another cup of coffee. It needs compassion. It needs a reset.

So ask yourself, "What kind of rest do I need today?" Not what's convenient. Not what's socially acceptable. But what your body, mind, and soul are begging for. Is it solitude? Movement? Sleep? Silence? Laughter?

Then give yourself permission. You're not lazy. You're not broken. You're just tired. You need to rest.

Anchor Truth

Rest is not a reward for hard work. It's a requirement for sustaining it. You can't live well if you never stop to breathe.

Prayer

God, I'm tired. I've given a lot. I've carried more than I let on. Help me release what's not mine and receive the rest I need. Remind me that even you paused.

Invitation

Choose one restorative action today. Just one. A walk, a nap, a slow breath, a meal in silence. Let it be your way of saying, "My health matters."

When You Feel Inadequate

"O Sovereign LORD," I said, "I can't speak for you! I'm too young!"

JEREMIAH 1:6

Inadequacy doesn't usually shout. It whispers: "You're not smart enough." "You don't belong here." "Someone else would do this better." It's a voice that echoes deep in the soul, especially when you're facing something that matters.

That's exactly where we find the prophet Jeremiah. When God called him to be a voice to the nations, his first response was fear cloaked in self-doubt. "I can't," he said. "I'm too young!" Too inexperienced. Too unqualified.

But Jeremiah's protest didn't disqualify him. In fact, it's what makes him relatable.

The feeling of inadequacy often traces back to early messaging—moments in childhood or adolescence when we internalized the belief that we weren't enough.

Maybe it was a critical parent. A teacher's disapproval. A painful comparison. Or maybe it's the perfectionism that keeps moving the goalpost just out of reach.

These beliefs become mental habits—distorted but familiar. We start defining ourselves by what we lack instead of who we are.

But notice what God didn't do with Jeremiah. He didn't say, "No, you're totally capable! You've got this on your own!" Instead, he said, "Don't be afraid . . . for I will be with you" (Jeremiah 1:8).

The antidote to inadequacy isn't self-confidence: It's *God-confidence*. It's knowing that your strength isn't the source of your calling. His presence is.

Your sense of "I can't" might be real. But God's presence is more real still.

Anchor Truth

Your feelings of inadequacy do not disqualify you from being used by God. His strength shines best through your weakness.

Prayer

God, I confess that I often feel inadequate, like I'm not enough. Remind me today that you are with me. I don't have to be perfect to be called. I just have to be willing. Fill my gaps with your grace.

Invitation

Where have you been holding back because of self-doubt? Take one small step today that says, "God, I trust you more than my fear." Speak. Show up. Move forward. Not because you're sure of yourself, but because you're sure of him.

Only the Real You Can Be Loved

We have spoken honestly with you, and our hearts are open to you.

2 CORINTHIANS 6:11

We all crave love. But many of us spend our lives offering only a curated version of ourselves—the polished, edited, approval-winning self we hope others will choose. We shrink certain parts. Overperform others. We keep our weird, our worry, and our wounds under wraps. And then we wonder why we feel alone—even in a crowded room or a committed relationship.

Here's the truth: Anything less than your full self might get applause, acceptance, even admiration. But it won't get you love. Not really. Because what others are loving isn't *you*. It's the mask. And that kind of love can't satisfy. It can't reach the places in you that are aching to be seen. It's like eating through a window—so close to nourishment, but never actually tasting it.

God's love isn't like that. He sees the unfiltered, unedited, totally human you. And he stays. No rejection. No revulsion. No rolling of the eyes. Just grace that says, "I know. And I'm not going anywhere."

When you risk authenticity in your human relationships, you give others the sacred chance to love you as you are, not as you wish you were. And only that kind of love can actually touch your loneliness.

Let people see you. Let them love the mess, the marvel, and the mystery that is you. Not everyone will, but the ones who do? Their love will change your life.

You can't be fully loved if you're only partially known. And you don't have to keep playing a part.

There is love on the other side of honesty.

Anchor Truth

You can't be truly loved until you let yourself be truly seen.

Prayer

God, I'm tired of hiding behind the version of me I think others want. Help me to live from the truth of your love and to offer others the real me. No mask required.

Invitation

Think of a relationship where you've been performing. What's one small way you could let your guard down this week, just a little? Try it. See what happens.

Grief Is What Love Feels Like After Loss

Jesus wept.

JOHN 11:35

Grief is what love feels like when it doesn't know where to go. It's the body aching for what the soul can no longer touch. The swirl of anger, numbness, confusion, and sadness that doesn't come in tidy stages but in relentless waves. It's waking up in the morning and forgetting for a moment—and then remembering.

Grief is not reserved for gravesides. It shows up in all kinds of losses: the relationship that slowly withered, the child you prayed for who never came, the version of life you thought you'd be living by now.

Grief is love interrupted, and it's a holy thing. And Jesus gets it. He didn't preach a sermon at the tomb of his friend. He didn't rattle off clichés about God's timing.

He wept. The Greek word used—*dakryō*—isn't a single stoic tear. It's full-body sobbing. The Son of God grieving in public.

Let that sink in.

Grief isn't a sign of weak faith. It's the overflow of deep love. You don't need to apologize for it. You don't need to rush through it. Grief doesn't ask to be fixed. It asks to be felt.

And here's the miracle: Your grief is not a detour from God's presence. It's a doorway to it. He's not waiting for you on the other side of this sorrow. He's *with* you in it—eyes wet, heart aching, holding the shattered pieces with tenderness and strength.

You don't grieve alone. And you won't always feel this broken. Because the same Jesus who wept also resurrects.

Anchor Truth

Grief is not a spiritual failure. It's proof that your heart loved deeply. And Jesus steps into it with you, not above it.

Prayer

God, thank you for being close to the brokenhearted. Thank you that I don't have to hide my sorrow from you. Help me feel what I need to feel today—without shame, without rush. Sit with me in it. Cry with me in it. Lead me through it.

Invitation

Wherever grief is surfacing in your life, name it. Whisper it. Write it down. Let it be seen. Let it be sacred. Even Jesus wept. So you can too.

Realistic, Not Resigned

We are pressed on every side by troubles, but we are not crushed. We are perplexed, but not driven to despair.

2 CORINTHIANS 4:8

Somewhere along the way, "being realistic" started to sound like giving up: *Don't get your hopes up. Don't expect too much. Just deal with what is.* But realism doesn't have to mean resignation. You can stare hardship in the face and still refuse to bow to despair.

That's the brilliance of Paul's words in 2 Corinthians. Pressed—but not crushed. Perplexed—but not in despair. He doesn't sugarcoat the pain. He just doesn't let it define the whole story.

Psychologists call this *tragic optimism*—a hope that persists even in suffering. Coined by Viktor Frankl, a Holocaust survivor and psychiatrist, it's the belief that meaning can emerge even from loss. That light can still find a way in. It's not blind hope. It's battled hope.

This is what makes Christian optimism different. It doesn't deny sorrow. It just insists that sorrow doesn't get the final word. You may feel squeezed, confused, delayed, discouraged. But you are not abandoned. And you're certainly not done.

Being optimistic doesn't mean faking a smile or ignoring the heaviness. It means anchoring yourself in something deeper than the pain—God's character, God's presence, God's ultimate renewal of all things.

So go ahead and tell the truth. Say, "This is hard. This hurts." And then say, "But I believe there's more." More healing. More grace. More life beyond this moment.

That's not naive. That's spiritual courage.

Anchor Truth

Faith doesn't deny reality. It redefines what's possible within it.

Prayer

God, I don't want to fake hope. But I do want to live like you're still at work, even when I can't see it. Help me hold on.

Invitation

Name one area of your life that feels unresolved or painful. Without rushing to fix it, ask, "What does it mean to hold hope here—even if I'm still waiting?"

Notes and Sources

JANUARY

1 *Connection isn't a luxury. It's a survival instinct.:* John Bowlby, "The Making and Breaking of Affectional Bonds," *The British Journal of Psychiatry* 130, no. 3 (1977): 201–210, https://doi.org/10.1192/bjp.130.3.201.

28 *Viktor Frankl . . . often taught:* Viktor E. Frankl, *Man's Search for Meaning,* rev. ed. (Washington Square Press, 1971), 164–165.

FEBRUARY

24 *Psychologist Gabriele Oettingen calls this mental contrasting:* Gabriele Oettingen, "Expectancy Effects on Behavior Depend on Self-Regulatory Thought," *Social Cognition* 18, no. 2 (2000): 101–129, https://doi.org/10.1521/soco.2000.18.2.101.

MARCH

6 *about 50 percent of your happiness:* Sonja Lyubomirsky et al., "Pursuing Happiness: The Architecture of Sustainable Change," *Review of General Psychology* 9, no. 2 (2005): 111–131, https://doi.org/10.1037/1089-2680.9.2.111.

25 *we say "the body keeps the score":* This phrasing was made popular by psychiatrist Bessel van der Kolk. See his work *The Body Keeps the Score* (Viking, 2014) for more information on trauma and its effects.

30 *people who asked more follow-up questions:* Karen Huang et al., "It Doesn't Hurt to Ask: Question-Asking Increases Liking," *Journal of Personality and Social Psychology* 113, no. 3 (2017): 430–452, https://doi.org/10.1037/pspi0000097.

APRIL

23 *"Authenticity is the daily practice":* Brené Brown, *The Gifts of Imperfection* (Hazelden, 2010), 50.

MAY

5 *the way two people handle a rupture:* John Gottman, *What Predicts Divorce?* (Lawrence Erlbaum Associates, 1994).

6 *giants of faith battled the shadows:* Roland H. Bainton, *Here I Stand: A Life of Martin Luther* (Abingdon-Cokesbury, 1950). Z. Schmoll, ed., *Spurgeon on Mental Health: Encouragement for Those in the Dark Valley* (Aneko Press, 2017). Mother Teresa, *Come Be My Light: The Private Writings of the "Saint of Calcutta"*, ed. Brian Kolodiejchuk (Doubleday, 2007). C. S. Lewis, *A Grief Observed* (Faber & Faber, 1961).

18 *David Brooks calls it* illumination*:* Brooks highlights this practice in chapter 3 of his book *How to Know a Person* (Random House, 2023).

JULY

13 *Brother Lawrence . . . famously found peace:* Lawrence of the Resurrection, "Third Letter," in *The Practice of the Presence of God*, trans. from French (Fleming H. Revel Company, 1985).

15 *Blaise Pascal . . . once wrote:* Blaise Pascal, "Of the Necessity of the Wager," in *Pensées*, (1657–58).

AUGUST

4 *doubts are the "ants in the pants" of faith:* Frederick Buechner, *Beyond Words: Daily Readings in the ABC's of Faith* (HarperCollins, 2004), 85.

17 *one study even found:* Martin Seligman et al., "Positive Psychology Progress: Empirical Validation of Interventions," *American Psychologist* 60, no. 5 (2005): 410–421, https://doi.org/10.1037/0003-066X.60.5.410.

SEPTEMBER

8 *the Bible mentions giving thanks:* This number comes from the combined usage of two words—one Hebrew (*yadah*), one Greek (*eucharisteō*). *Yadah* appears 111 times in the Old Testament and is often translated "praise," "[give] thanks," or "confess." *Eucharisteō* appears 38 times in the New Testament and is usually translated as "give thanks."

OCTOBER

4 *One study from the University of Illinois even found:* Rosalba Hernandez et al., "Optimism and Cardiovascular Health: Multi-Ethnic Study of Atherosclerosis (MESA)," *Health Behavior and Policy Review* 2, no. 1 (2015): 62–73, https://doi.org/10.14485/HBPR.2.1.6.

4 *Psychologist Martin Seligman calls it explanatory style:* Christopher Peterson and Martin E. Seligman, "Causal Explanations as a Risk Factor for Depression: Theory and Evidence," *Psychological Review* 91, no. 3 (1984): 347–374, https://doi.org/10.1037/0033-295X.91.3.347.

12 *the most hopeful people are often the most realistic:* George A. Bonanno, "Loss, Trauma, and Human Resilience: Have We Underestimated the Human Capacity to Thrive After Extremely Aversive Events?," *American Psychologist* 59, no. 1 (2004): 20–28, https://doi.org/10.1037/0003-066X.59.1.20. Shelley E. Taylor and David A. Armor, "Positive Illusions and Coping with Adversity," *Journal of Personality* 64, no. 4 (1996): 873–898, https://doi.org/10.1111/j.1467-6494.1996.tb00947.x.

19 *social circuits in the brain can be reignited:* Louis Cozolino, *The Neuroscience of Human Relationships: Attachment and the Developing Social Brain*, 2nd ed. (W. W. Norton & Company, 2014). Stephen W. Porges, *The Polyvagal Theory: Neurophysiological Foundations of Emotions, Attachment, Communication, and Self-Regulation* (W. W. Norton & Company, 2011).

DECEMBER

25 *meaningful relationships are the single greatest predictor of well-being:* Robert Waldinger and Marc Schulz, *The Good Life: Lessons from the World's Longest Scientific Study of Happiness* (Simon & Schuster, 2023).

31 *Coined by Victor Frankl:* Viktor E. Frankl, "The Case for a Tragic Optimism" (postscript 1984), in *Man's Search for Meaning*, trans. Helen Pisano (Beacon Press, 2006).

About the Authors

Drs. Les and Leslie Parrott are #1 *New York Times* bestselling authors and psychologists. Their books include *The Love Language That Matters Most*; *Healthy Me, Healthy Us*; and the award-winning *Saving Your Marriage Before It Starts*. Their pioneering assessments have been used by millions and include the free MyHeartChart.com. Their work has been featured in *The New York Times* and *USA Today* as well as on CNN, *Good Morning America*, *TODAY*, *The View*, and *Oprah*. They live in Seattle and can be found online at LesAndLeslie.com.